HIROAKI

SAMURA

4

LISTEN
TO ME!

STORY & CAS

Sapporo, Hokkaido. One night at a bar, Minare Koda has her heartbroken ramblings secretly recorded by a local FM radio station director, Mato, who then airs the audio the following day. Minare storms into the station in a burst of fury, only to be duped by Mato into doing an impromptu talk show explaining her severe remarks. The segment turns out to be a big hit, leading Mato to make Minare an official offer to have her own show. And so begins the daily struggle to produce her shoestring operation of a radio program. One night, Minare meets with her senior Madoka Chishiro, who hands her the outline for a mysterious project...

Minare Koda

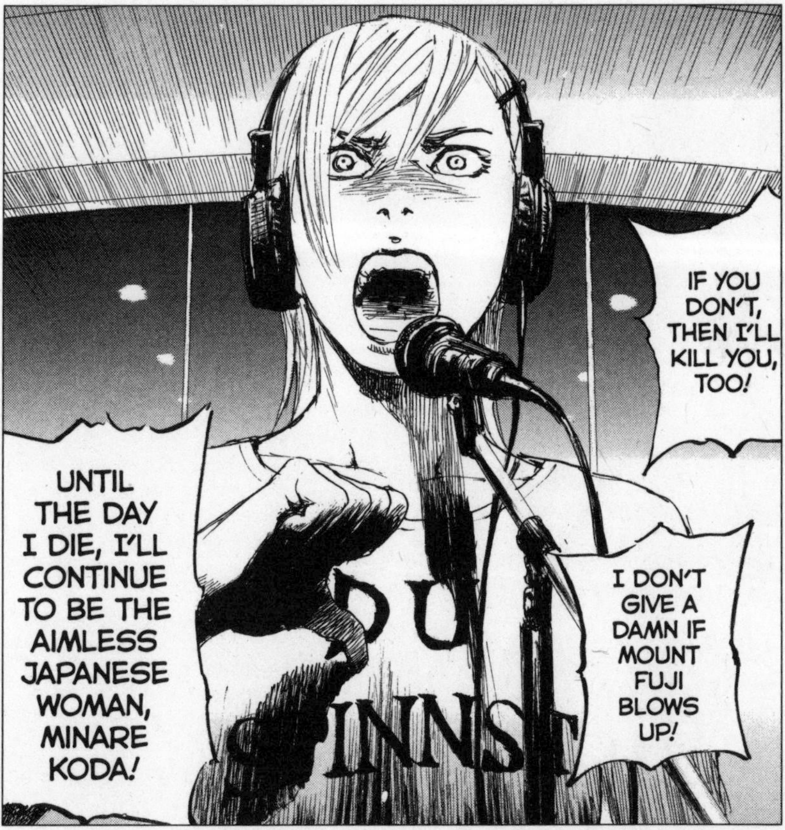
IF YOU DON'T, THEN I'LL KILL YOU, TOO!
UNTIL THE DAY I DIE, I'LL CONTINUE TO BE THE AIMLESS JAPANESE WOMAN, MINARE KODA!
I DON'T GIVE A DAMN IF MOUNT FUJI BLOWS UP!
DU
INNST

The protagonist. Lives in Sapporo, a bustling city on Japan's chilly, northern island of Hokkaido. Born and raised in the coastal city of Kushiro. Currently 26 and single. Her day job as a waitress at the soup curry restaurant VOYAGER is in jeopardy. Causes all sorts of trouble in trying to execute ideas for her show.

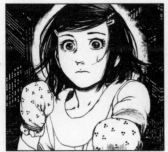

Mizuho Nanba

Assistant director at MRS. Currently letting Minare stay with her after Minare was kicked out of her apartment. Really kind-hearted.

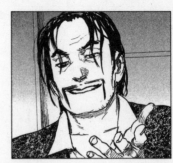

Kanetsugu Mato

A director at the FM station Moiwayama Radio (MRS). Saw potential in Minare's conversational ability and scouted her for the radio business.

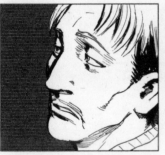

Katsumi Kureko

A scriptwriter for MRS and a veteran of the industry. Primarily works as an erotica novelist. Supposedly goes way back with Mato.

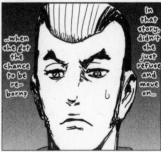

In that story, didn't she just refuse and move on...
...when she got the chance to be re-born?

Chuuya Nakahara

An employee at VOYAGER. Supposedly in love with Minare, but invited Makie to stay at his place. She's still there now.

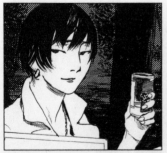

Madoka Chishiro

A radio host at Moiwayama Radio Station. Extremely skilled and has a good relationship with scriptwriter Kureko. A master at provocation.

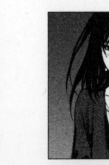

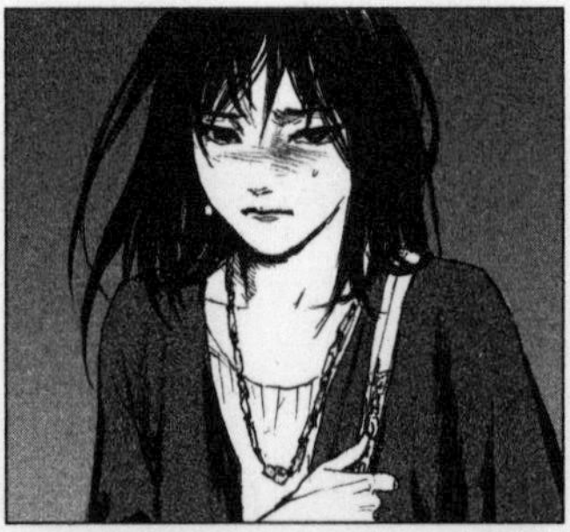

Makie Tachibana

A beautiful woman working at VOYAGER to help pay for the car accident caused by her brother. Not the most skilled swordsperson in this manga, nor affiliated with the Itto-ryu.

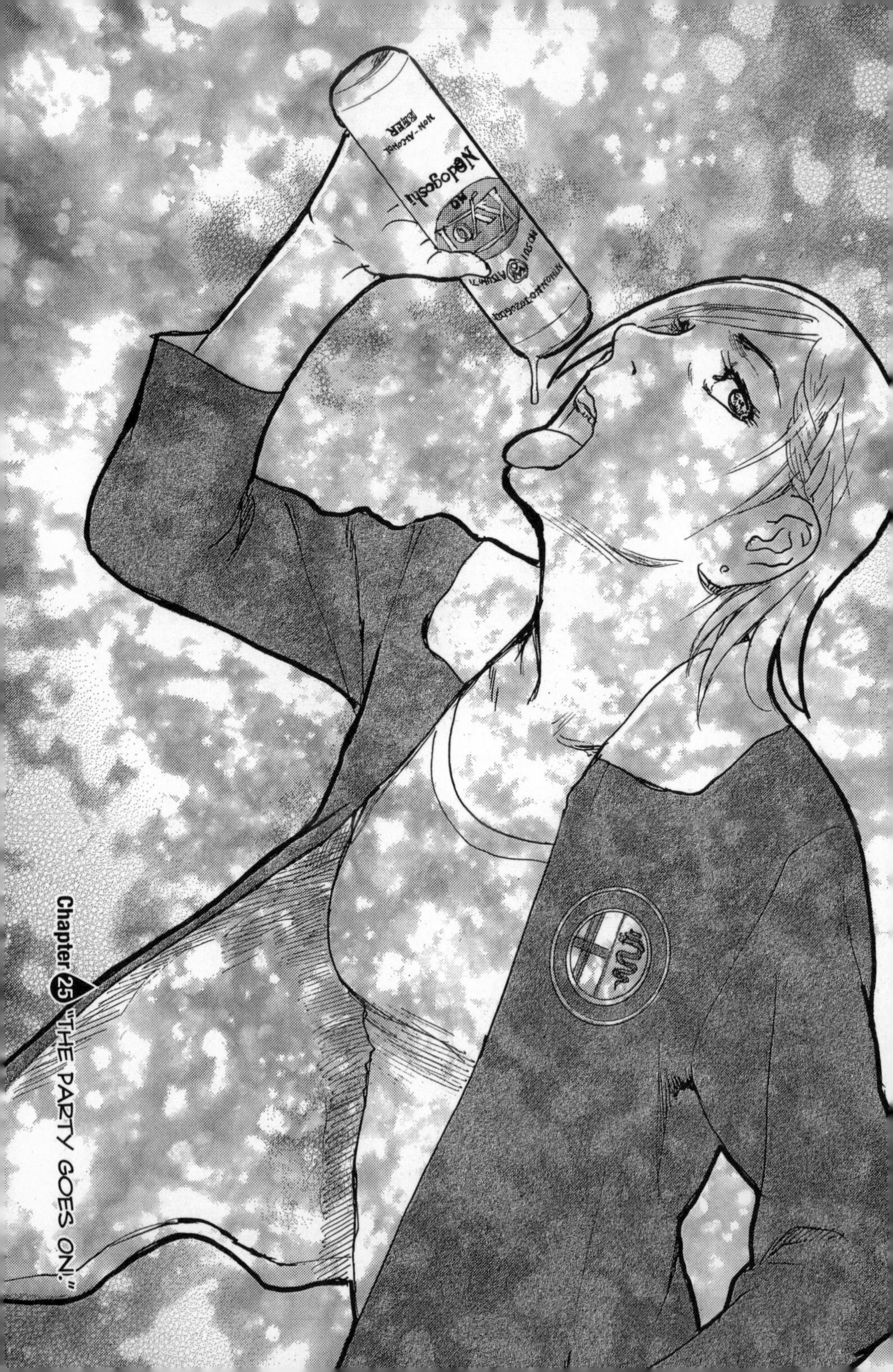
Chapter 25 "THE PARTY GOES ON."

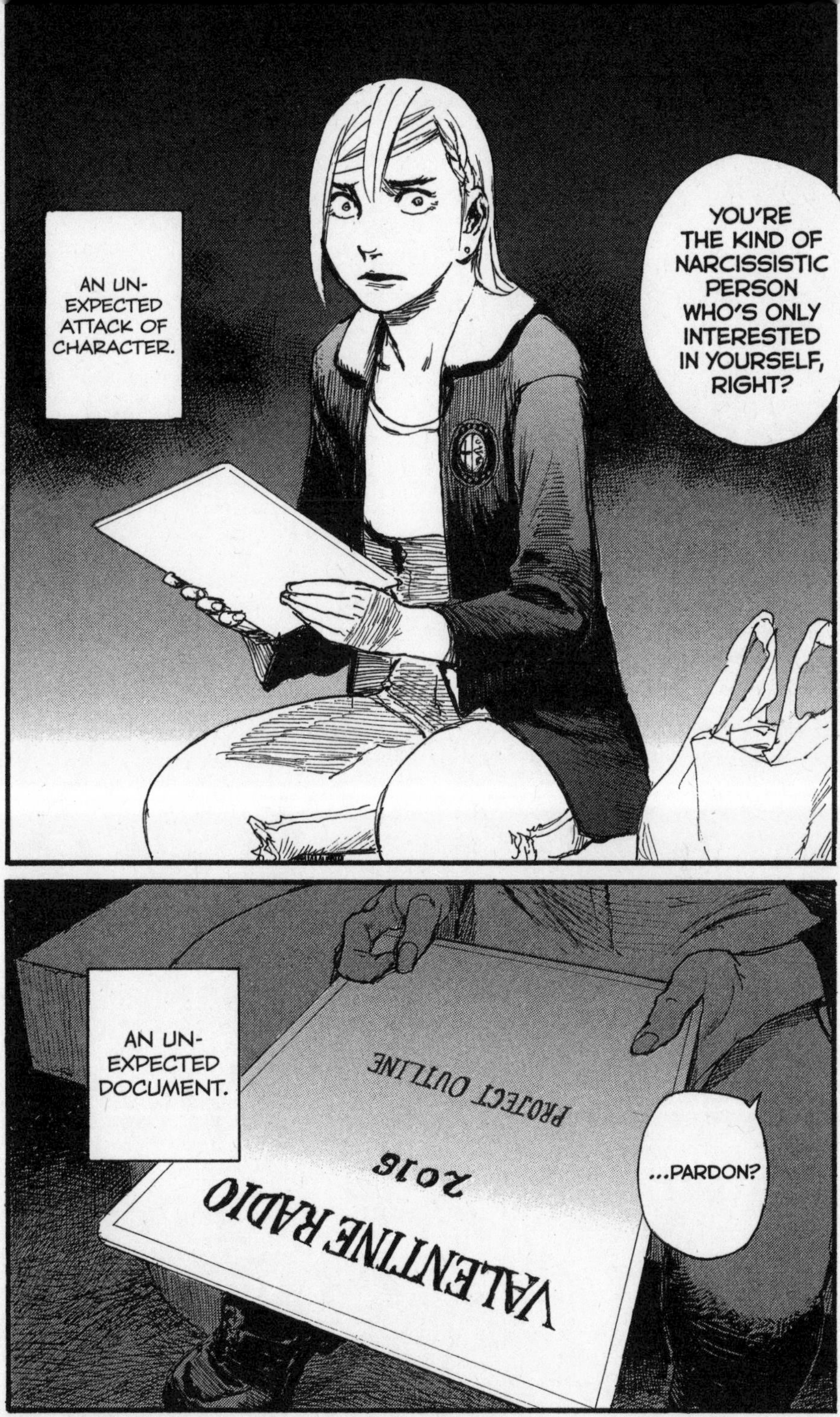
YOU'RE THE KIND OF NARCISSISTIC PERSON WHO'S ONLY INTERESTED IN YOURSELF, RIGHT?
AN UN-EXPECTED ATTACK OF CHARACTER.
...PARDON?
AN UN-EXPECTED DOCUMENT.
VALENTINE RADIO
2016
PROJECT OUTLINE

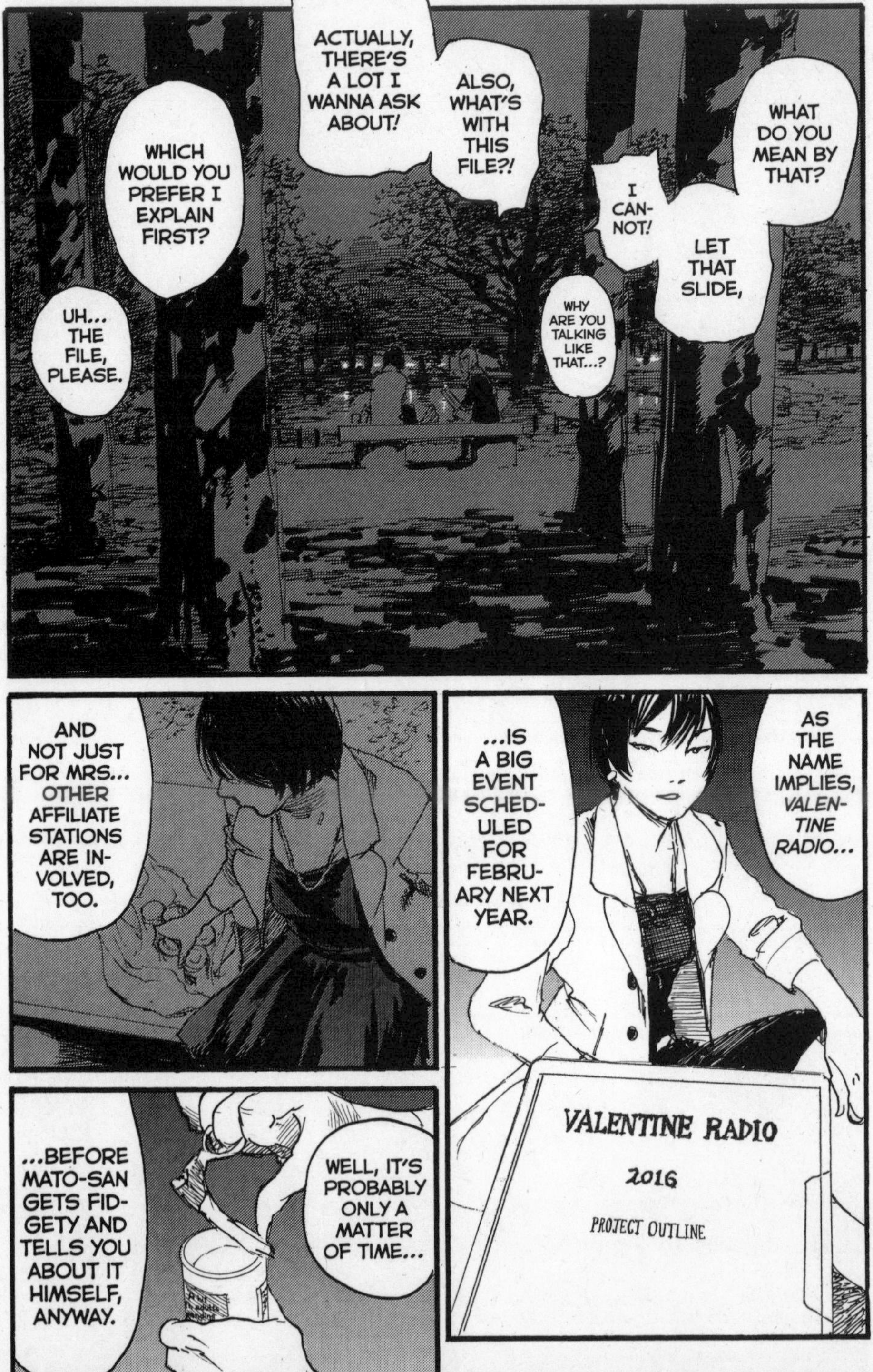
WHAT DO YOU MEAN BY THAT?
I CANNOT!
LET THAT SLIDE,
WHY ARE YOU TALKING LIKE THAT...?
ALSO, WHAT'S WITH THIS FILE?!
ACTUALLY, THERE'S A LOT I WANNA ASK ABOUT!
WHICH WOULD YOU PREFER I EXPLAIN FIRST?
UH... THE FILE, PLEASE.
AS THE NAME IMPLIES, VALENTINE RADIO...
...IS A BIG EVENT SCHEDULED FOR FEBRUARY NEXT YEAR.
VALENTINE RADIO
2016
PROJECT OUTLINE
AND NOT JUST FOR MRS... OTHER AFFILIATE STATIONS ARE INVOLVED, TOO.
WELL, IT'S PROBABLY ONLY A MATTER OF TIME...
...BEFORE MATO-SAN GETS FIDGETY AND TELLS YOU ABOUT IT HIMSELF, ANYWAY.

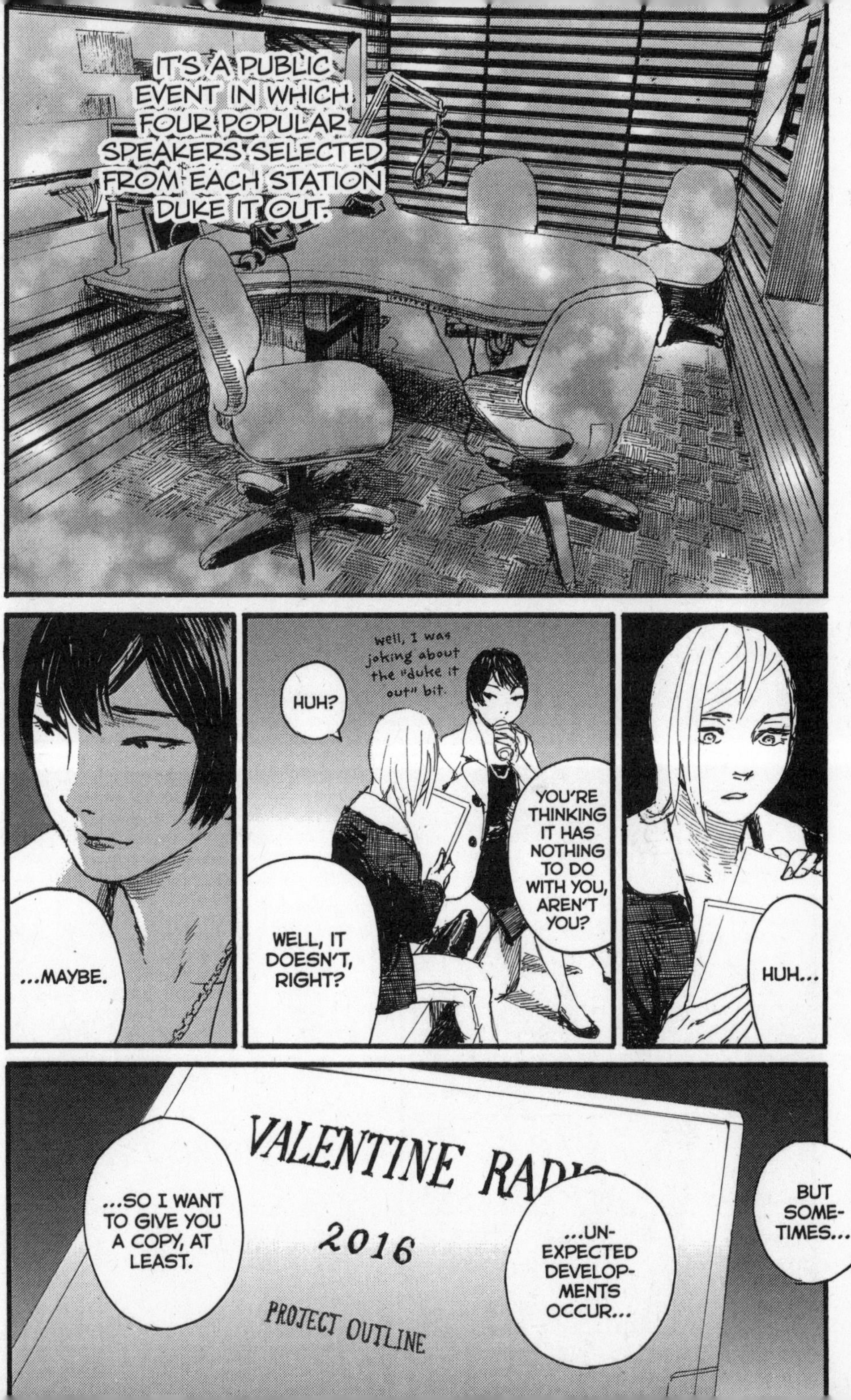
IT'S A PUBLIC EVENT IN WHICH FOUR POPULAR SPEAKERS SELECTED FROM EACH STATION DUKE IT OUT.
HUH...
well, I was joking about the "duke it out" bit.
HUH?
YOU'RE THINKING IT HAS NOTHING TO DO WITH YOU, AREN'T YOU?
WELL, IT DOESN'T, RIGHT?
...MAYBE.
BUT SOME-TIMES...
...UN-EXPECTED DEVELOP-MENTS OCCUR...
VALENTINE RADI
2016
PROJECT OUTLINE
...SO I WANT TO GIVE YOU A COPY, AT LEAST.

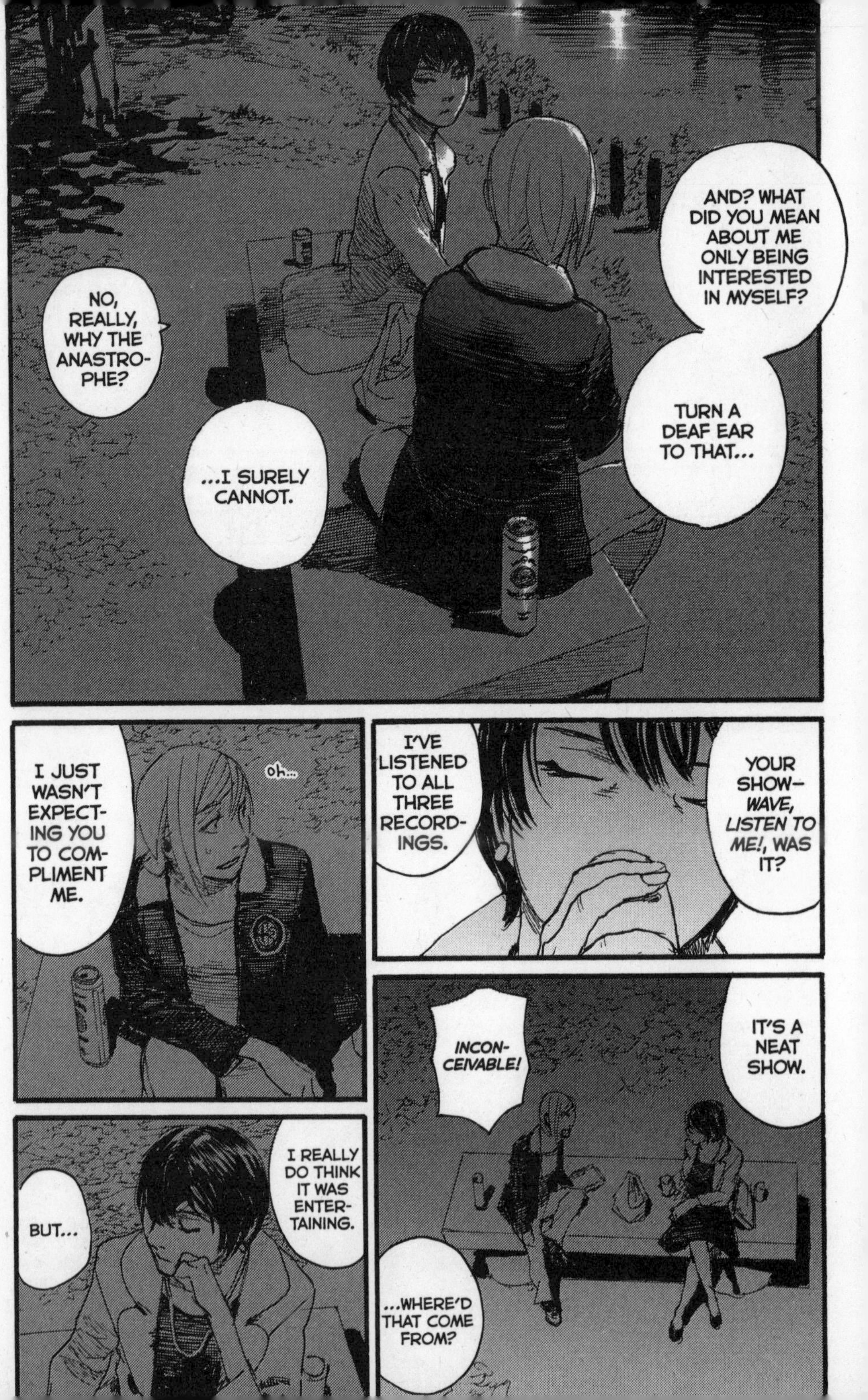
AND? WHAT DID YOU MEAN ABOUT ME ONLY BEING INTERESTED IN MYSELF?
TURN A DEAF EAR TO THAT...
...I SURELY CANNOT.
NO, REALLY, WHY THE ANASTROPHE?
YOUR SHOW—*WAVE, LISTEN TO ME!*, WAS IT?
I'VE LISTENED TO ALL THREE RECORDINGS.
IT'S A NEAT SHOW.
INCONCEIVABLE!
...WHERE'D THAT COME FROM?
oh...
I JUST WASN'T EXPECTING YOU TO COMPLIMENT ME.
I REALLY DO THINK IT WAS ENTERTAINING.
BUT...

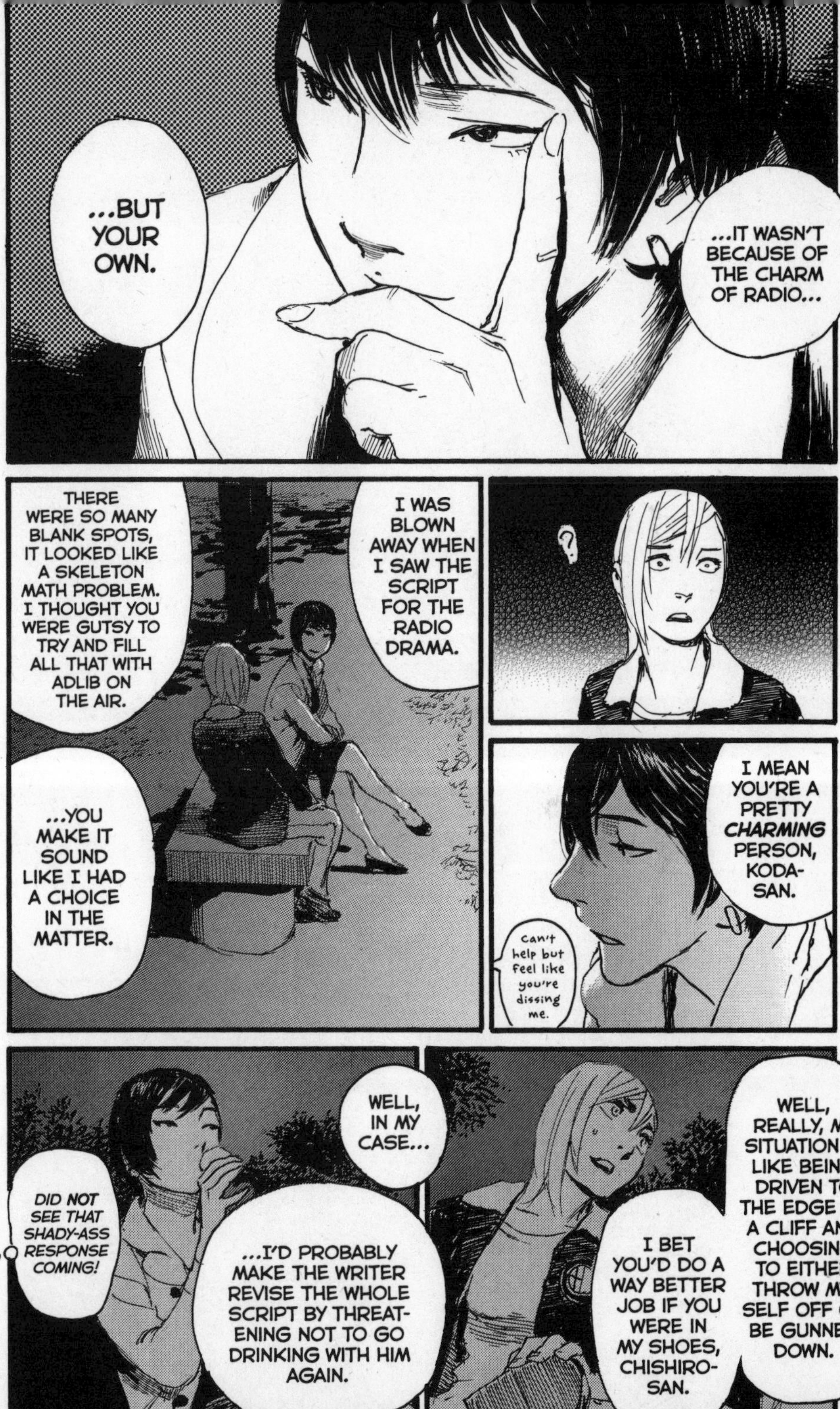
...IT WASN'T BECAUSE OF THE CHARM OF RADIO...
...BUT YOUR OWN.
?
I MEAN YOU'RE A PRETTY *CHARMING* PERSON, KODA-SAN.
Can't help but feel like you're dissing me.
I WAS BLOWN AWAY WHEN I SAW THE SCRIPT FOR THE RADIO DRAMA.
THERE WERE SO MANY BLANK SPOTS, IT LOOKED LIKE A SKELETON MATH PROBLEM. I THOUGHT YOU WERE GUTSY TO TRY AND FILL ALL THAT WITH ADLIB ON THE AIR.
...YOU MAKE IT SOUND LIKE I HAD A CHOICE IN THE MATTER.
WELL, REALLY, MY SITUATION IS LIKE BEING DRIVEN TO THE EDGE OF A CLIFF AND CHOOSING TO EITHER THROW MY-SELF OFF OR BE GUNNED DOWN.
I BET YOU'D DO A WAY BETTER JOB IF YOU WERE IN MY SHOES, CHISHIRO-SAN.
WELL, IN MY CASE...
...I'D PROBABLY MAKE THE WRITER REVISE THE WHOLE SCRIPT BY THREAT-ENING NOT TO GO DRINKING WITH HIM AGAIN.
DID NOT SEE THAT SHADY-ASS RESPONSE COMING!

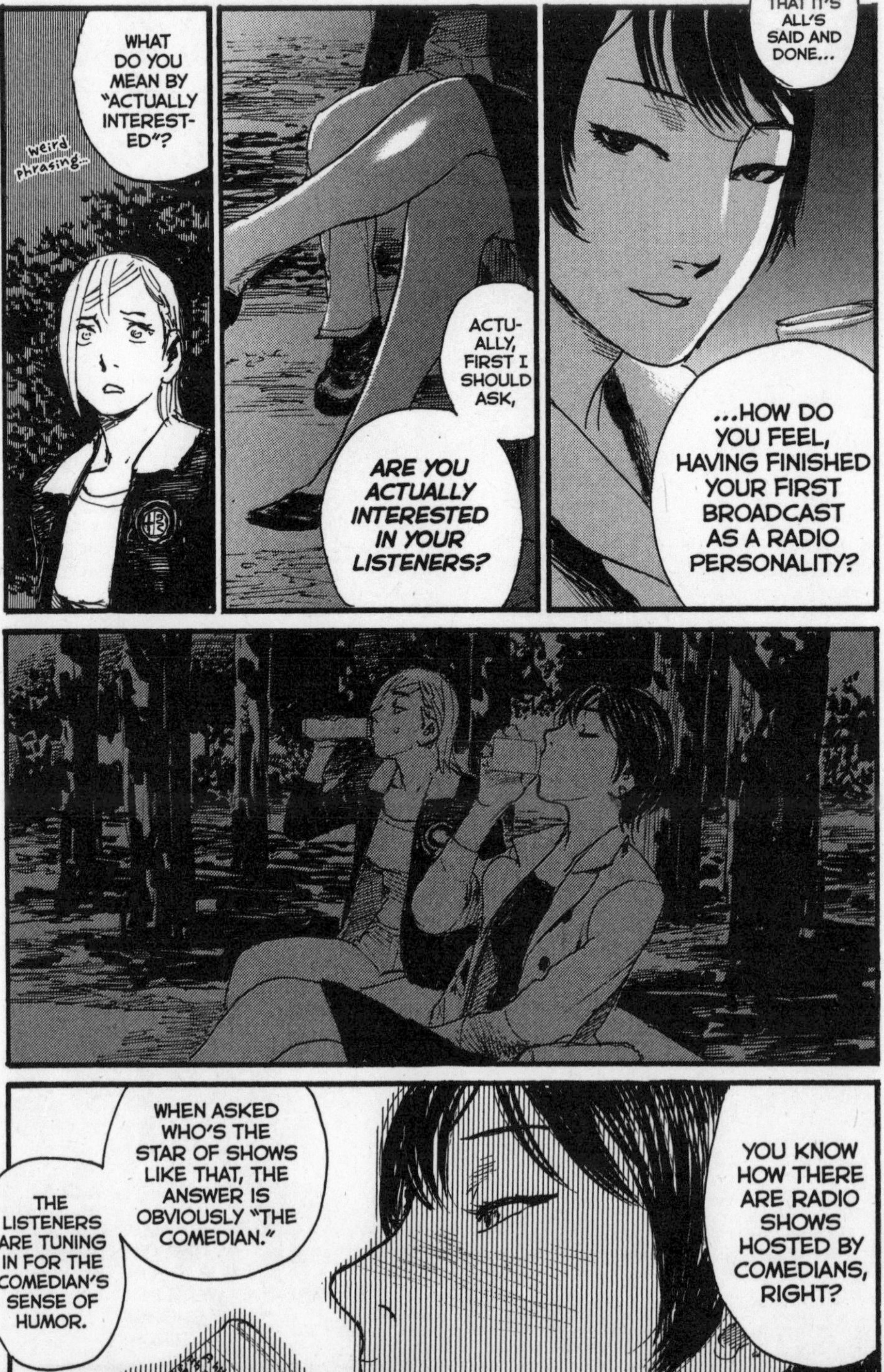
SO, NOW THAT IT'S ALL'S SAID AND DONE...
...HOW DO YOU FEEL, HAVING FINISHED YOUR FIRST BROADCAST AS A RADIO PERSONALITY?
ACTU-ALLY, FIRST I SHOULD ASK,
ARE YOU ACTUALLY INTERESTED IN YOUR LISTENERS?
WHAT DO YOU MEAN BY "ACTUALLY INTEREST-ED"?
weird phrasing...
YOU KNOW HOW THERE ARE RADIO SHOWS HOSTED BY COMEDIANS, RIGHT?
WHEN ASKED WHO'S THE STAR OF SHOWS LIKE THAT, THE ANSWER IS OBVIOUSLY "THE COMEDIAN."
THE LISTENERS ARE TUNING IN FOR THE COMEDIAN'S SENSE OF HUMOR.

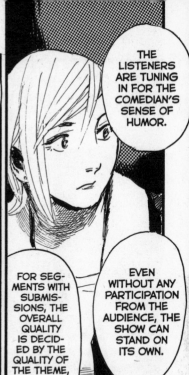

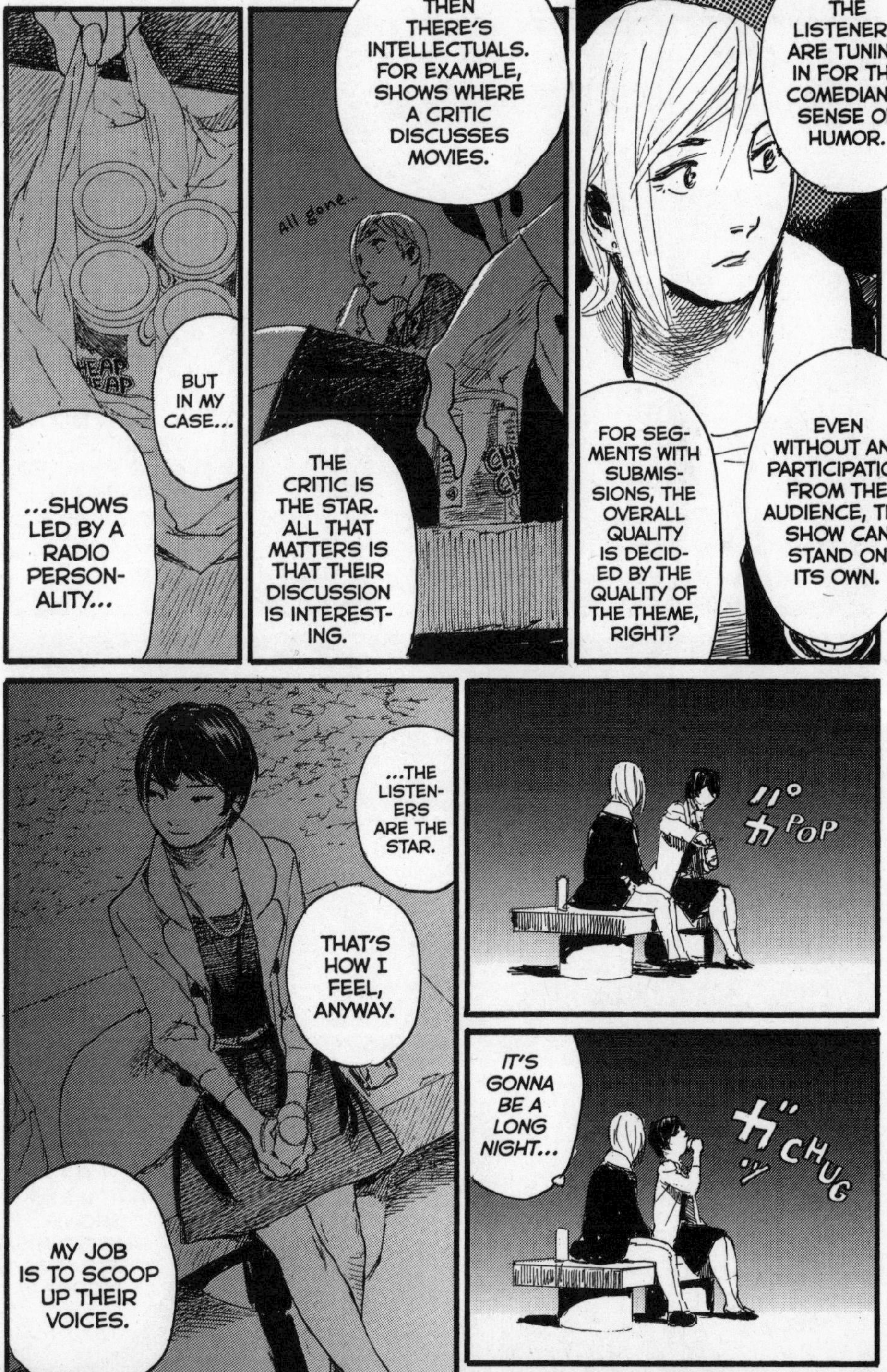
THE LISTENERS ARE TUNING IN FOR THE COMEDIAN'S SENSE OF HUMOR.
EVEN WITHOUT ANY PARTICIPATION FROM THE AUDIENCE, THE SHOW CAN STAND ON ITS OWN.
FOR SEGMENTS WITH SUBMISSIONS, THE OVERALL QUALITY IS DECIDED BY THE QUALITY OF THE THEME, RIGHT?
THEN THERE'S INTELLECTUALS. FOR EXAMPLE, SHOWS WHERE A CRITIC DISCUSSES MOVIES.
All gone...
THE CRITIC IS THE STAR. ALL THAT MATTERS IS THAT THEIR DISCUSSION IS INTERESTING.
BUT IN MY CASE...
...SHOWS LED BY A RADIO PERSONALITY...
パカ POP
IT'S GONNA BE A LONG NIGHT...
ガッ CHUG
...THE LISTENERS ARE THE STAR.
THAT'S HOW I FEEL, ANYWAY.
MY JOB IS TO SCOOP UP THEIR VOICES.

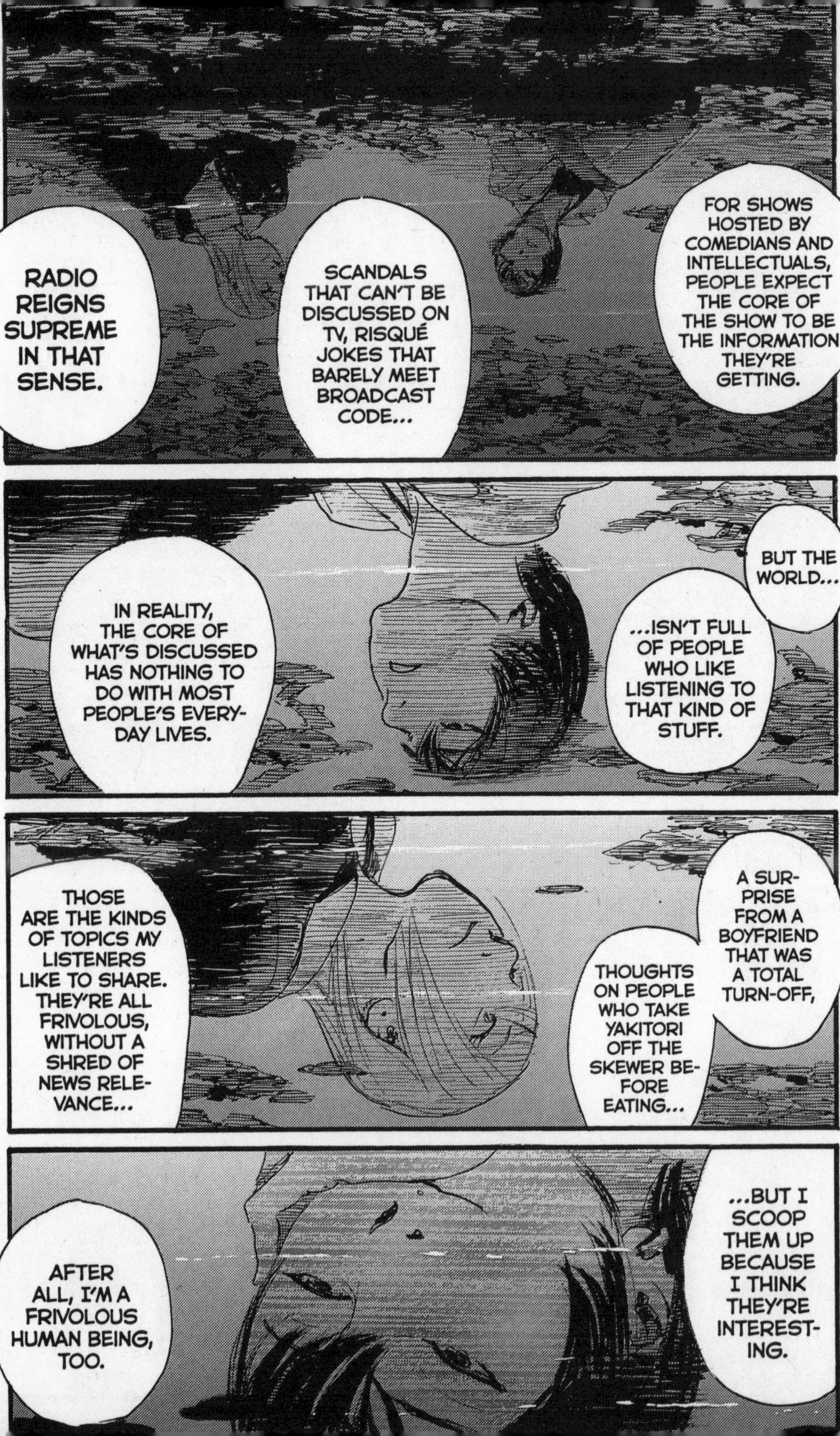
FOR SHOWS HOSTED BY COMEDIANS AND INTELLECTUALS, PEOPLE EXPECT THE CORE OF THE SHOW TO BE THE INFORMATION THEY'RE GETTING.
SCANDALS THAT CAN'T BE DISCUSSED ON TV, RISQUÉ JOKES THAT BARELY MEET BROADCAST CODE...
RADIO REIGNS SUPREME IN THAT SENSE.
BUT THE WORLD...
...ISN'T FULL OF PEOPLE WHO LIKE LISTENING TO THAT KIND OF STUFF.
IN REALITY, THE CORE OF WHAT'S DISCUSSED HAS NOTHING TO DO WITH MOST PEOPLE'S EVERY-DAY LIVES.
A SUR-PRISE FROM A BOYFRIEND THAT WAS A TOTAL TURN-OFF,
THOUGHTS ON PEOPLE WHO TAKE YAKITORI OFF THE SKEWER BE-FORE EATING...
THOSE ARE THE KINDS OF TOPICS MY LISTENERS LIKE TO SHARE. THEY'RE ALL FRIVOLOUS, WITHOUT A SHRED OF NEWS RELE-VANCE...
...BUT I SCOOP THEM UP BECAUSE I THINK THEY'RE INTEREST-ING.
AFTER ALL, I'M A FRIVOLOUS HUMAN BEING, TOO.

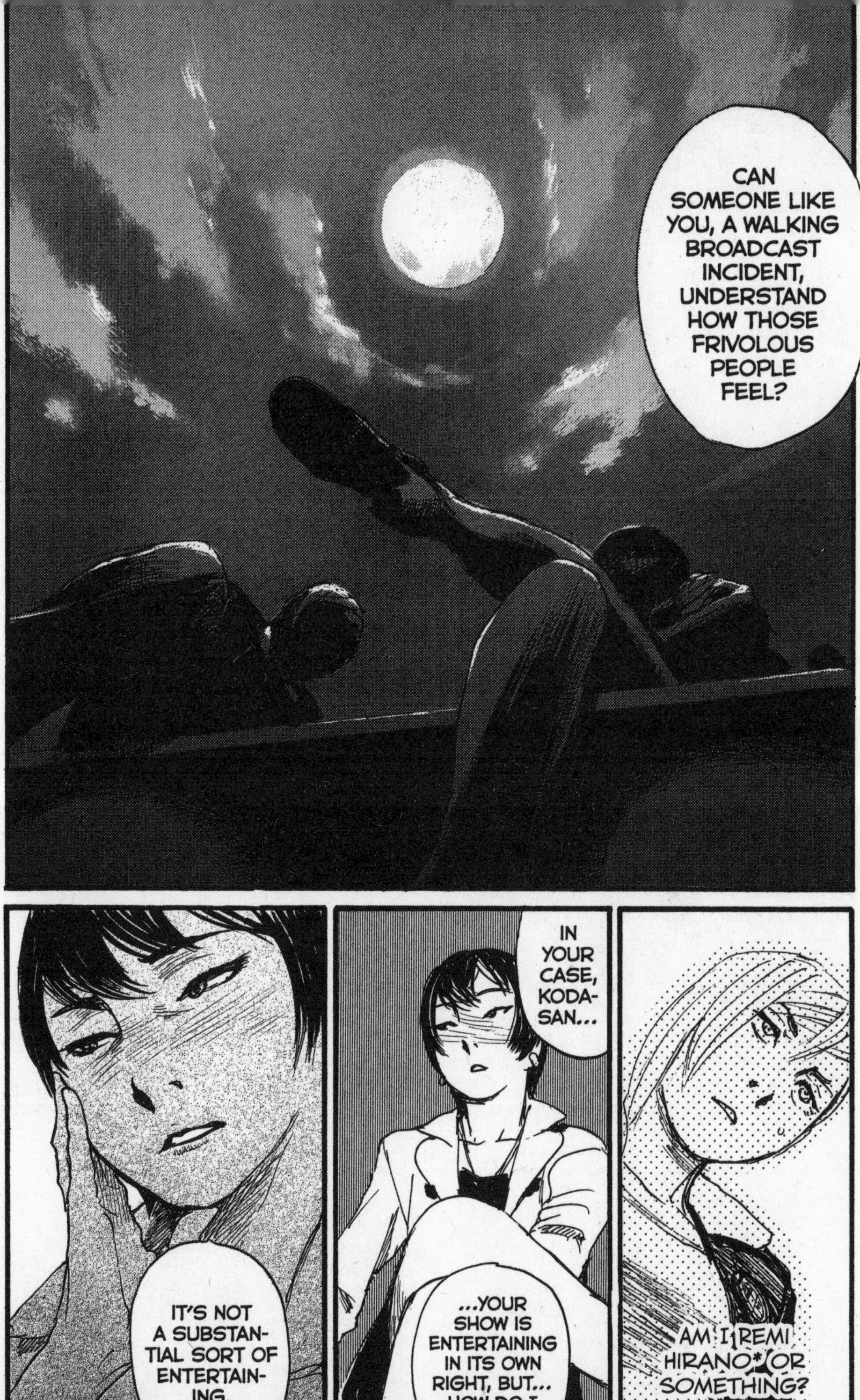
CAN SOMEONE LIKE YOU, A WALKING BROADCAST INCIDENT, UNDERSTAND HOW THOSE FRIVOLOUS PEOPLE FEEL?
AM I REMI HIRANO* OR SOMETHING?
IN YOUR CASE, KODA-SAN...
...YOUR SHOW IS ENTERTAINING IN ITS OWN RIGHT, BUT... HOW DO I PUT IT?
IT'S NOT A SUBSTAN-TIAL SORT OF ENTERTAIN-ING.

*A CHEF AND TV PERSONALITY WITH A PENCHANT FOR FLUBS ON AIR.

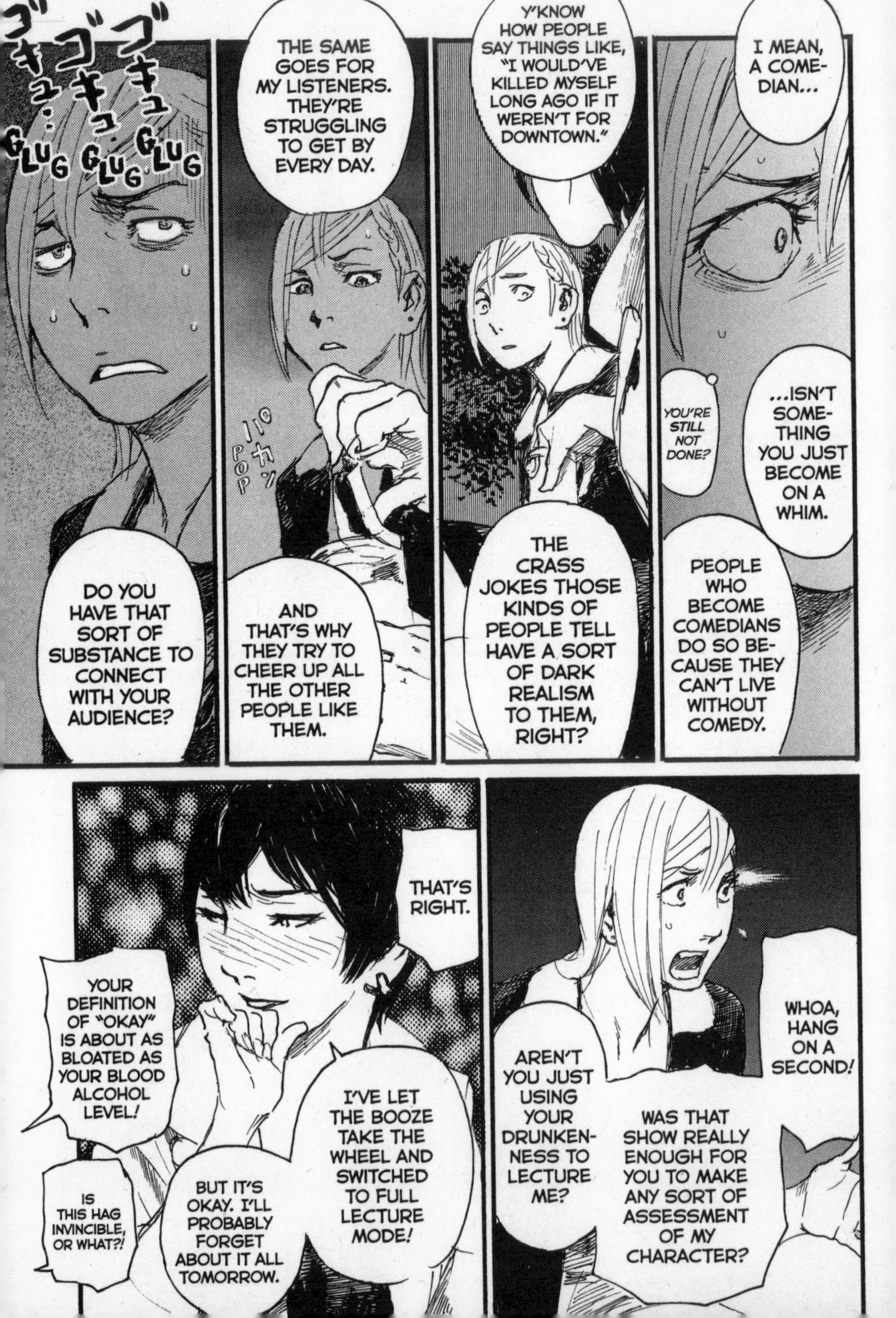
I MEAN, A COMEDIAN...
...ISN'T SOMETHING YOU JUST BECOME ON A WHIM.
YOU'RE STILL NOT DONE?
PEOPLE WHO BECOME COMEDIANS DO SO BECAUSE THEY CAN'T LIVE WITHOUT COMEDY.
Y'KNOW HOW PEOPLE SAY THINGS LIKE, "I WOULD'VE KILLED MYSELF LONG AGO IF IT WEREN'T FOR DOWNTOWN."
THE CRASS JOKES THOSE KINDS OF PEOPLE TELL HAVE A SORT OF DARK REALISM TO THEM, RIGHT?
THE SAME GOES FOR MY LISTENERS. THEY'RE STRUGGLING TO GET BY EVERY DAY.
パカッ POP
AND THAT'S WHY THEY TRY TO CHEER UP ALL THE OTHER PEOPLE LIKE THEM.
ゴキュ ゴキュ ゴキュ GLUG GLUG GLUG
DO YOU HAVE THAT SORT OF SUBSTANCE TO CONNECT WITH YOUR AUDIENCE?
WHOA, HANG ON A SECOND!
WAS THAT SHOW REALLY ENOUGH FOR YOU TO MAKE ANY SORT OF ASSESSMENT OF MY CHARACTER?
AREN'T YOU JUST USING YOUR DRUNKENNESS TO LECTURE ME?
THAT'S RIGHT.
I'VE LET THE BOOZE TAKE THE WHEEL AND SWITCHED TO FULL LECTURE MODE!
BUT IT'S OKAY. I'LL PROBABLY FORGET ABOUT IT ALL TOMORROW.
YOUR DEFINITION OF "OKAY" IS ABOUT AS BLOATED AS YOUR BLOOD ALCOHOL LEVEL!
IS THIS HAG INVINCIBLE, OR WHAT?!

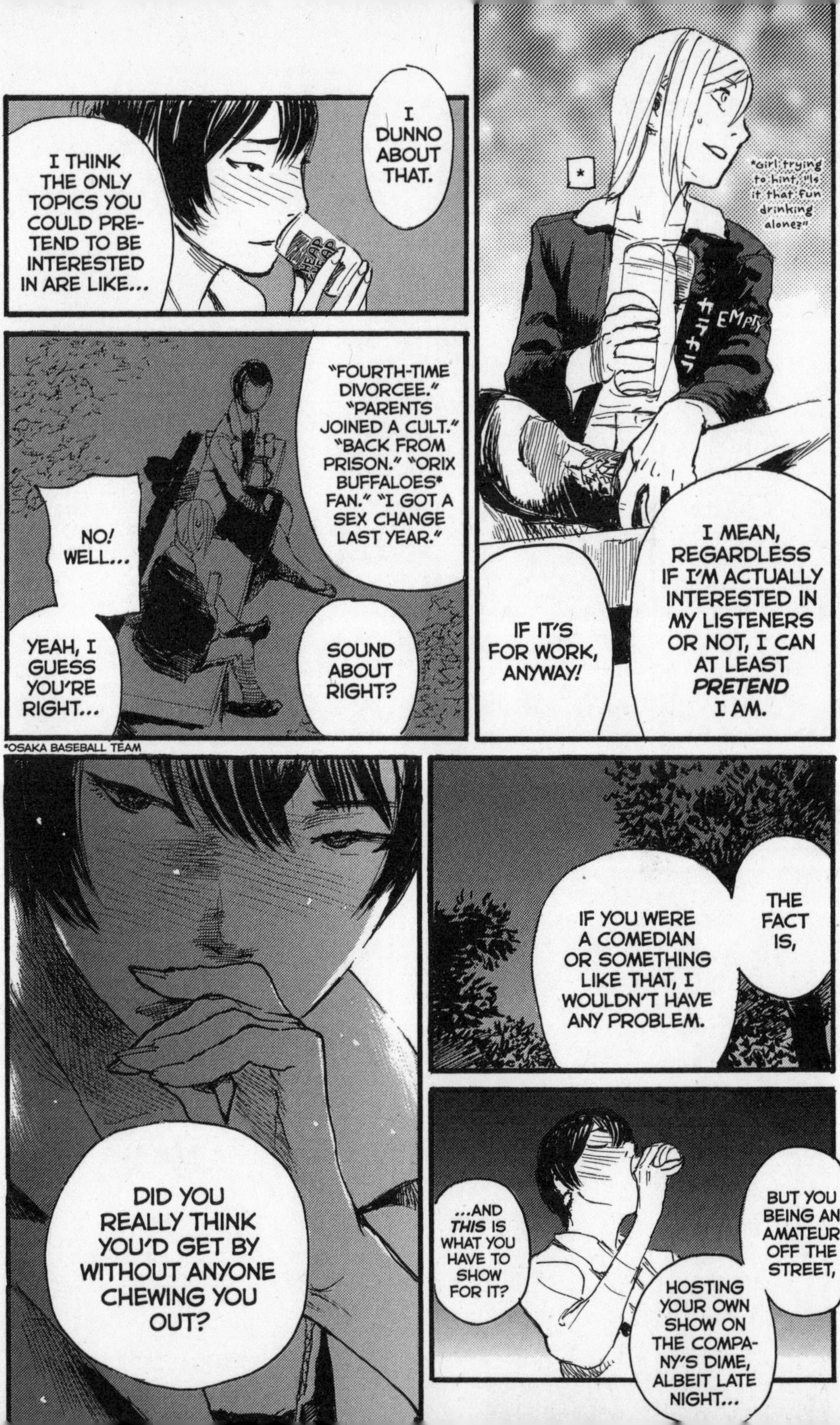
*
*Girl trying to hint, "Is it that fun drinking alone?"
EMPTY
I MEAN, REGARDLESS IF I'M ACTUALLY INTERESTED IN MY LISTENERS OR NOT, I CAN AT LEAST *PRETEND* I AM.
IF IT'S FOR WORK, ANYWAY!
I DUNNO ABOUT THAT.
I THINK THE ONLY TOPICS YOU COULD PRETEND TO BE INTERESTED IN ARE LIKE...
"FOURTH-TIME DIVORCEE." "PARENTS JOINED A CULT." "BACK FROM PRISON." "ORIX BUFFALOES* FAN." "I GOT A SEX CHANGE LAST YEAR."
NO! WELL...
SOUND ABOUT RIGHT?
YEAH, I GUESS YOU'RE RIGHT...
*OSAKA BASEBALL TEAM
THE FACT IS,
IF YOU WERE A COMEDIAN OR SOMETHING LIKE THAT, I WOULDN'T HAVE ANY PROBLEM.
BUT YOU BEING AN AMATEUR OFF THE STREET,
HOSTING YOUR OWN SHOW ON THE COMPANY'S DIME, ALBEIT LATE NIGHT...
...AND *THIS* IS WHAT YOU HAVE TO SHOW FOR IT?
DID YOU REALLY THINK YOU'D GET BY WITHOUT ANYONE CHEWING YOU OUT?

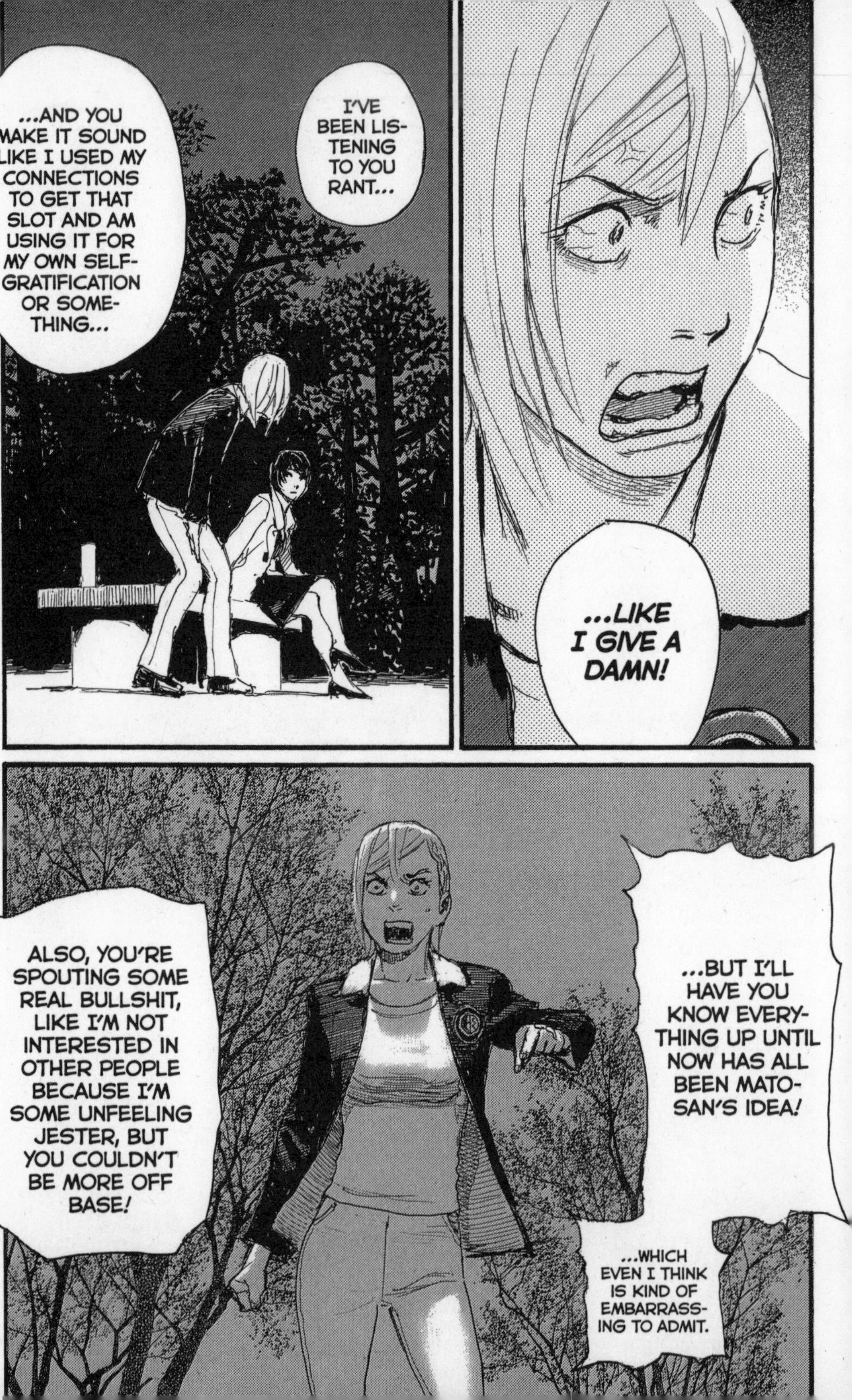
...LIKE I GIVE A DAMN!
I'VE BEEN LISTENING TO YOU RANT...
...AND YOU MAKE IT SOUND LIKE I USED MY CONNECTIONS TO GET THAT SLOT AND AM USING IT FOR MY OWN SELF-GRATIFICATION OR SOMETHING...
ALSO, YOU'RE SPOUTING SOME REAL BULLSHIT, LIKE I'M NOT INTERESTED IN OTHER PEOPLE BECAUSE I'M SOME UNFEELING JESTER, BUT YOU COULDN'T BE MORE OFF BASE!
...BUT I'LL HAVE YOU KNOW EVERYTHING UP UNTIL NOW HAS ALL BEEN MATO-SAN'S IDEA!
...WHICH EVEN I THINK IS KIND OF EMBARRASSING TO ADMIT.

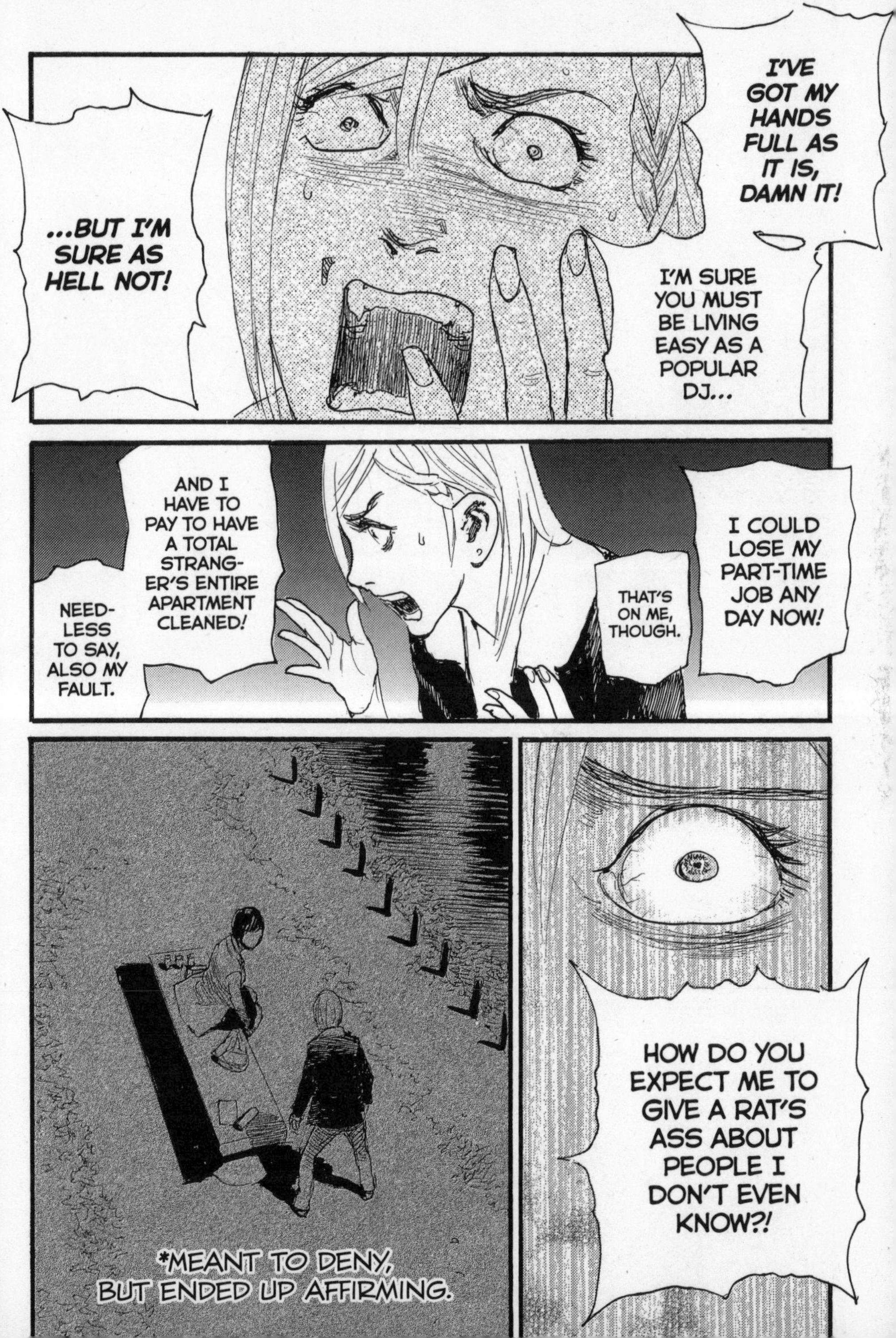
I'VE GOT MY HANDS FULL AS IT IS, DAMN IT!
I'M SURE YOU MUST BE LIVING EASY AS A POPULAR DJ...
...BUT I'M SURE AS HELL NOT!
I COULD LOSE MY PART-TIME JOB ANY DAY NOW!
THAT'S ON ME, THOUGH.
AND I HAVE TO PAY TO HAVE A TOTAL STRANGER'S ENTIRE APARTMENT CLEANED!
NEEDLESS TO SAY, ALSO MY FAULT.
HOW DO YOU EXPECT ME TO GIVE A RAT'S ASS ABOUT PEOPLE I DON'T EVEN KNOW?!
*MEANT TO DENY, BUT ENDED UP AFFIRMING.

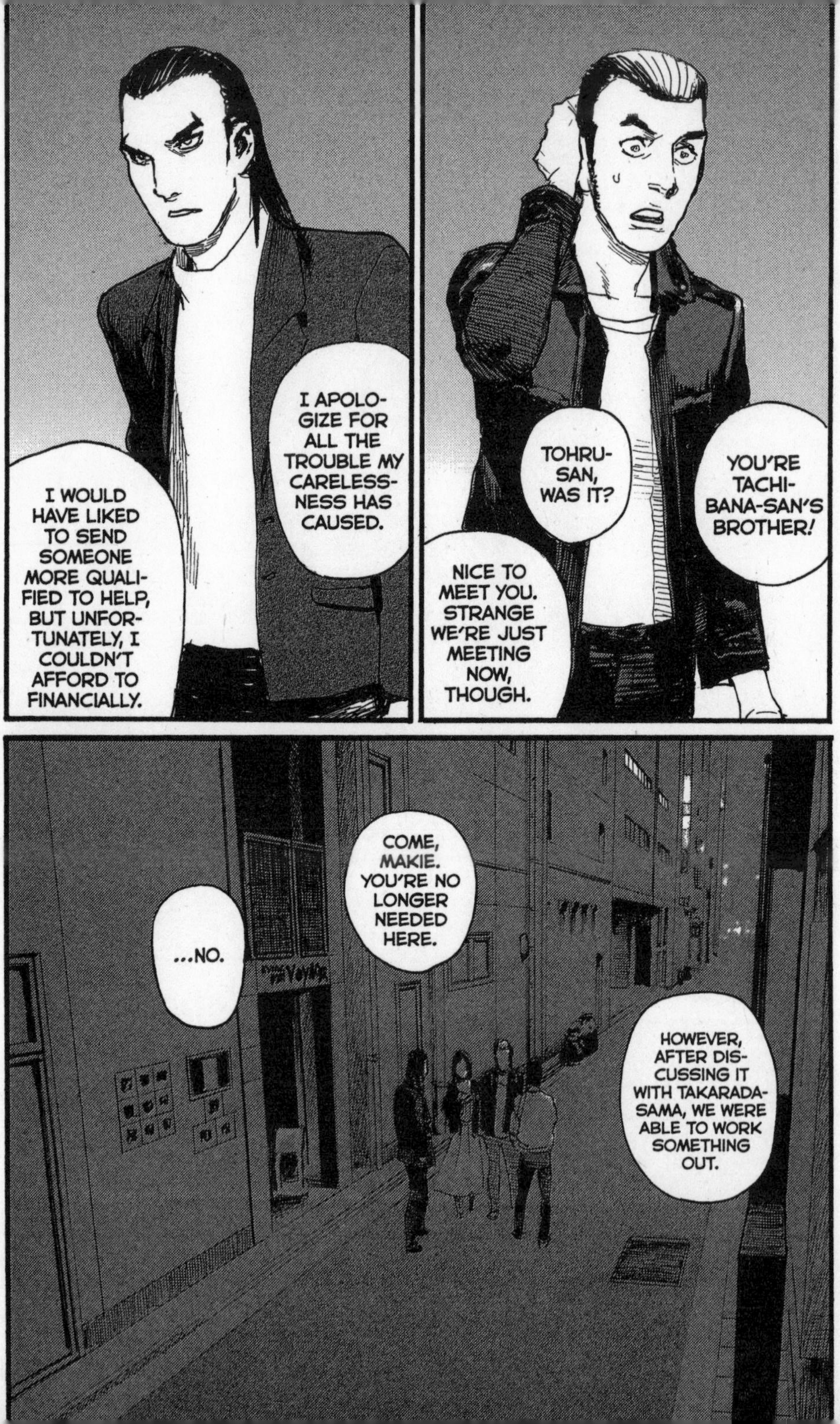

YOU'RE TACHI-BANA-SAN'S BROTHER!
TOHRU-SAN, WAS IT?
NICE TO MEET YOU. STRANGE WE'RE JUST MEETING NOW, THOUGH.
I APOLO-GIZE FOR ALL THE TROUBLE MY CARELESS-NESS HAS CAUSED.
I WOULD HAVE LIKED TO SEND SOMEONE MORE QUALI-FIED TO HELP, BUT UNFOR-TUNATELY, I COULDN'T AFFORD TO FINANCIALLY.
HOWEVER, AFTER DIS-CUSSING IT WITH TAKARADA-SAMA, WE WERE ABLE TO WORK SOMETHING OUT.
COME, MAKIE. YOU'RE NO LONGER NEEDED HERE.
...NO.

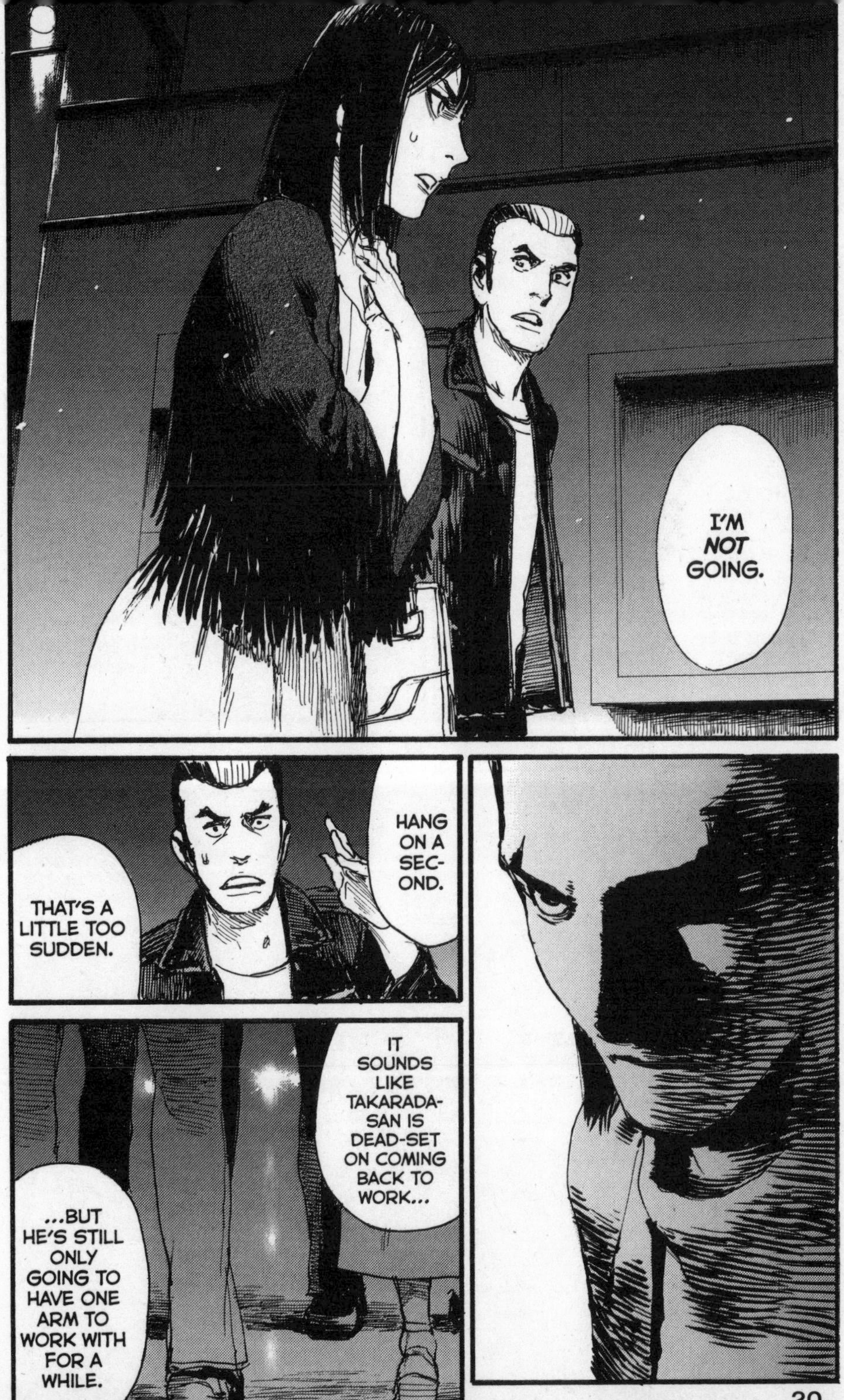
I'M *NOT* GOING.
HANG ON A SEC-OND.
THAT'S A LITTLE TOO SUDDEN.
IT SOUNDS LIKE TAKARADA-SAN IS DEAD-SET ON COMING BACK TO WORK...
...BUT HE'S STILL ONLY GOING TO HAVE ONE ARM TO WORK WITH FOR A WHILE.

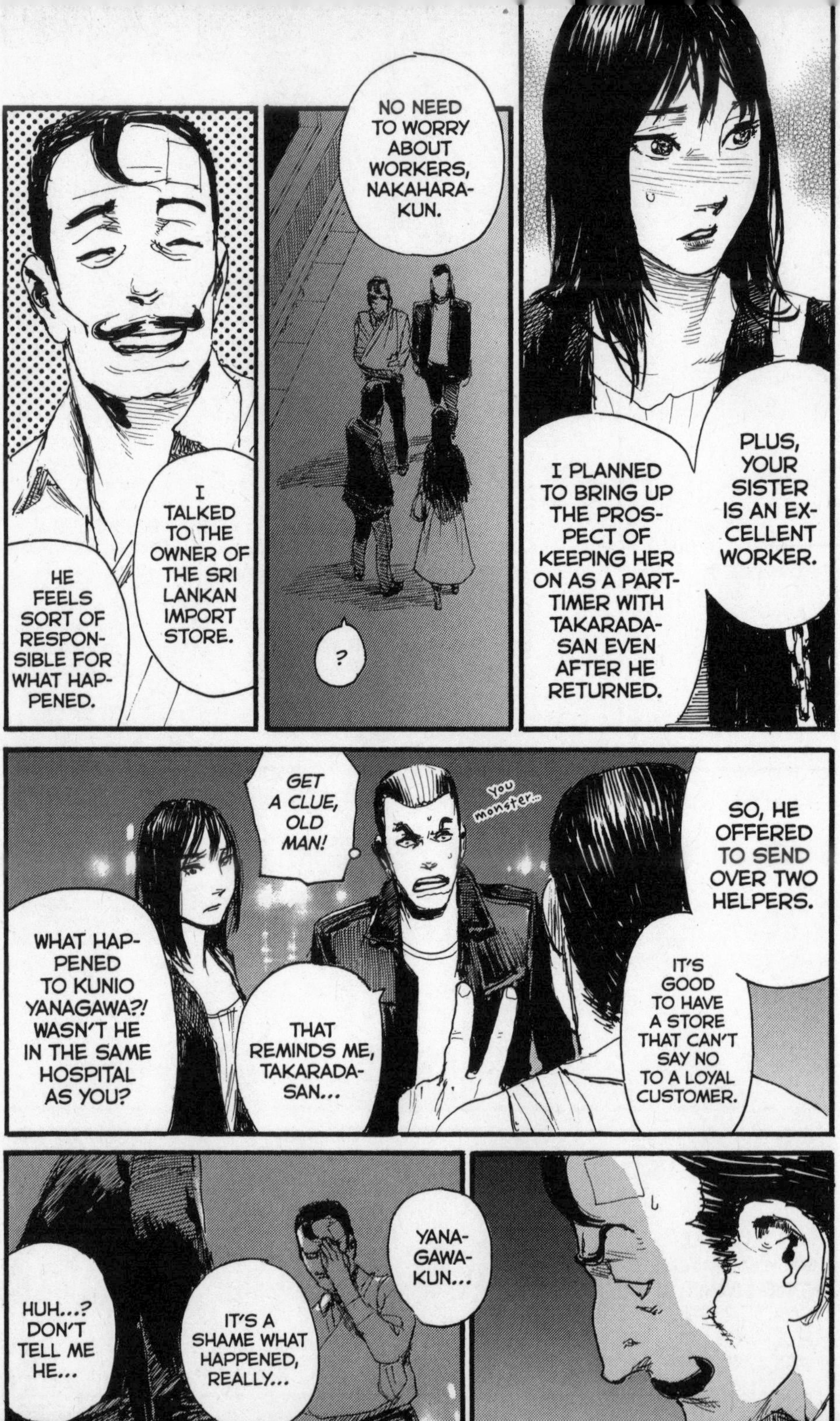
PLUS, YOUR SISTER IS AN EXCELLENT WORKER.
I PLANNED TO BRING UP THE PROSPECT OF KEEPING HER ON AS A PART-TIMER WITH TAKARADA-SAN EVEN AFTER HE RETURNED.
NO NEED TO WORRY ABOUT WORKERS, NAKAHARA-KUN.
?
I TALKED TO THE OWNER OF THE SRI LANKAN IMPORT STORE.
HE FEELS SORT OF RESPONSIBLE FOR WHAT HAPPENED.
SO, HE OFFERED TO SEND OVER TWO HELPERS.
IT'S GOOD TO HAVE A STORE THAT CAN'T SAY NO TO A LOYAL CUSTOMER.
You monster...
GET A CLUE, OLD MAN!
THAT REMINDS ME, TAKARADA-SAN...
WHAT HAPPENED TO KUNIO YANAGAWA?! WASN'T HE IN THE SAME HOSPITAL AS YOU?
YANAGAWA-KUN...
IT'S A SHAME WHAT HAPPENED, REALLY...
HUH...? DON'T TELL ME HE...

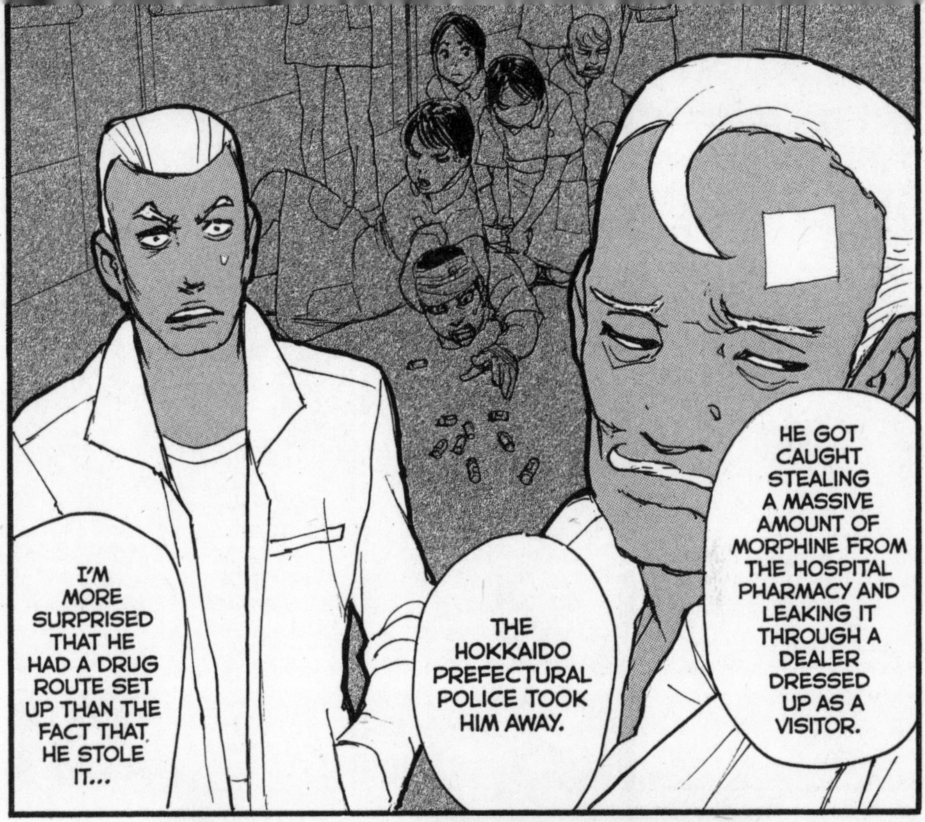
HE GOT CAUGHT STEALING A MASSIVE AMOUNT OF MORPHINE FROM THE HOSPITAL PHARMACY AND LEAKING IT THROUGH A DEALER DRESSED UP AS A VISITOR.
THE HOKKAIDO PREFECTURAL POLICE TOOK HIM AWAY.
I'M MORE SURPRISED THAT HE HAD A DRUG ROUTE SET UP THAN THE FACT THAT HE STOLE IT...

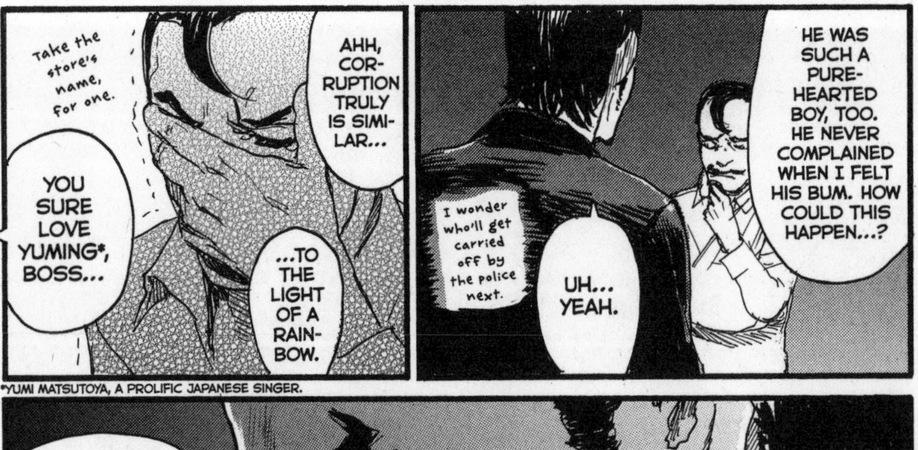
HE WAS SUCH A PURE-HEARTED BOY, TOO. HE NEVER COMPLAINED WHEN I FELT HIS BUM. HOW COULD THIS HAPPEN...?
UH... YEAH.
I wonder who'll get carried off by the police next.
AHH, CORRUPTION TRULY IS SIMILAR...
...TO THE LIGHT OF A RAINBOW.
Take the store's name, for one.
YOU SURE LOVE YUMING*, BOSS...

*YUMI MATSUTOYA, A PROLIFIC JAPANESE SINGER.

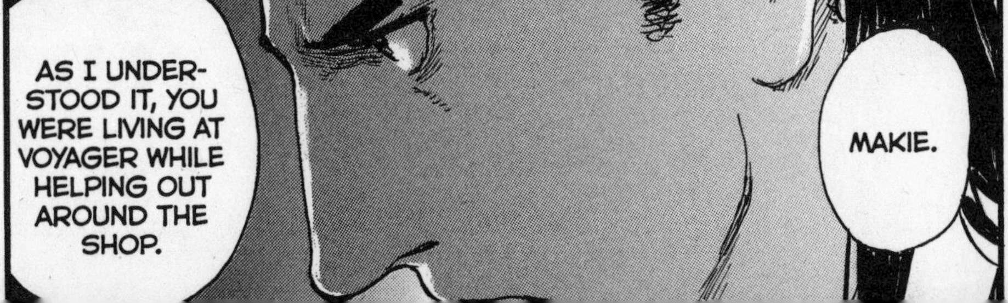
MAKIE.
AS I UNDERSTOOD IT, YOU WERE LIVING AT VOYAGER WHILE HELPING OUT AROUND THE SHOP.

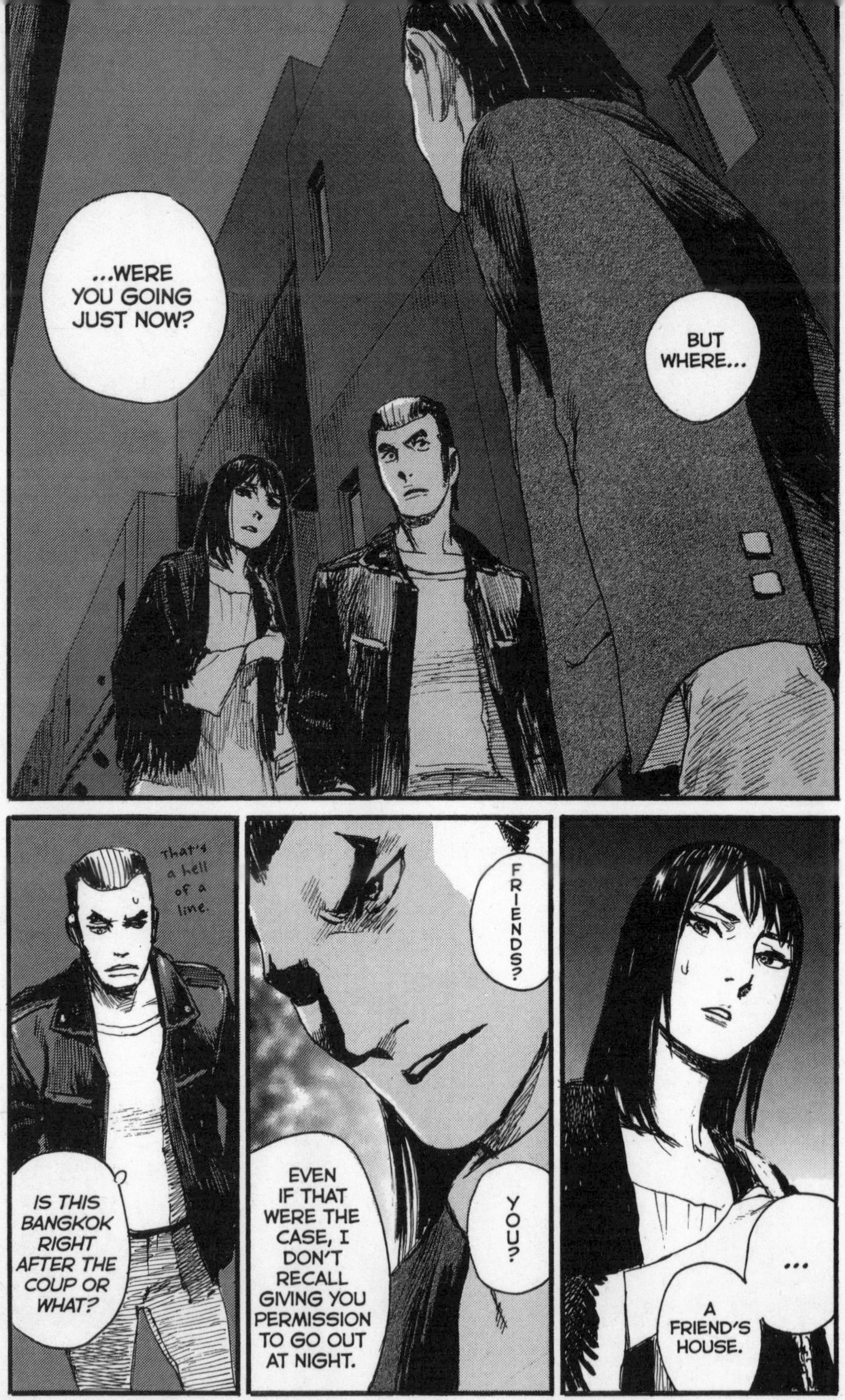
BUT WHERE...
...WERE YOU GOING JUST NOW?
...
A FRIEND'S HOUSE.
FRIENDS?
YOU?
EVEN IF THAT WERE THE CASE, I DON'T RECALL GIVING YOU PERMISSION TO GO OUT AT NIGHT.
That's a hell of a line.
IS THIS BANGKOK RIGHT AFTER THE COUP OR WHAT?

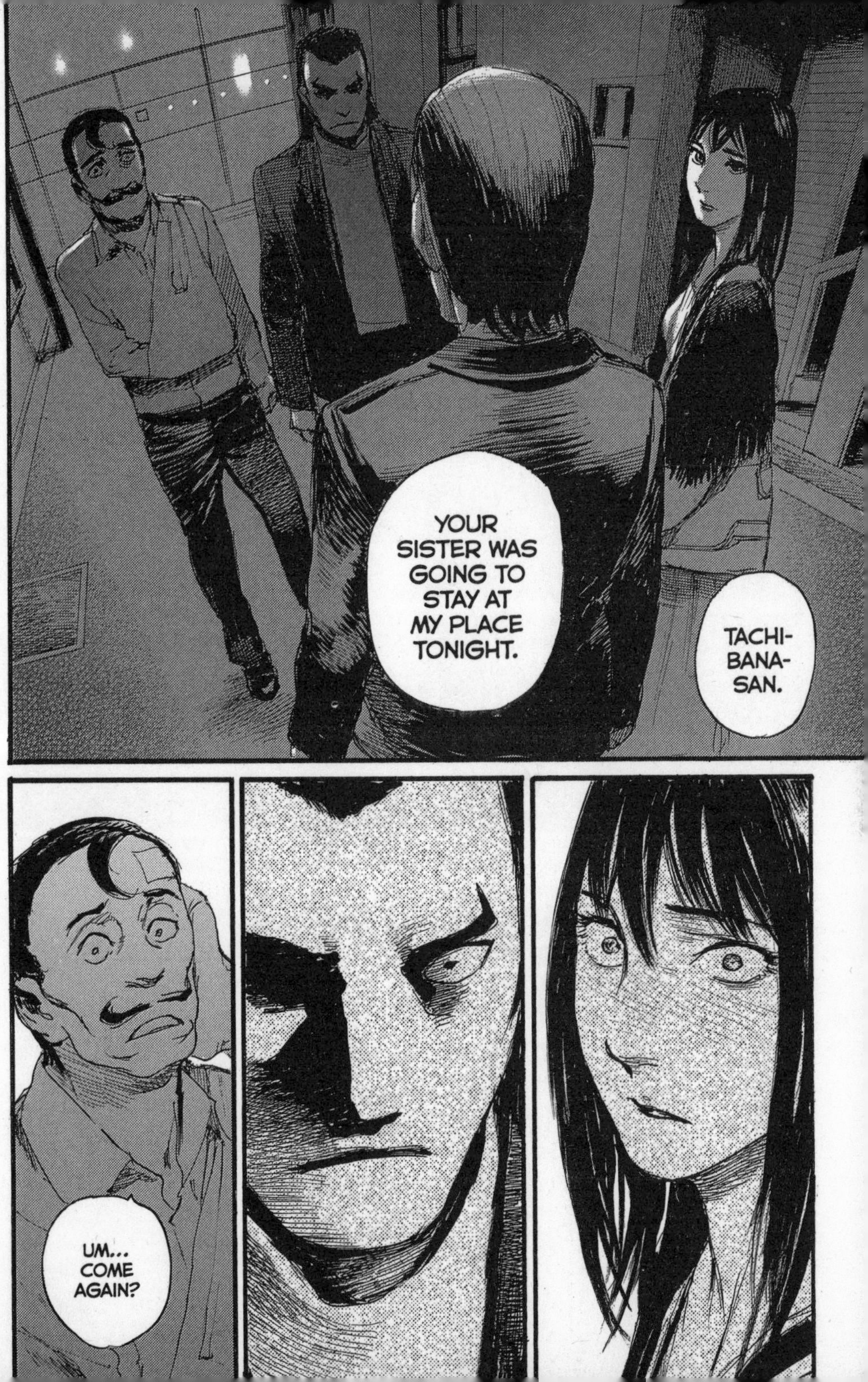
TACHI-BANA-SAN.
YOUR SISTER WAS GOING TO STAY AT MY PLACE TONIGHT.
UM... COME AGAIN?

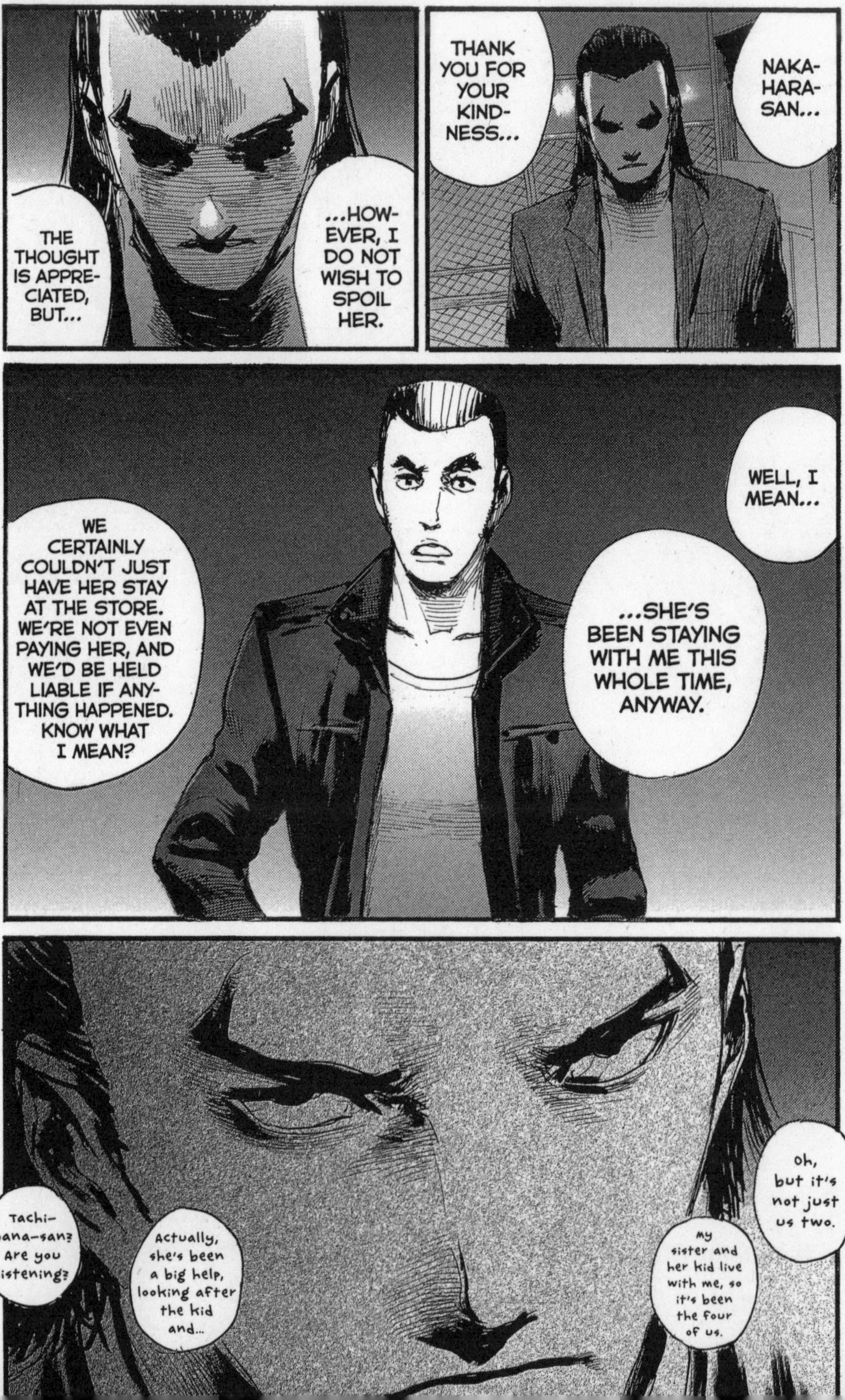
NAKAHARA-SAN...
THANK YOU FOR YOUR KINDNESS...
...HOWEVER, I DO NOT WISH TO SPOIL HER.
THE THOUGHT IS APPRECIATED, BUT...
WELL, I MEAN...
...SHE'S BEEN STAYING WITH ME THIS WHOLE TIME, ANYWAY.
WE CERTAINLY COULDN'T JUST HAVE HER STAY AT THE STORE. WE'RE NOT EVEN PAYING HER, AND WE'D BE HELD LIABLE IF ANYTHING HAPPENED. KNOW WHAT I MEAN?
Oh, but it's not just us two.
My sister and her kid live with me, so it's been the four of us.
Actually, she's been a big help, looking after the kid and...
Tachibana-san? Are you listening?

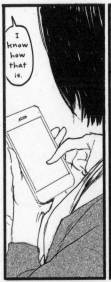

CLUNK CLONK
It's late, but I'm hungry...
I know how that is.
Cheers
09-30-2015 12:52
I'll be home late tonight. Madoka Chishiro asked me to meet her in Maruyama Park… I'll get her before she gets me! Don't wait up.
Hey! Don't ignore us!

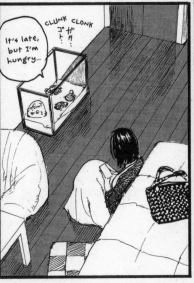

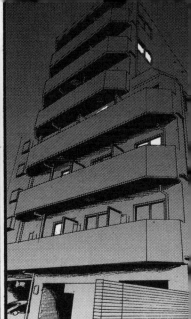

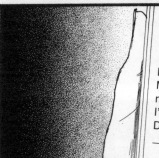

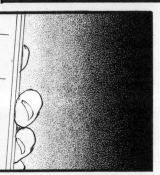

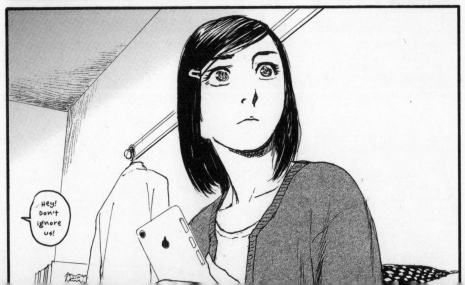

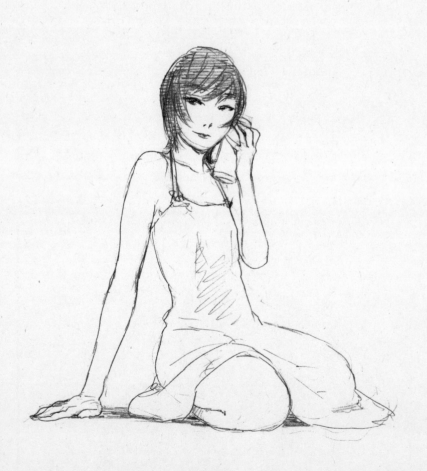

wave
LISTEN TO ME!

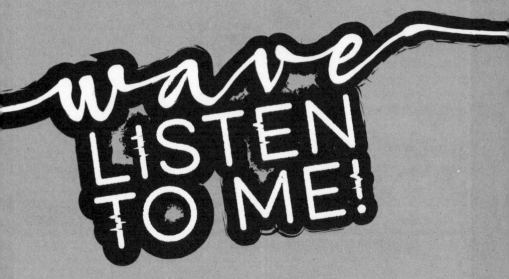

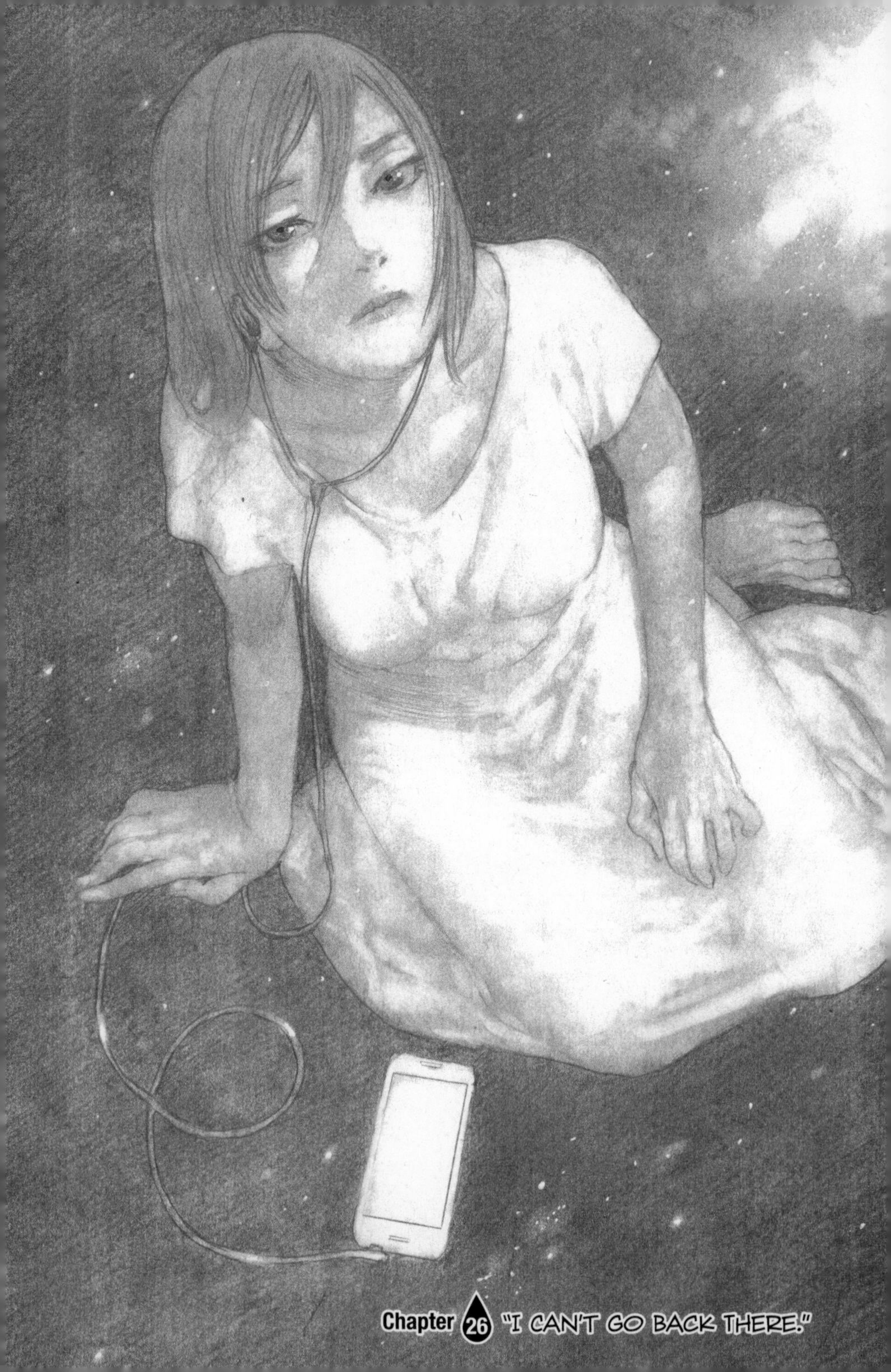
Chapter 26 "I CAN'T GO BACK THERE."

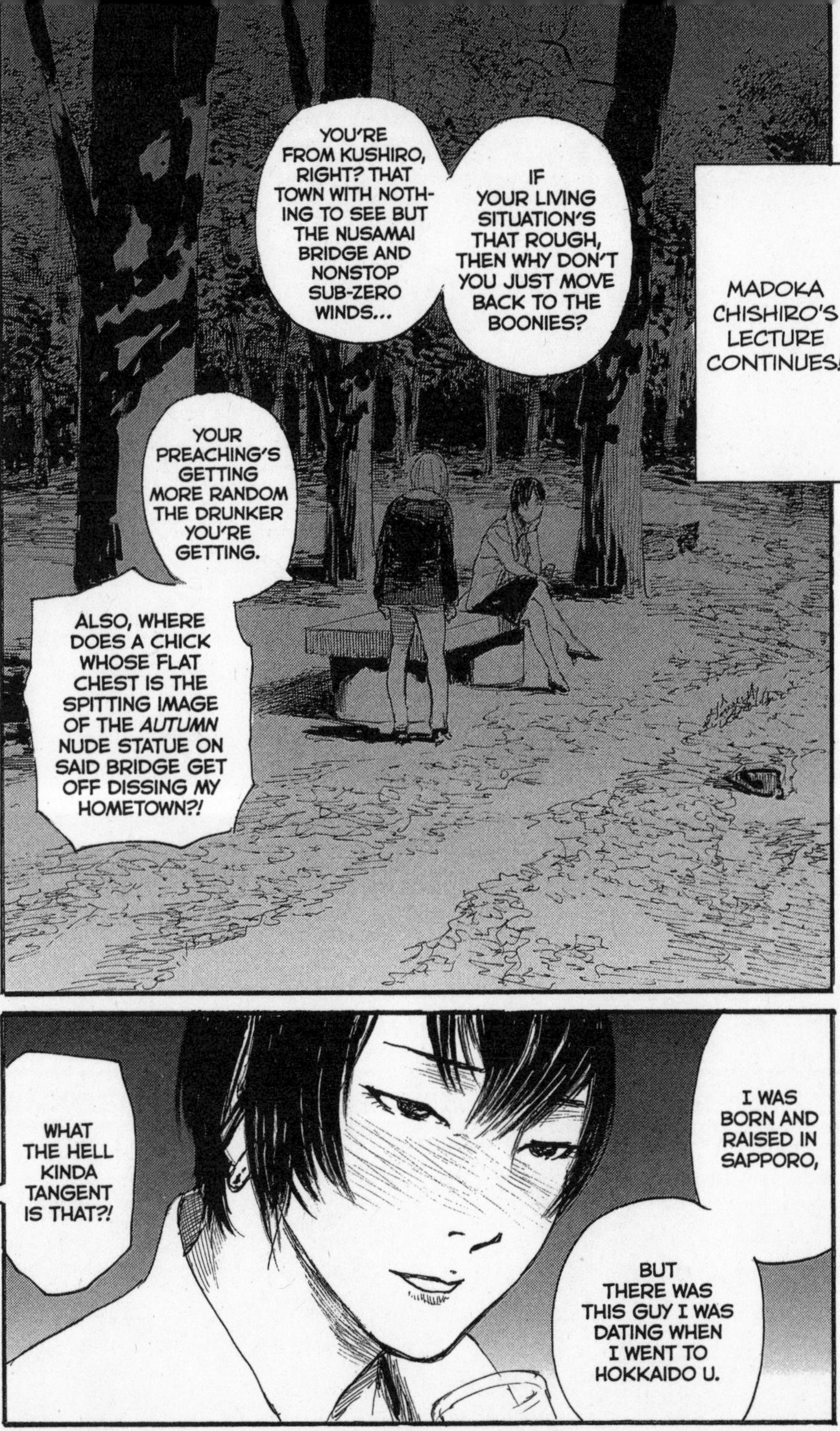
MADOKA CHISHIRO'S LECTURE CONTINUES!
IF YOUR LIVING SITUATION'S THAT ROUGH, THEN WHY DON'T YOU JUST MOVE BACK TO THE BOONIES?
YOU'RE FROM KUSHIRO, RIGHT? THAT TOWN WITH NOTHING TO SEE BUT THE NUSAMAI BRIDGE AND NONSTOP SUB-ZERO WINDS...
YOUR PREACHING'S GETTING MORE RANDOM THE DRUNKER YOU'RE GETTING.
ALSO, WHERE DOES A CHICK WHOSE FLAT CHEST IS THE SPITTING IMAGE OF THE *AUTUMN* NUDE STATUE ON SAID BRIDGE GET OFF DISSING MY HOMETOWN?!
I WAS BORN AND RAISED IN SAPPORO,
BUT THERE WAS THIS GUY I WAS DATING WHEN I WENT TO HOKKAIDO U.
WHAT THE HELL KINDA TANGENT IS THAT?!

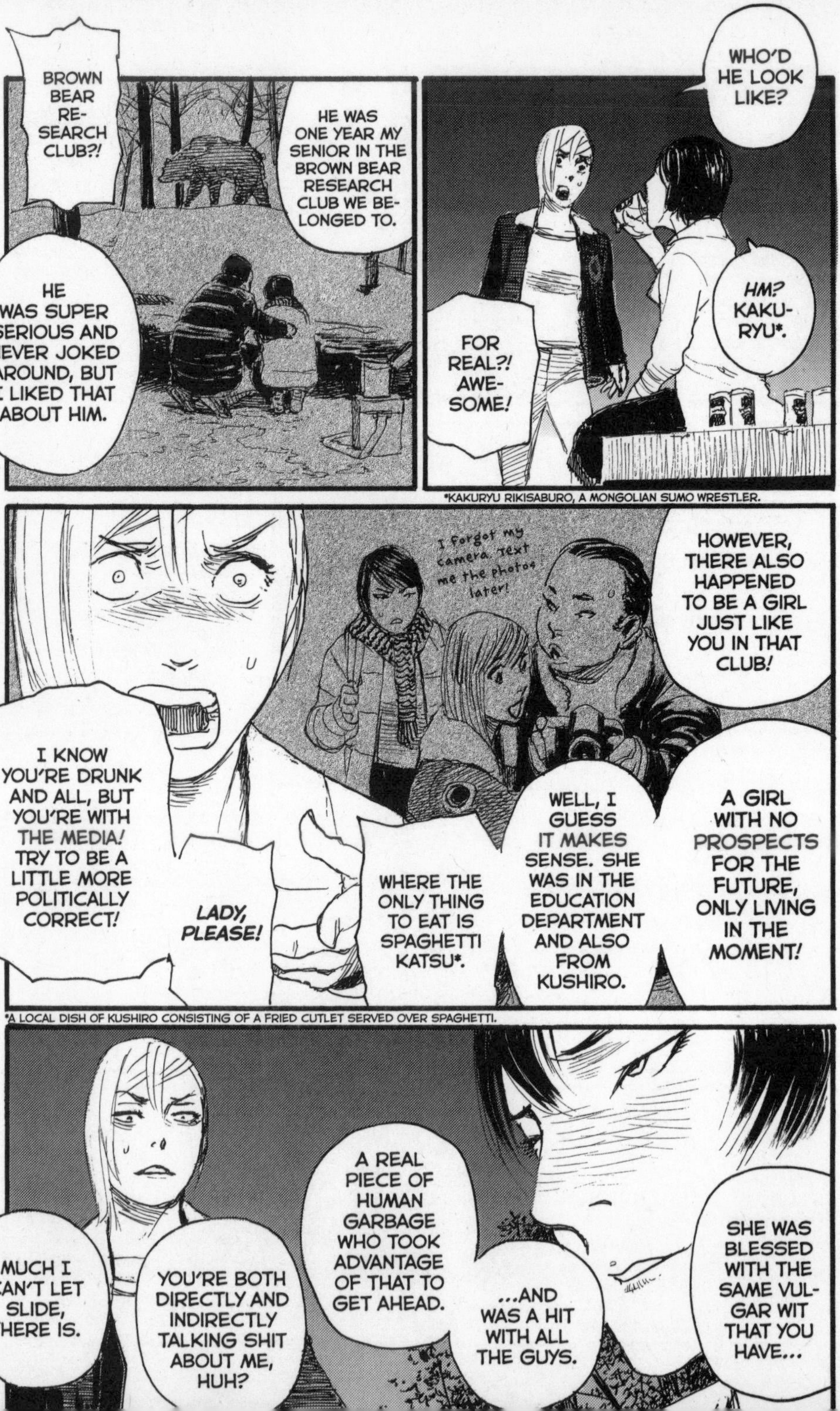
WHO'D HE LOOK LIKE?
HM? KAKURYU*.
FOR REAL?! AWESOME!
HE WAS ONE YEAR MY SENIOR IN THE BROWN BEAR RESEARCH CLUB WE BELONGED TO.
BROWN BEAR RESEARCH CLUB?!
HE WAS SUPER SERIOUS AND NEVER JOKED AROUND, BUT I LIKED THAT ABOUT HIM.
HOWEVER, THERE ALSO HAPPENED TO BE A GIRL JUST LIKE YOU IN THAT CLUB!
I forgot my camera. Text me the photos later!
A GIRL WITH NO PROSPECTS FOR THE FUTURE, ONLY LIVING IN THE MOMENT!
WELL, I GUESS IT MAKES SENSE. SHE WAS IN THE EDUCATION DEPARTMENT AND ALSO FROM KUSHIRO.
WHERE THE ONLY THING TO EAT IS SPAGHETTI KATSU*.
LADY, PLEASE!
I KNOW YOU'RE DRUNK AND ALL, BUT YOU'RE WITH THE MEDIA! TRY TO BE A LITTLE MORE POLITICALLY CORRECT!
SHE WAS BLESSED WITH THE SAME VULGAR WIT THAT YOU HAVE...
...AND WAS A HIT WITH ALL THE GUYS.
A REAL PIECE OF HUMAN GARBAGE WHO TOOK ADVANTAGE OF THAT TO GET AHEAD.
YOU'RE BOTH DIRECTLY AND INDIRECTLY TALKING SHIT ABOUT ME, HUH?
MUCH I CAN'T LET SLIDE, THERE IS.

*KAKURYU RIKISABURO, A MONGOLIAN SUMO WRESTLER.

*A LOCAL DISH OF KUSHIRO CONSISTING OF A FRIED CUTLET SERVED OVER SPAGHETTI.

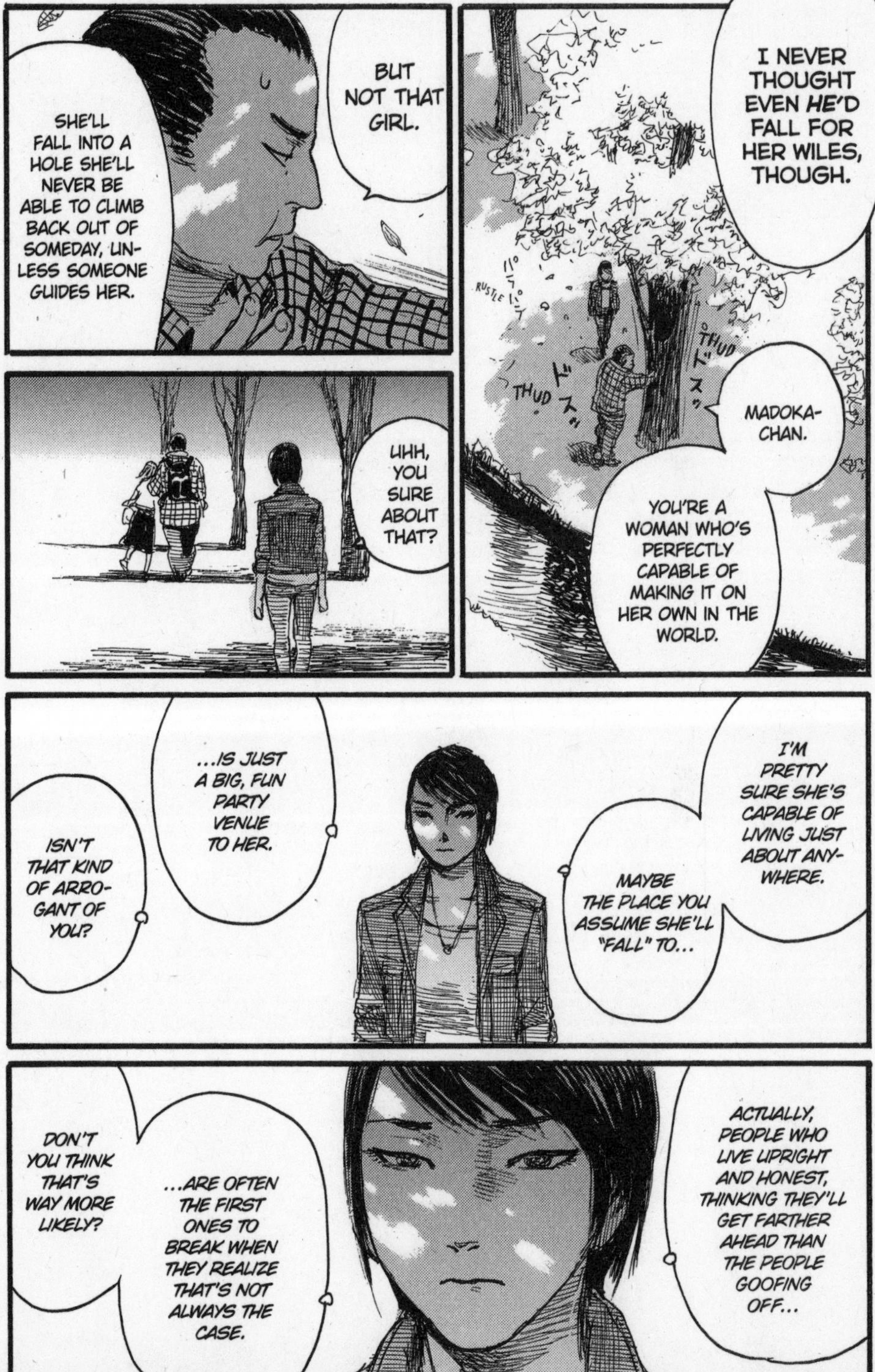
I NEVER THOUGHT EVEN HE'D FALL FOR HER WILES, THOUGH.
RUSTLE
THUD
THUD
MADOKA-CHAN.
YOU'RE A WOMAN WHO'S PERFECTLY CAPABLE OF MAKING IT ON HER OWN IN THE WORLD.
BUT NOT THAT GIRL.
SHE'LL FALL INTO A HOLE SHE'LL NEVER BE ABLE TO CLIMB BACK OUT OF SOMEDAY, UNLESS SOMEONE GUIDES HER.
UHH, YOU SURE ABOUT THAT?
I'M PRETTY SURE SHE'S CAPABLE OF LIVING JUST ABOUT ANYWHERE.
MAYBE THE PLACE YOU ASSUME SHE'LL "FALL" TO...
...IS JUST A BIG, FUN PARTY VENUE TO HER.
ISN'T THAT KIND OF ARROGANT OF YOU?
ACTUALLY, PEOPLE WHO LIVE UPRIGHT AND HONEST, THINKING THEY'LL GET FARTHER AHEAD THAN THE PEOPLE GOOFING OFF...
...ARE OFTEN THE FIRST ONES TO BREAK WHEN THEY REALIZE THAT'S NOT ALWAYS THE CASE.
DON'T YOU THINK THAT'S WAY MORE LIKELY?

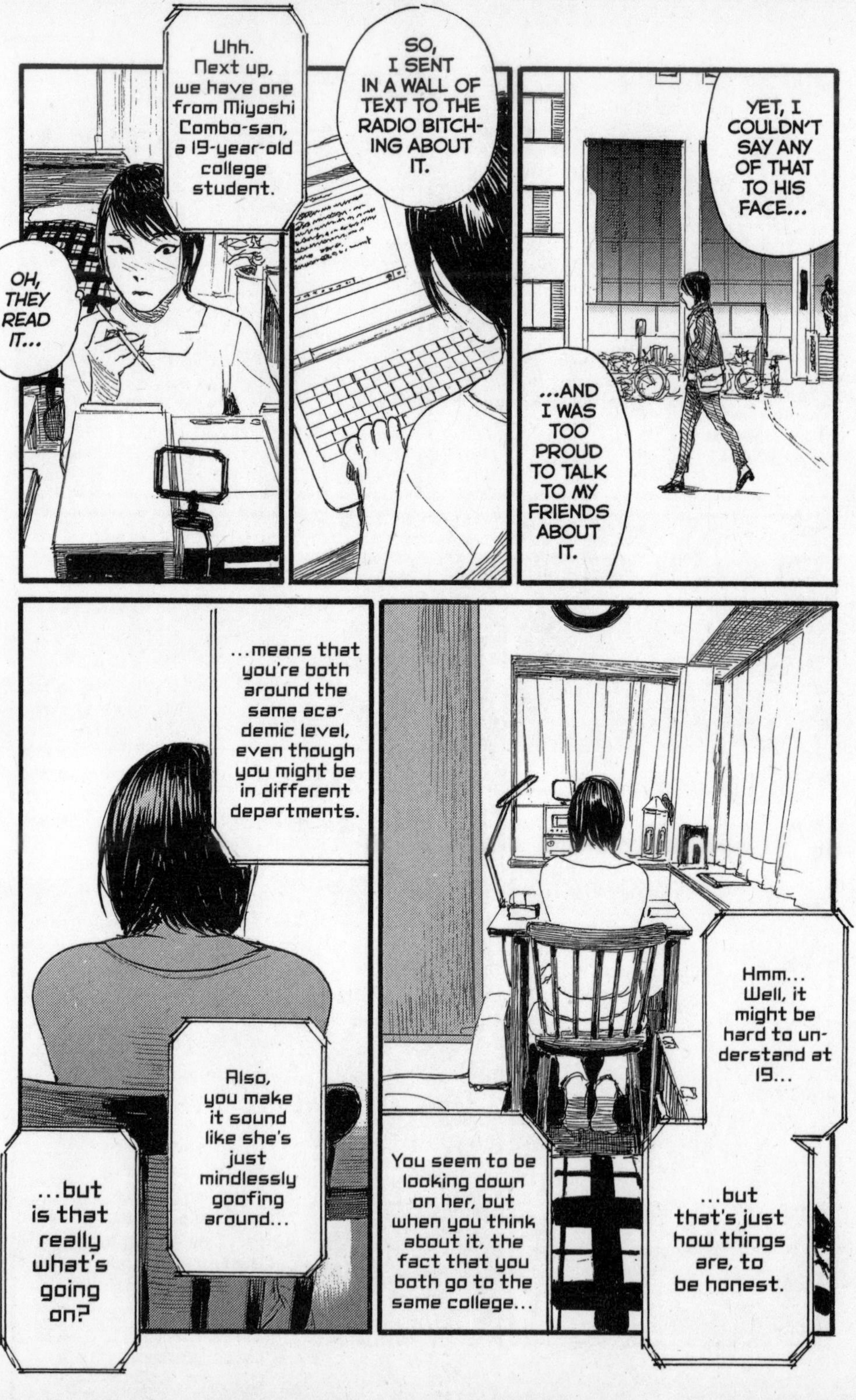
YET, I COULDN'T SAY ANY OF THAT TO HIS FACE...
...AND I WAS TOO PROUD TO TALK TO MY FRIENDS ABOUT IT.
SO, I SENT IN A WALL OF TEXT TO THE RADIO BITCHING ABOUT IT.
Uhh. Next up, we have one from Miyoshi Combo-san, a 19-year-old college student.
OH, THEY READ IT...
Hmm... Well, it might be hard to understand at 19...
...but that's just how things are, to be honest.
You seem to be looking down on her, but when you think about it, the fact that you both go to the same college...
...means that you're both around the same academic level, even though you might be in different departments.
Also, you make it sound like she's just mindlessly goofing around...
...but is that really what's going on?

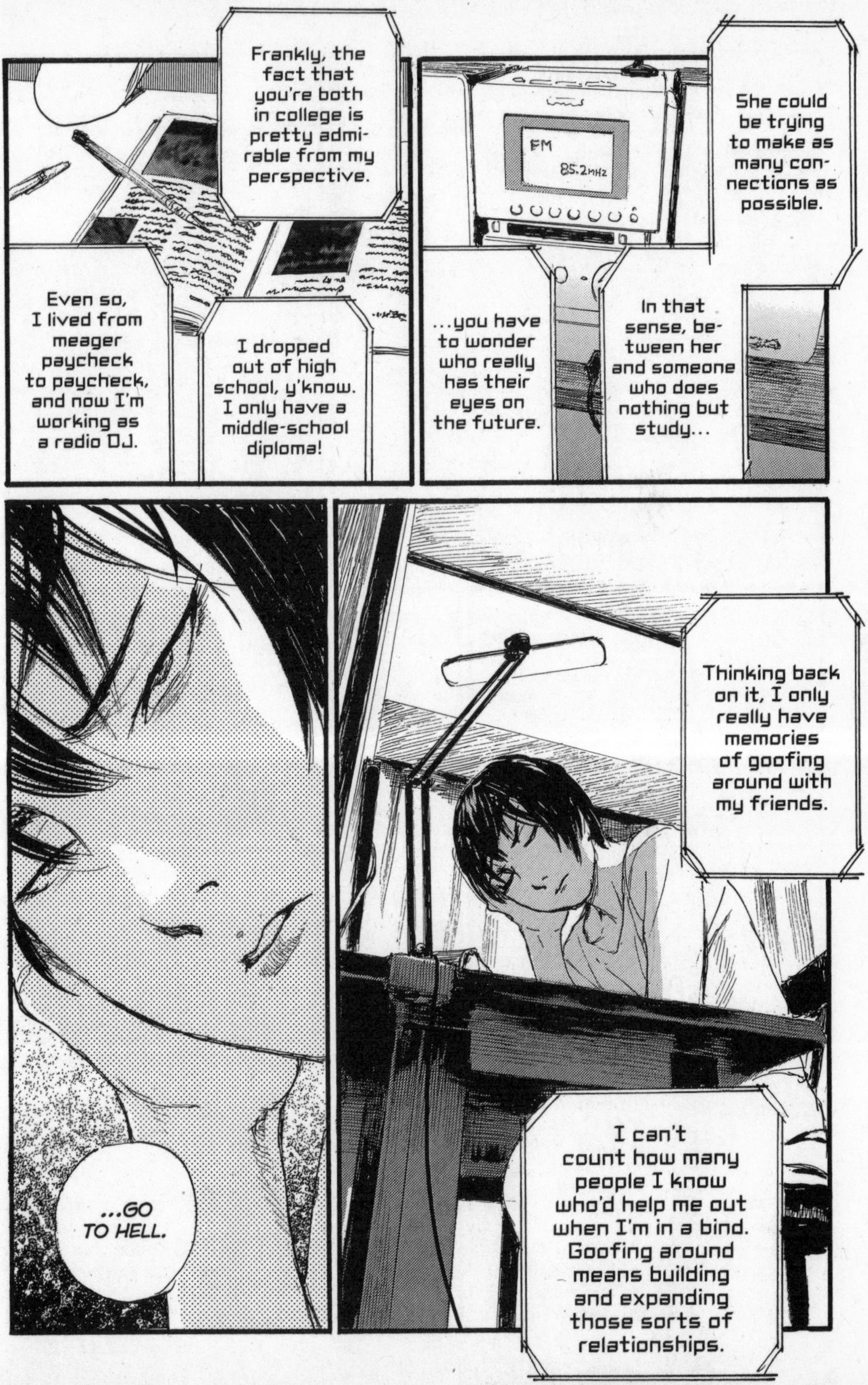
She could be trying to make as many connections as possible.
In that sense, between her and someone who does nothing but study...
...you have to wonder who really has their eyes on the future.
FM 85.2MHz
Frankly, the fact that you're both in college is pretty admirable from my perspective.
I dropped out of high school, y'know. I only have a middle-school diploma!
Even so, I lived from meager paycheck to paycheck, and now I'm working as a radio DJ.
Thinking back on it, I only really have memories of goofing around with my friends.
I can't count how many people I know who'd help me out when I'm in a bind. Goofing around means building and expanding those sorts of relationships.
...GO TO HELL.

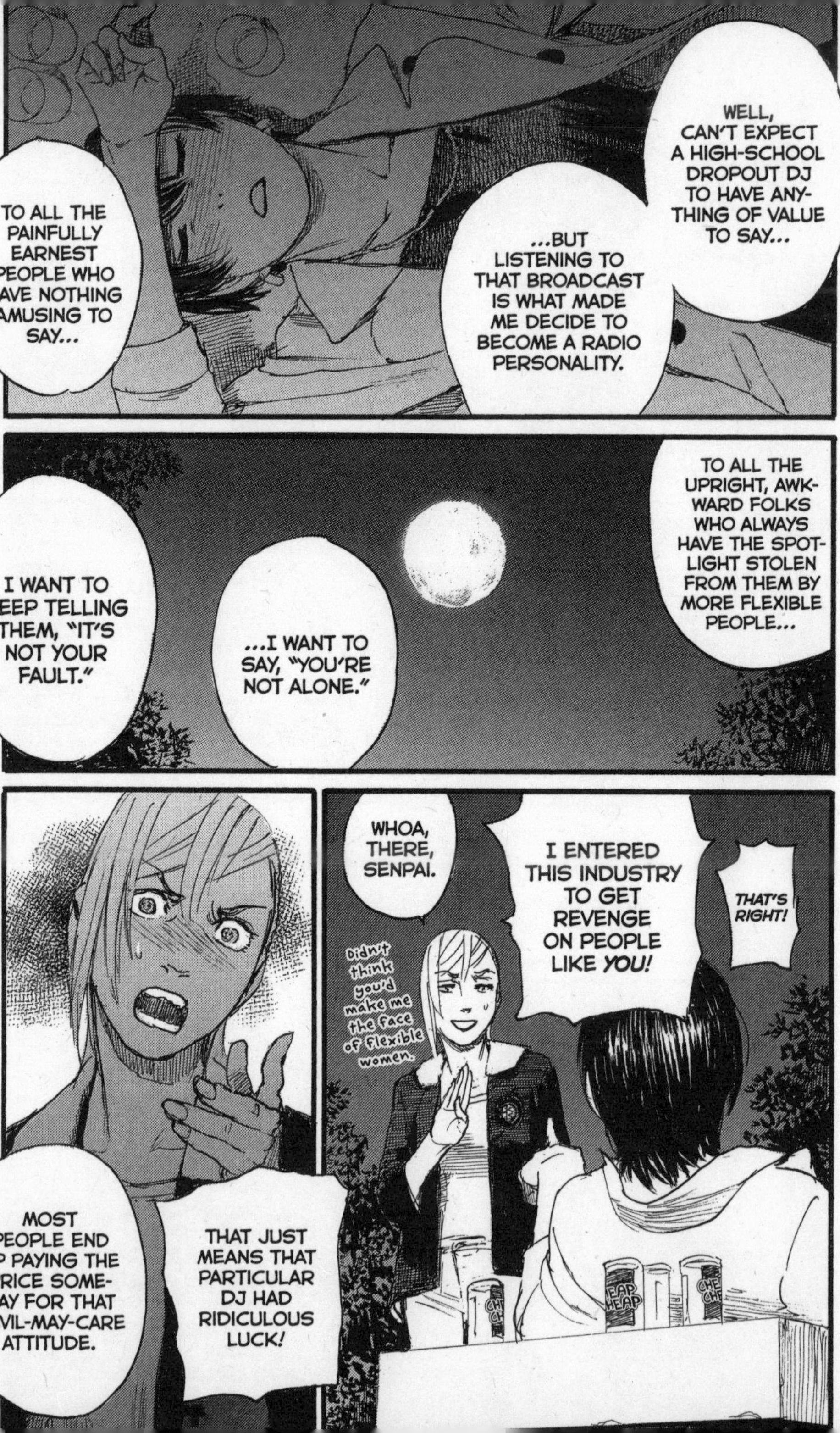
WELL, CAN'T EXPECT A HIGH-SCHOOL DROPOUT DJ TO HAVE ANY-THING OF VALUE TO SAY...
...BUT LISTENING TO THAT BROADCAST IS WHAT MADE ME DECIDE TO BECOME A RADIO PERSONALITY.
TO ALL THE PAINFULLY EARNEST PEOPLE WHO HAVE NOTHING AMUSING TO SAY...
TO ALL THE UPRIGHT, AWK-WARD FOLKS WHO ALWAYS HAVE THE SPOT-LIGHT STOLEN FROM THEM BY MORE FLEXIBLE PEOPLE...
...I WANT TO SAY, "YOU'RE NOT ALONE."
I WANT TO KEEP TELLING THEM, "IT'S NOT YOUR FAULT."
THAT'S RIGHT!
I ENTERED THIS INDUSTRY TO GET REVENGE ON PEOPLE LIKE *YOU*!
WHOA, THERE, SENPAI.
Didn't think you'd make me the face of flexible women.
THAT JUST MEANS THAT PARTICULAR DJ HAD RIDICULOUS LUCK!
MOST PEOPLE END UP PAYING THE PRICE SOME-DAY FOR THAT DEVIL-MAY-CARE ATTITUDE.

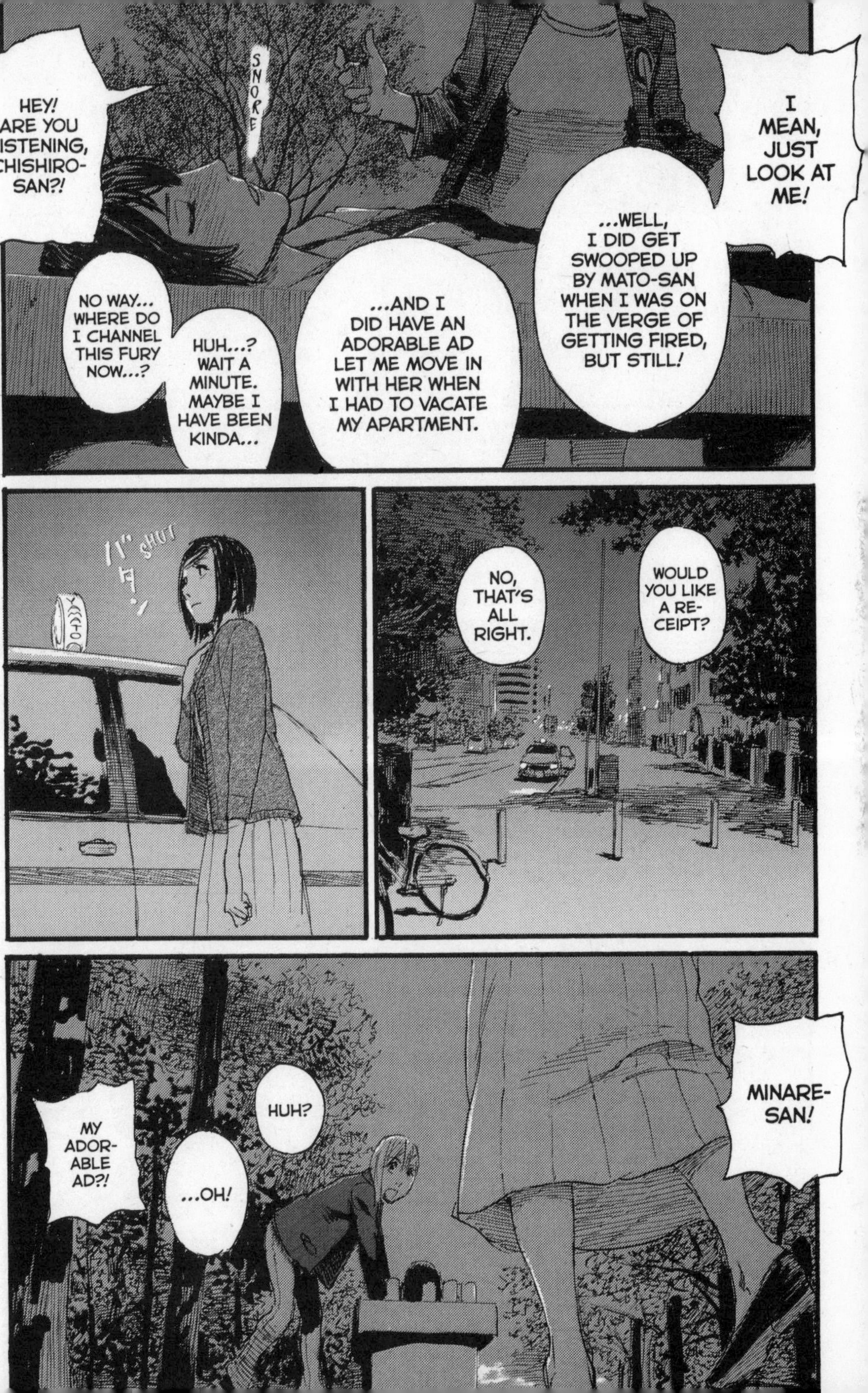
I MEAN, JUST LOOK AT ME!
...WELL, I DID GET SWOOPED UP BY MATO-SAN WHEN I WAS ON THE VERGE OF GETTING FIRED, BUT STILL!
...AND I DID HAVE AN ADORABLE AD LET ME MOVE IN WITH HER WHEN I HAD TO VACATE MY APARTMENT.
HUH...? WAIT A MINUTE. MAYBE I HAVE BEEN KINDA...
NO WAY... WHERE DO I CHANNEL THIS FURY NOW...?
HEY! ARE YOU LISTENING, CHISHIRO-SAN?!
SNORE
WOULD YOU LIKE A RE-CEIPT?
NO, THAT'S ALL RIGHT.
SHUT
YAMATO
MINARE-SAN!
HUH?
...OH!
MY ADOR-ABLE AD?!

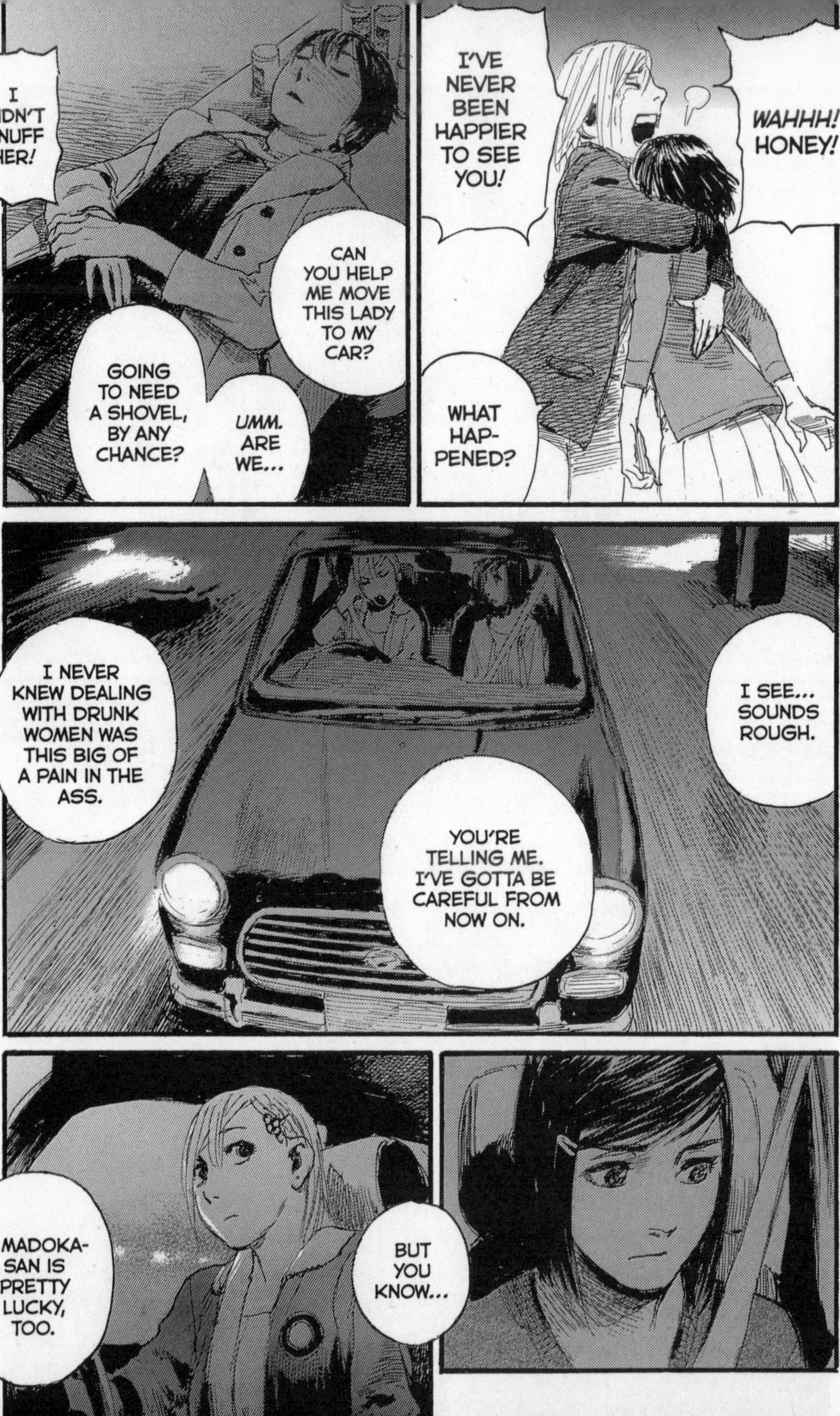
WAHHH! HONEY!
I'VE NEVER BEEN HAPPIER TO SEE YOU!
WHAT HAP-PENED?
CAN YOU HELP ME MOVE THIS LADY TO MY CAR?
UMM. ARE WE...
GOING TO NEED A SHOVEL, BY ANY CHANCE?
I DIDN'T SNUFF HER!
I NEVER KNEW DEALING WITH DRUNK WOMEN WAS THIS BIG OF A PAIN IN THE ASS.
I SEE... SOUNDS ROUGH.
YOU'RE TELLING ME. I'VE GOTTA BE CAREFUL FROM NOW ON.
BUT YOU KNOW...
...MADOKA-SAN IS PRETTY LUCKY, TOO.

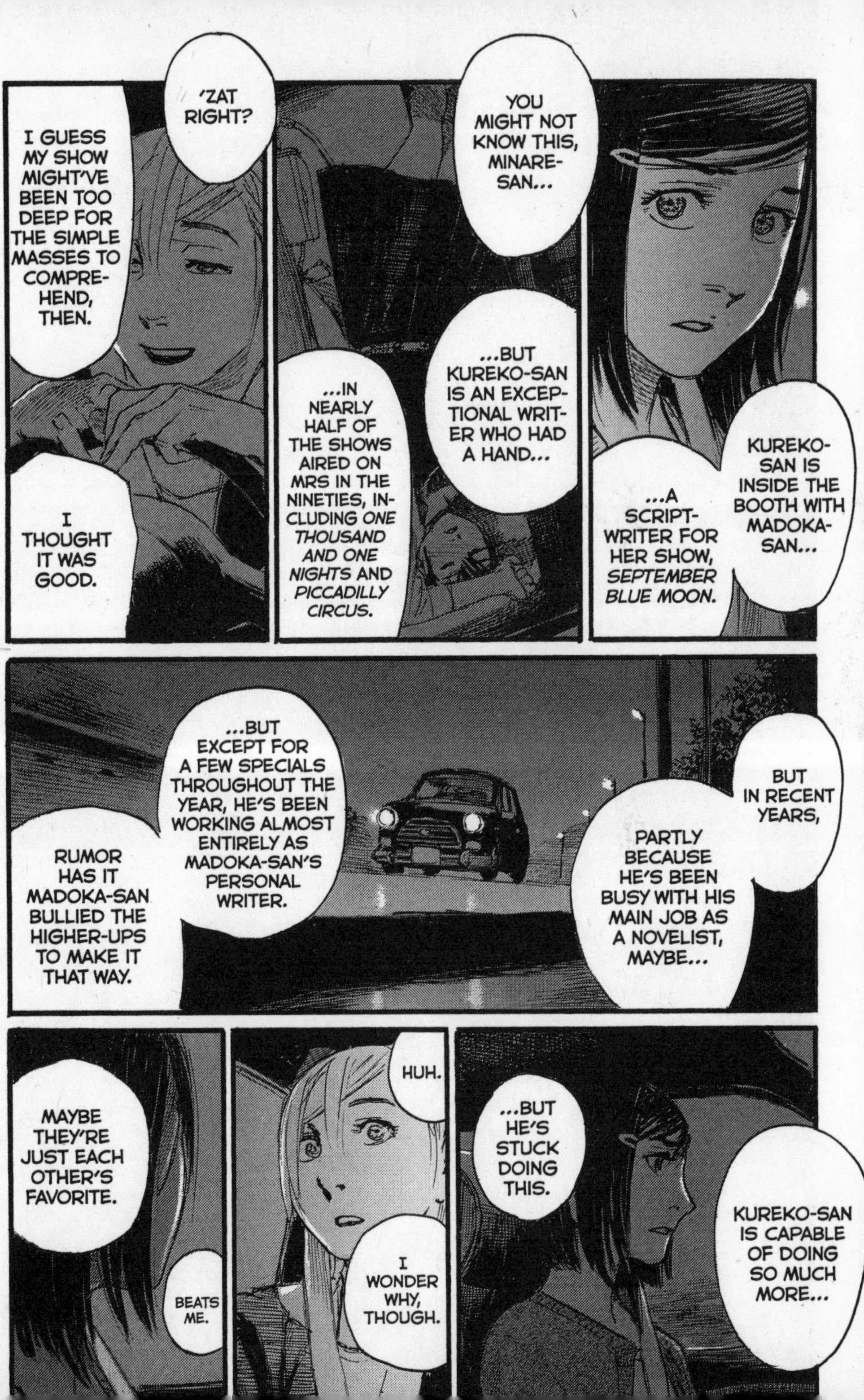
YOU MIGHT NOT KNOW THIS, MINARE-SAN...
KUREKO-SAN IS INSIDE THE BOOTH WITH MADOKA-SAN...
...A SCRIPT-WRITER FOR HER SHOW, *SEPTEMBER BLUE MOON.*
...BUT KUREKO-SAN IS AN EXCEP-TIONAL WRIT-ER WHO HAD A HAND...
...IN NEARLY HALF OF THE SHOWS AIRED ON MRS IN THE NINETIES, IN-CLUDING *ONE THOUSAND AND ONE NIGHTS* AND *PICCADILLY CIRCUS.*
'ZAT RIGHT?
I GUESS MY SHOW MIGHT'VE BEEN TOO DEEP FOR THE SIMPLE MASSES TO COMPRE-HEND, THEN.
I THOUGHT IT WAS GOOD.
BUT IN RECENT YEARS,
PARTLY BECAUSE HE'S BEEN BUSY WITH HIS MAIN JOB AS A NOVELIST, MAYBE...
...BUT EXCEPT FOR A FEW SPECIALS THROUGHOUT THE YEAR, HE'S BEEN WORKING ALMOST ENTIRELY AS MADOKA-SAN'S PERSONAL WRITER.
RUMOR HAS IT MADOKA-SAN BULLIED THE HIGHER-UPS TO MAKE IT THAT WAY.
KUREKO-SAN IS CAPABLE OF DOING SO MUCH MORE...
...BUT HE'S STUCK DOING THIS.
HUH.
I WONDER WHY, THOUGH.
MAYBE THEY'RE JUST EACH OTHER'S FAVORITE.
BEATS ME.

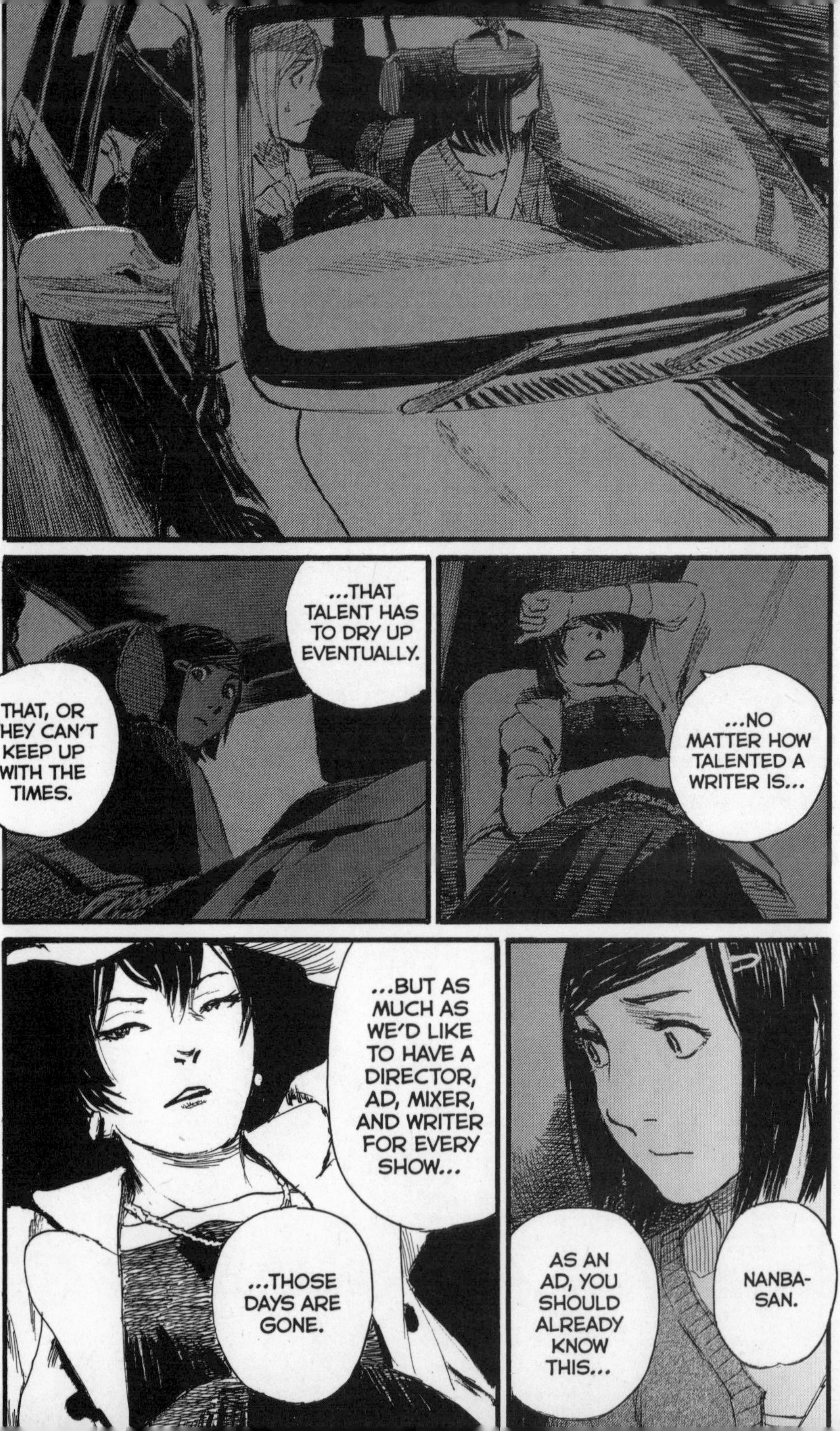
...NO MATTER HOW TALENTED A WRITER IS...
...THAT TALENT HAS TO DRY UP EVENTUALLY.
THAT, OR THEY CAN'T KEEP UP WITH THE TIMES.
NANBA-SAN.
AS AN AD, YOU SHOULD ALREADY KNOW THIS...
...BUT AS MUCH AS WE'D LIKE TO HAVE A DIRECTOR, AD, MIXER, AND WRITER FOR EVERY SHOW...
...THOSE DAYS ARE GONE.

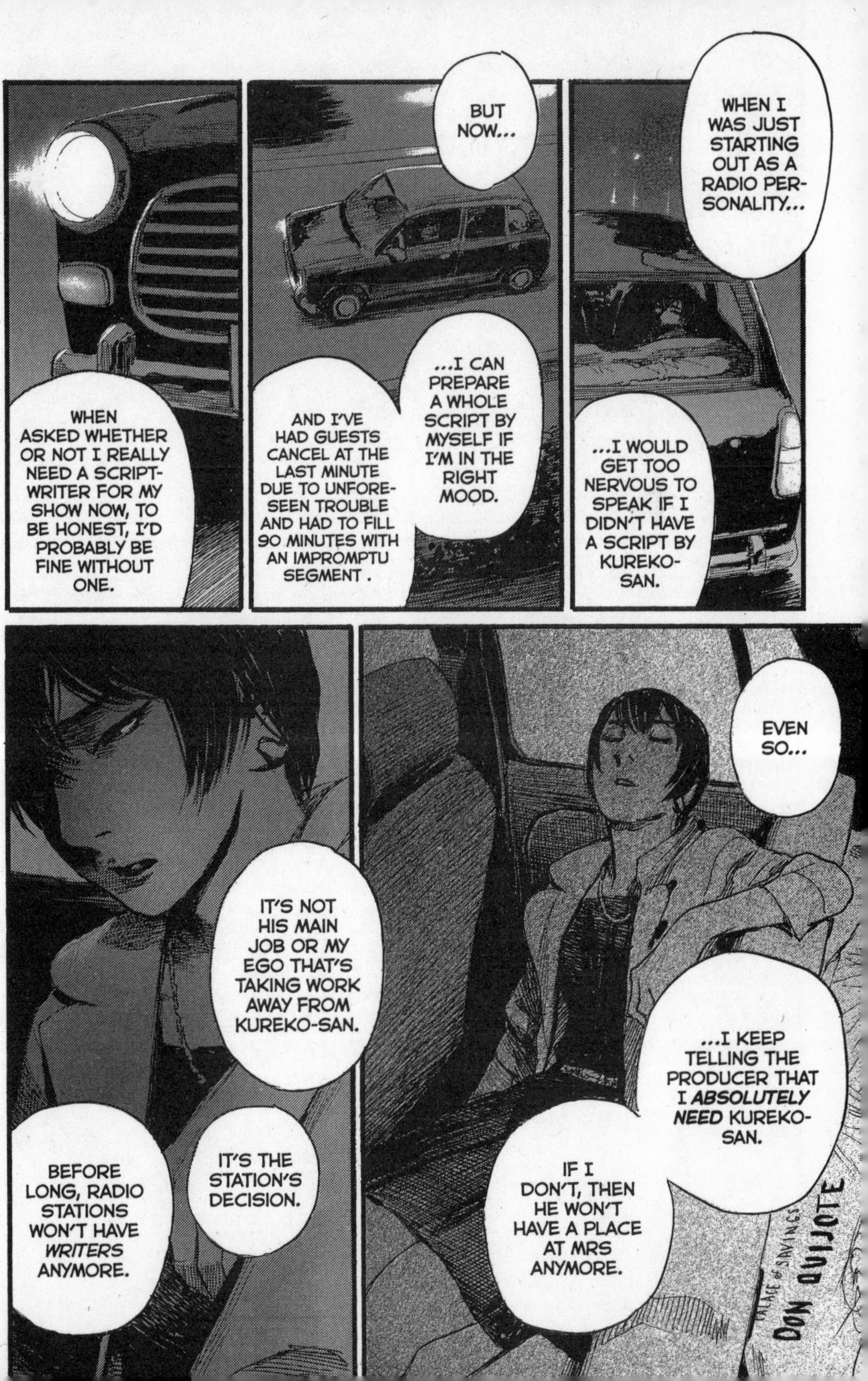
WHEN I WAS JUST STARTING OUT AS A RADIO PERSONALITY...
...I WOULD GET TOO NERVOUS TO SPEAK IF I DIDN'T HAVE A SCRIPT BY KUREKO-SAN.
BUT NOW...
...I CAN PREPARE A WHOLE SCRIPT BY MYSELF IF I'M IN THE RIGHT MOOD.
AND I'VE HAD GUESTS CANCEL AT THE LAST MINUTE DUE TO UNFORESEEN TROUBLE AND HAD TO FILL 90 MINUTES WITH AN IMPROMPTU SEGMENT .
WHEN ASKED WHETHER OR NOT I REALLY NEED A SCRIPTWRITER FOR MY SHOW NOW, TO BE HONEST, I'D PROBABLY BE FINE WITHOUT ONE.
EVEN SO...
...I KEEP TELLING THE PRODUCER THAT I *ABSOLUTELY NEED* KUREKO-SAN.
IF I DON'T, THEN HE WON'T HAVE A PLACE AT MRS ANYMORE.
PALACE of SAVINGS
DON QUIJOTE
IT'S NOT HIS MAIN JOB OR MY EGO THAT'S TAKING WORK AWAY FROM KUREKO-SAN.
IT'S THE STATION'S DECISION.
BEFORE LONG, RADIO STATIONS WON'T HAVE *WRITERS* ANYMORE.

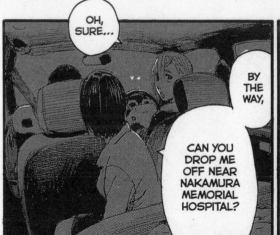

OH, SURE...
BY THE WAY,
CAN YOU DROP ME OFF NEAR NAKAMURA MEMORIAL HOSPITAL?
WHERE WERE YOU HEADED, ANYWAY?
MOUNT ICHAN-KOPPE.
AND WHAT'S IN THIS DON QUIJOTE BAG?
A SHOVEL...
...YOU REALLY WERE GOING TO BURY ME, WEREN'T YOU?
I'M SO SORRY, NAKA-HARA-SAN!
UMM... HOW'S YOUR NECK?
I'M FINE, NO BIGGIE. I JUST GOT STRUNG UP A LITTLE.

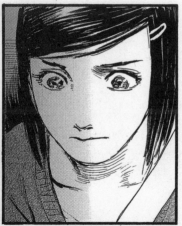

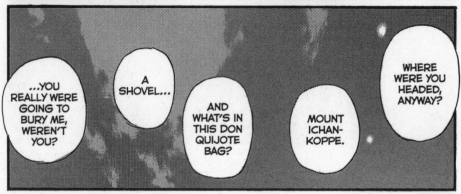

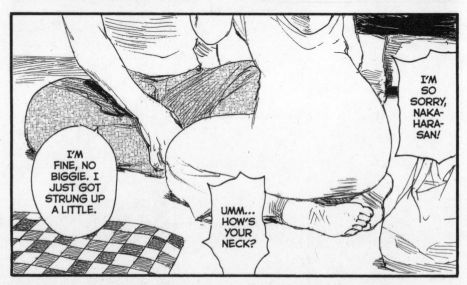

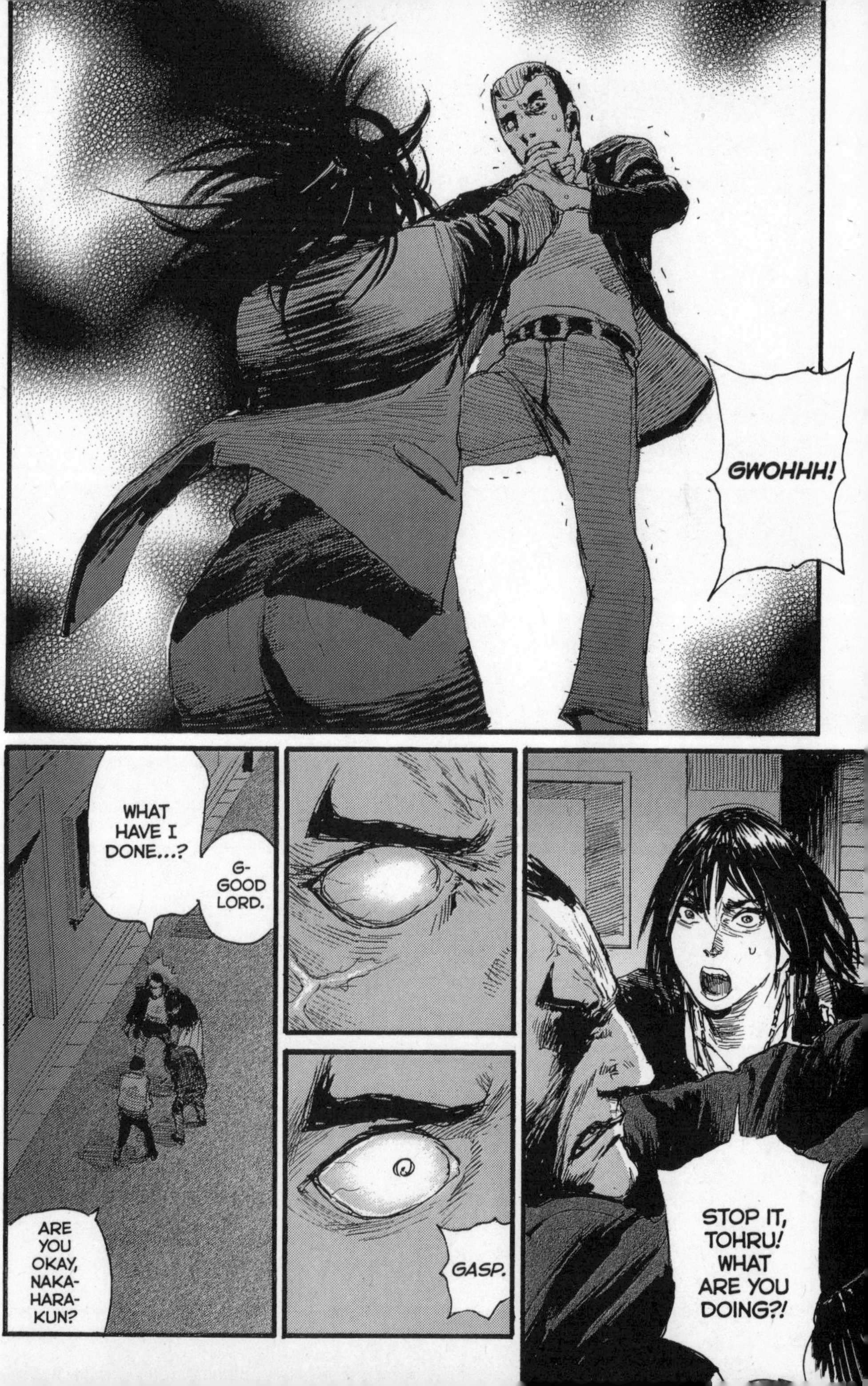
GWOHHH!
STOP IT, TOHRU! WHAT ARE YOU DOING?!
GASP.
WHAT HAVE I DONE...?
G-GOOD LORD.
ARE YOU OKAY, NAKAHARA-KUN?

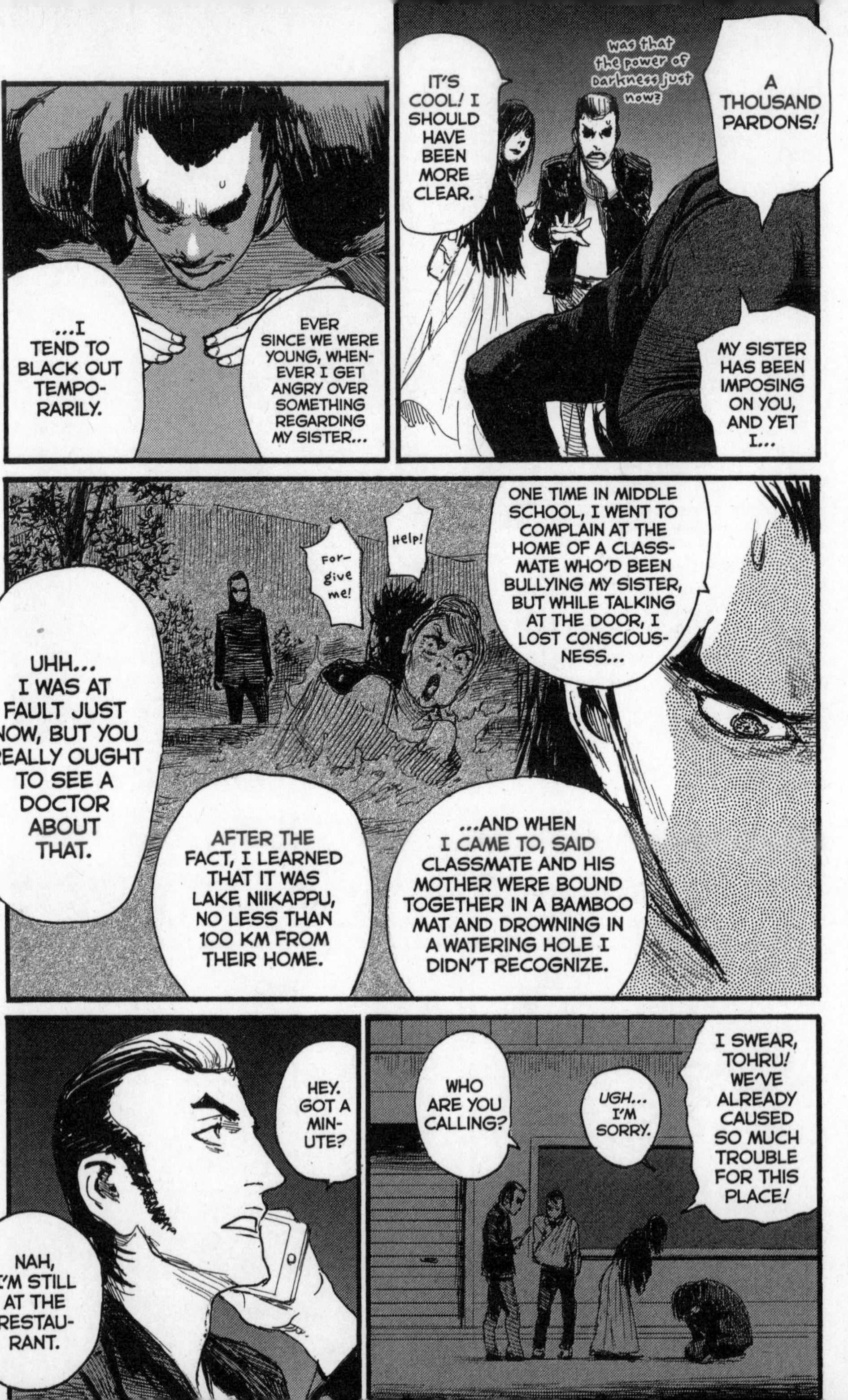
A THOUSAND PARDONS!
MY SISTER HAS BEEN IMPOSING ON YOU, AND YET I...
was that the power of darkness just now?
IT'S COOL! I SHOULD HAVE BEEN MORE CLEAR.
EVER SINCE WE WERE YOUNG, WHEN-EVER I GET ANGRY OVER SOMETHING REGARDING MY SISTER...
...I TEND TO BLACK OUT TEMPO-RARILY.
ONE TIME IN MIDDLE SCHOOL, I WENT TO COMPLAIN AT THE HOME OF A CLASS-MATE WHO'D BEEN BULLYING MY SISTER, BUT WHILE TALKING AT THE DOOR, I LOST CONSCIOUS-NESS...
Help!
For-give me!
...AND WHEN I CAME TO, SAID CLASSMATE AND HIS MOTHER WERE BOUND TOGETHER IN A BAMBOO MAT AND DROWNING IN A WATERING HOLE I DIDN'T RECOGNIZE.
AFTER THE FACT, I LEARNED THAT IT WAS LAKE NIIKAPPU, NO LESS THAN 100 KM FROM THEIR HOME.
UHH... I WAS AT FAULT JUST NOW, BUT YOU REALLY OUGHT TO SEE A DOCTOR ABOUT THAT.
I SWEAR, TOHRU! WE'VE ALREADY CAUSED SO MUCH TROUBLE FOR THIS PLACE!
UGH... I'M SORRY.
WHO ARE YOU CALLING?
HEY. GOT A MIN-UTE?
NAH, I'M STILL AT THE RESTAU-RANT.

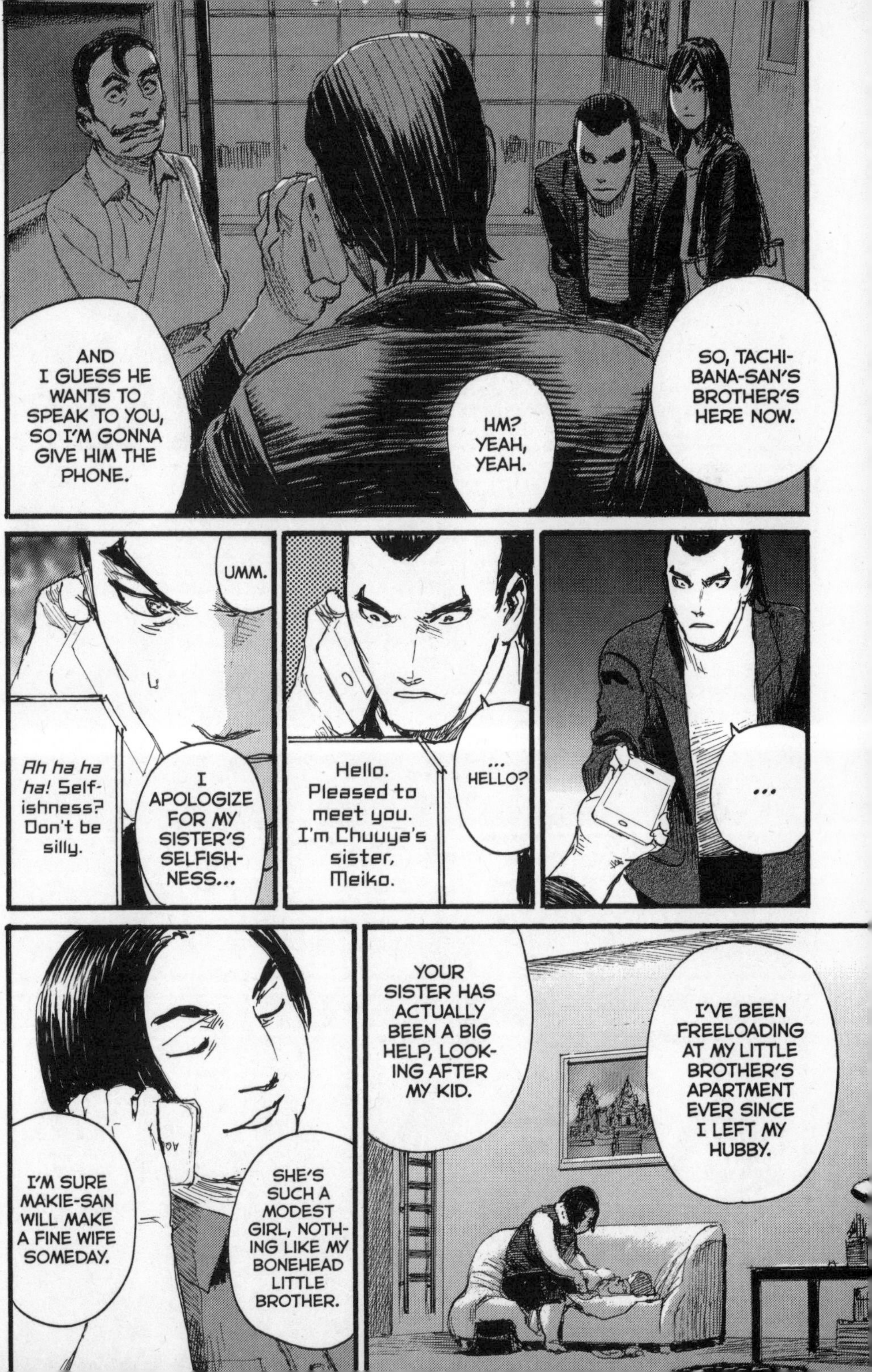
SO, TACHIBANA-SAN'S BROTHER'S HERE NOW.
HM? YEAH, YEAH.
AND I GUESS HE WANTS TO SPEAK TO YOU, SO I'M GONNA GIVE HIM THE PHONE.
...
... HELLO?
Hello. Pleased to meet you. I'm Chuuya's sister, Meiko.
UMM.
I APOLOGIZE FOR MY SISTER'S SELFISHNESS...
Ah ha ha ha! Selfishness? Don't be silly.
I'VE BEEN FREELOADING AT MY LITTLE BROTHER'S APARTMENT EVER SINCE I LEFT MY HUBBY.
YOUR SISTER HAS ACTUALLY BEEN A BIG HELP, LOOKING AFTER MY KID.
SHE'S SUCH A MODEST GIRL, NOTHING LIKE MY BONEHEAD LITTLE BROTHER.
I'M SURE MAKIE-SAN WILL MAKE A FINE WIFE SOMEDAY.

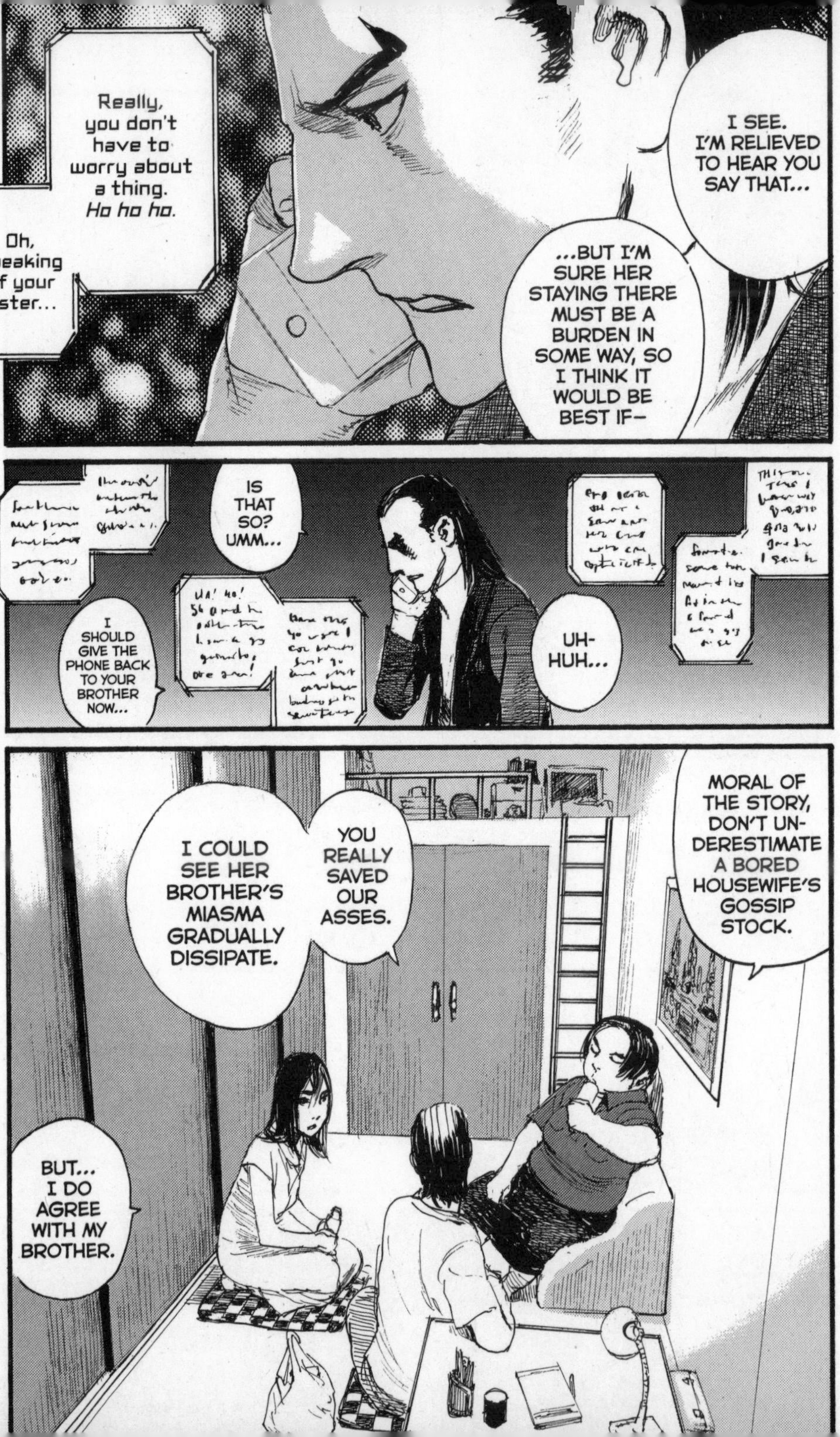
I SEE. I'M RELIEVED TO HEAR YOU SAY THAT...
...BUT I'M SURE HER STAYING THERE MUST BE A BURDEN IN SOME WAY, SO I THINK IT WOULD BE BEST IF–
Really, you don't have to worry about a thing. *Ho ho ho.*
Oh, speaking of your sister...
IS THAT SO? UMM...
UH-HUH...
I SHOULD GIVE THE PHONE BACK TO YOUR BROTHER NOW...
MORAL OF THE STORY, DON'T UN-DERESTIMATE A BORED HOUSEWIFE'S GOSSIP STOCK.
YOU REALLY SAVED OUR ASSES.
I COULD SEE HER BROTHER'S MIASMA GRADUALLY DISSIPATE.
BUT... I DO AGREE WITH MY BROTHER.

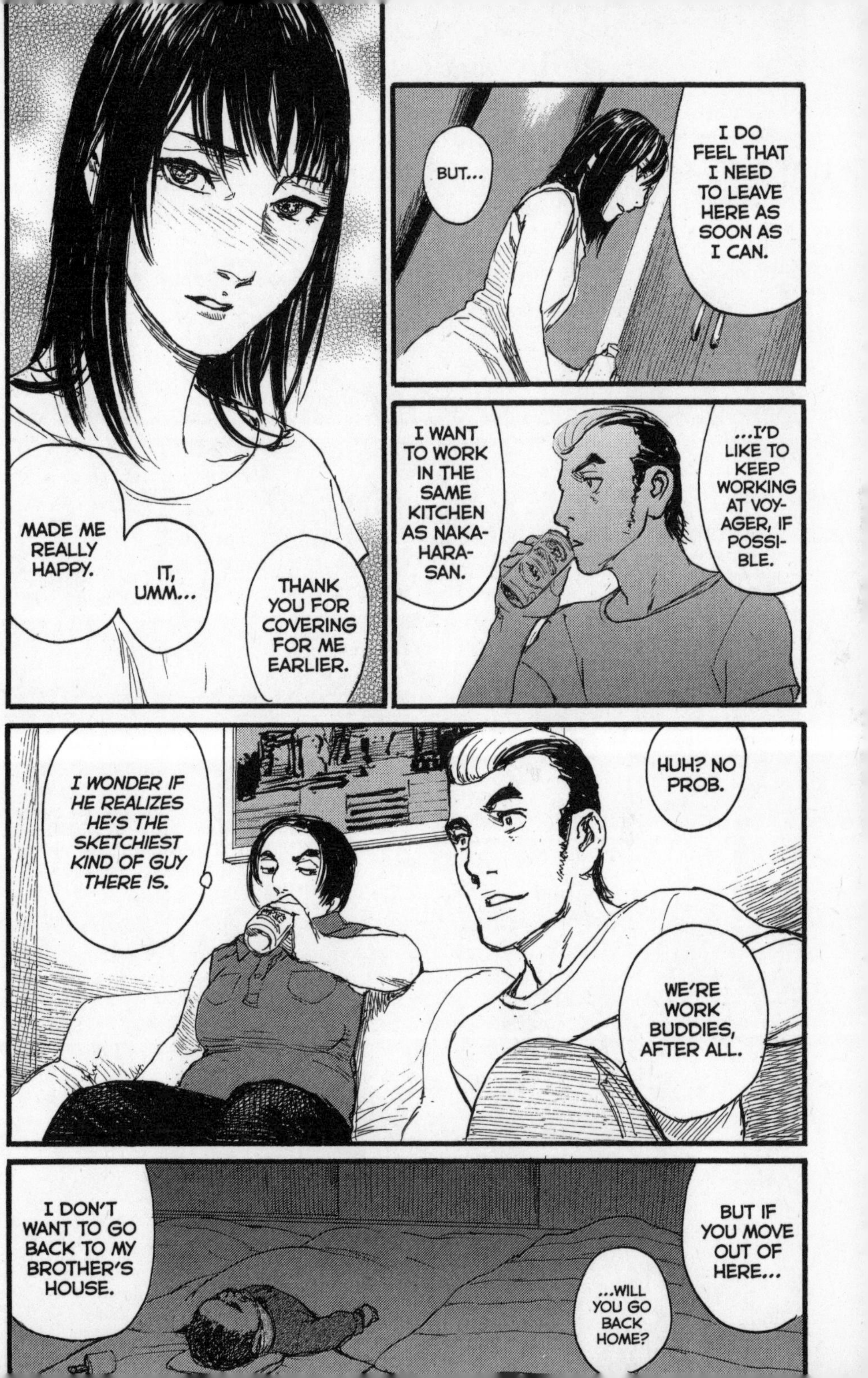
I DO FEEL THAT I NEED TO LEAVE HERE AS SOON AS I CAN.
BUT...
...I'D LIKE TO KEEP WORKING AT VOYAGER, IF POSSIBLE.
I WANT TO WORK IN THE SAME KITCHEN AS NAKAHARA-SAN.
THANK YOU FOR COVERING FOR ME EARLIER.
IT, UMM...
MADE ME REALLY HAPPY.
HUH? NO PROB.
WE'RE WORK BUDDIES, AFTER ALL.
I WONDER IF HE REALIZES HE'S THE SKETCHIEST KIND OF GUY THERE IS.
BUT IF YOU MOVE OUT OF HERE...
...WILL YOU GO BACK HOME?
I DON'T WANT TO GO BACK TO MY BROTHER'S HOUSE.

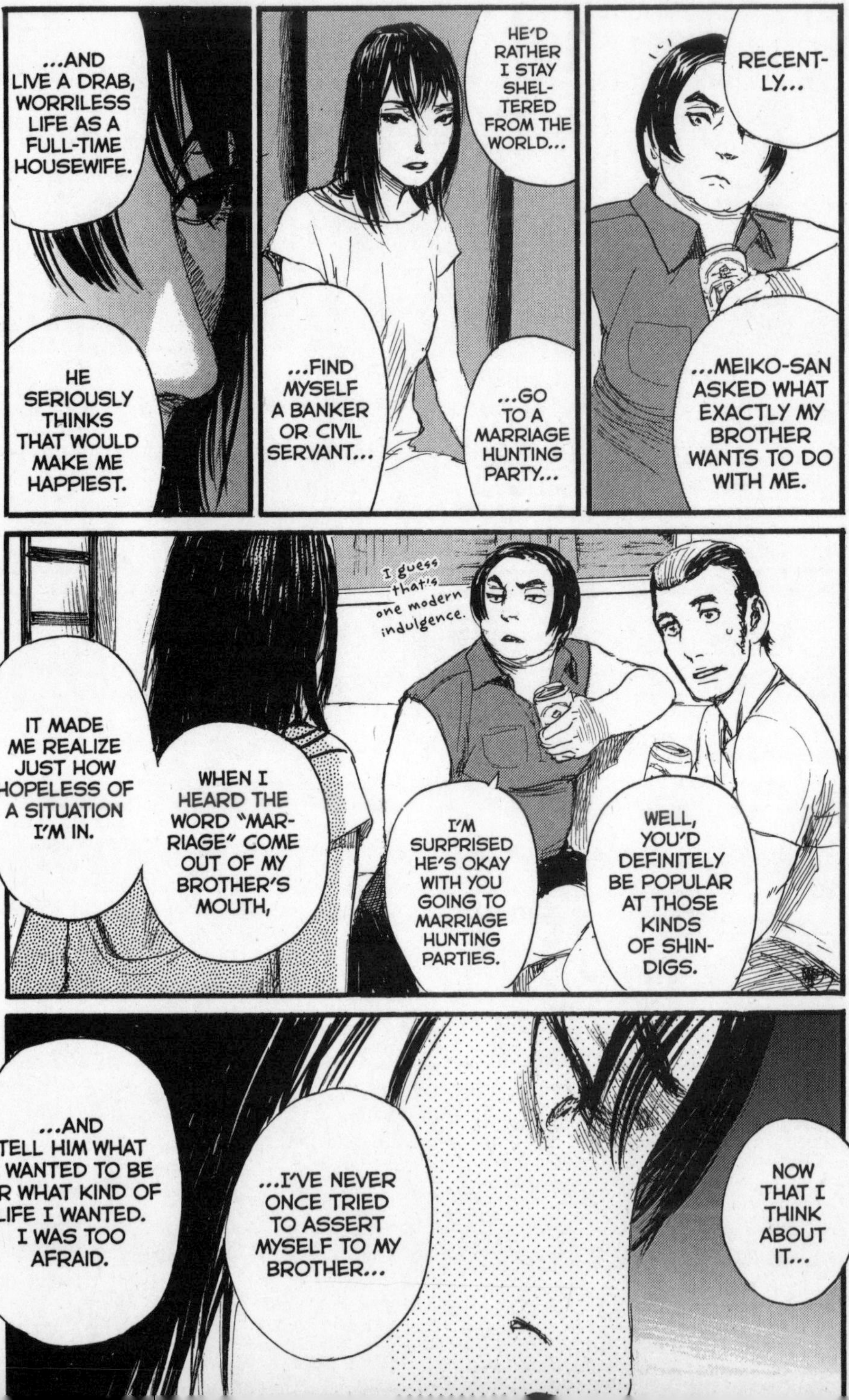
RECENTLY...
...MEIKO-SAN ASKED WHAT EXACTLY MY BROTHER WANTS TO DO WITH ME.
HE'D RATHER I STAY SHELTERED FROM THE WORLD...
...GO TO A MARRIAGE HUNTING PARTY...
...FIND MYSELF A BANKER OR CIVIL SERVANT...
...AND LIVE A DRAB, WORRILESS LIFE AS A FULL-TIME HOUSEWIFE.
HE SERIOUSLY THINKS THAT WOULD MAKE ME HAPPIEST.
WELL, YOU'D DEFINITELY BE POPULAR AT THOSE KINDS OF SHINDIGS.
I'M SURPRISED HE'S OKAY WITH YOU GOING TO MARRIAGE HUNTING PARTIES.
I guess that's one modern indulgence.
WHEN I HEARD THE WORD "MARRIAGE" COME OUT OF MY BROTHER'S MOUTH,
IT MADE ME REALIZE JUST HOW HOPELESS OF A SITUATION I'M IN.
NOW THAT I THINK ABOUT IT...
...I'VE NEVER ONCE TRIED TO ASSERT MYSELF TO MY BROTHER...
...AND TELL HIM WHAT I WANTED TO BE OR WHAT KIND OF LIFE I WANTED. I WAS TOO AFRAID.

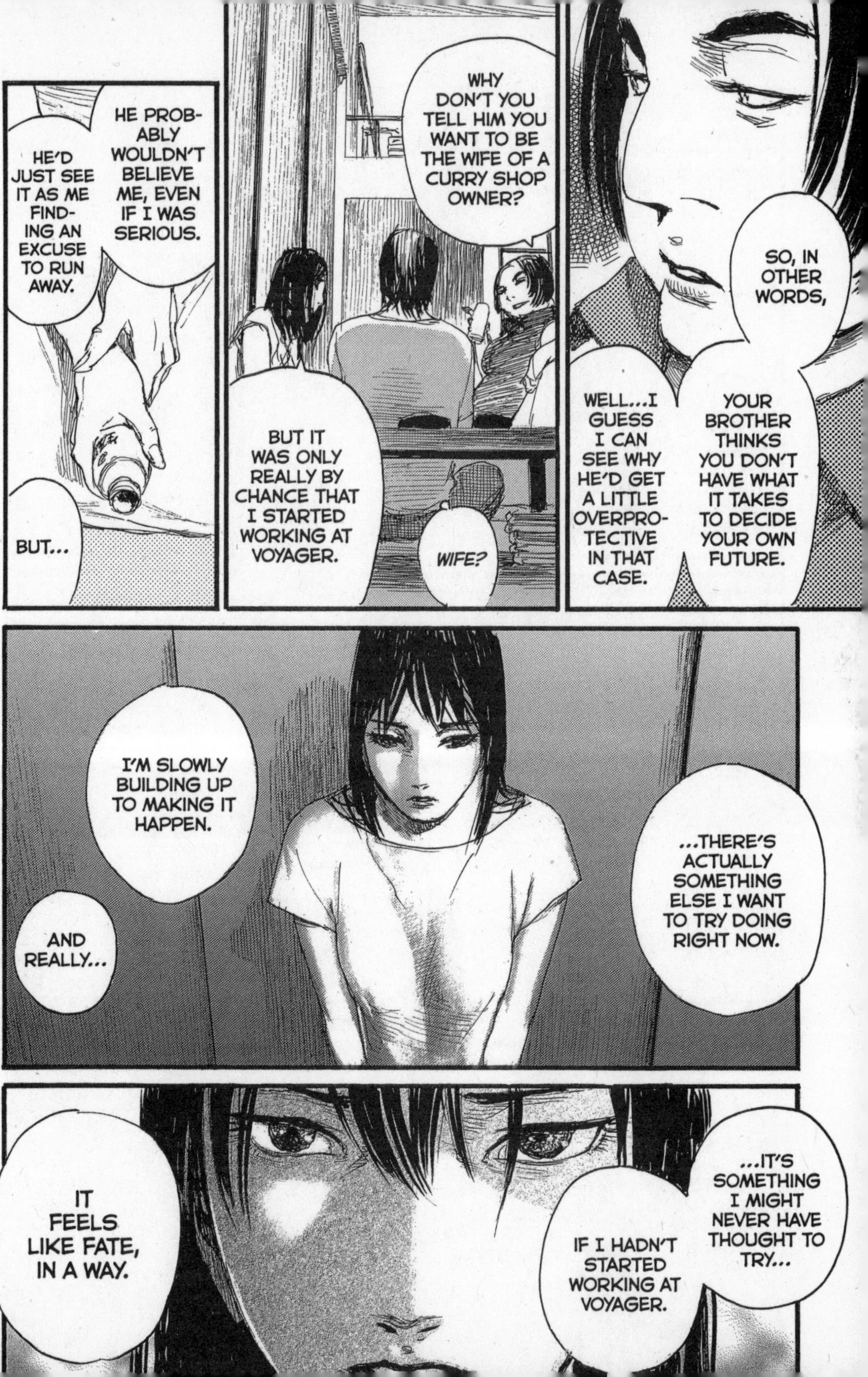
SO, IN OTHER WORDS,
YOUR BROTHER THINKS YOU DON'T HAVE WHAT IT TAKES TO DECIDE YOUR OWN FUTURE.
WELL...I GUESS I CAN SEE WHY HE'D GET A LITTLE OVERPRO-TECTIVE IN THAT CASE.
WHY DON'T YOU TELL HIM YOU WANT TO BE THE WIFE OF A CURRY SHOP OWNER?
WIFE?
BUT IT WAS ONLY REALLY BY CHANCE THAT I STARTED WORKING AT VOYAGER.
HE PROB-ABLY WOULDN'T BELIEVE ME, EVEN IF I WAS SERIOUS.
HE'D JUST SEE IT AS ME FIND-ING AN EXCUSE TO RUN AWAY.
BUT...
...THERE'S ACTUALLY SOMETHING ELSE I WANT TO TRY DOING RIGHT NOW.
I'M SLOWLY BUILDING UP TO MAKING IT HAPPEN.
AND REALLY...
...IT'S SOMETHING I MIGHT NEVER HAVE THOUGHT TO TRY...
IF I HADN'T STARTED WORKING AT VOYAGER.
IT FEELS LIKE FATE, IN A WAY.

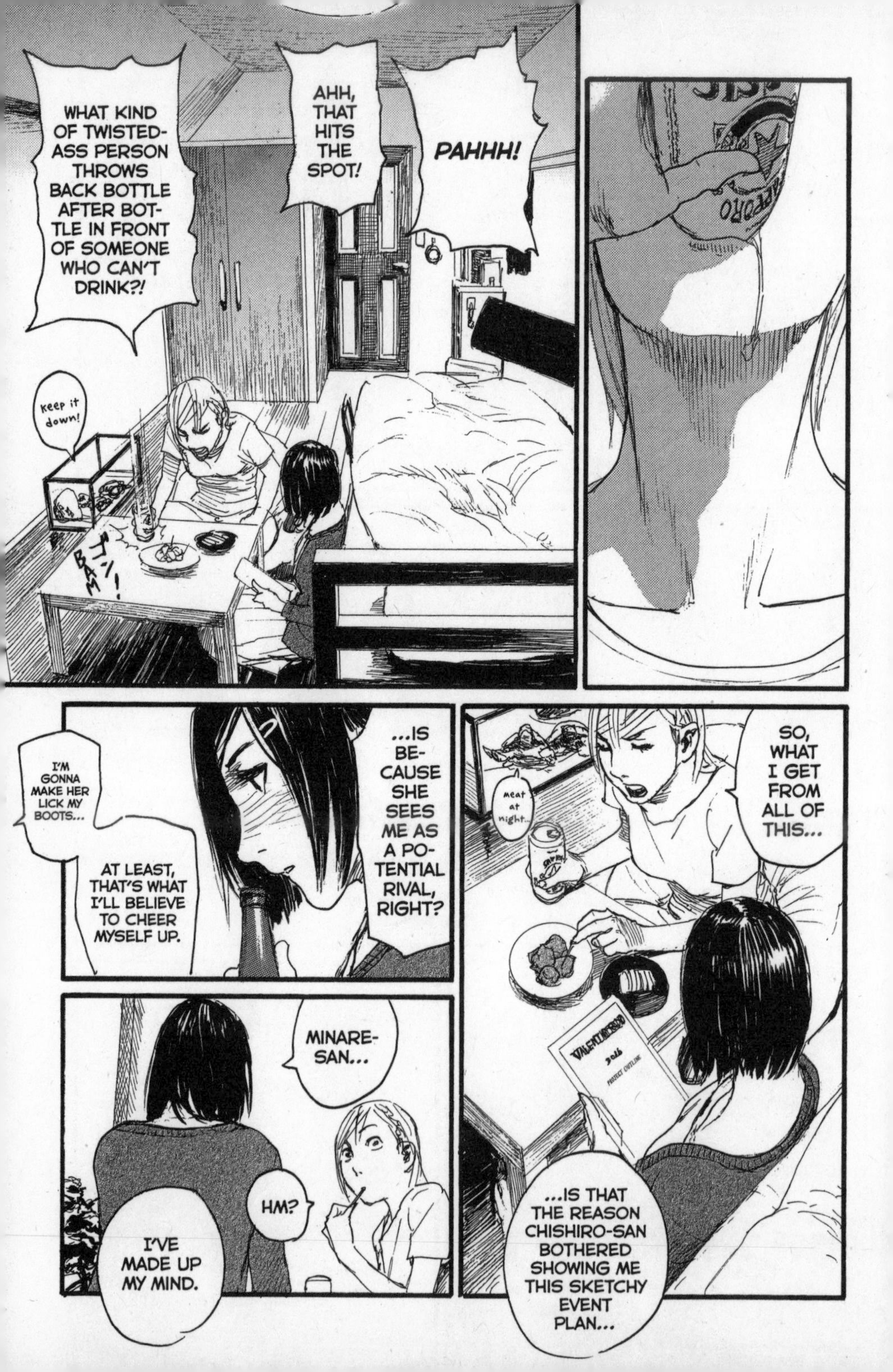
PAHHH!
AHH, THAT HITS THE SPOT!
WHAT KIND OF TWISTED-ASS PERSON THROWS BACK BOTTLE AFTER BOTTLE IN FRONT OF SOMEONE WHO CAN'T DRINK?!
keep it down!
BAM
SO, WHAT I GET FROM ALL OF THIS...
meat at night...
...IS THAT THE REASON CHISHIRO-SAN BOTHERED SHOWING ME THIS SKETCHY EVENT PLAN...
...IS BE-CAUSE SHE SEES ME AS A PO-TENTIAL RIVAL, RIGHT?
I'M GONNA MAKE HER LICK MY BOOTS...
AT LEAST, THAT'S WHAT I'LL BELIEVE TO CHEER MYSELF UP.
MINARE-SAN...
HM?
I'VE MADE UP MY MIND.

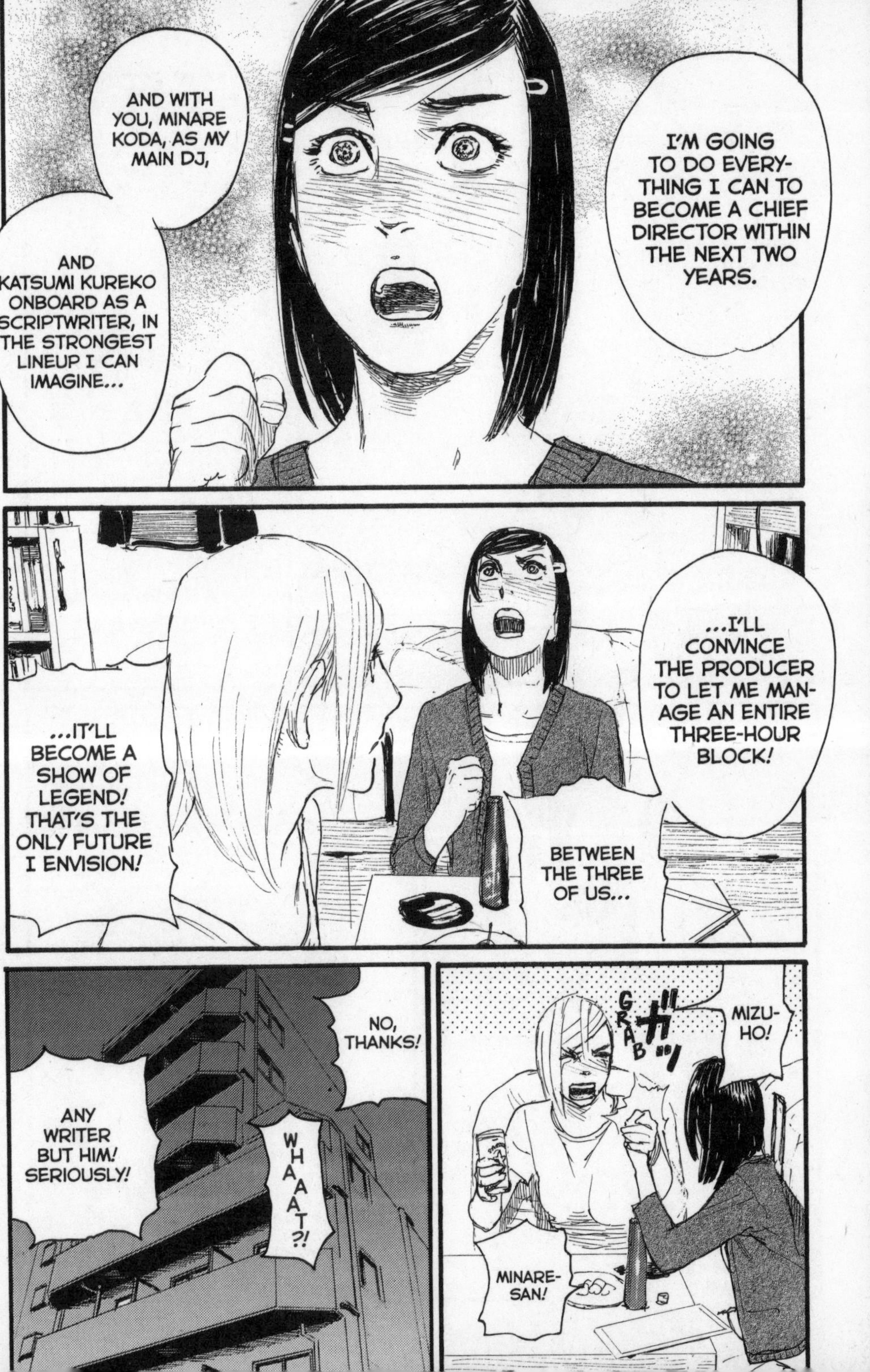
I'M GOING TO DO EVERYTHING I CAN TO BECOME A CHIEF DIRECTOR WITHIN THE NEXT TWO YEARS.
AND WITH YOU, MINARE KODA, AS MY MAIN DJ,
AND KATSUMI KUREKO ONBOARD AS A SCRIPTWRITER, IN THE STRONGEST LINEUP I CAN IMAGINE...
...I'LL CONVINCE THE PRODUCER TO LET ME MANAGE AN ENTIRE THREE-HOUR BLOCK!
BETWEEN THE THREE OF US...
...IT'LL BECOME A SHOW OF LEGEND! THAT'S THE ONLY FUTURE I ENVISION!
MIZUHO!
GRAB
MINARE-SAN!
NO, THANKS!
WHAAAT?!
ANY WRITER BUT HIM! SERIOUSLY!

Chapter 27 "THINGS WON'T PLAY OUT."

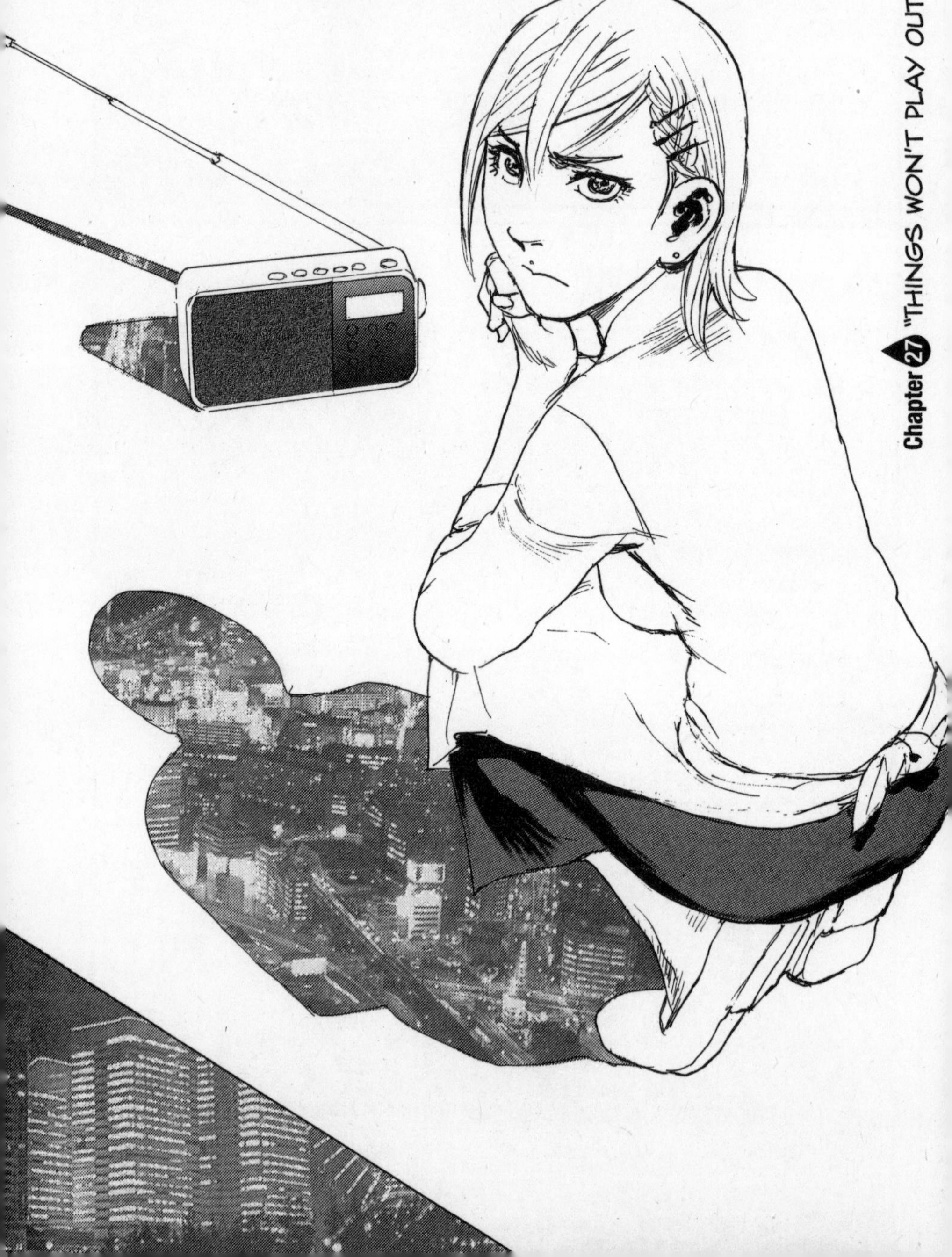

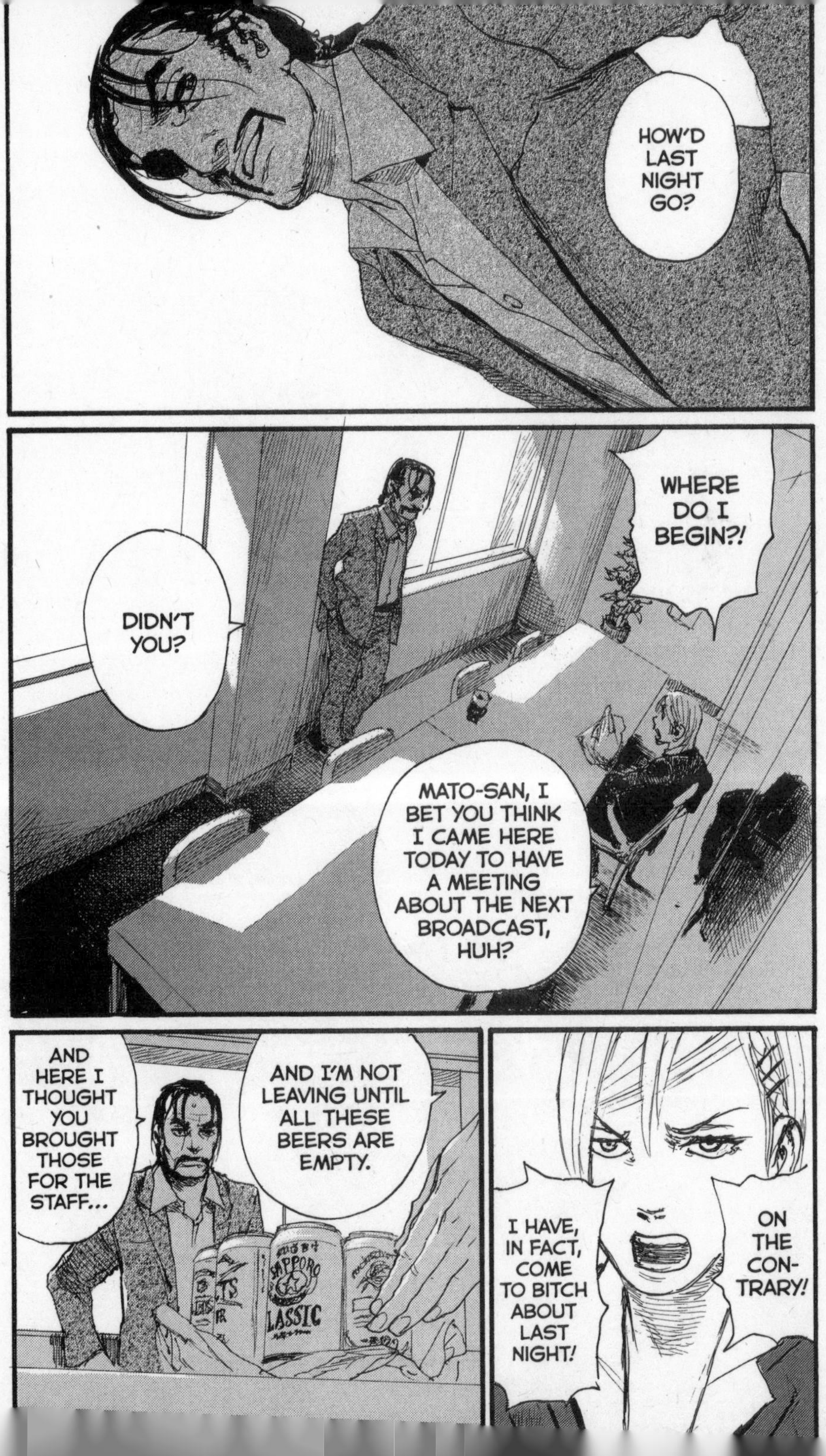
HOW'D LAST NIGHT GO?
WHERE DO I BEGIN?!
MATO-SAN, I BET YOU THINK I CAME HERE TODAY TO HAVE A MEETING ABOUT THE NEXT BROADCAST, HUH?
DIDN'T YOU?
ON THE CON-TRARY!
I HAVE, IN FACT, COME TO BITCH ABOUT LAST NIGHT!
AND I'M NOT LEAVING UNTIL ALL THESE BEERS ARE EMPTY.
AND HERE I THOUGHT YOU BROUGHT THOSE FOR THE STAFF...

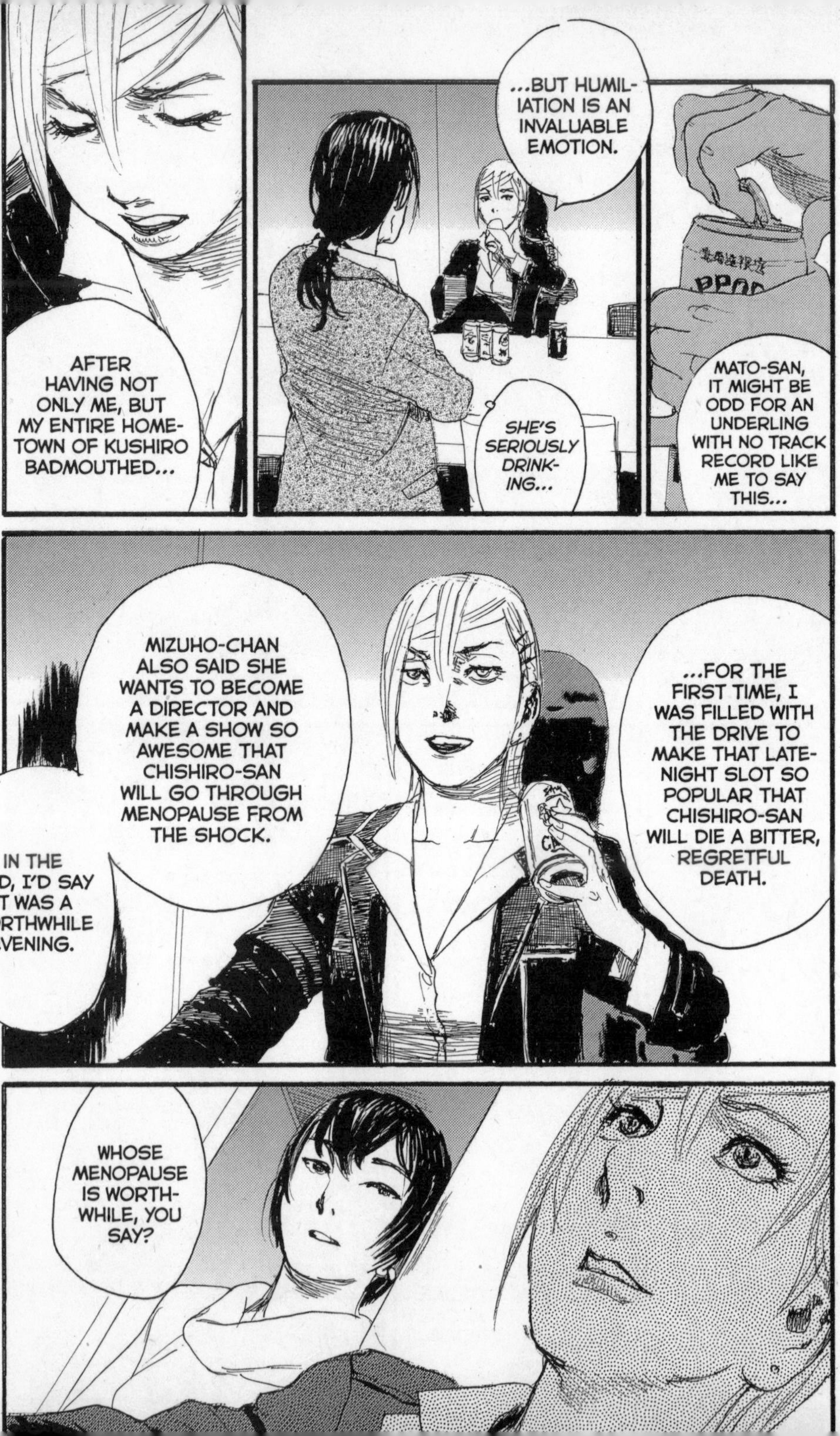
MATO-SAN, IT MIGHT BE ODD FOR AN UNDERLING WITH NO TRACK RECORD LIKE ME TO SAY THIS...
...BUT HUMIL-IATION IS AN INVALUABLE EMOTION.
SHE'S SERIOUSLY DRINK-ING...
AFTER HAVING NOT ONLY ME, BUT MY ENTIRE HOME-TOWN OF KUSHIRO BADMOUTHED...
...FOR THE FIRST TIME, I WAS FILLED WITH THE DRIVE TO MAKE THAT LATE-NIGHT SLOT SO POPULAR THAT CHISHIRO-SAN WILL DIE A BITTER, REGRETFUL DEATH.
MIZUHO-CHAN ALSO SAID SHE WANTS TO BECOME A DIRECTOR AND MAKE A SHOW SO AWESOME THAT CHISHIRO-SAN WILL GO THROUGH MENOPAUSE FROM THE SHOCK.
IN THE END, I'D SAY IT WAS A WORTHWHILE EVENING.
WHOSE MENOPAUSE IS WORTH-WHILE, YOU SAY?

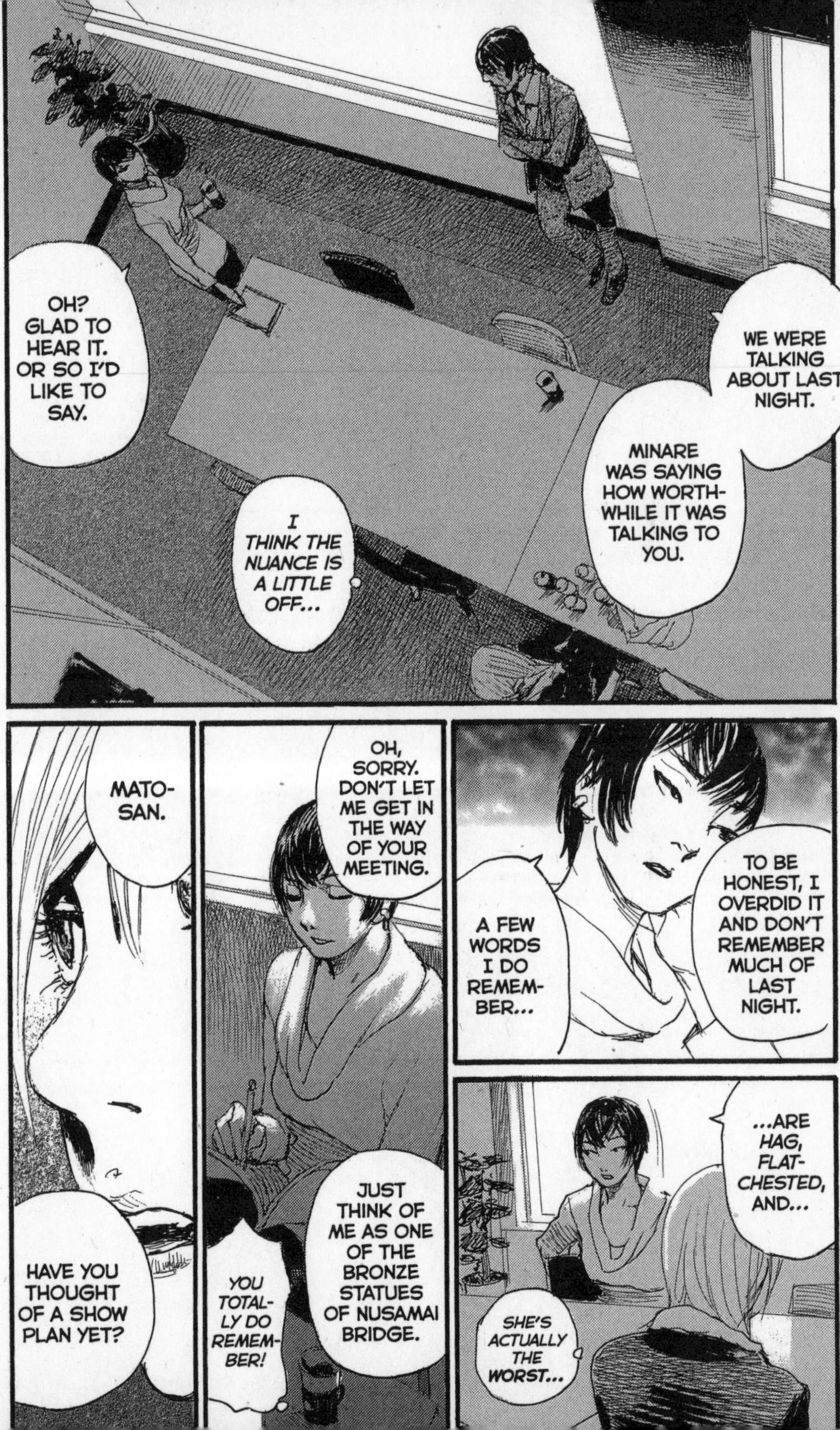
WE WERE TALKING ABOUT LAST NIGHT.
MINARE WAS SAYING HOW WORTHWHILE IT WAS TALKING TO YOU.
OH? GLAD TO HEAR IT. OR SO I'D LIKE TO SAY.
I THINK THE NUANCE IS A LITTLE OFF...
TO BE HONEST, I OVERDID IT AND DON'T REMEMBER MUCH OF LAST NIGHT.
A FEW WORDS I DO REMEMBER...
...ARE HAG, FLAT-CHESTED, AND...
SHE'S ACTUALLY THE WORST...
OH, SORRY. DON'T LET ME GET IN THE WAY OF YOUR MEETING.
JUST THINK OF ME AS ONE OF THE BRONZE STATUES OF NUSAMAI BRIDGE.
YOU TOTALLY DO REMEMBER!
MATO-SAN.
HAVE YOU THOUGHT OF A SHOW PLAN YET?

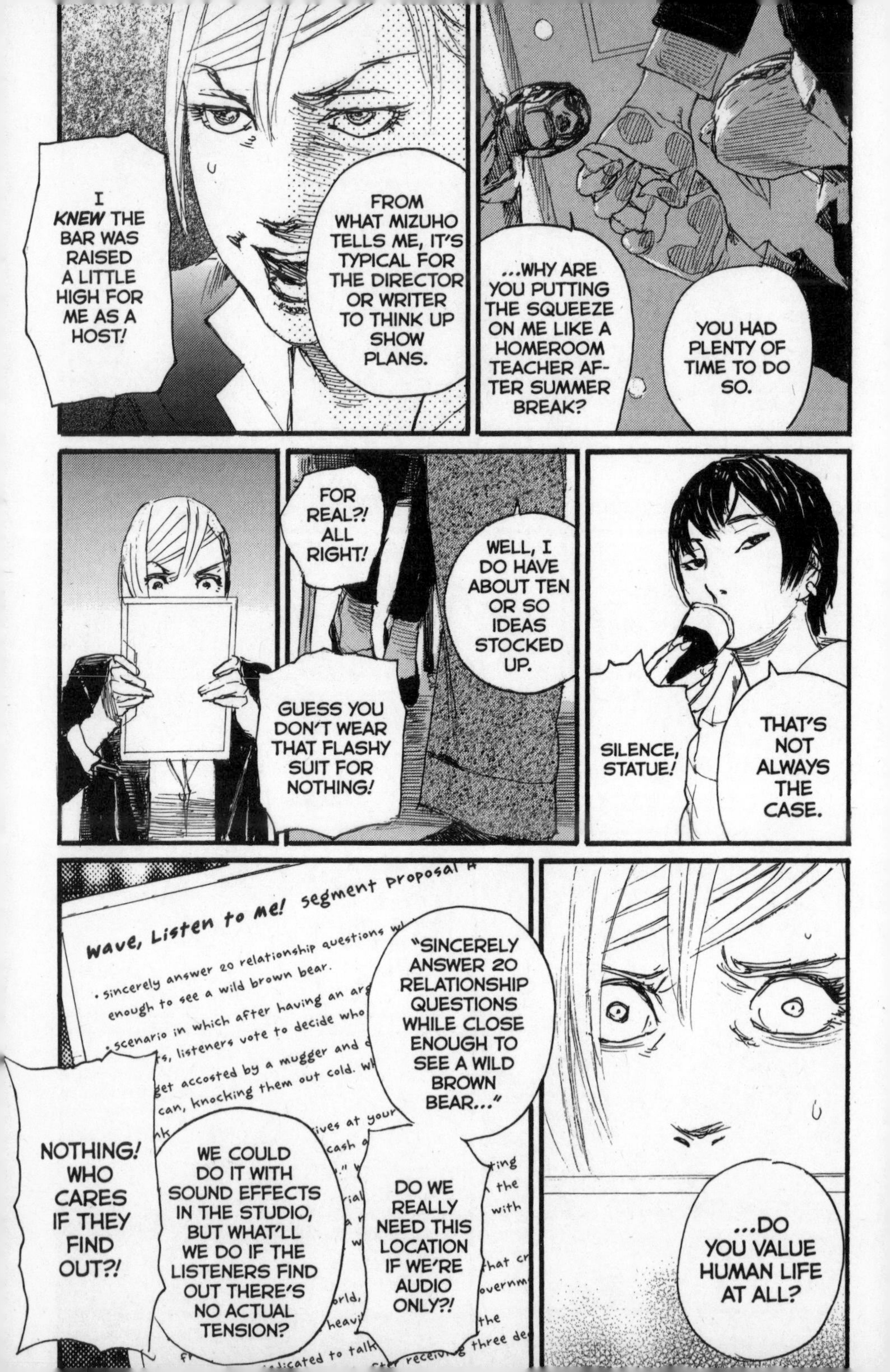
YOU HAD PLENTY OF TIME TO DO SO.
...WHY ARE YOU PUTTING THE SQUEEZE ON ME LIKE A HOMEROOM TEACHER AF-TER SUMMER BREAK?
FROM WHAT MIZUHO TELLS ME, IT'S TYPICAL FOR THE DIRECTOR OR WRITER TO THINK UP SHOW PLANS.
I *KNEW* THE BAR WAS RAISED A LITTLE HIGH FOR ME AS A HOST!
THAT'S NOT ALWAYS THE CASE.
SILENCE, STATUE!
WELL, I DO HAVE ABOUT TEN OR SO IDEAS STOCKED UP.
FOR REAL?! ALL RIGHT!
GUESS YOU DON'T WEAR THAT FLASHY SUIT FOR NOTHING!
...DO YOU VALUE HUMAN LIFE AT ALL?
Wave, Listen to me! segment proposal
• sincerely answer 20 relationship questions
enough to see a wild brown bear.
• scenario in which after having an
listeners vote to decide who
get accosted by a mugger and
can, knocking them out cold.
"SINCERELY ANSWER 20 RELATIONSHIP QUESTIONS WHILE CLOSE ENOUGH TO SEE A WILD BROWN BEAR..."
DO WE REALLY NEED THIS LOCATION IF WE'RE AUDIO ONLY?!
WE COULD DO IT WITH SOUND EFFECTS IN THE STUDIO, BUT WHAT'LL WE DO IF THE LISTENERS FIND OUT THERE'S NO ACTUAL TENSION?
NOTHING! WHO CARES IF THEY FIND OUT?!

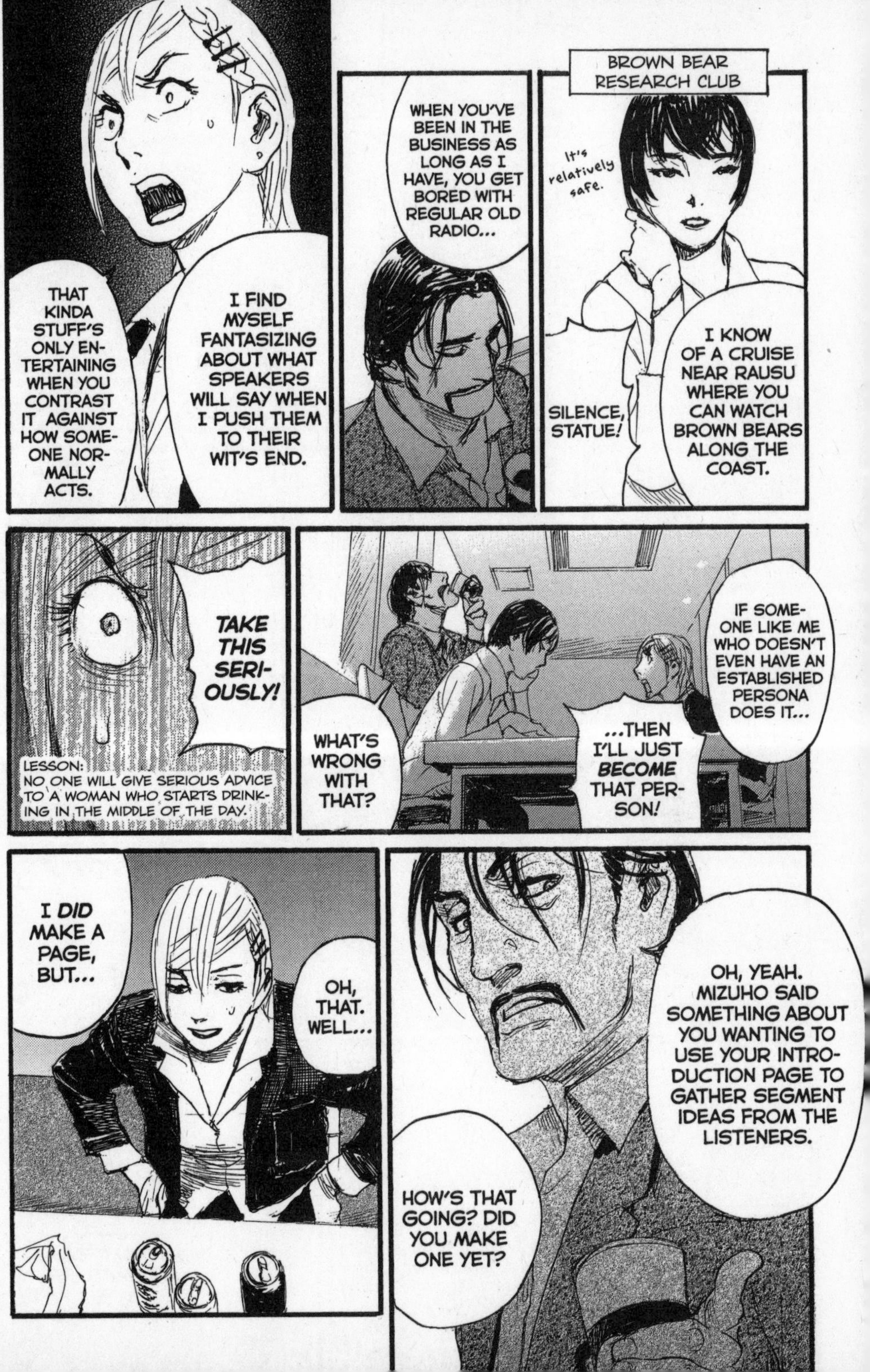
BROWN BEAR RESEARCH CLUB
I KNOW OF A CRUISE NEAR RAUSU WHERE YOU CAN WATCH BROWN BEARS ALONG THE COAST.
It's relatively safe.
SILENCE, STATUE!
WHEN YOU'VE BEEN IN THE BUSINESS AS LONG AS I HAVE, YOU GET BORED WITH REGULAR OLD RADIO...
I FIND MYSELF FANTASIZING ABOUT WHAT SPEAKERS WILL SAY WHEN I PUSH THEM TO THEIR WIT'S END.
THAT KINDA STUFF'S ONLY ENTERTAINING WHEN YOU CONTRAST IT AGAINST HOW SOMEONE NORMALLY ACTS.
IF SOMEONE LIKE ME WHO DOESN'T EVEN HAVE AN ESTABLISHED PERSONA DOES IT...
...THEN I'LL JUST *BECOME* THAT PERSON!
WHAT'S WRONG WITH THAT?
TAKE THIS SERIOUSLY!
LESSON: NO ONE WILL GIVE SERIOUS ADVICE TO A WOMAN WHO STARTS DRINKING IN THE MIDDLE OF THE DAY.
OH, YEAH. MIZUHO SAID SOMETHING ABOUT YOU WANTING TO USE YOUR INTRODUCTION PAGE TO GATHER SEGMENT IDEAS FROM THE LISTENERS.
HOW'S THAT GOING? DID YOU MAKE ONE YET?
OH, THAT. WELL...
I *DID* MAKE A PAGE, BUT...

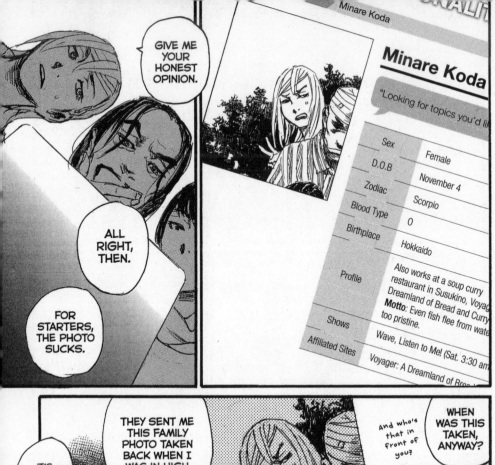

GIVE ME YOUR HONEST OPINION.

ALL RIGHT, THEN.

FOR STARTERS, THE PHOTO SUCKS.

Minare Koda

"Looking for topics you'd li[ke]

Sex		Female
D.O.B		November 4
Zodiac		Scorpio
Blood Type		O
Birthplace		Hokkaido
Profile		Also works at a soup curry restaurant in Susukino, Voyag[er] Dreamland of Bread and Curry. **Motto**: Even fish flee from wate[r] too pristine.
Shows		Wave, Listen to Me! (Sat. 3:30 am
Affiliated Sites		Voyager: A Dreamland of Bre[ad]

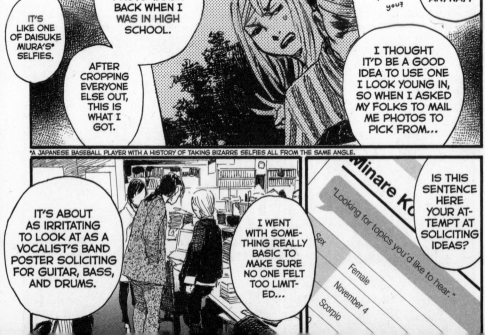

IT'S LIKE ONE OF DAISUKE MIURA'S* SELFIES.

THEY SENT ME THIS FAMILY PHOTO TAKEN BACK WHEN I WAS IN HIGH SCHOOL.

AFTER CROPPING EVERYONE ELSE OUT, THIS IS WHAT I GOT.

And who's that in front of you?

WHEN WAS THIS TAKEN, ANYWAY?

I THOUGHT IT'D BE A GOOD IDEA TO USE ONE I LOOK YOUNG IN, SO WHEN I ASKED MY FOLKS TO MAIL ME PHOTOS TO PICK FROM...

*A JAPANESE BASEBALL PLAYER WITH A HISTORY OF TAKING BIZARRE SELFIES ALL FROM THE SAME ANGLE.

IT'S ABOUT AS IRRITATING TO LOOK AT AS A VOCALIST'S BAND POSTER SOLICITING FOR GUITAR, BASS, AND DRUMS.

I WENT WITH SOMETHING REALLY BASIC TO MAKE SURE NO ONE FELT TOO LIMITED...

IS THIS SENTENCE HERE YOUR ATTEMPT AT SOLICITING IDEAS?

Minare Ko[da]

"Looking for topics you'd like to hear."

Sex

Female

November 4

Scorpio

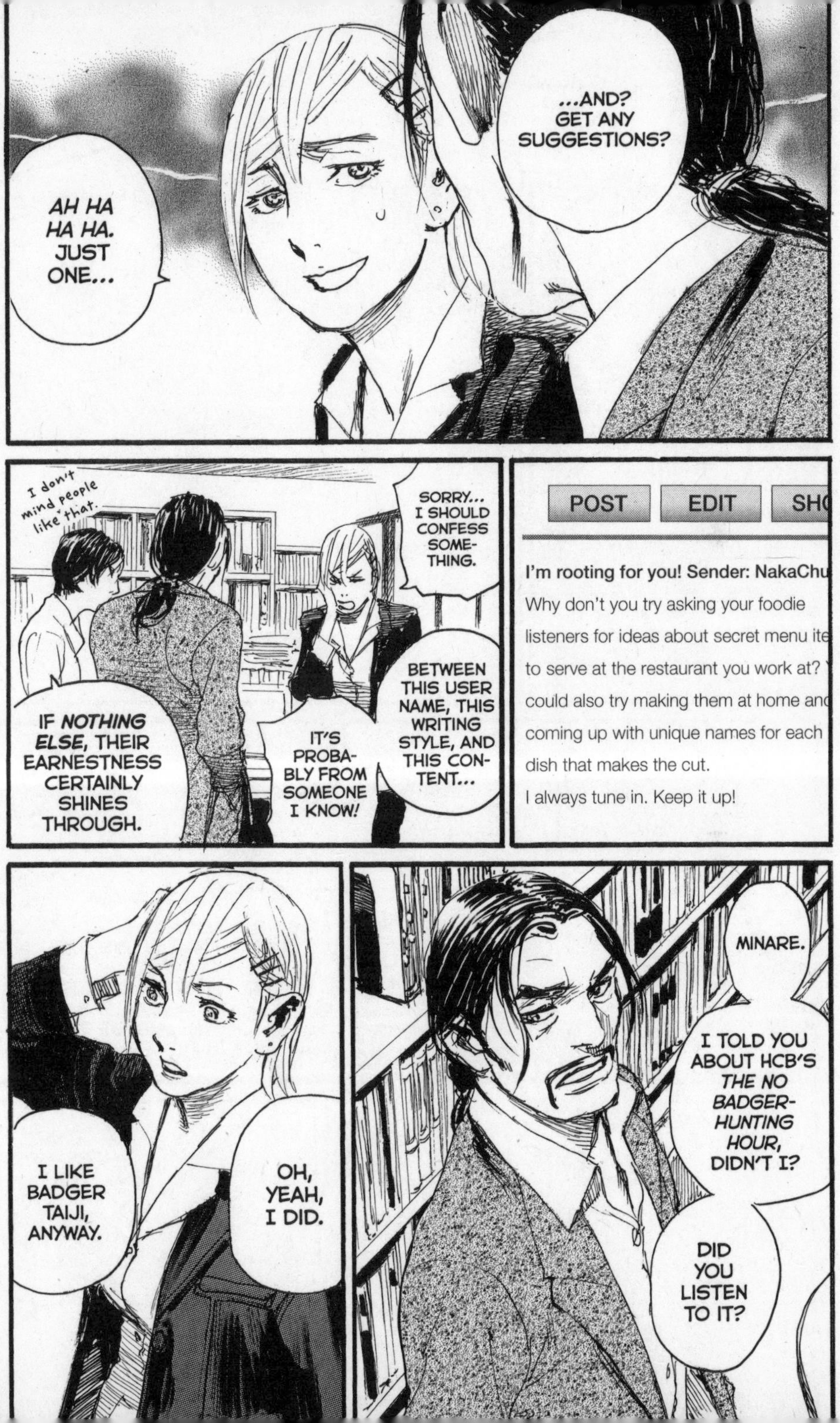
...AND? GET ANY SUGGESTIONS?
AH HA HA HA. JUST ONE...
POST
EDIT
SHO
I'm rooting for you! Sender: NakaChu
Why don't you try asking your foodie
listeners for ideas about secret menu ite
to serve at the restaurant you work at?
could also try making them at home and
coming up with unique names for each
dish that makes the cut.
I always tune in. Keep it up!
SORRY... I SHOULD CONFESS SOME-THING.
BETWEEN THIS USER NAME, THIS WRITING STYLE, AND THIS CON-TENT...
IT'S PROBA-BLY FROM SOMEONE I KNOW!
I don't mind people like that.
IF NOTHING ELSE, THEIR EARNESTNESS CERTAINLY SHINES THROUGH.
MINARE.
I TOLD YOU ABOUT HCB'S THE NO BADGER-HUNTING HOUR, DIDN'T I?
DID YOU LISTEN TO IT?
OH, YEAH, I DID.
I LIKE BADGER TAIJI, ANYWAY.

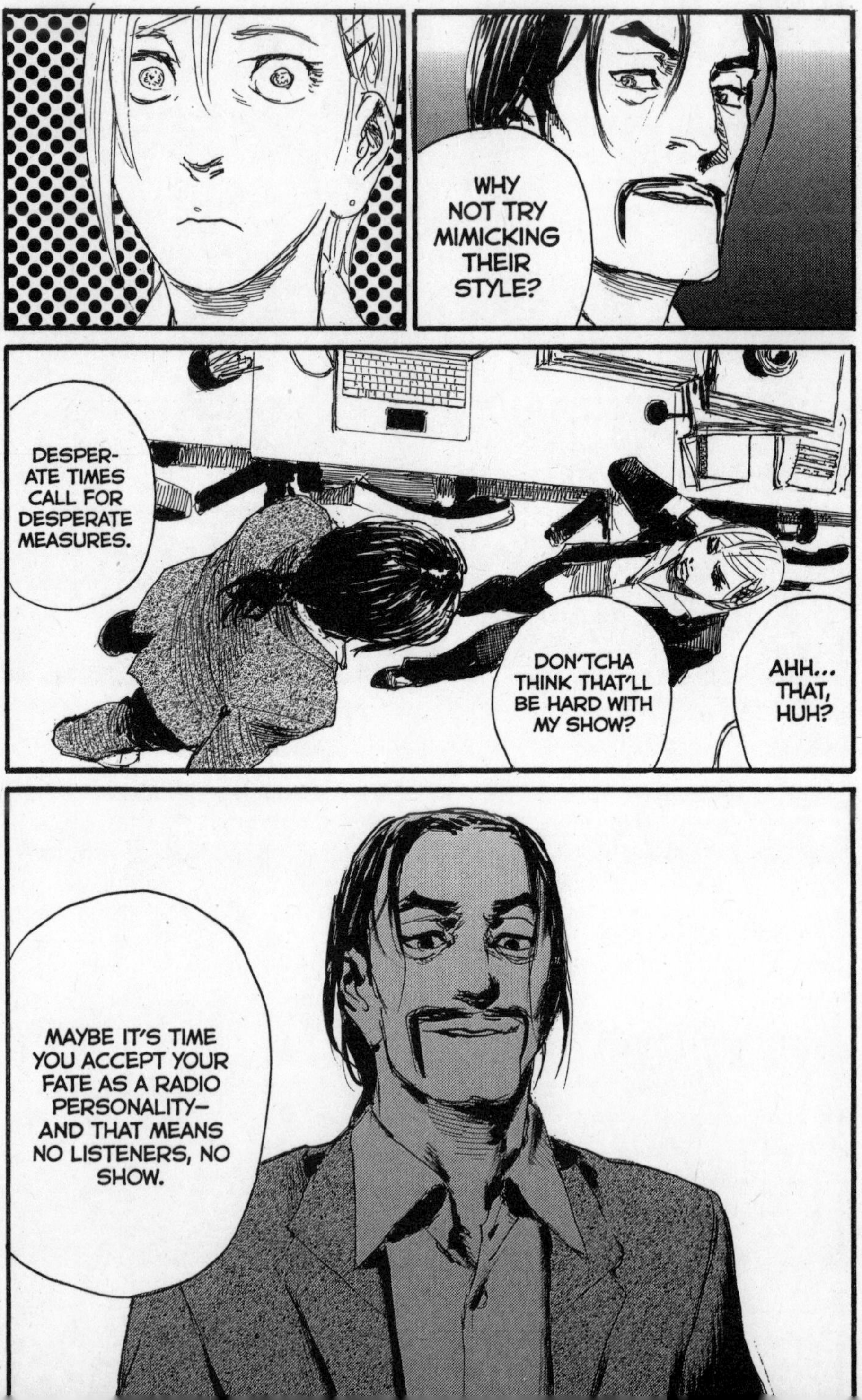
WHY NOT TRY MIMICKING THEIR STYLE?
AHH... THAT, HUH?
DON'TCHA THINK THAT'LL BE HARD WITH MY SHOW?
DESPER-ATE TIMES CALL FOR DESPERATE MEASURES.
MAYBE IT'S TIME YOU ACCEPT YOUR FATE AS A RADIO PERSONALITY—AND THAT MEANS NO LISTENERS, NO SHOW.

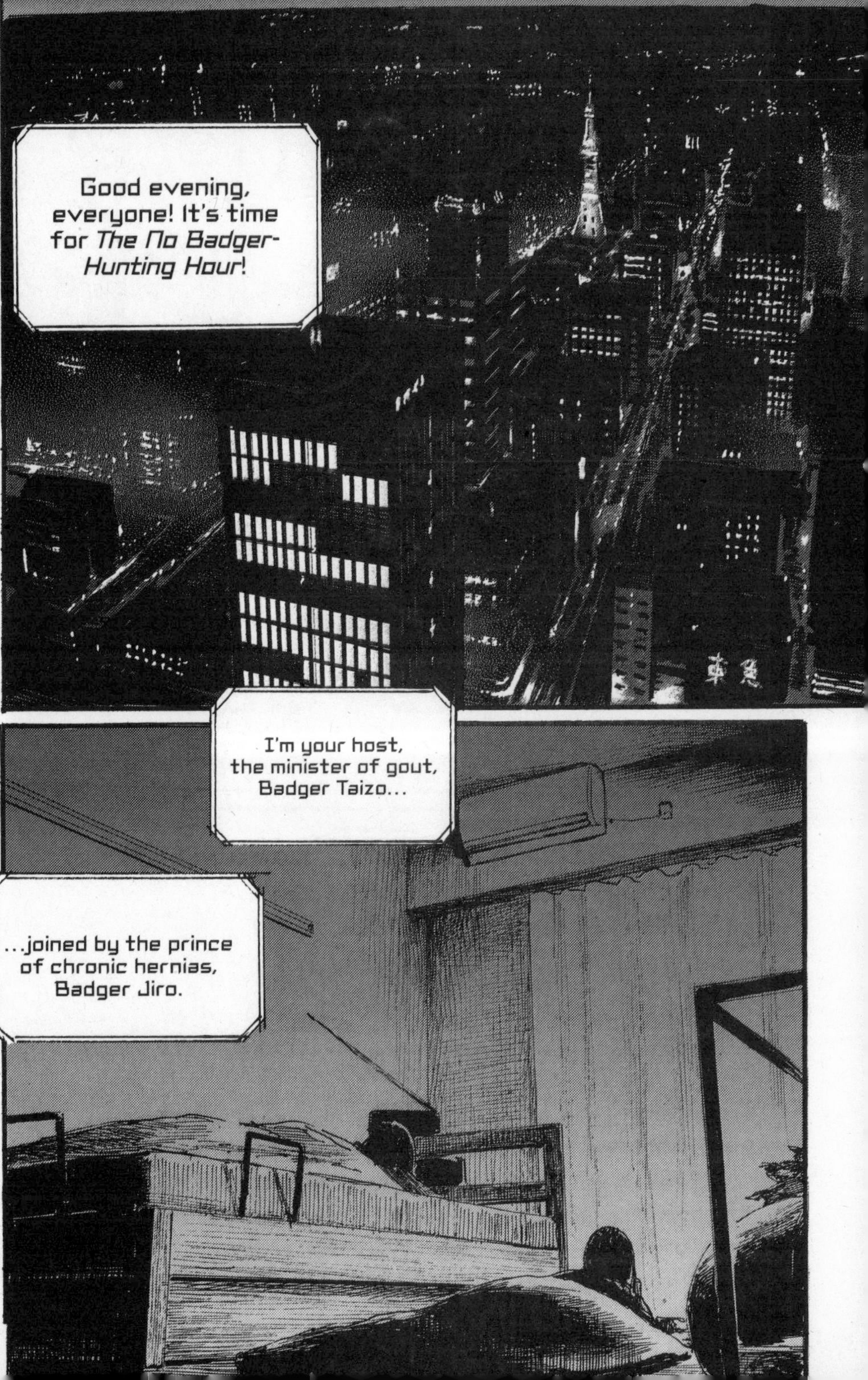
Good evening, everyone! It's time for *The No Badger-Hunting Hour*!
I'm your host, the minister of gout, Badger Taizo...
...joined by the prince of chronic hernias, Badger Jiro.

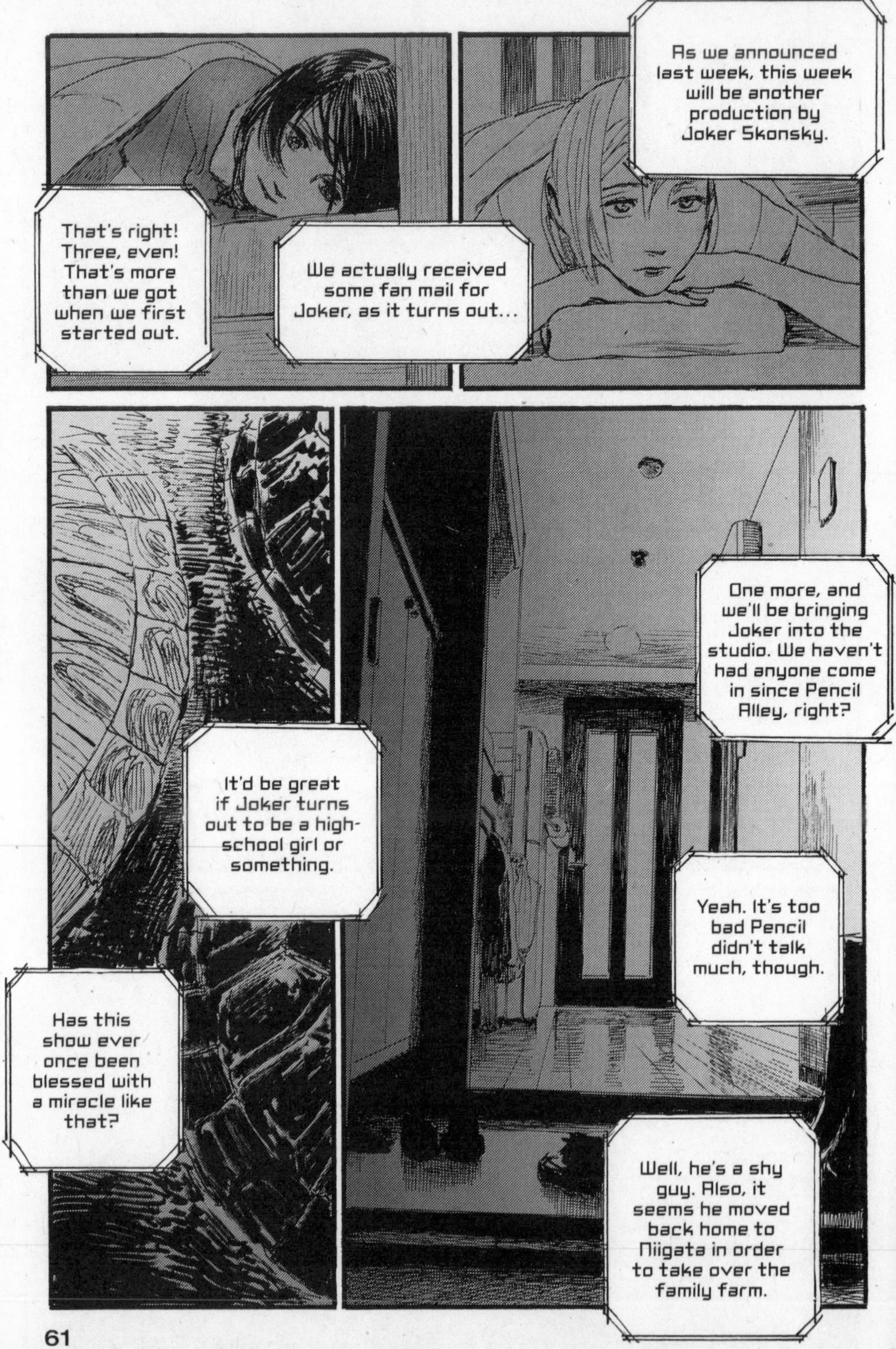
As we announced last week, this week will be another production by Joker Skonsky.
We actually received some fan mail for Joker, as it turns out...
That's right! Three, even! That's more than we got when we first started out.
One more, and we'll be bringing Joker into the studio. We haven't had anyone come in since Pencil Alley, right?
Yeah. It's too bad Pencil didn't talk much, though.
Well, he's a shy guy. Also, it seems he moved back home to Niigata in order to take over the family farm.
It'd be great if Joker turns out to be a high-school girl or something.
Has this show ever once been blessed with a miracle like that?

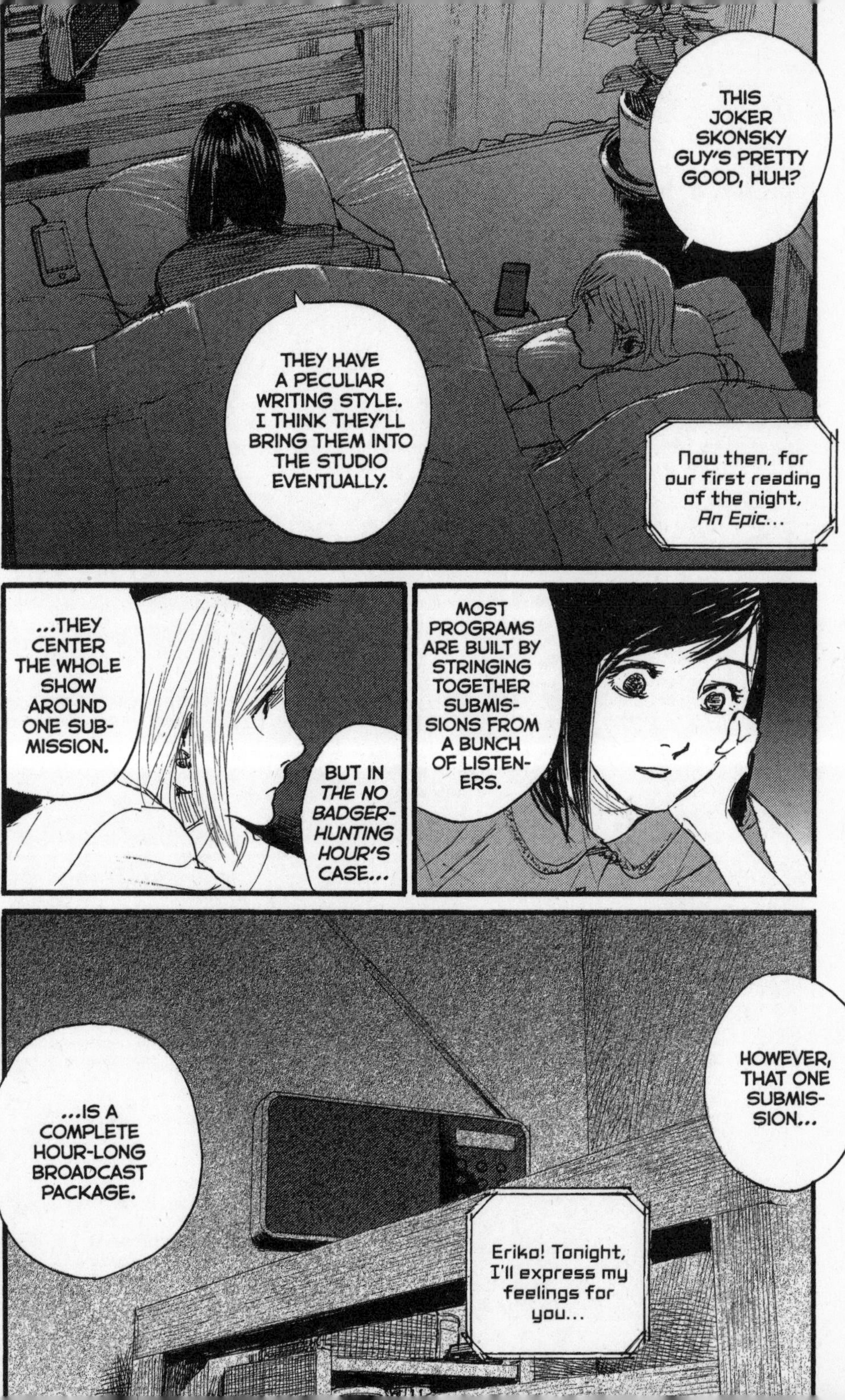
THIS JOKER SKONSKY GUY'S PRETTY GOOD, HUH?
THEY HAVE A PECULIAR WRITING STYLE. I THINK THEY'LL BRING THEM INTO THE STUDIO EVENTUALLY.
Now then, for our first reading of the night, *An Epic*...
MOST PROGRAMS ARE BUILT BY STRINGING TOGETHER SUBMISSIONS FROM A BUNCH OF LISTENERS.
BUT IN *THE NO BADGER-HUNTING HOUR'S* CASE...
...THEY CENTER THE WHOLE SHOW AROUND ONE SUBMISSION.
HOWEVER, THAT ONE SUBMISSION...
...IS A COMPLETE HOUR-LONG BROADCAST PACKAGE.
Eriko! Tonight, I'll express my feelings for you...

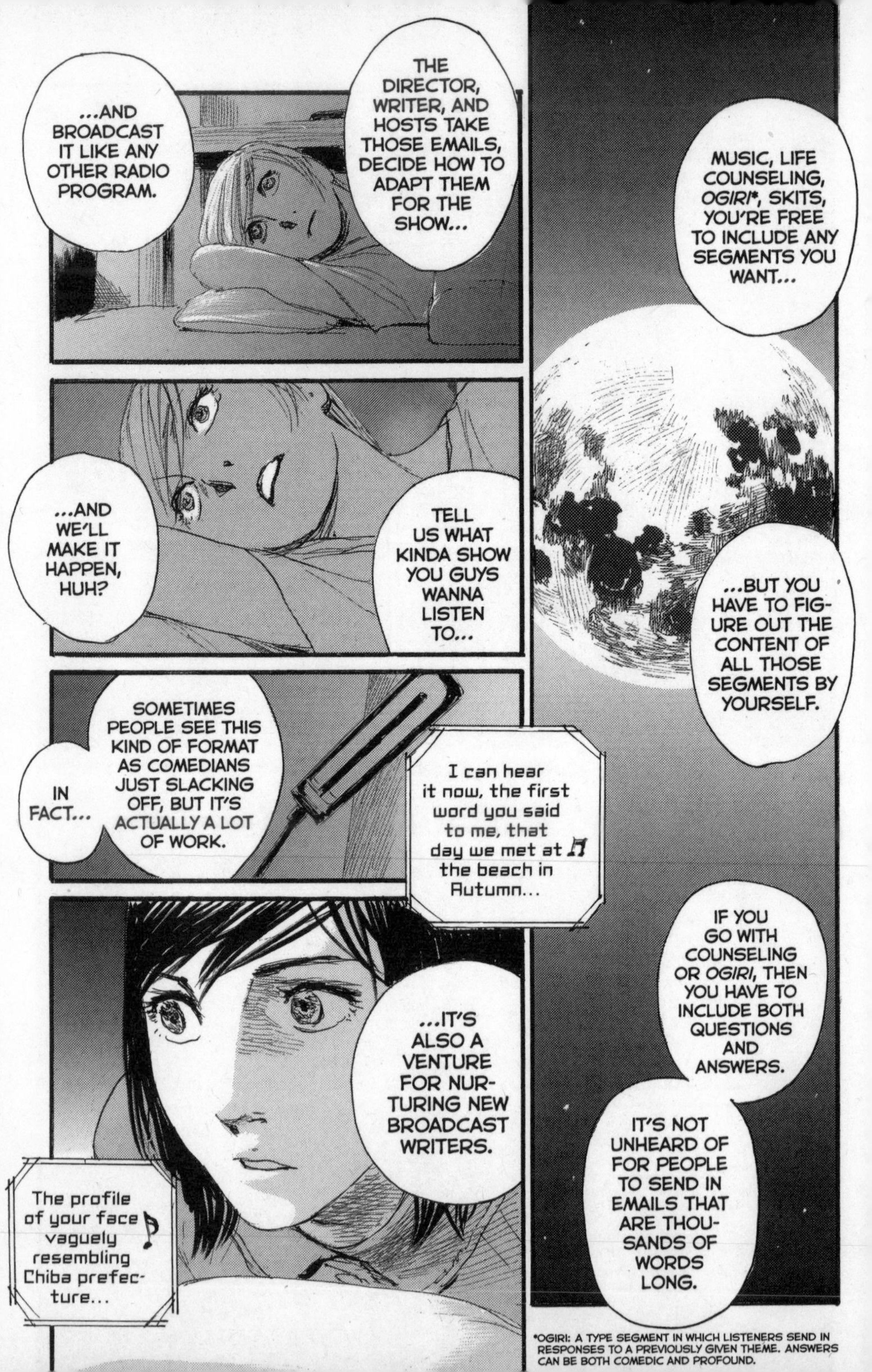
MUSIC, LIFE COUNSELING, OGIRI*, SKITS, YOU'RE FREE TO INCLUDE ANY SEGMENTS YOU WANT...
...BUT YOU HAVE TO FIG-URE OUT THE CONTENT OF ALL THOSE SEGMENTS BY YOURSELF.
IF YOU GO WITH COUNSELING OR OGIRI, THEN YOU HAVE TO INCLUDE BOTH QUESTIONS AND ANSWERS.
IT'S NOT UNHEARD OF FOR PEOPLE TO SEND IN EMAILS THAT ARE THOU-SANDS OF WORDS LONG.
THE DIRECTOR, WRITER, AND HOSTS TAKE THOSE EMAILS, DECIDE HOW TO ADAPT THEM FOR THE SHOW...
...AND BROADCAST IT LIKE ANY OTHER RADIO PROGRAM.
TELL US WHAT KINDA SHOW YOU GUYS WANNA LISTEN TO...
...AND WE'LL MAKE IT HAPPEN, HUH?
I can hear it now, the first word you said to me, that day we met at the beach in Autumn...
SOMETIMES PEOPLE SEE THIS KIND OF FORMAT AS COMEDIANS JUST SLACKING OFF, BUT IT'S ACTUALLY A LOT OF WORK.
IN FACT...
...IT'S ALSO A VENTURE FOR NUR-TURING NEW BROADCAST WRITERS.
The profile of your face vaguely resembling Chiba prefec-ture...

*OGIRI: A TYPE SEGMENT IN WHICH LISTENERS SEND IN RESPONSES TO A PREVIOUSLY GIVEN THEME. ANSWERS CAN BE BOTH COMEDIC AND PROFOUND.

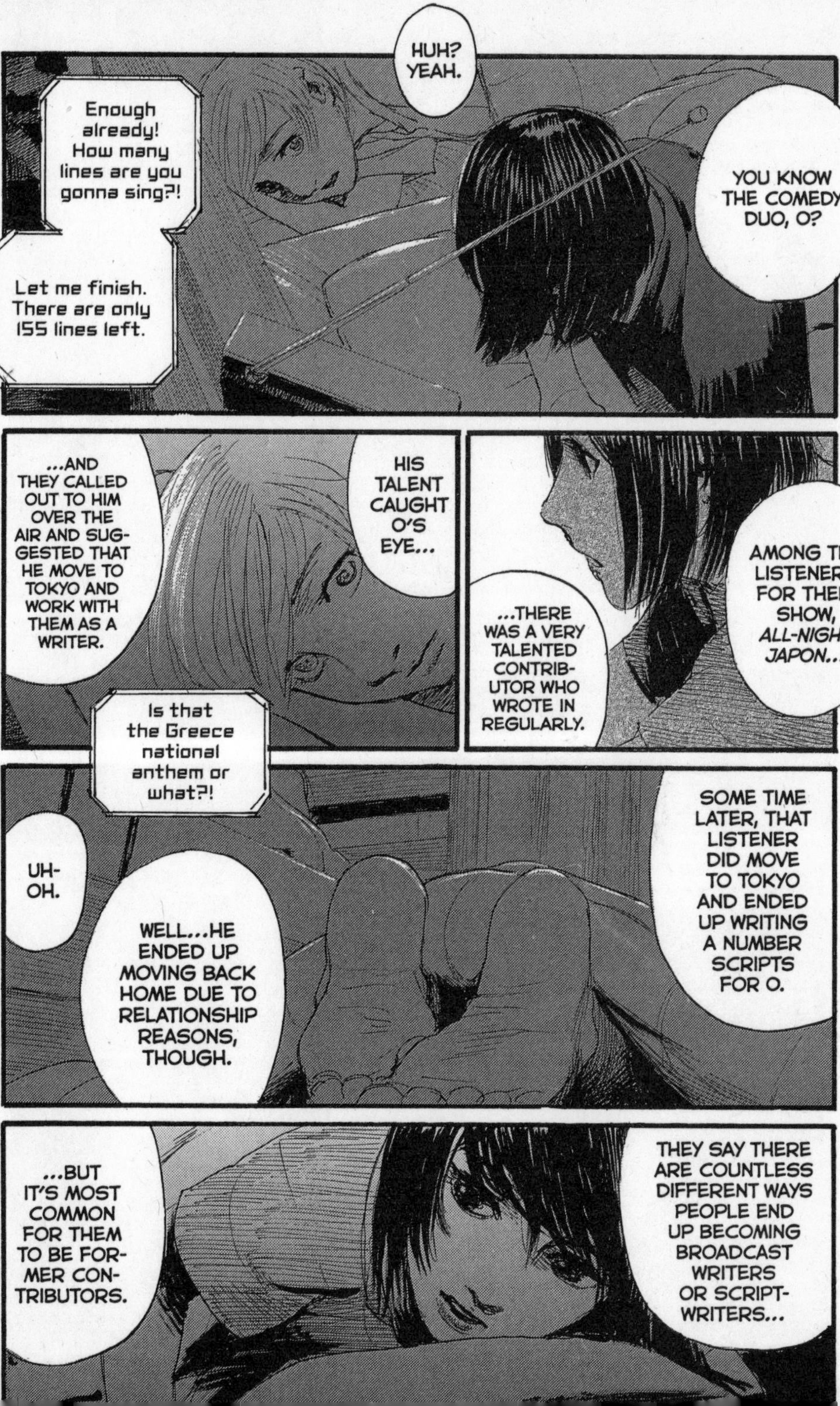
YOU KNOW THE COMEDY DUO, O?
HUH? YEAH.
Enough already! How many lines are you gonna sing?!
Let me finish. There are only 155 lines left.
AMONG THE LISTENERS FOR THEIR SHOW, *ALL-NIGHT JAPON*...
...THERE WAS A VERY TALENTED CONTRIB-UTOR WHO WROTE IN REGULARLY.
HIS TALENT CAUGHT O'S EYE...
...AND THEY CALLED OUT TO HIM OVER THE AIR AND SUG-GESTED THAT HE MOVE TO TOKYO AND WORK WITH THEM AS A WRITER.
Is that the Greece national anthem or what?!
SOME TIME LATER, THAT LISTENER DID MOVE TO TOKYO AND ENDED UP WRITING A NUMBER SCRIPTS FOR O.
WELL...HE ENDED UP MOVING BACK HOME DUE TO RELATIONSHIP REASONS, THOUGH.
UH-OH.
THEY SAY THERE ARE COUNTLESS DIFFERENT WAYS PEOPLE END UP BECOMING BROADCAST WRITERS OR SCRIPT-WRITERS...
...BUT IT'S MOST COMMON FOR THEM TO BE FOR-MER CON-TRIBUTORS.

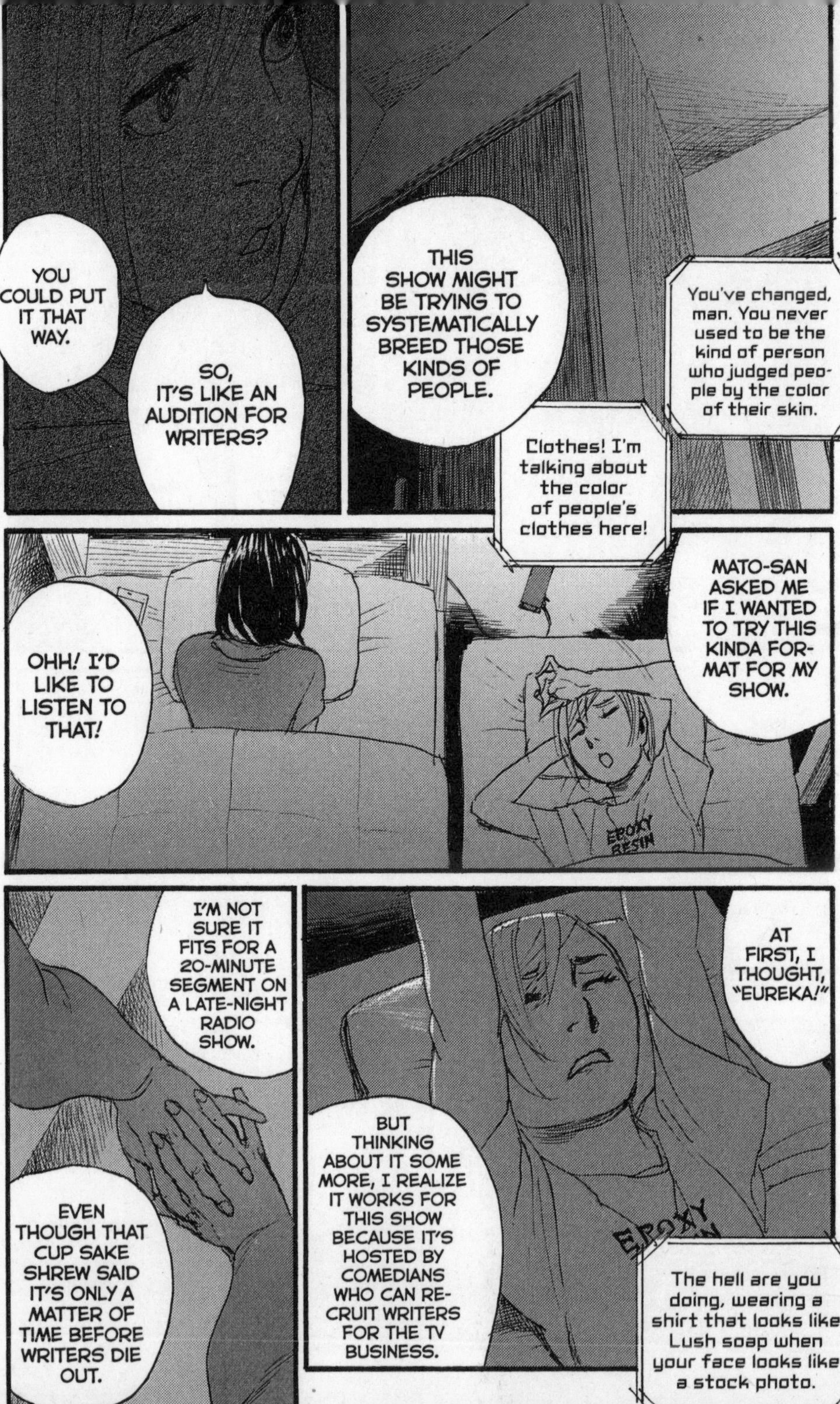
THIS SHOW MIGHT BE TRYING TO SYSTEMATICALLY BREED THOSE KINDS OF PEOPLE.
You've changed, man. You never used to be the kind of person who judged people by the color of their skin.
Clothes! I'm talking about the color of people's clothes here!
SO, IT'S LIKE AN AUDITION FOR WRITERS?
YOU COULD PUT IT THAT WAY.
MATO-SAN ASKED ME IF I WANTED TO TRY THIS KINDA FORMAT FOR MY SHOW.
EPOXY RESIN
OHH! I'D LIKE TO LISTEN TO THAT!
AT FIRST, I THOUGHT, "EUREKA!"
BUT THINKING ABOUT IT SOME MORE, I REALIZE IT WORKS FOR THIS SHOW BECAUSE IT'S HOSTED BY COMEDIANS WHO CAN RECRUIT WRITERS FOR THE TV BUSINESS.
The hell are you doing, wearing a shirt that looks like Lush soap when your face looks like a stock photo.
I'M NOT SURE IT FITS FOR A 20-MINUTE SEGMENT ON A LATE-NIGHT RADIO SHOW.
EVEN THOUGH THAT CUP SAKE SHREW SAID IT'S ONLY A MATTER OF TIME BEFORE WRITERS DIE OUT.

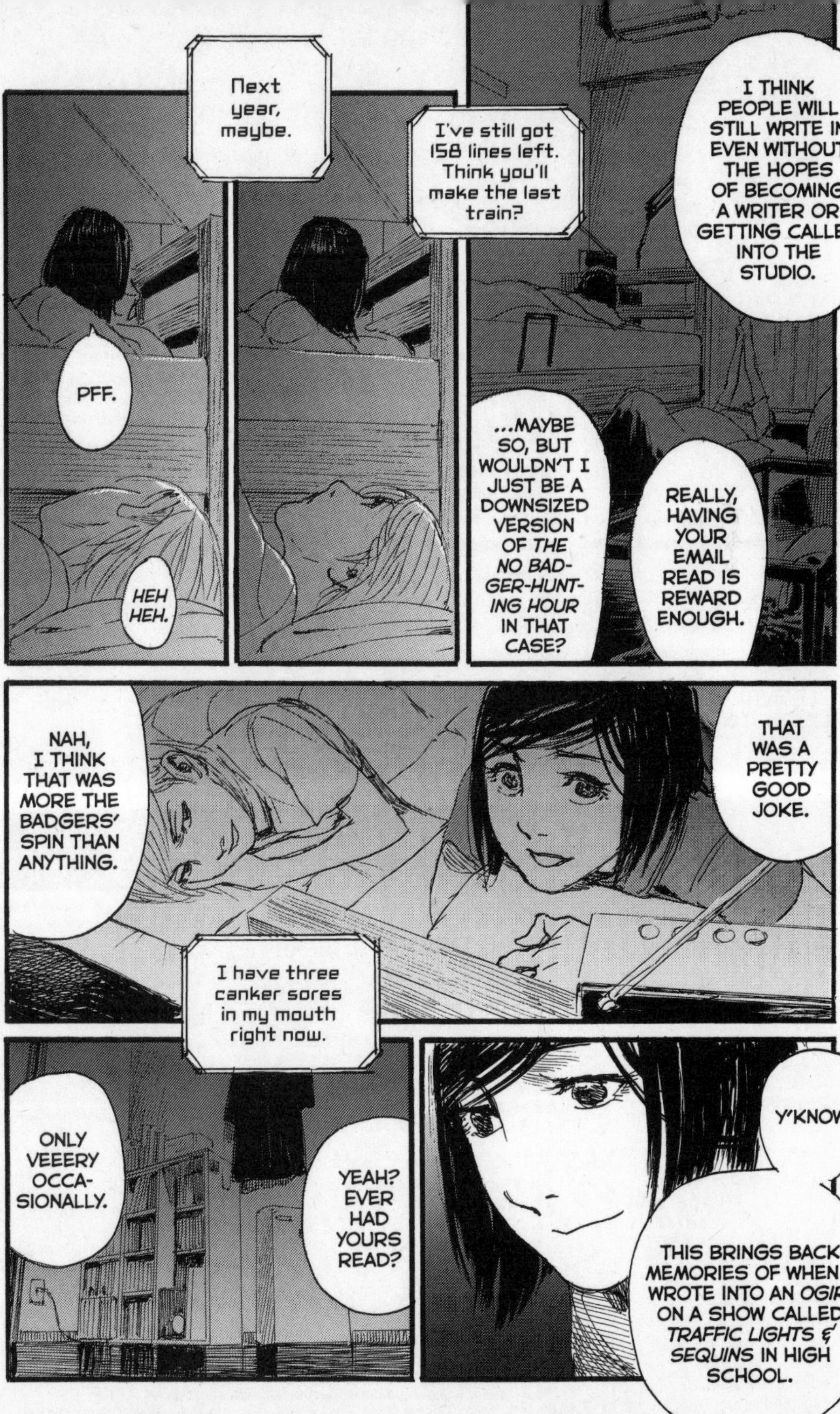
I THINK PEOPLE WILL STILL WRITE IN EVEN WITHOUT THE HOPES OF BECOMING A WRITER OR GETTING CALLED INTO THE STUDIO.
REALLY, HAVING YOUR EMAIL READ IS REWARD ENOUGH.
...MAYBE SO, BUT WOULDN'T I JUST BE A DOWNSIZED VERSION OF *THE NO BADGER-HUNTING HOUR* IN THAT CASE?
I've still got 158 lines left. Think you'll make the last train?
Next year, maybe.
PFF.
HEH HEH.
THAT WAS A PRETTY GOOD JOKE.
NAH, I THINK THAT WAS MORE THE BADGERS' SPIN THAN ANYTHING.
I have three canker sores in my mouth right now.
Y'KNOW,
THIS BRINGS BACK MEMORIES OF WHEN I WROTE INTO AN *OGIRI* ON A SHOW CALLED *TRAFFIC LIGHTS & SEQUINS* IN HIGH SCHOOL.
YEAH? EVER HAD YOURS READ?
ONLY VEEERY OCCA-SIONALLY.

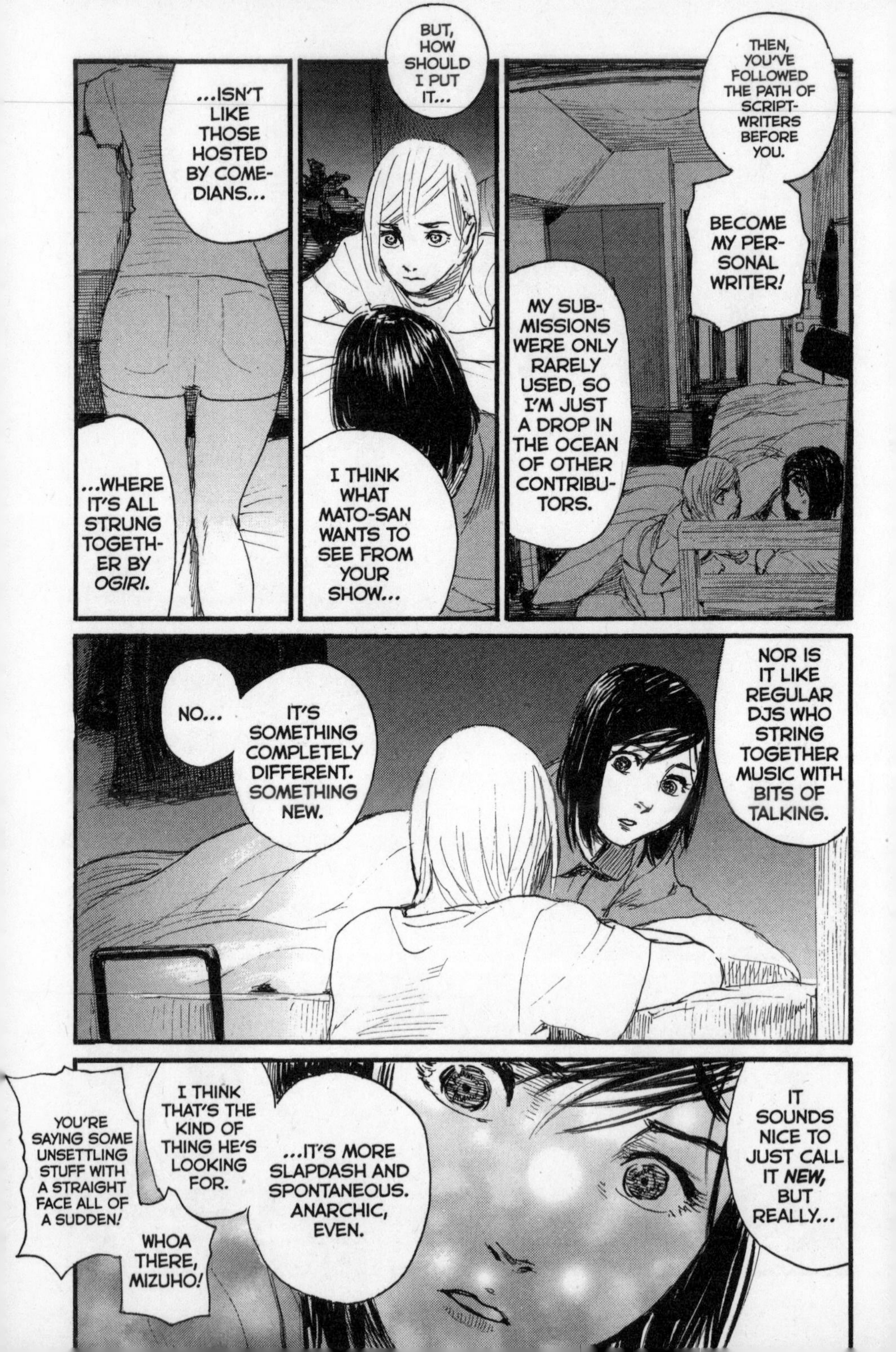

THEN, YOU'VE FOLLOWED THE PATH OF SCRIPT-WRITERS BEFORE YOU.
BECOME MY PERSONAL WRITER!
MY SUBMISSIONS WERE ONLY RARELY USED, SO I'M JUST A DROP IN THE OCEAN OF OTHER CONTRIBUTORS.
BUT, HOW SHOULD I PUT IT...
I THINK WHAT MATO-SAN WANTS TO SEE FROM YOUR SHOW...
...ISN'T LIKE THOSE HOSTED BY COMEDIANS...
...WHERE IT'S ALL STRUNG TOGETHER BY *OGIRI*.
NOR IS IT LIKE REGULAR DJS WHO STRING TOGETHER MUSIC WITH BITS OF TALKING.
NO... IT'S SOMETHING COMPLETELY DIFFERENT. SOMETHING NEW.
IT SOUNDS NICE TO JUST CALL IT *NEW*, BUT REALLY...
...IT'S MORE SLAPDASH AND SPONTANEOUS. ANARCHIC, EVEN.
I THINK THAT'S THE KIND OF THING HE'S LOOKING FOR.
WHOA THERE, MIZUHO!
YOU'RE SAYING SOME UNSETTLING STUFF WITH A STRAIGHT FACE ALL OF A SUDDEN!

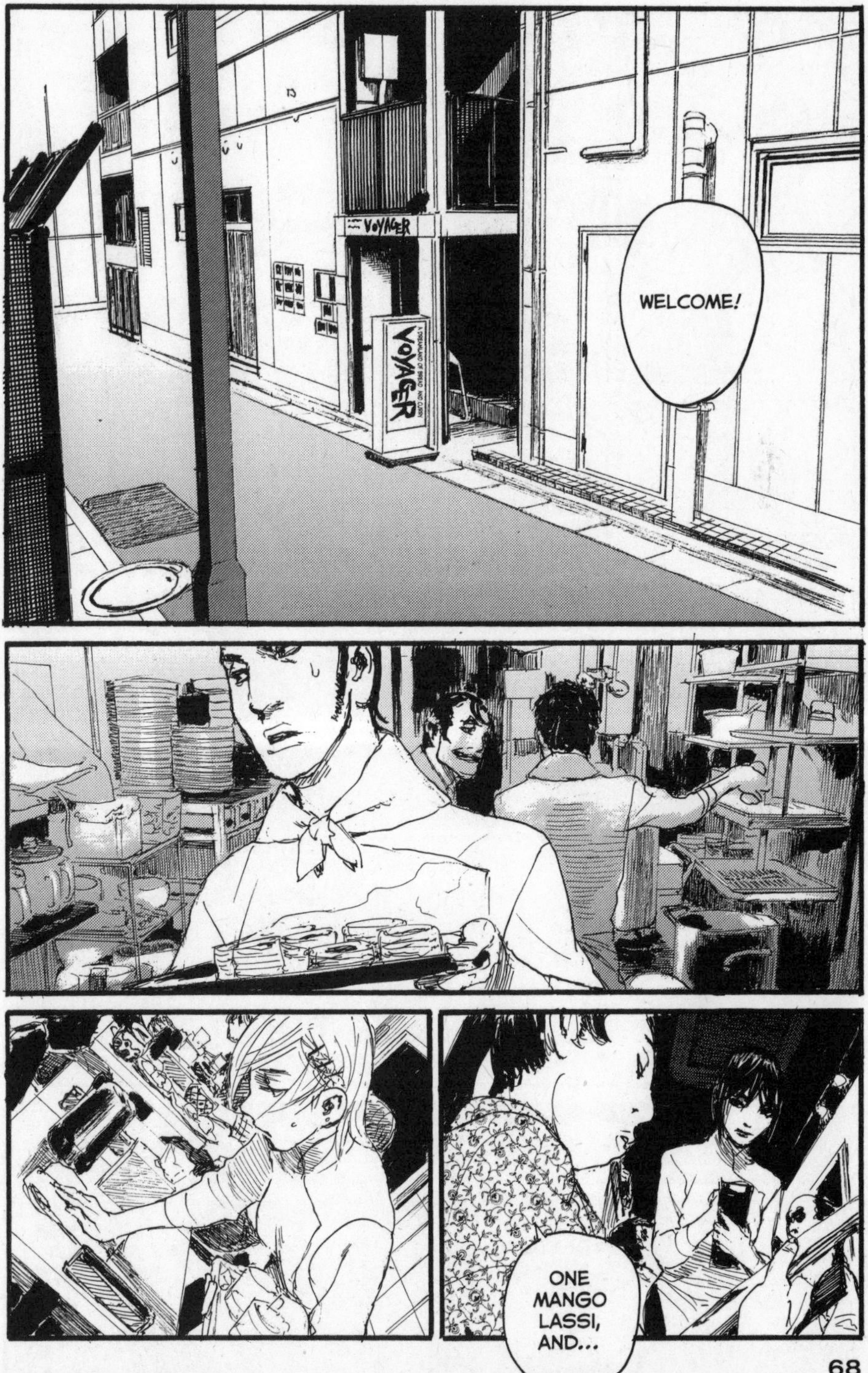
VOYAGER
VOYAGER
A DREAMLAND OF BREAD AND CURRY
WELCOME!
ONE MANGO LASSI, AND...

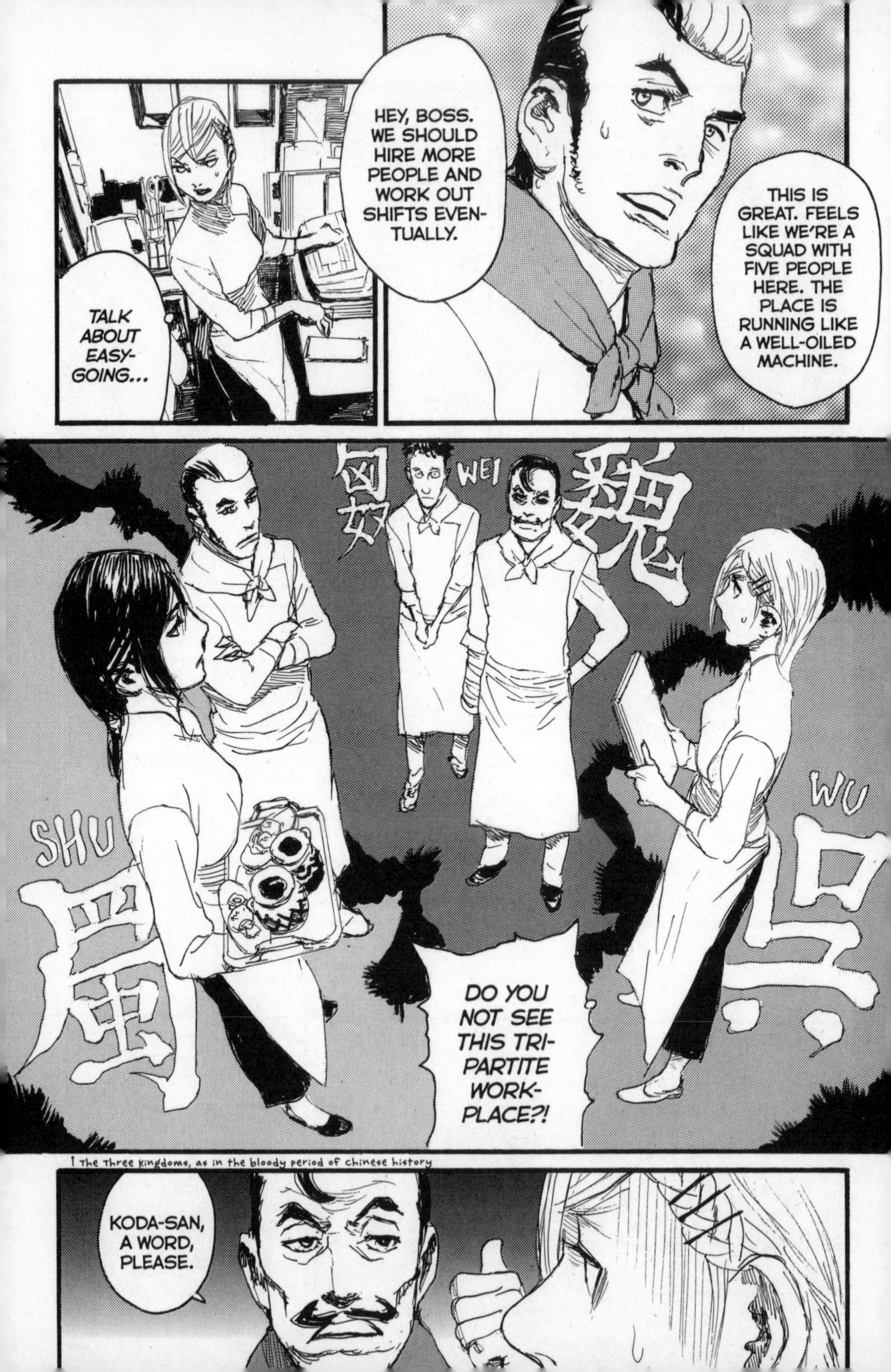
THIS IS GREAT. FEELS LIKE WE'RE A SQUAD WITH FIVE PEOPLE HERE. THE PLACE IS RUNNING LIKE A WELL-OILED MACHINE.
HEY, BOSS. WE SHOULD HIRE MORE PEOPLE AND WORK OUT SHIFTS EVEN-TUALLY.
TALK ABOUT EASY-GOING...
WEI
魏
WU
呉
SHU
蜀
DO YOU NOT SEE THIS TRI-PARTITE WORK-PLACE?!
† The Three Kingdoms, as in the bloody period of Chinese history
KODA-SAN, A WORD, PLEASE.

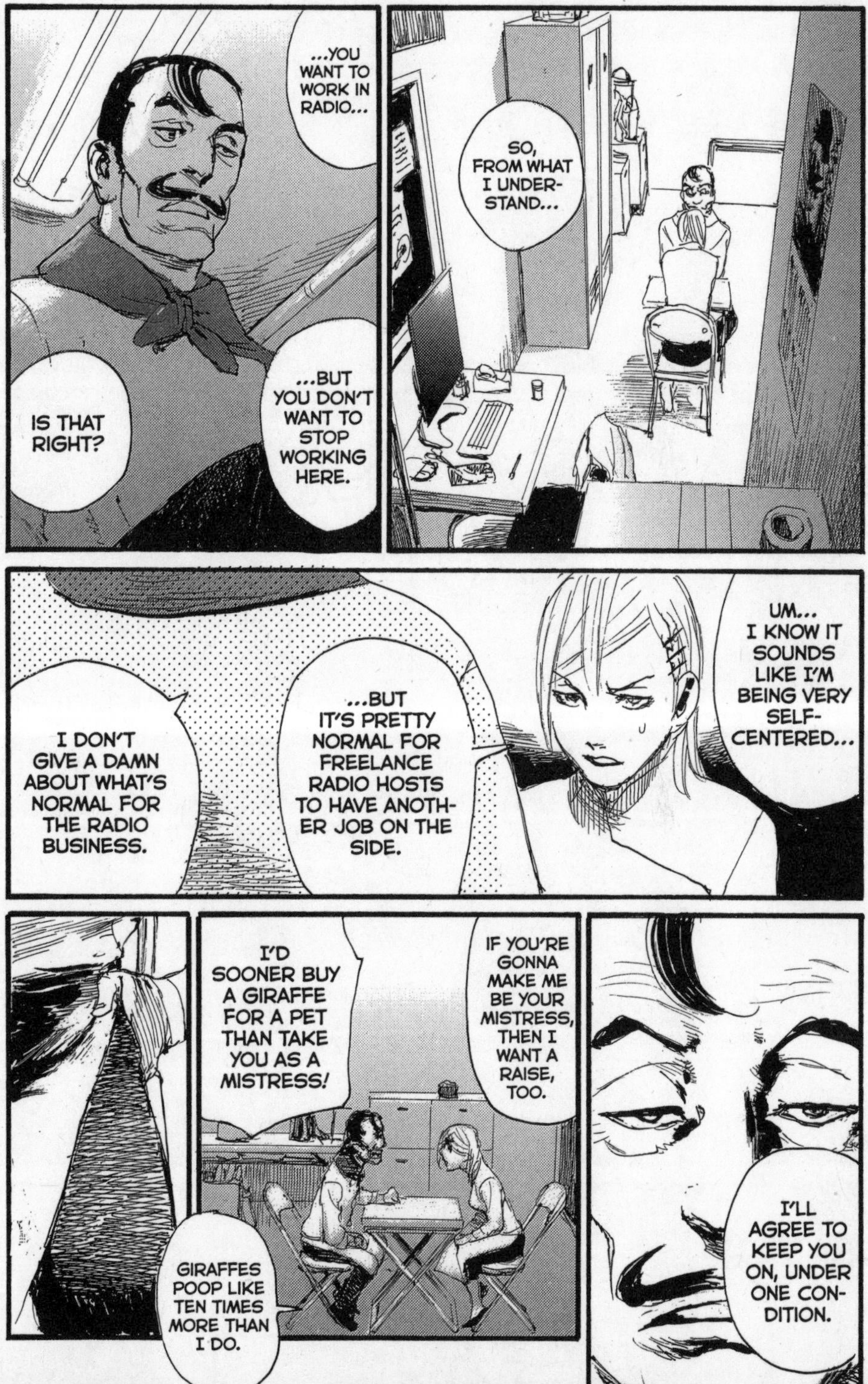
SO, FROM WHAT I UNDERSTAND...
...YOU WANT TO WORK IN RADIO...
...BUT YOU DON'T WANT TO STOP WORKING HERE.
IS THAT RIGHT?
UM... I KNOW IT SOUNDS LIKE I'M BEING VERY SELF-CENTERED...
...BUT IT'S PRETTY NORMAL FOR FREELANCE RADIO HOSTS TO HAVE ANOTHER JOB ON THE SIDE.
I DON'T GIVE A DAMN ABOUT WHAT'S NORMAL FOR THE RADIO BUSINESS.
I'LL AGREE TO KEEP YOU ON, UNDER ONE CONDITION.
IF YOU'RE GONNA MAKE ME BE YOUR MISTRESS, THEN I WANT A RAISE, TOO.
I'D SOONER BUY A GIRAFFE FOR A PET THAN TAKE YOU AS A MISTRESS!
GIRAFFES POOP LIKE TEN TIMES MORE THAN I DO.

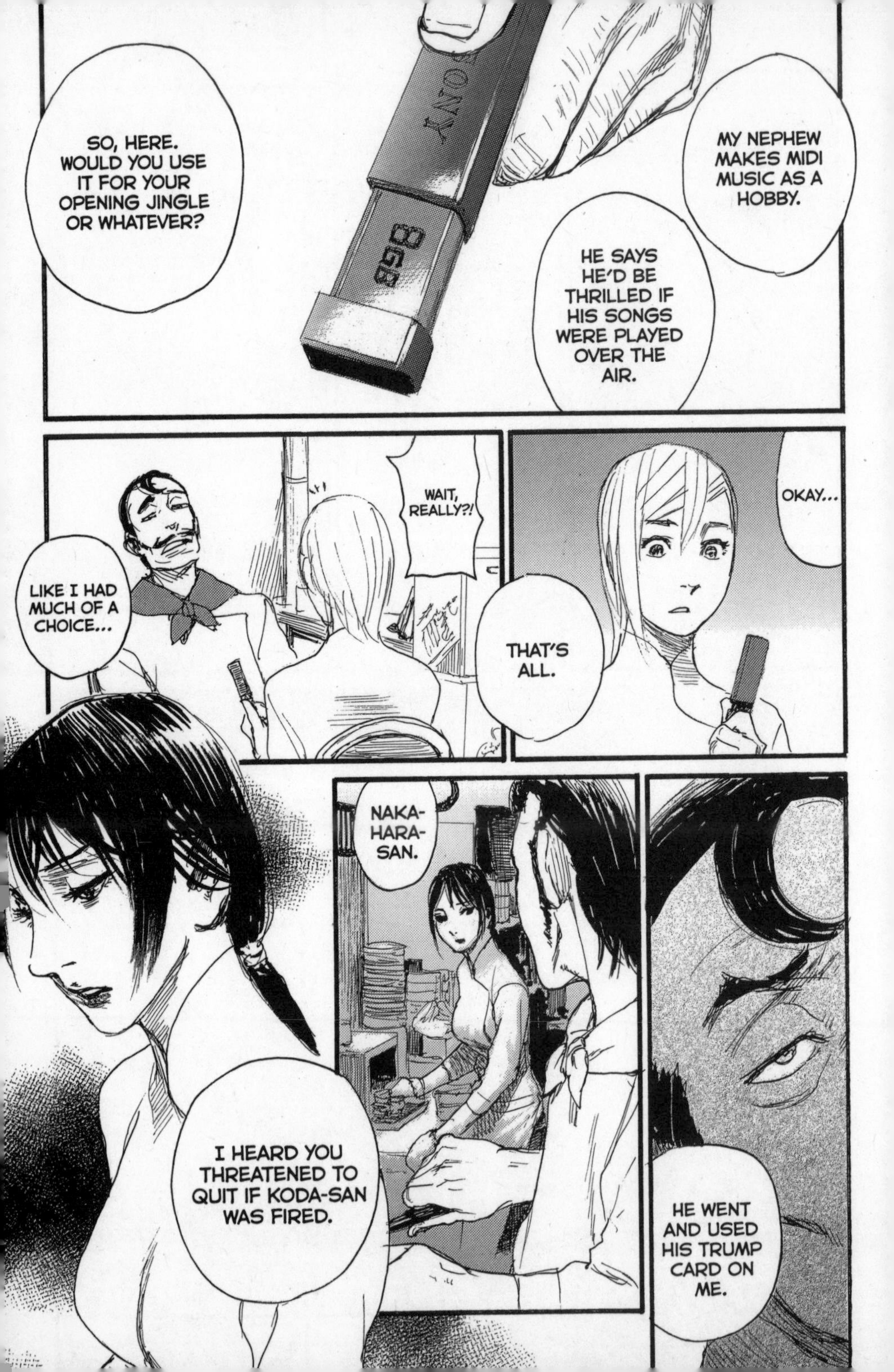
SONY
8GB
MY NEPHEW MAKES MIDI MUSIC AS A HOBBY.
HE SAYS HE'D BE THRILLED IF HIS SONGS WERE PLAYED OVER THE AIR.
SO, HERE. WOULD YOU USE IT FOR YOUR OPENING JINGLE OR WHATEVER?
OKAY...
THAT'S ALL.
WAIT, REALLY?!
LIKE I HAD MUCH OF A CHOICE...
HE WENT AND USED HIS TRUMP CARD ON ME.
NAKA-HARA-SAN.
I HEARD YOU THREATENED TO QUIT IF KODA-SAN WAS FIRED.

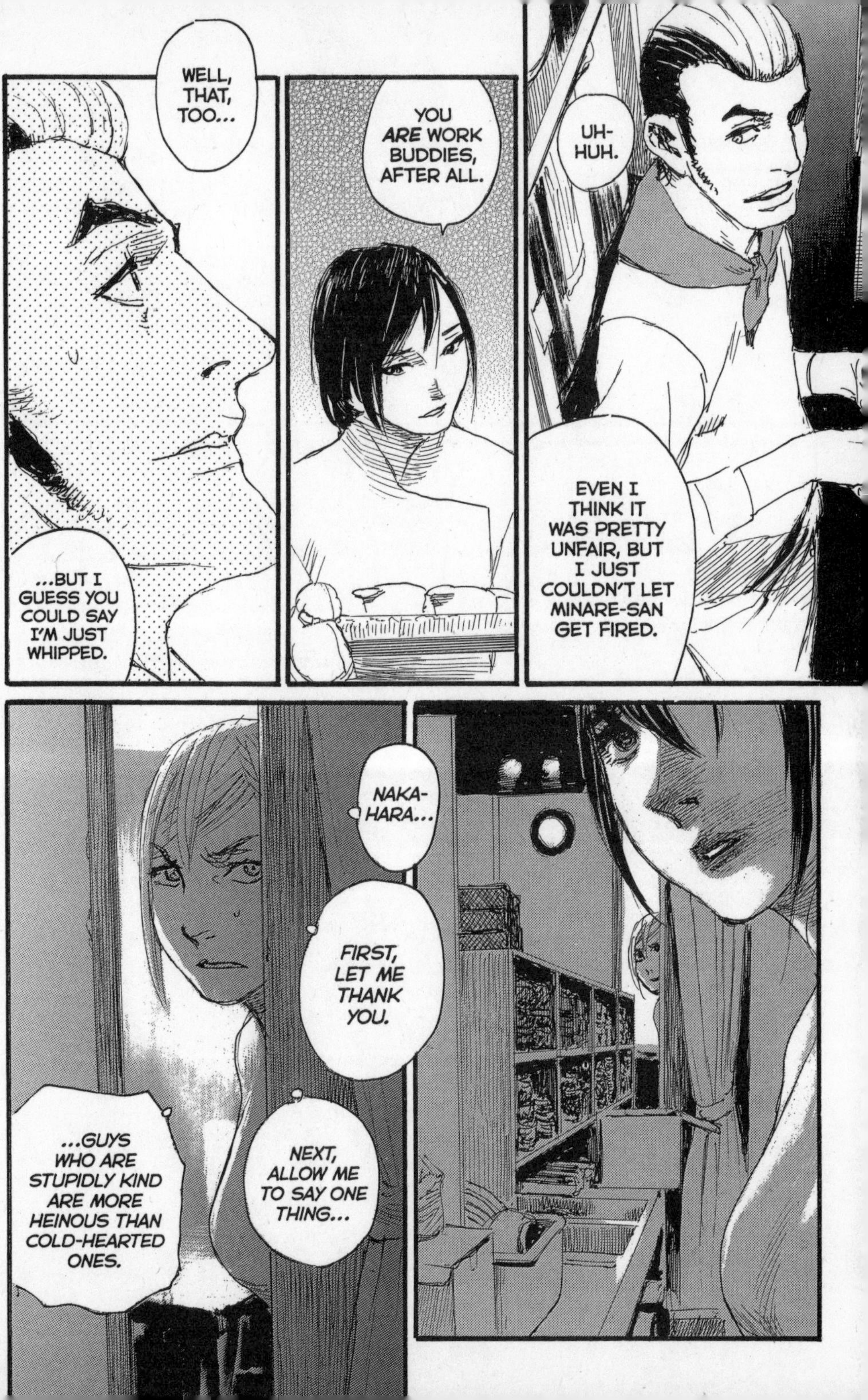
UH-HUH.
EVEN I THINK IT WAS PRETTY UNFAIR, BUT I JUST COULDN'T LET MINARE-SAN GET FIRED.
YOU *ARE* WORK BUDDIES, AFTER ALL.
WELL, THAT, TOO...
...BUT I GUESS YOU COULD SAY I'M JUST WHIPPED.
NAKA-HARA...
FIRST, LET ME THANK YOU.
NEXT, ALLOW ME TO SAY ONE THING...
...GUYS WHO ARE STUPIDLY KIND ARE MORE HEINOUS THAN COLD-HEARTED ONES.

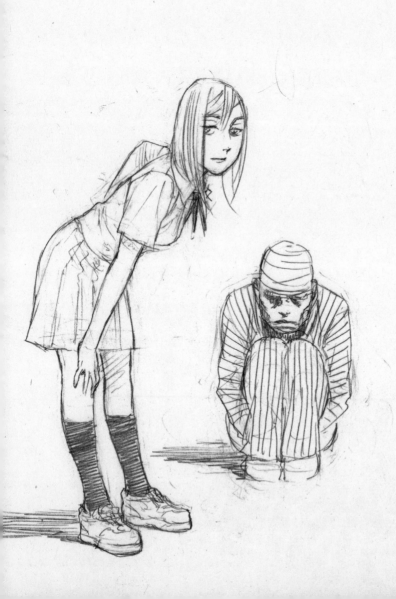

wave
LISTEN
TO ME!

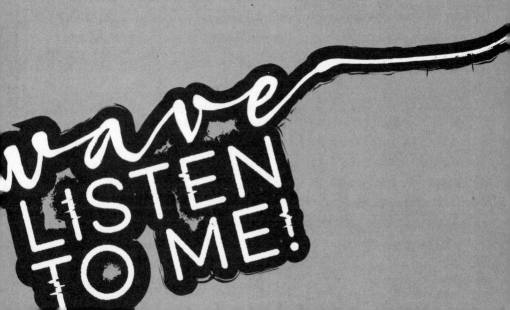

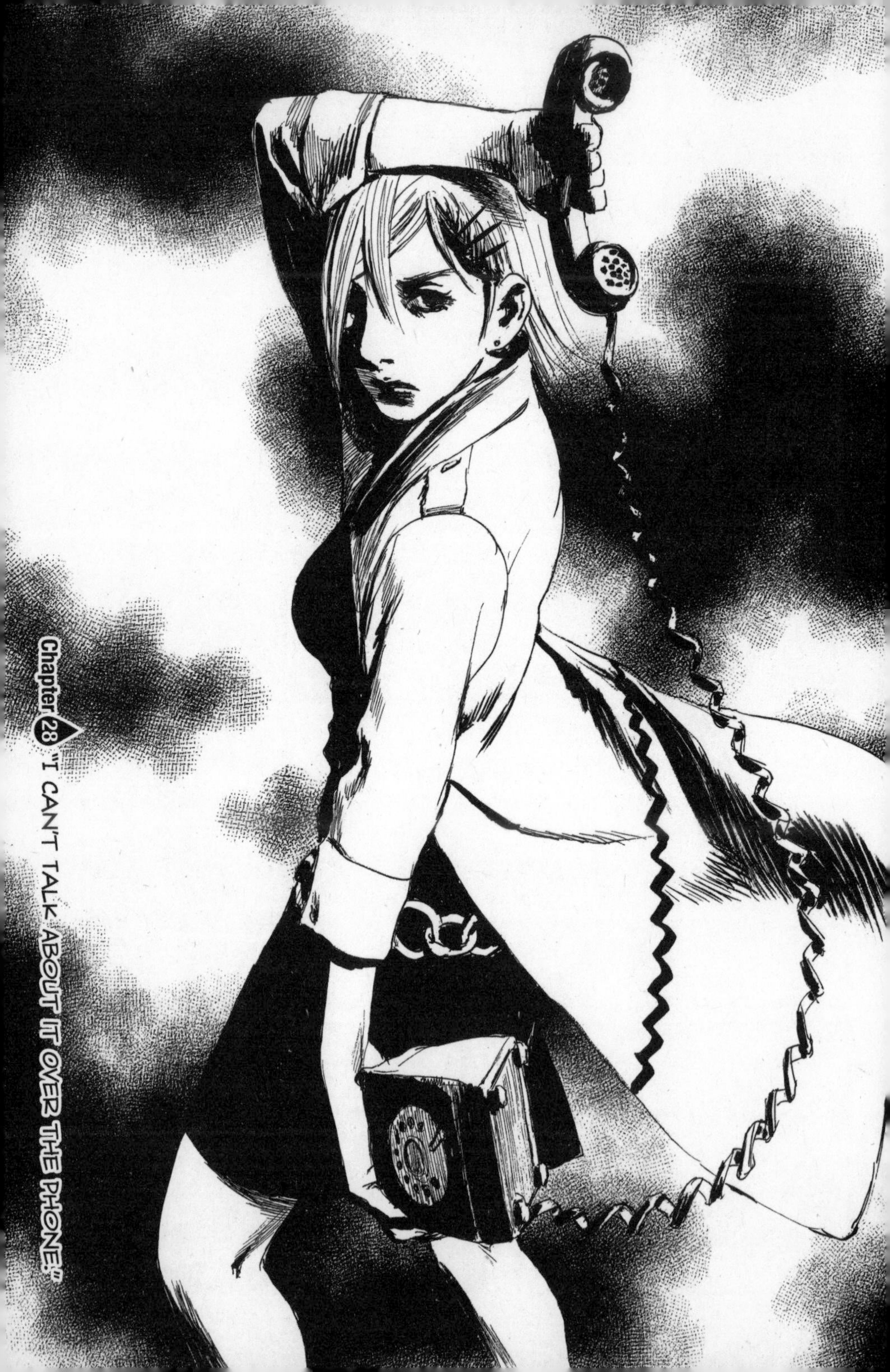
Chapter 28 "I CAN'T TALK ABOUT IT OVER THE PHONE"

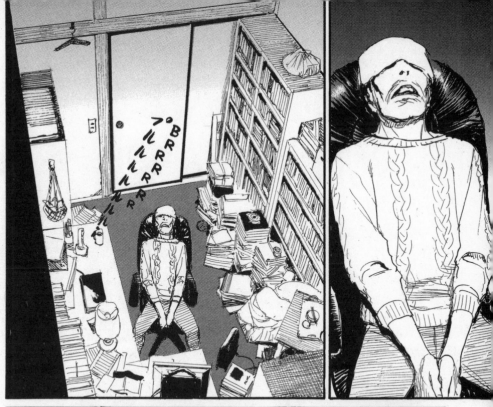

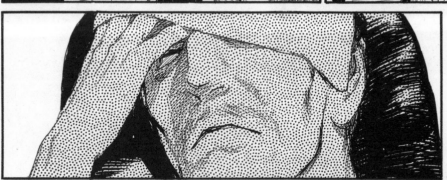

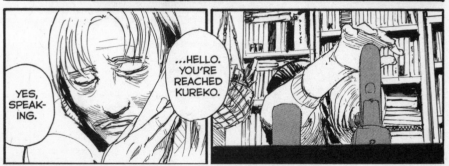

...HELLO. YOU'RE REACHED KUREKO.

YES, SPEAK- ING.

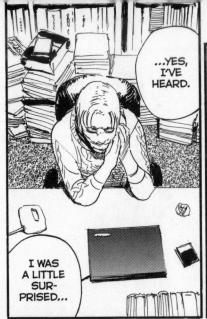

...YES, I'VE HEARD.

I WAS A LITTLE SUR- PRISED...

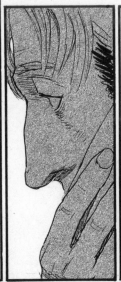

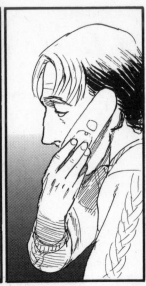

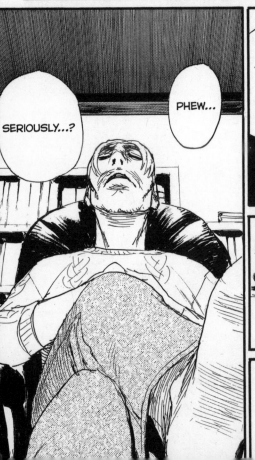

SERIOUSLY...?

PHEW...

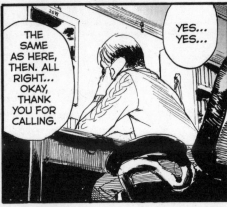

THE SAME AS HERE, THEN. ALL RIGHT... OKAY, THANK YOU FOR CALLING.

YES... YES...

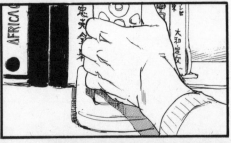

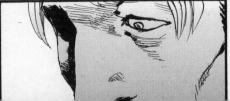

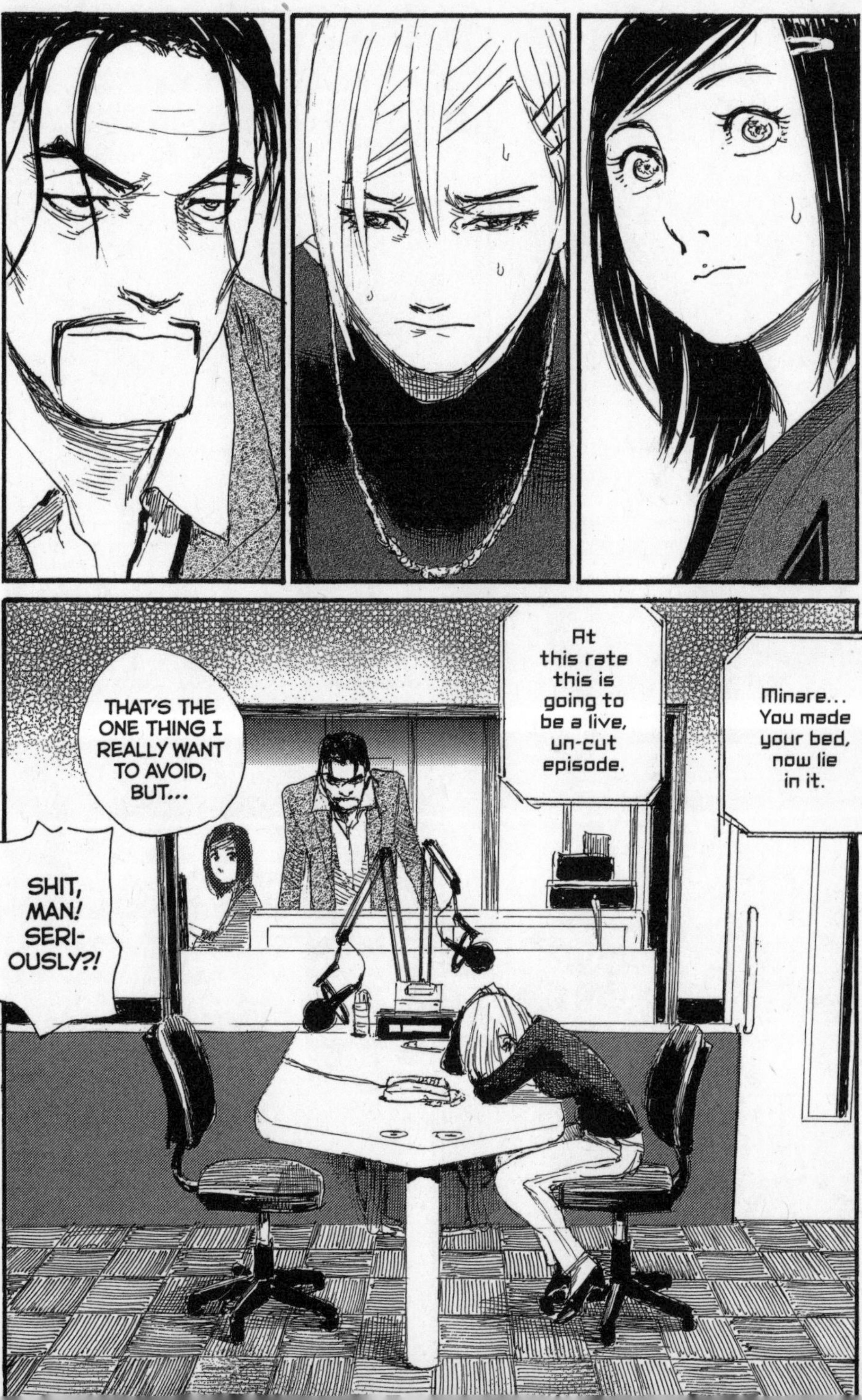
Minare... You made your bed, now lie in it.
At this rate this is going to be a live, un-cut episode.
THAT'S THE ONE THING I REALLY WANT TO AVOID, BUT...
SHIT, MAN! SERIOUSLY?!

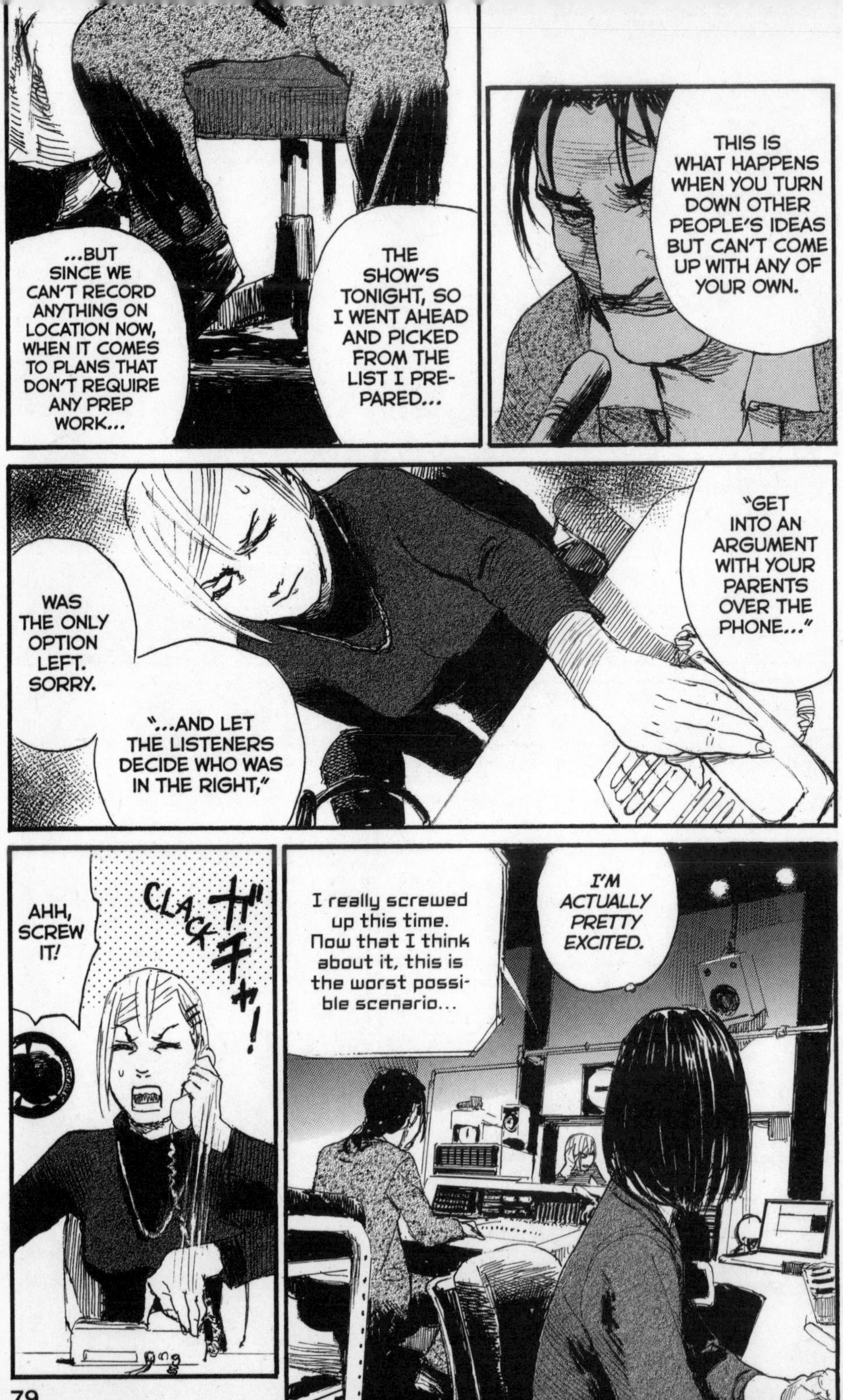
THIS IS WHAT HAPPENS WHEN YOU TURN DOWN OTHER PEOPLE'S IDEAS BUT CAN'T COME UP WITH ANY OF YOUR OWN.
...BUT SINCE WE CAN'T RECORD ANYTHING ON LOCATION NOW, WHEN IT COMES TO PLANS THAT DON'T REQUIRE ANY PREP WORK...
THE SHOW'S TONIGHT, SO I WENT AHEAD AND PICKED FROM THE LIST I PRE-PARED...
"GET INTO AN ARGUMENT WITH YOUR PARENTS OVER THE PHONE..."
"...AND LET THE LISTENERS DECIDE WHO WAS IN THE RIGHT,"
WAS THE ONLY OPTION LEFT. SORRY.
I'M ACTUALLY PRETTY EXCITED.
I really screwed up this time. Now that I think about it, this is the worst possi-ble scenario...
ガチャ!
CLACK
AHH, SCREW IT!

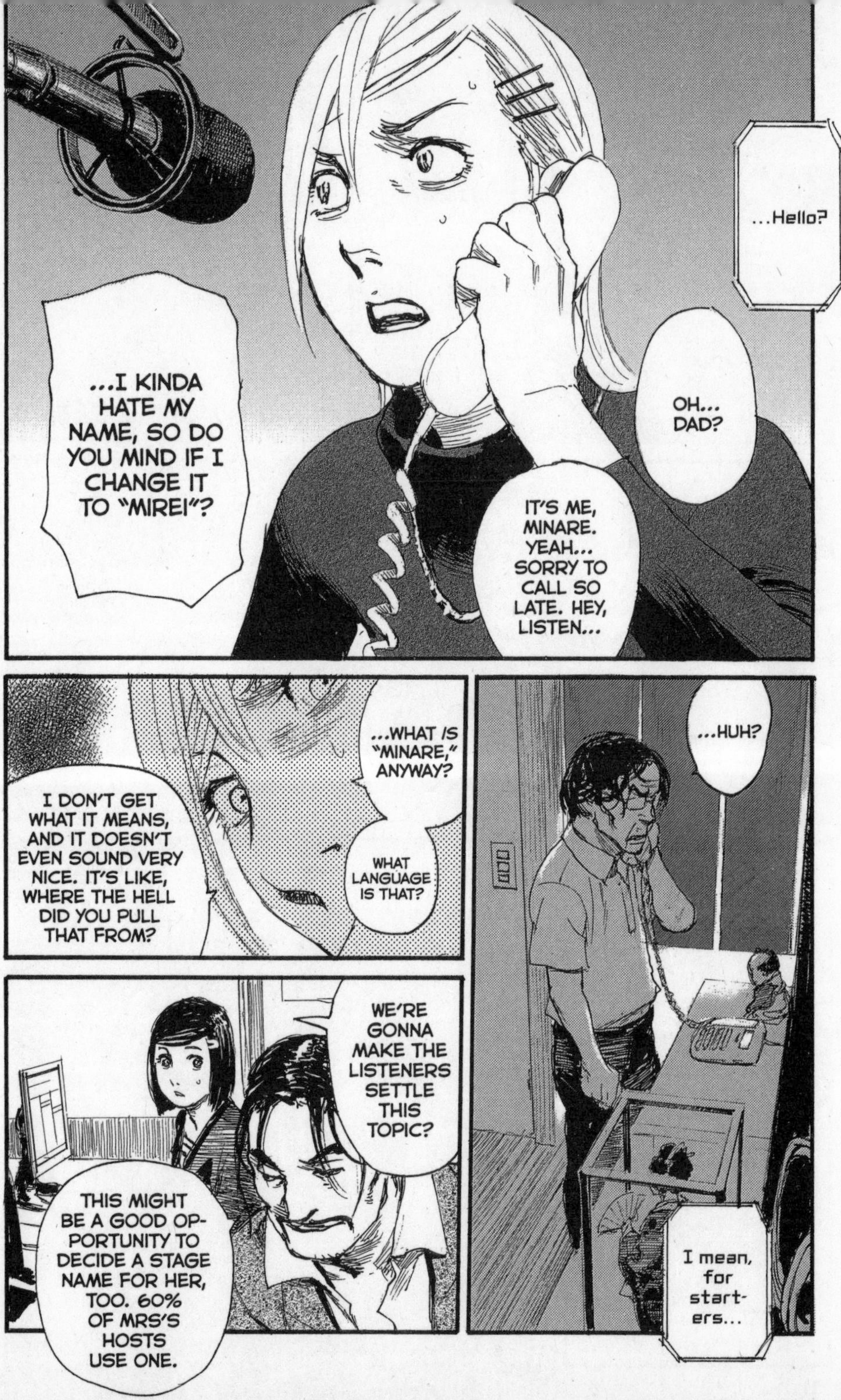
...Hello?
OH... DAD?
IT'S ME, MINARE. YEAH... SORRY TO CALL SO LATE. HEY, LISTEN...
...I KINDA HATE MY NAME, SO DO YOU MIND IF I CHANGE IT TO "MIREI"?
...HUH?
I mean, for starters...
...WHAT IS "MINARE," ANYWAY?
WHAT LANGUAGE IS THAT?
I DON'T GET WHAT IT MEANS, AND IT DOESN'T EVEN SOUND VERY NICE. IT'S LIKE, WHERE THE HELL DID YOU PULL THAT FROM?
WE'RE GONNA MAKE THE LISTENERS SETTLE THIS TOPIC?
THIS MIGHT BE A GOOD OP-PORTUNITY TO DECIDE A STAGE NAME FOR HER, TOO. 60% OF MRS'S HOSTS USE ONE.

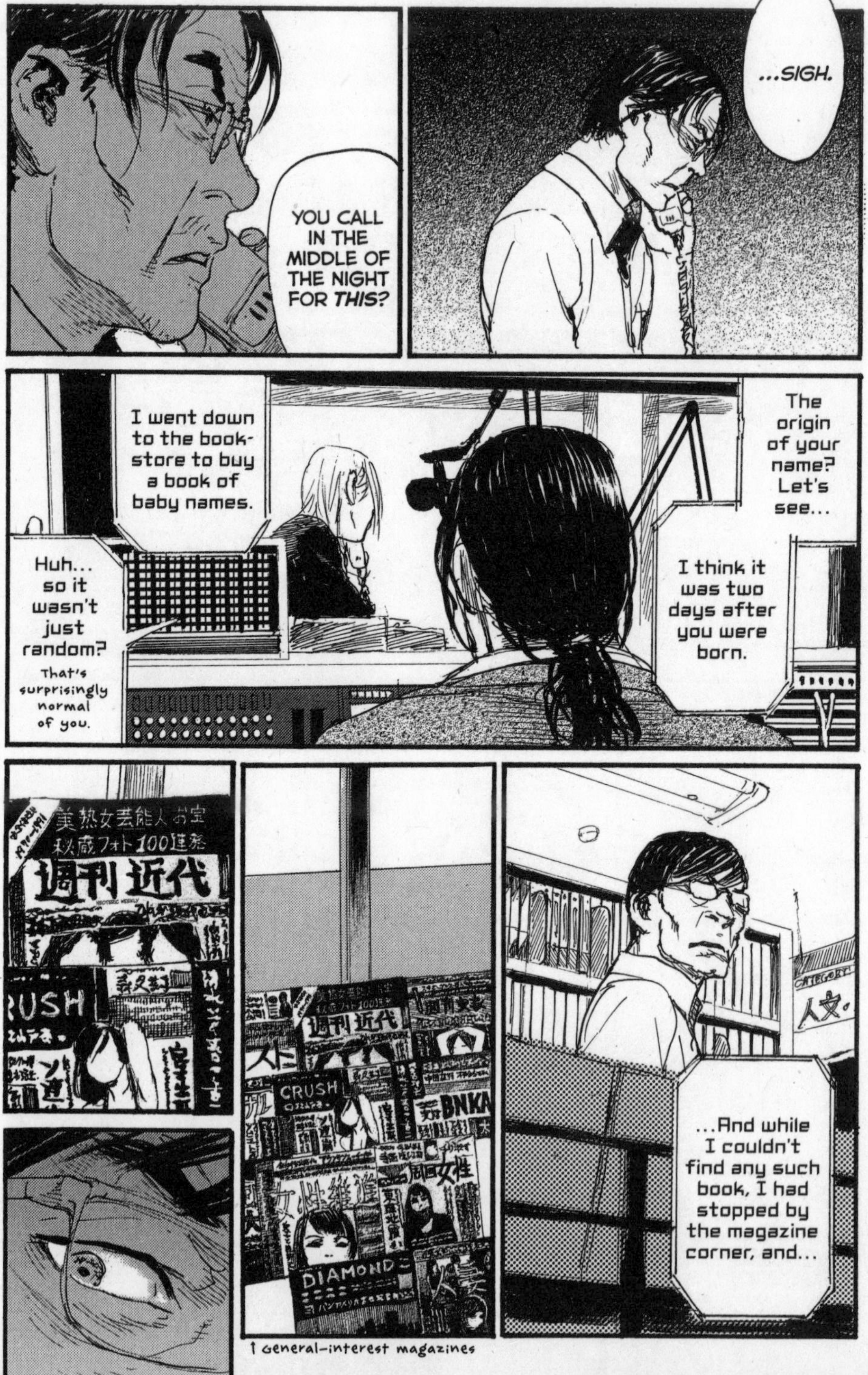
...SIGH.
YOU CALL IN THE MIDDLE OF THE NIGHT FOR *THIS*?
The origin of your name? Let's see...
I think it was two days after you were born.
I went down to the bookstore to buy a book of baby names.
Huh... so it wasn't just random?
That's surprisingly normal of you.
...And while I couldn't find any such book, I had stopped by the magazine corner, and...
週刊近代
CRUSH
DIAMOND
CRUSH
週刊近代
人文
↑General-interest magazines

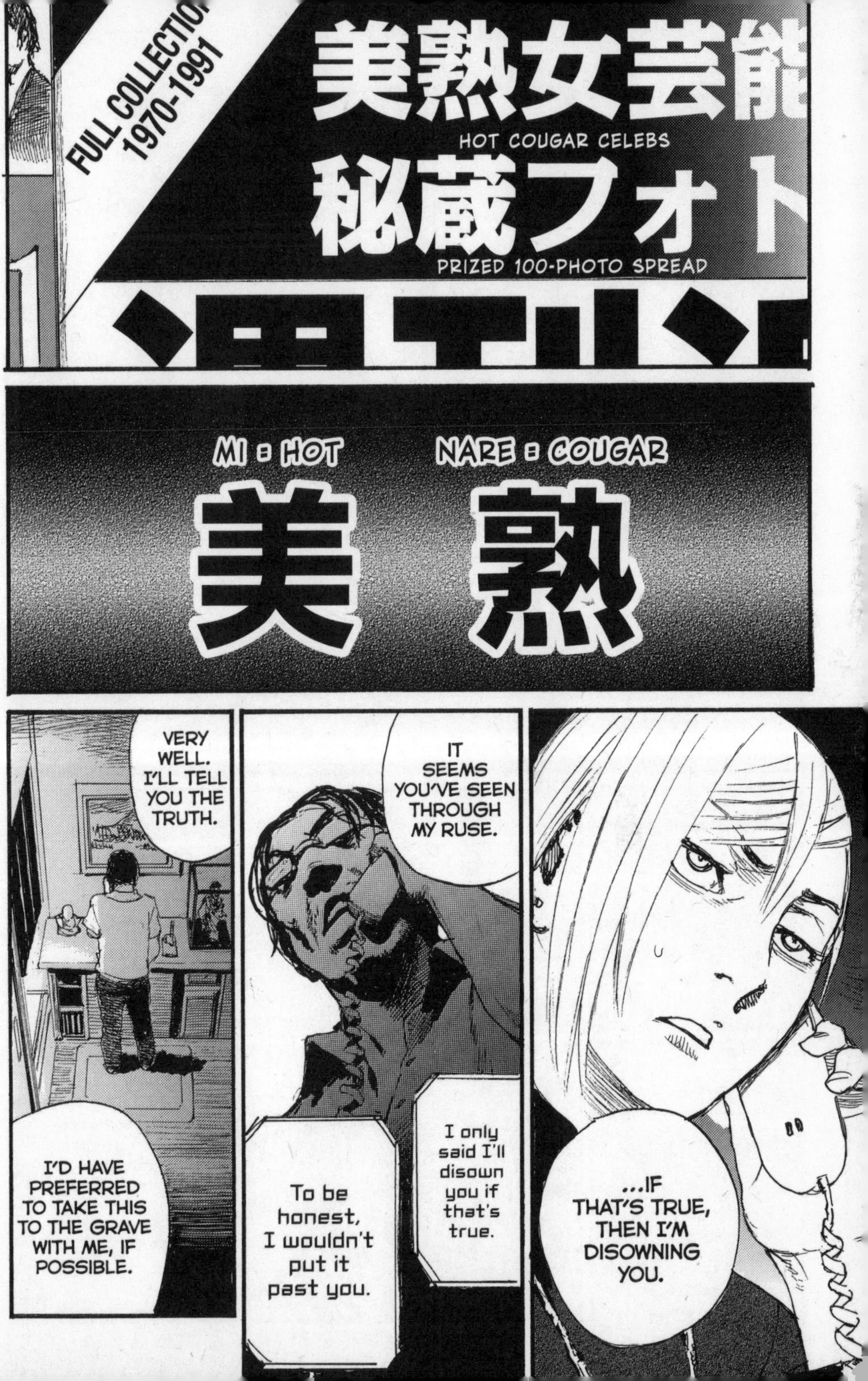
FULL COLLECTIO
1970-1991
美熟女芸能
HOT COUGAR CELEBS
秘蔵フォト
PRIZED 100-PHOTO SPREAD
MI : HOT
NARE : COUGAR
美熟
...IF THAT'S TRUE, THEN I'M DISOWNING YOU.
IT SEEMS YOU'VE SEEN THROUGH MY RUSE.
I only said I'll disown you if that's true.
To be honest, I wouldn't put it past you.
VERY WELL. I'LL TELL YOU THE TRUTH.
I'D HAVE PREFERRED TO TAKE THIS TO THE GRAVE WITH ME, IF POSSIBLE.

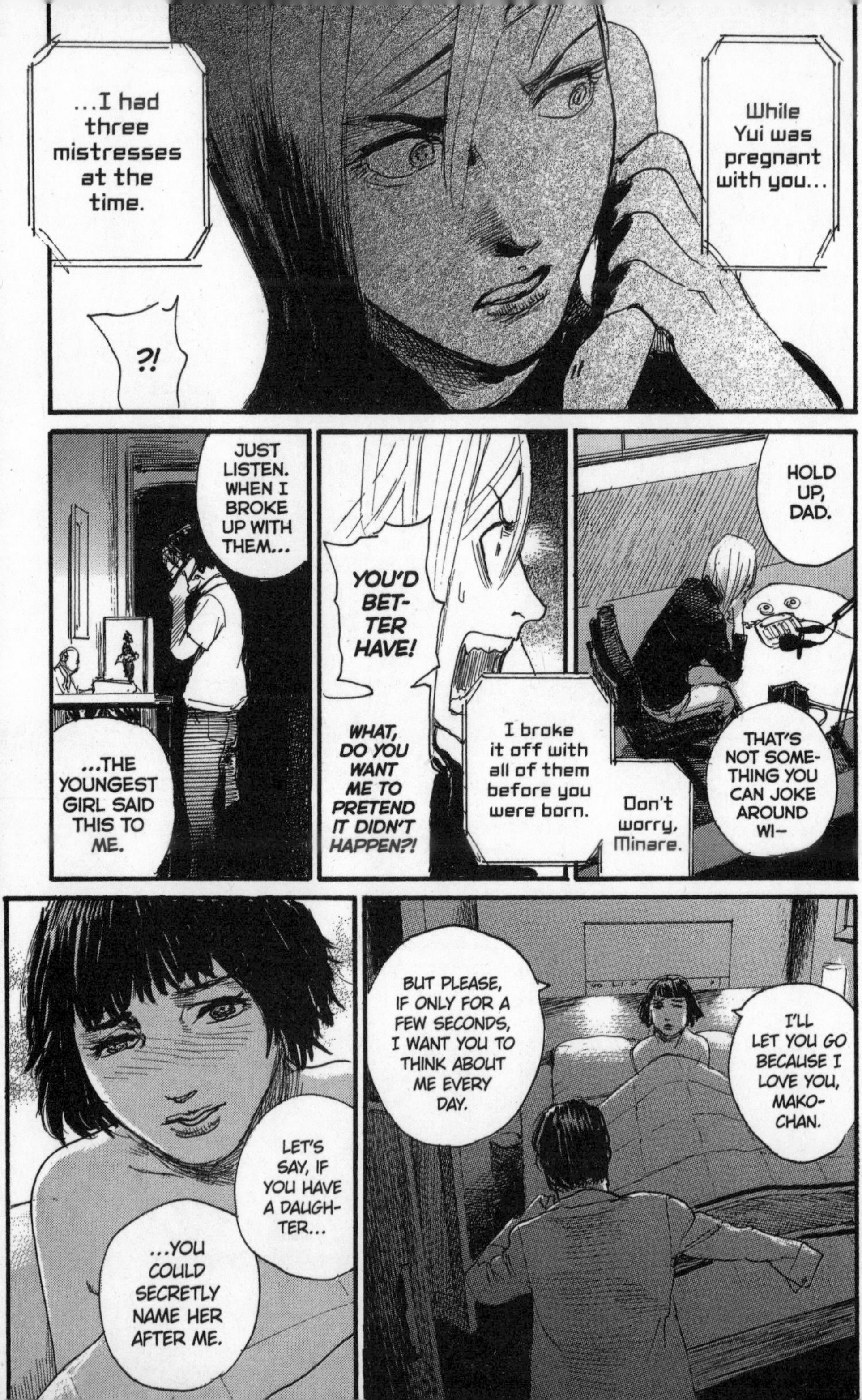
While Yui was pregnant with you...
...I had three mistresses at the time.
?!
HOLD UP, DAD.
THAT'S NOT SOMETHING YOU CAN JOKE AROUND WI–
Don't worry, Minare.
I broke it off with all of them before you were born.
YOU'D BETTER HAVE!
WHAT, DO YOU WANT ME TO PRETEND IT DIDN'T HAPPEN?!
JUST LISTEN. WHEN I BROKE UP WITH THEM...
...THE YOUNGEST GIRL SAID THIS TO ME.
I'LL LET YOU GO BECAUSE I LOVE YOU, MAKO-CHAN.
BUT PLEASE, IF ONLY FOR A FEW SECONDS, I WANT YOU TO THINK ABOUT ME EVERY DAY.
LET'S SAY, IF YOU HAVE A DAUGHTER...
...YOU COULD SECRETLY NAME HER AFTER ME.

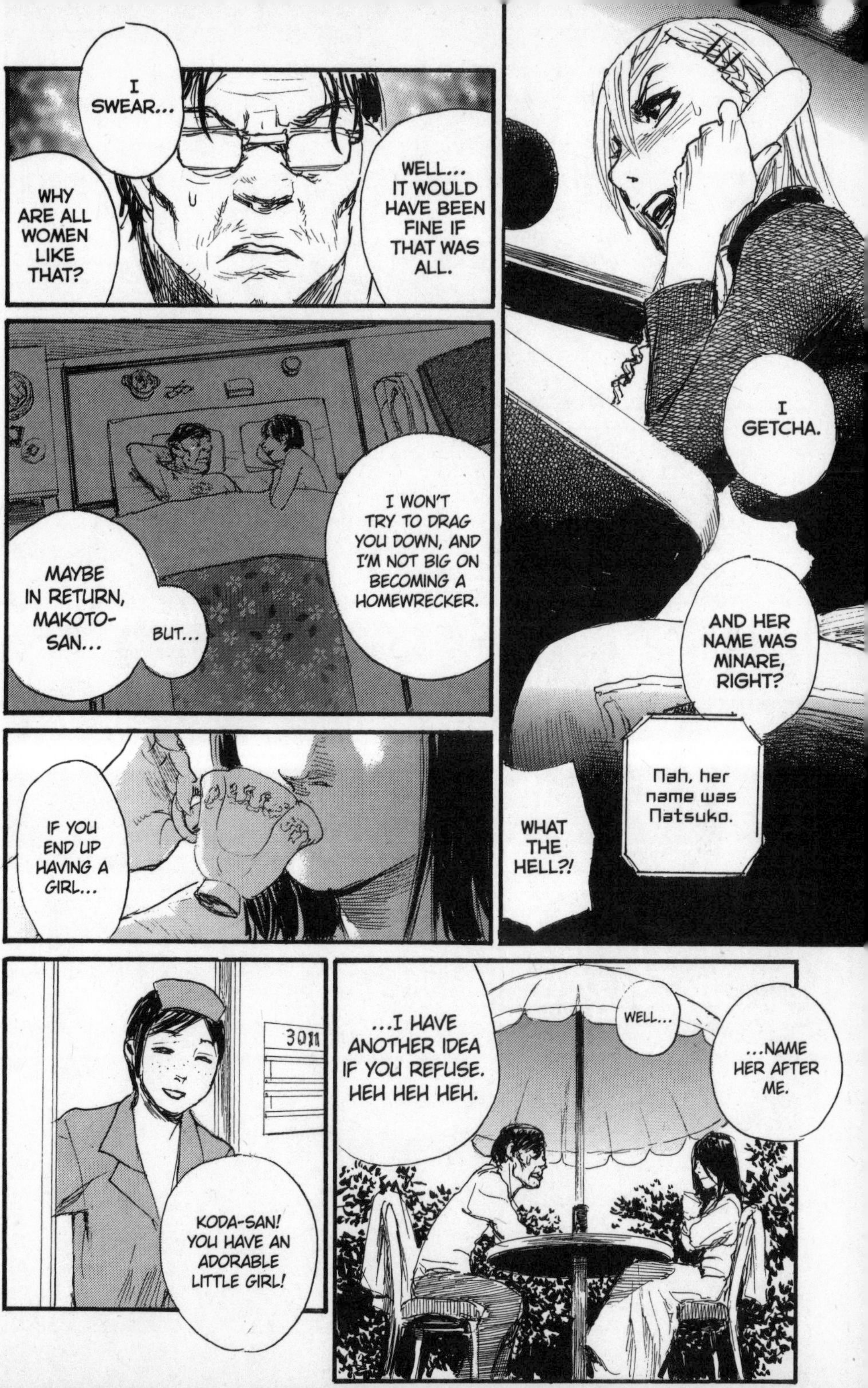

I GETCHA.
AND HER NAME WAS MINARE, RIGHT?
Nah, her name was Natsuko.
WHAT THE HELL?!
I SWEAR...
WHY ARE ALL WOMEN LIKE THAT?
WELL... IT WOULD HAVE BEEN FINE IF THAT WAS ALL.
I WON'T TRY TO DRAG YOU DOWN, AND I'M NOT BIG ON BECOMING A HOMEWRECKER.
BUT...
MAYBE IN RETURN, MAKOTO-SAN...
IF YOU END UP HAVING A GIRL...
WELL...
...NAME HER AFTER ME.
...I HAVE ANOTHER IDEA IF YOU REFUSE. HEH HEH HEH.
3011
KODA-SAN! YOU HAVE AN ADORABLE LITTLE GIRL!

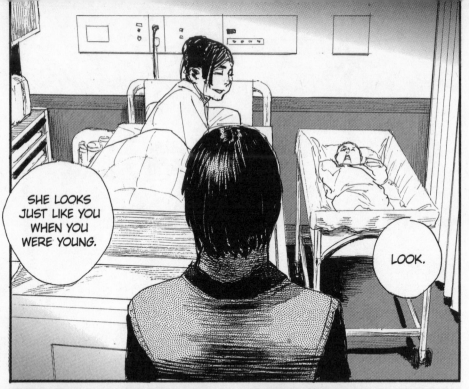

SHE LOOKS JUST LIKE YOU WHEN YOU WERE YOUNG.

LOOK.

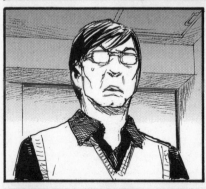

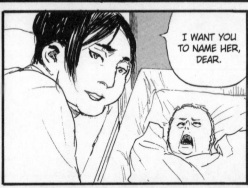

I WANT YOU TO NAME HER, DEAR.

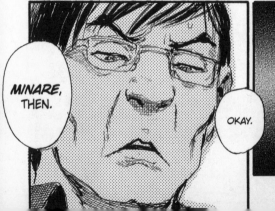

MINARE, THEN.

OKAY.

Michiru Natsuko Reiko

UHH...

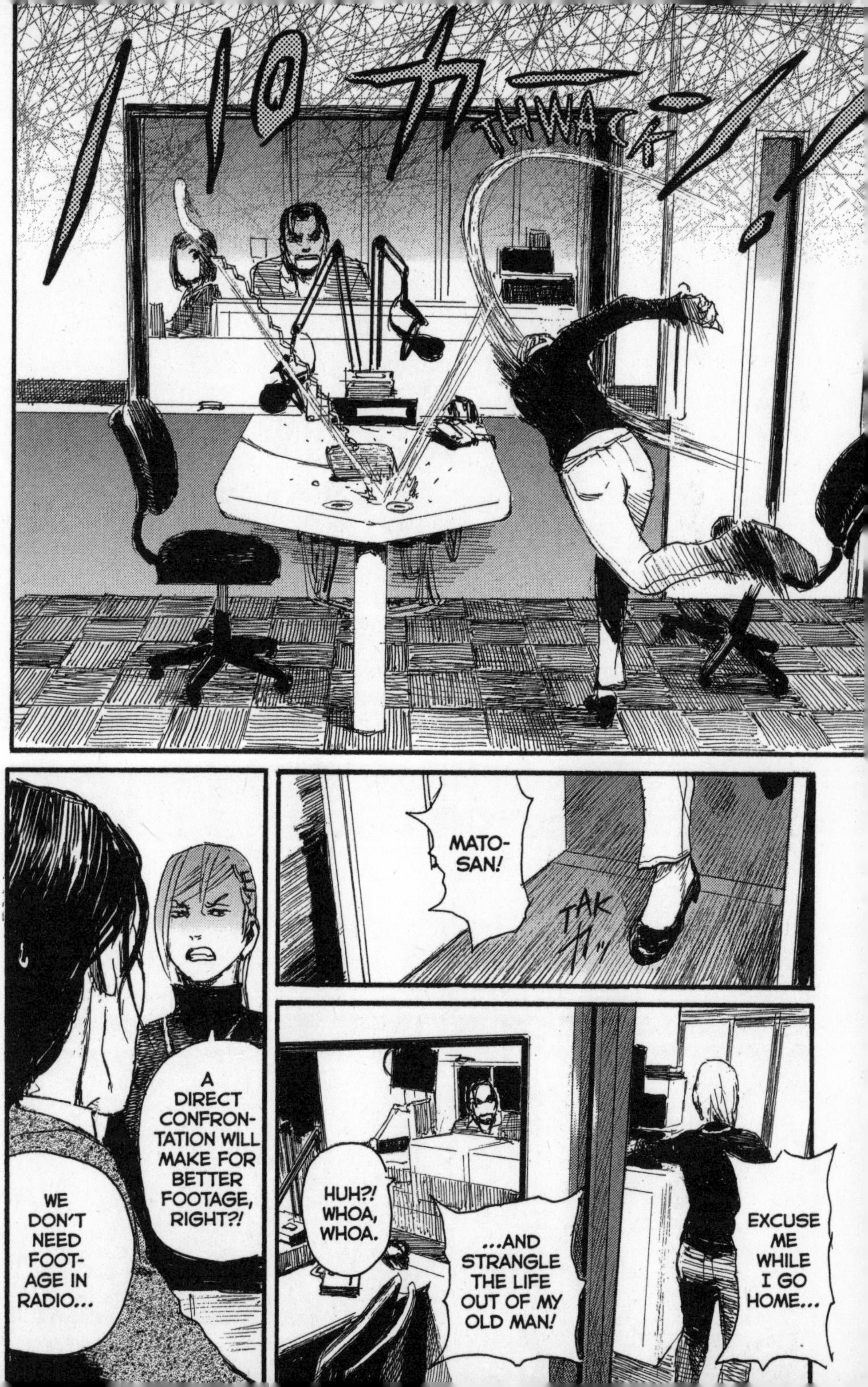
THWACK
MATO-SAN!
TAK
EXCUSE ME WHILE I GO HOME...
...AND STRANGLE THE LIFE OUT OF MY OLD MAN!
HUH?! WHOA, WHOA.
A DIRECT CONFRONTATION WILL MAKE FOR BETTER FOOTAGE, RIGHT?!
WE DON'T NEED FOOTAGE IN RADIO...

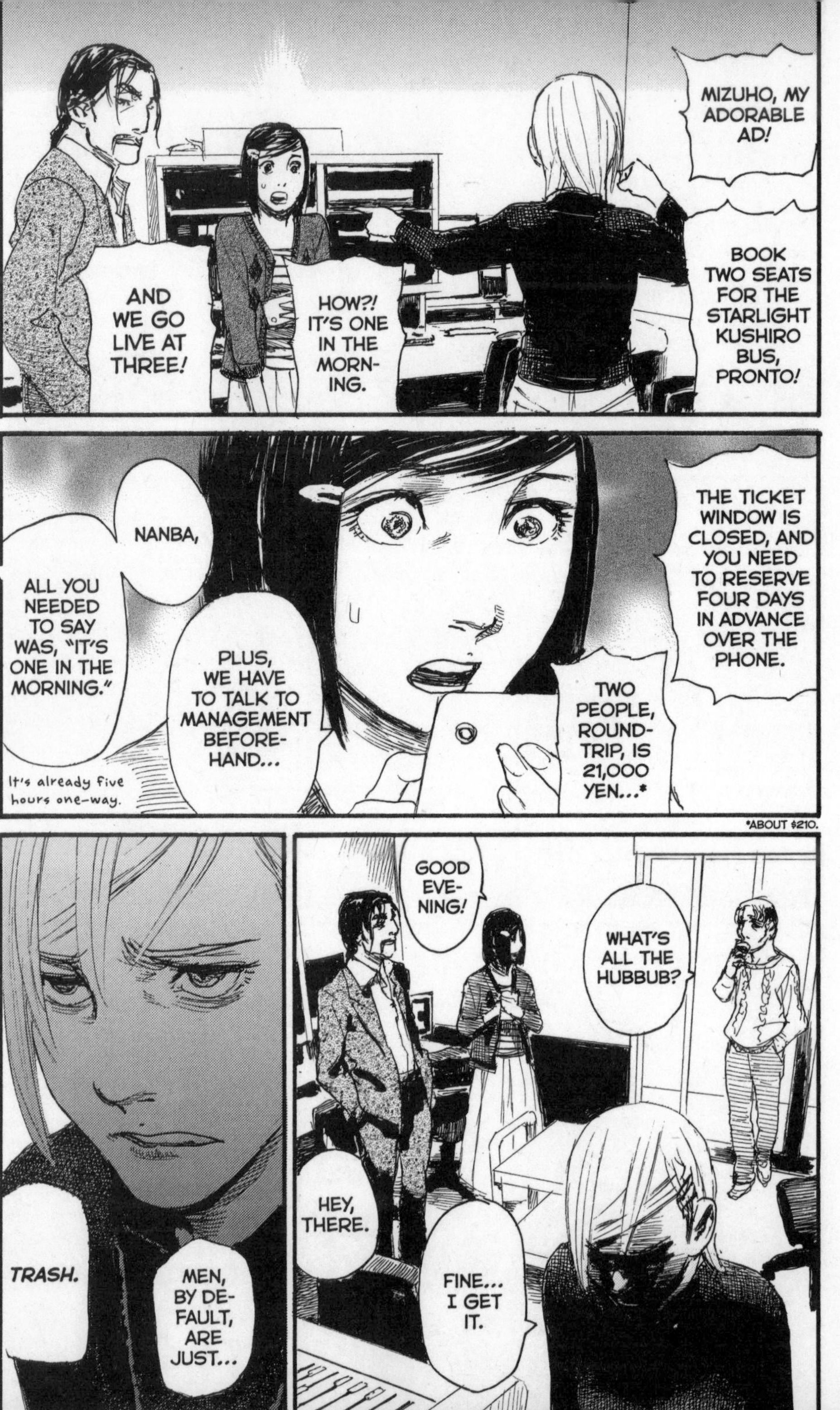
MIZUHO, MY ADORABLE AD!
BOOK TWO SEATS FOR THE STARLIGHT KUSHIRO BUS, PRONTO!
HOW?! IT'S ONE IN THE MORNING.
AND WE GO LIVE AT THREE!
THE TICKET WINDOW IS CLOSED, AND YOU NEED TO RESERVE FOUR DAYS IN ADVANCE OVER THE PHONE.
TWO PEOPLE, ROUND-TRIP, IS 21,000 YEN...*
PLUS, WE HAVE TO TALK TO MANAGEMENT BEFOREHAND...
NANBA,
ALL YOU NEEDED TO SAY WAS, "IT'S ONE IN THE MORNING."
It's already five hours one-way.
GOOD EVENING!
WHAT'S ALL THE HUBBUB?
HEY, THERE.
FINE... I GET IT.
MEN, BY DEFAULT, ARE JUST...
TRASH.

*ABOUT $210.

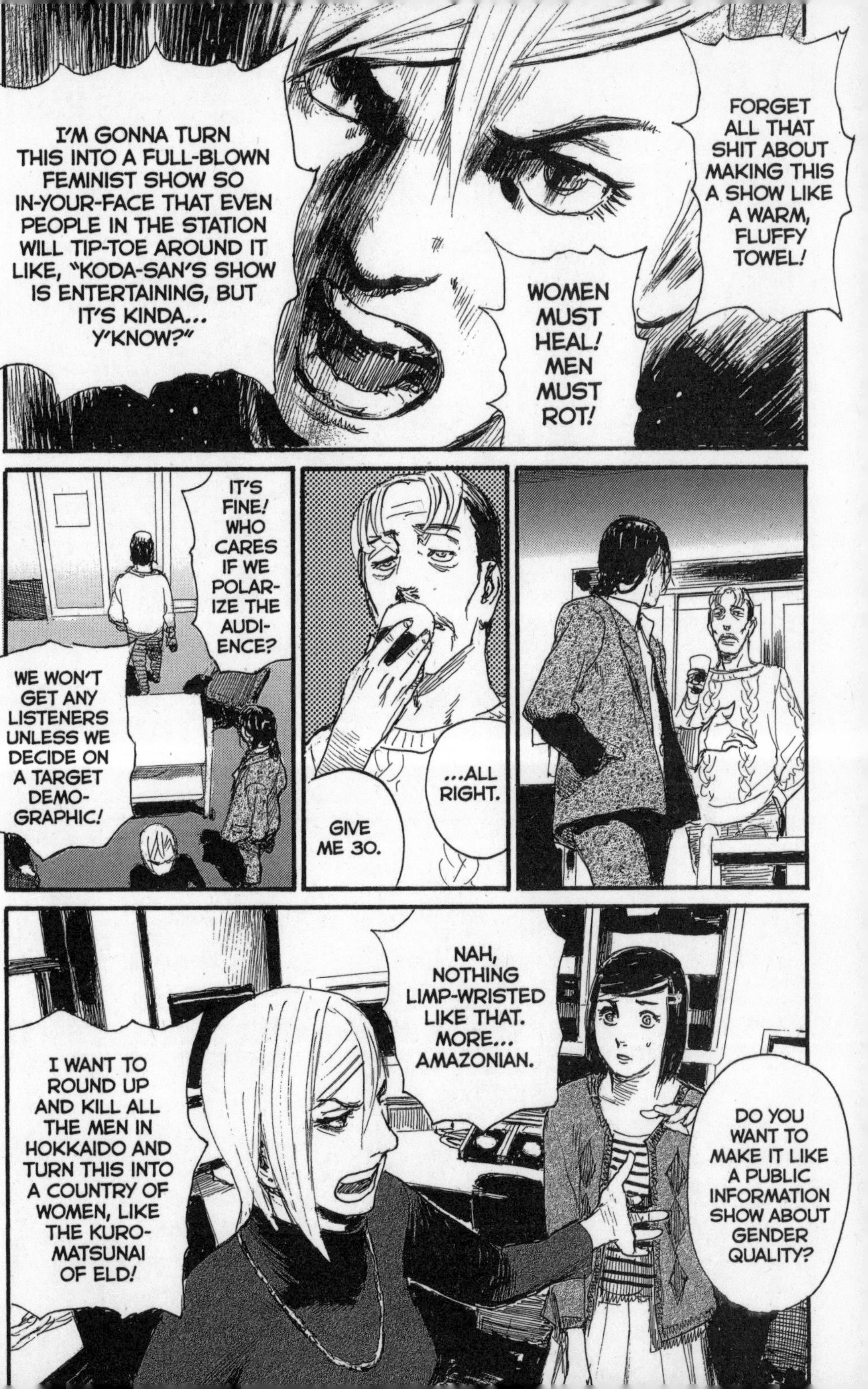

FORGET ALL THAT SHIT ABOUT MAKING THIS A SHOW LIKE A WARM, FLUFFY TOWEL!
WOMEN MUST HEAL! MEN MUST ROT!
I'M GONNA TURN THIS INTO A FULL-BLOWN FEMINIST SHOW SO IN-YOUR-FACE THAT EVEN PEOPLE IN THE STATION WILL TIP-TOE AROUND IT LIKE, "KODA-SAN'S SHOW IS ENTERTAINING, BUT IT'S KINDA... Y'KNOW?"
...ALL RIGHT.
GIVE ME 30.
IT'S FINE! WHO CARES IF WE POLARIZE THE AUDIENCE?
WE WON'T GET ANY LISTENERS UNLESS WE DECIDE ON A TARGET DEMOGRAPHIC!
DO YOU WANT TO MAKE IT LIKE A PUBLIC INFORMATION SHOW ABOUT GENDER QUALITY?
NAH, NOTHING LIMP-WRISTED LIKE THAT. MORE... AMAZONIAN.
I WANT TO ROUND UP AND KILL ALL THE MEN IN HOKKAIDO AND TURN THIS INTO A COUNTRY OF WOMEN, LIKE THE KURO-MATSUNAI OF ELD!

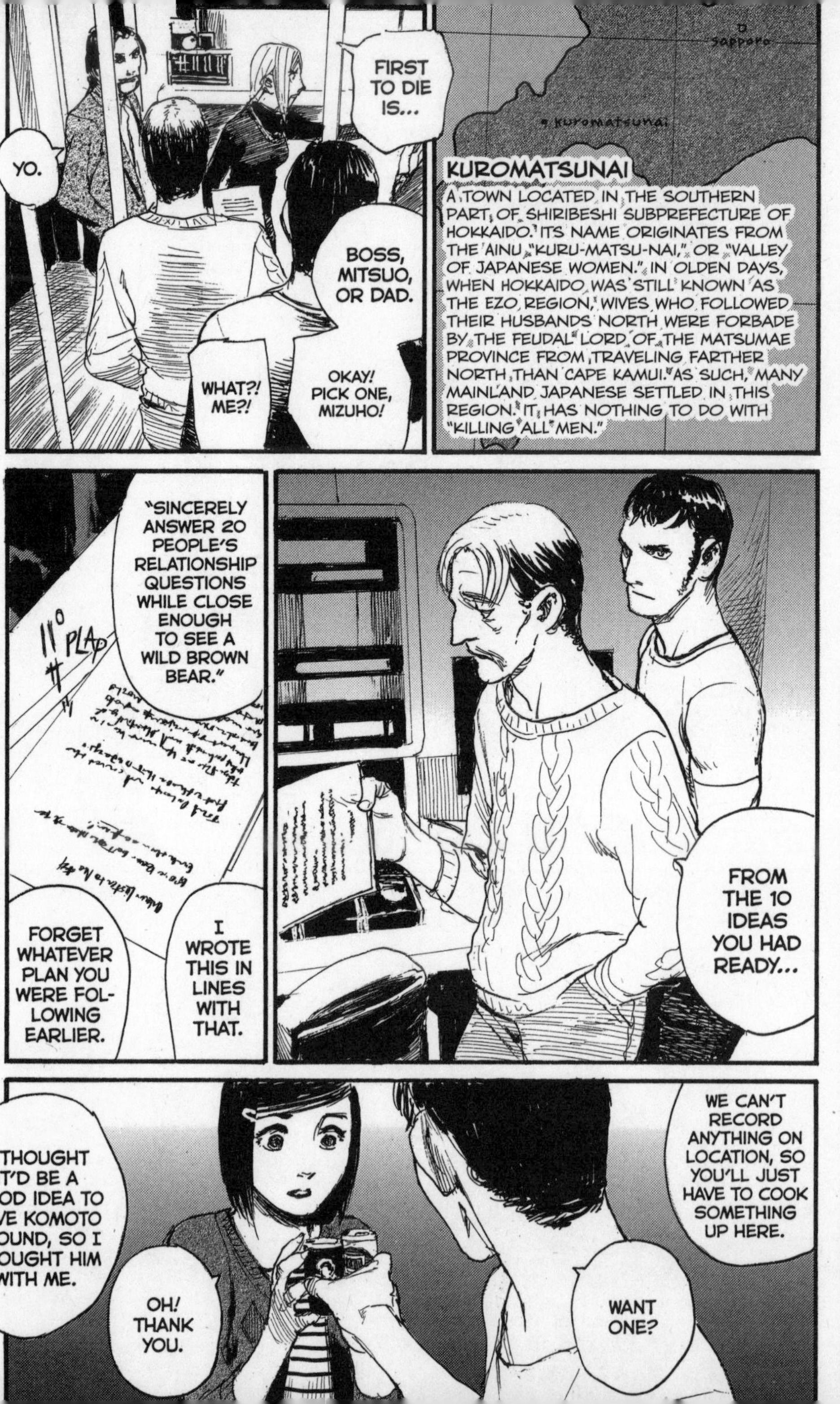
Sapporo
Kuromatsunai
KUROMATSUNAI
A TOWN LOCATED IN THE SOUTHERN PART OF SHIRIBESHI SUBPREFECTURE OF HOKKAIDO. ITS NAME ORIGINATES FROM THE AINU "KURU-MATSU-NAI," OR "VALLEY OF JAPANESE WOMEN." IN OLDEN DAYS, WHEN HOKKAIDO WAS STILL KNOWN AS THE EZO REGION, WIVES WHO FOLLOWED THEIR HUSBANDS NORTH WERE FORBADE BY THE FEUDAL LORD OF THE MATSUMAE PROVINCE FROM TRAVELING FARTHER NORTH THAN CAPE KAMUI. AS SUCH, MANY MAINLAND JAPANESE SETTLED IN THIS REGION. IT HAS NOTHING TO DO WITH "KILLING ALL MEN."
FIRST TO DIE IS...
BOSS, MITSUO, OR DAD.
YO.
OKAY! PICK ONE, MIZUHO!
WHAT?! ME?!
FROM THE 10 IDEAS YOU HAD READY...
"SINCERELY ANSWER 20 PEOPLE'S RELATIONSHIP QUESTIONS WHILE CLOSE ENOUGH TO SEE A WILD BROWN BEAR."
PLAP
I WROTE THIS IN LINES WITH THAT.
FORGET WHATEVER PLAN YOU WERE FOL-LOWING EARLIER.
WE CAN'T RECORD ANYTHING ON LOCATION, SO YOU'LL JUST HAVE TO COOK SOMETHING UP HERE.
I THOUGHT IT'D BE A GOOD IDEA TO HAVE KOMOTO AROUND, SO I BROUGHT HIM WITH ME.
WANT ONE?
OH! THANK YOU.

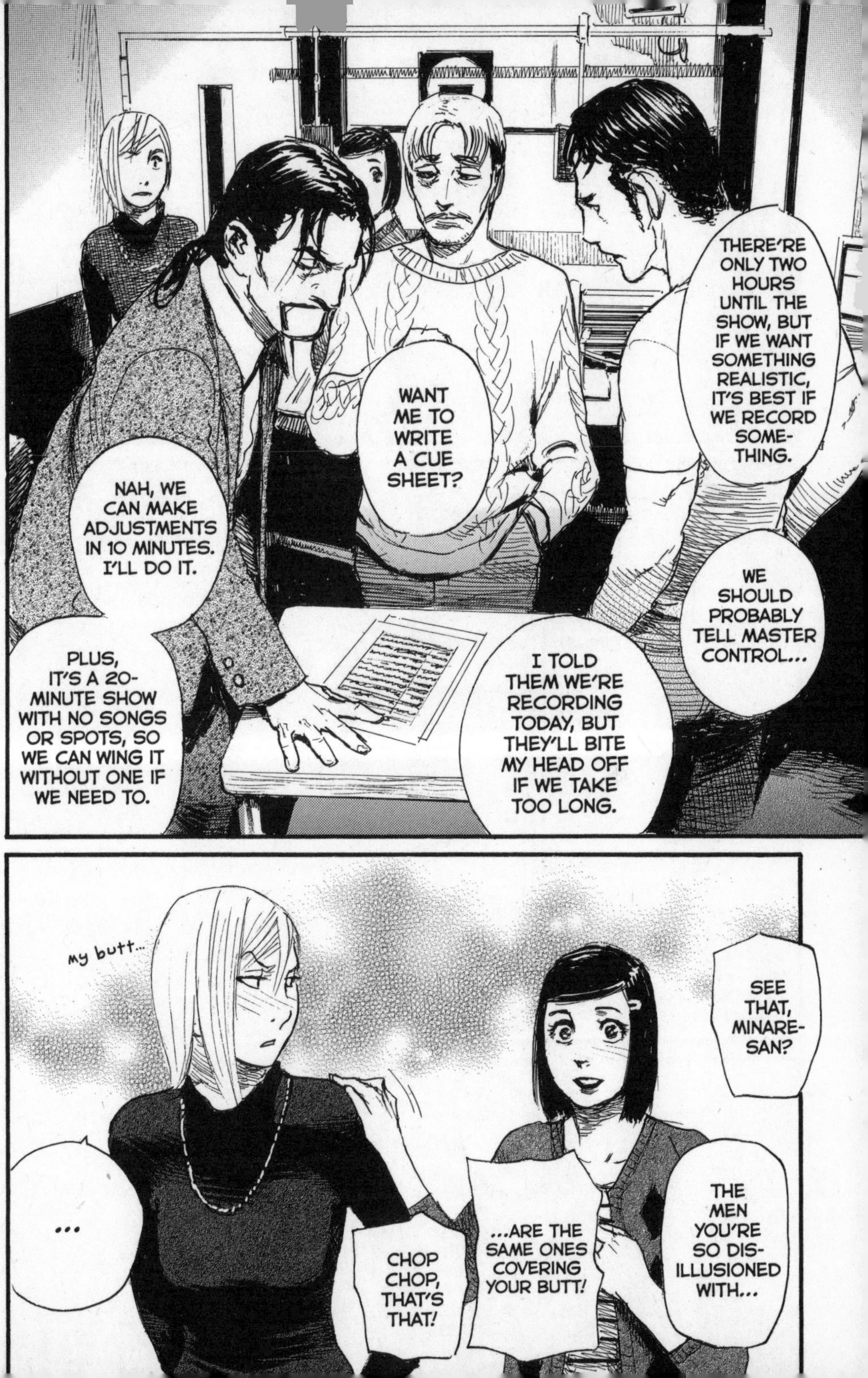
THERE'RE ONLY TWO HOURS UNTIL THE SHOW, BUT IF WE WANT SOMETHING REALISTIC, IT'S BEST IF WE RECORD SOME-THING.
WANT ME TO WRITE A CUE SHEET?
NAH, WE CAN MAKE ADJUSTMENTS IN 10 MINUTES. I'LL DO IT.
WE SHOULD PROBABLY TELL MASTER CONTROL...
I TOLD THEM WE'RE RECORDING TODAY, BUT THEY'LL BITE MY HEAD OFF IF WE TAKE TOO LONG.
PLUS, IT'S A 20-MINUTE SHOW WITH NO SONGS OR SPOTS, SO WE CAN WING IT WITHOUT ONE IF WE NEED TO.
SEE THAT, MINARE-SAN?
my butt...
THE MEN YOU'RE SO DIS-ILLUSIONED WITH...
...ARE THE SAME ONES COVERING YOUR BUTT!
CHOP CHOP, THAT'S THAT!
...

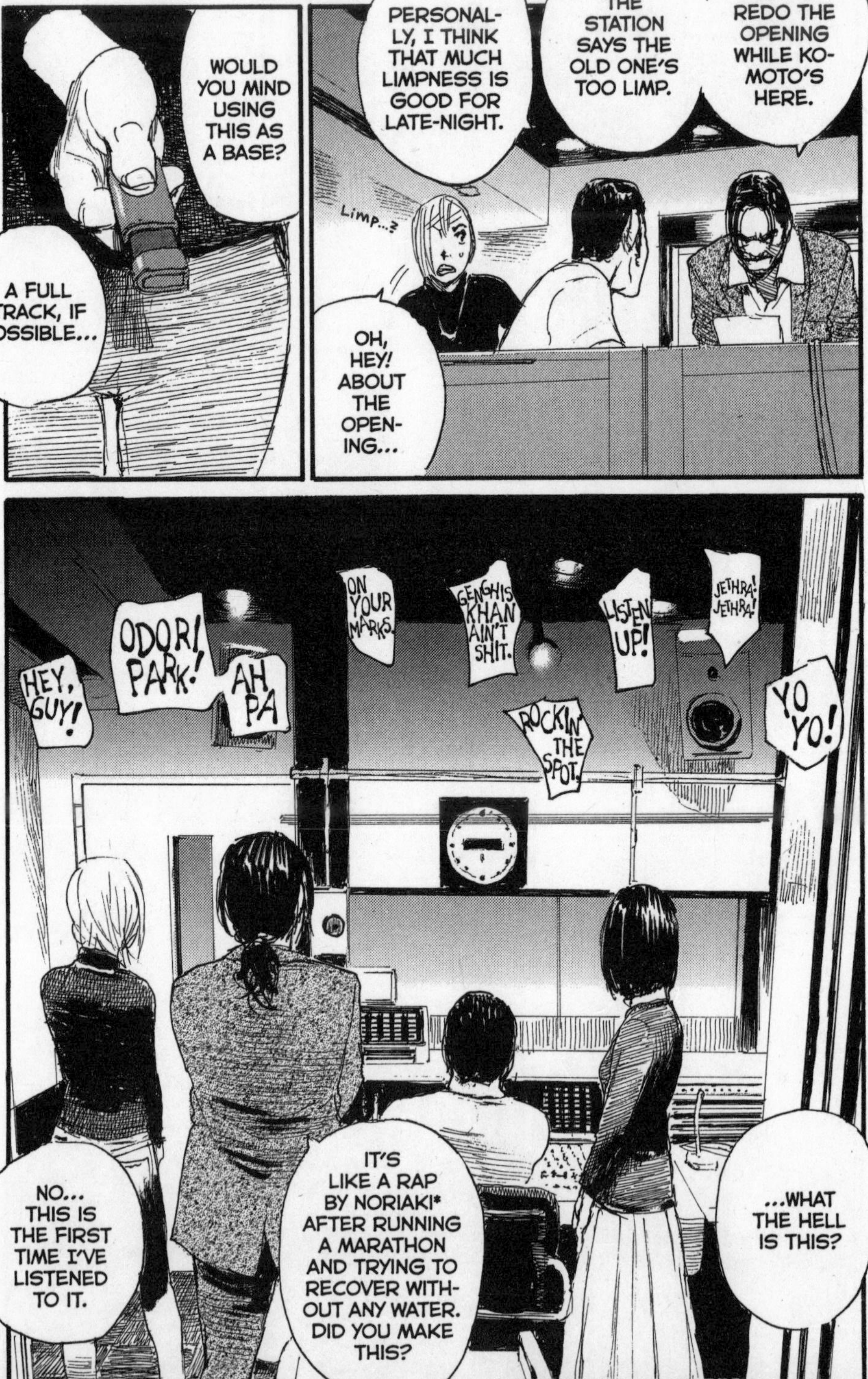
LET'S REDO THE OPENING WHILE KO-MOTO'S HERE.
THE STATION SAYS THE OLD ONE'S TOO LIMP.
PERSONAL-LY, I THINK THAT MUCH LIMPNESS IS GOOD FOR LATE-NIGHT.
Limp...?
OH, HEY! ABOUT THE OPEN-ING...
WOULD YOU MIND USING THIS AS A BASE?
A FULL TRACK, IF POSSIBLE...
YO YO!
JETHRA! JETHRA!
LISTEN UP!
GENGHIS KHAN AIN'T SHIT.
ROCKIN' THE SPOT.
ON YOUR MARKS.
AH PA
ODORI PARK!
HEY, GUY!
...WHAT THE HELL IS THIS?
IT'S LIKE A RAP BY NORIAKI* AFTER RUNNING A MARATHON AND TRYING TO RECOVER WITH-OUT ANY WATER. DID YOU MAKE THIS?
NO... THIS IS THE FIRST TIME I'VE LISTENED TO IT.

*A JAPANESE RAPPER/VOCALIST ACTIVE FROM 2004-2009.

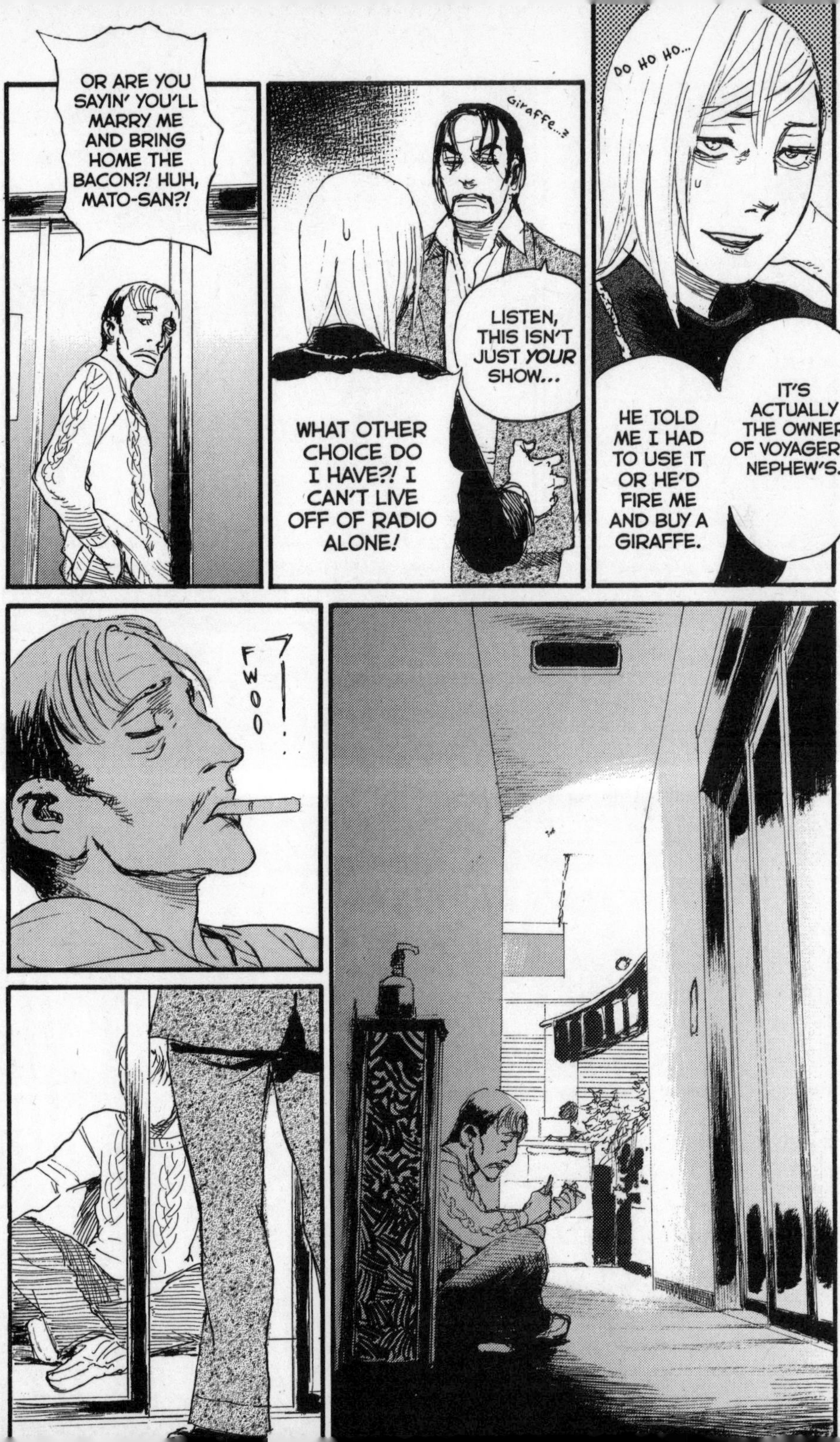
DO HO HO...
IT'S ACTUALLY THE OWNER OF VOYAGER'S NEPHEW'S.
HE TOLD ME I HAD TO USE IT OR HE'D FIRE ME AND BUY A GIRAFFE.
Giraffe...?
LISTEN, THIS ISN'T JUST *YOUR* SHOW...
WHAT OTHER CHOICE DO I HAVE?! I CAN'T LIVE OFF OF RADIO ALONE!
OR ARE YOU SAYIN' YOU'LL MARRY ME AND BRING HOME THE BACON?! HUH, MATO-SAN?!
FWOO

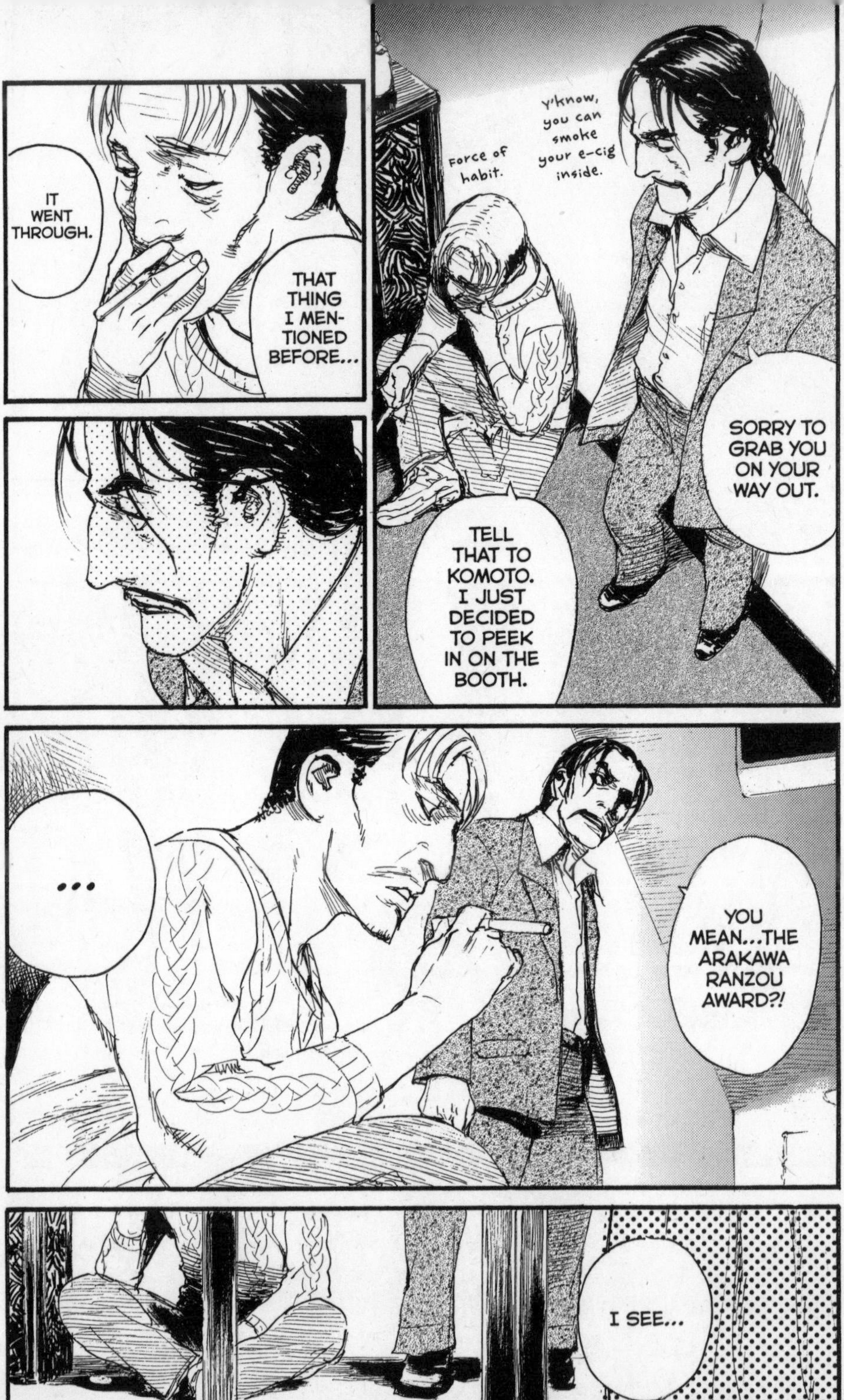
Y'know, you can smoke your e-cig inside.
Force of habit.
SORRY TO GRAB YOU ON YOUR WAY OUT.
TELL THAT TO KOMOTO. I JUST DECIDED TO PEEK IN ON THE BOOTH.
THAT THING I MENTIONED BEFORE...
IT WENT THROUGH.
YOU MEAN...THE ARAKAWA RANZOU AWARD?!
...
I SEE...

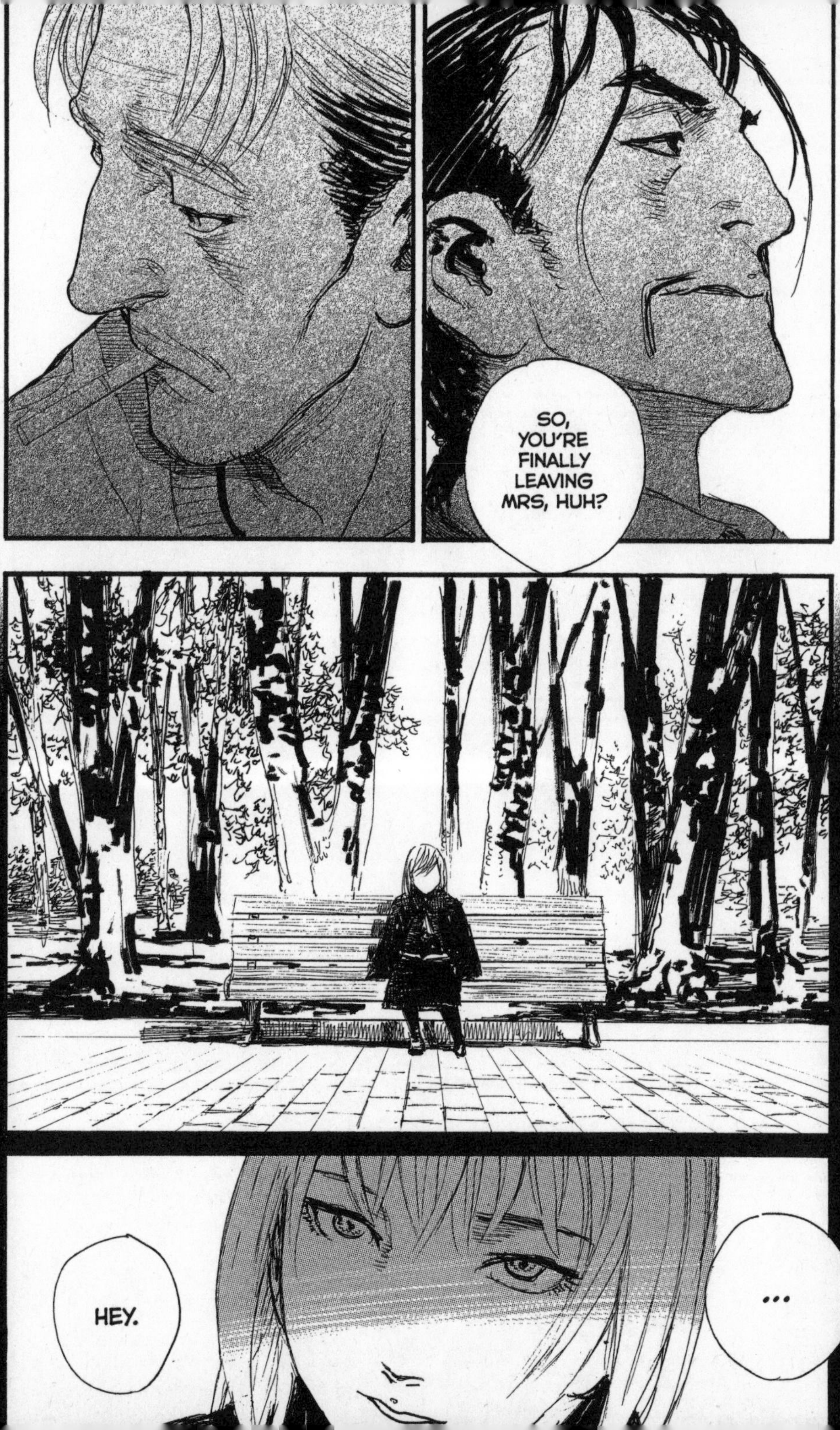
SO, YOU'RE FINALLY LEAVING MRS, HUH?
...
HEY.

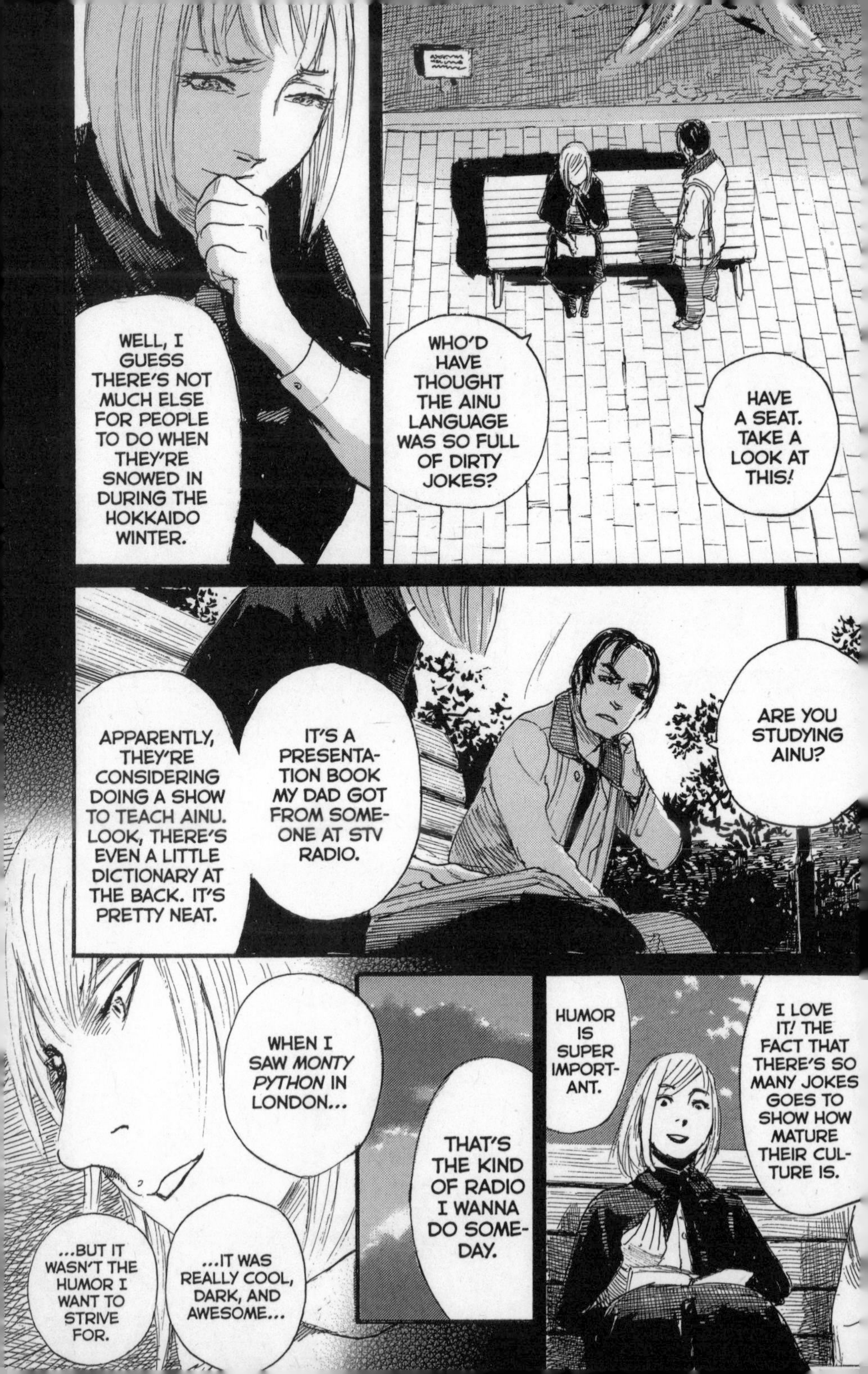

HAVE A SEAT. TAKE A LOOK AT THIS!
WHO'D HAVE THOUGHT THE AINU LANGUAGE WAS SO FULL OF DIRTY JOKES?
WELL, I GUESS THERE'S NOT MUCH ELSE FOR PEOPLE TO DO WHEN THEY'RE SNOWED IN DURING THE HOKKAIDO WINTER.
ARE YOU STUDYING AINU?
IT'S A PRESENTATION BOOK MY DAD GOT FROM SOMEONE AT STV RADIO.
APPARENTLY, THEY'RE CONSIDERING DOING A SHOW TO TEACH AINU. LOOK, THERE'S EVEN A LITTLE DICTIONARY AT THE BACK. IT'S PRETTY NEAT.
I LOVE IT! THE FACT THAT THERE'S SO MANY JOKES GOES TO SHOW HOW MATURE THEIR CULTURE IS.
HUMOR IS SUPER IMPORTANT.
THAT'S THE KIND OF RADIO I WANNA DO SOMEDAY.
WHEN I SAW *MONTY PYTHON* IN LONDON...
...IT WAS REALLY COOL, DARK, AND AWESOME...
...BUT IT WASN'T THE HUMOR I WANT TO STRIVE FOR.

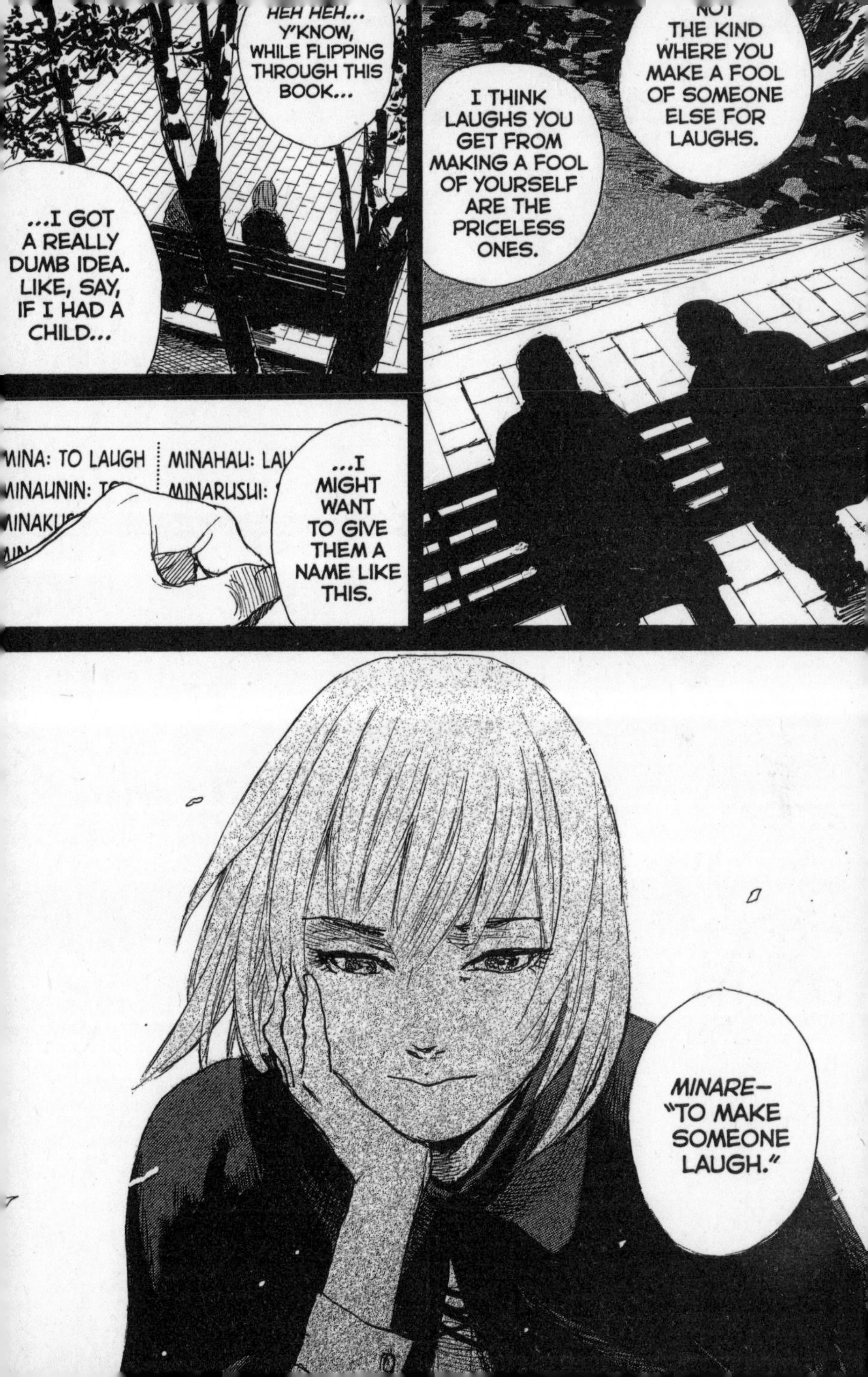
NOT THE KIND WHERE YOU MAKE A FOOL OF SOMEONE ELSE FOR LAUGHS.
I THINK LAUGHS YOU GET FROM MAKING A FOOL OF YOURSELF ARE THE PRICELESS ONES.
HEH HEH... Y'KNOW, WHILE FLIPPING THROUGH THIS BOOK...
...I GOT A REALLY DUMB IDEA. LIKE, SAY, IF I HAD A CHILD...
...I MIGHT WANT TO GIVE THEM A NAME LIKE THIS.
MINA: TO LAUGH
MINARE— "TO MAKE SOMEONE LAUGH."

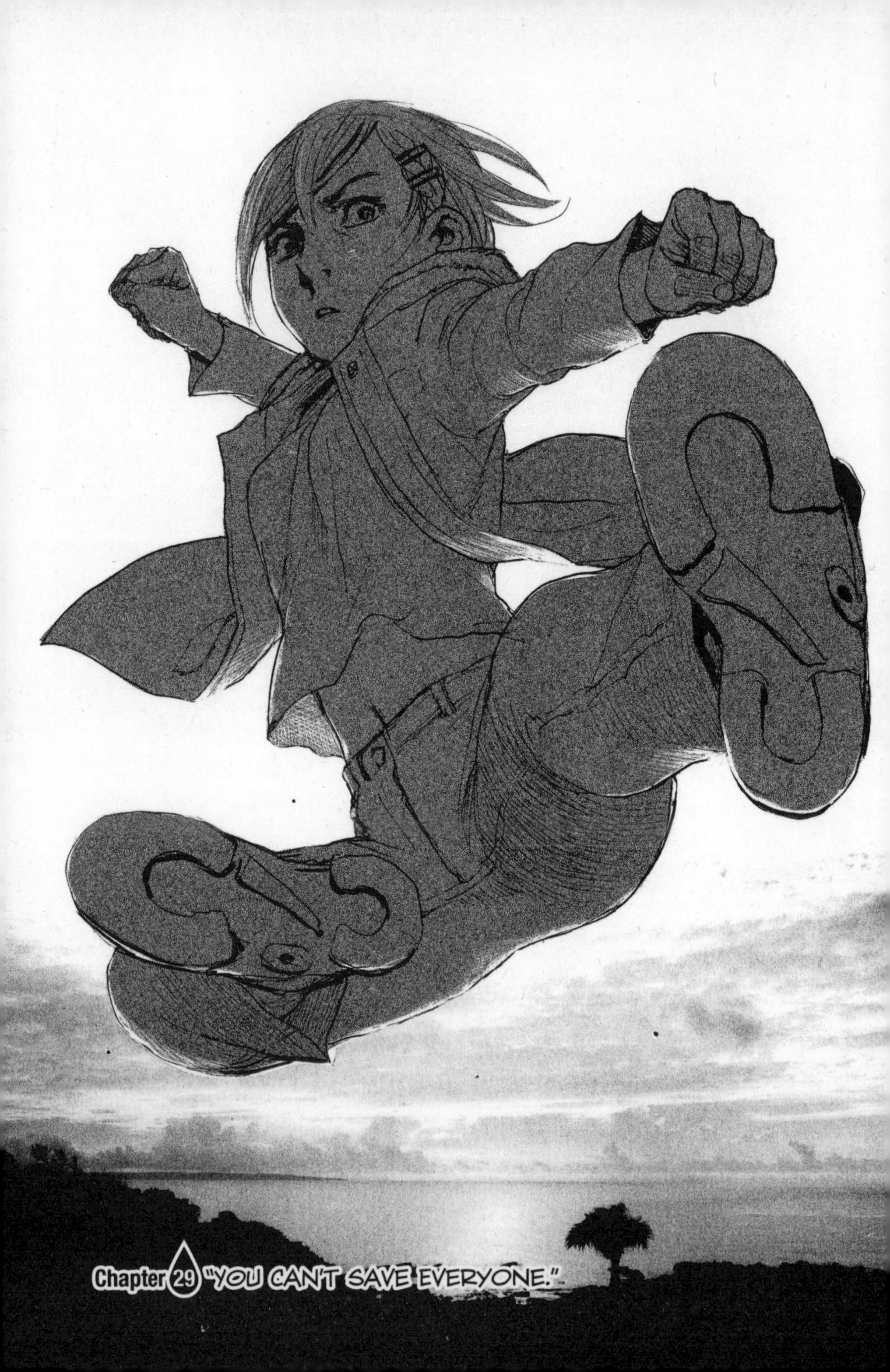

Chapter 29 "YOU CAN'T SAVE EVERYONE."

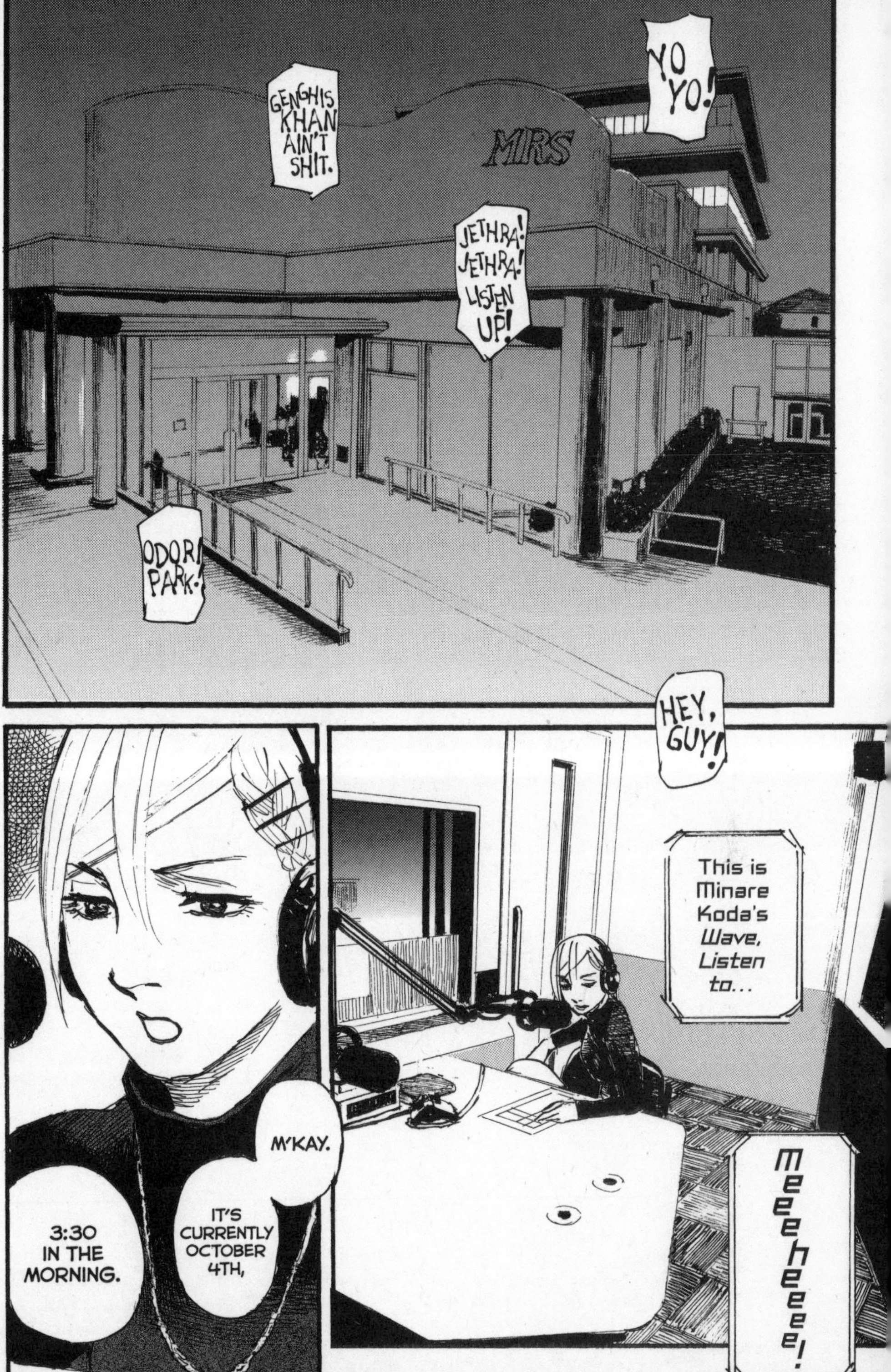
YO YO!
GENGHIS KHAN AIN'T SHIT.
MRS
JETHRA! JETHRA! LISTEN UP!
ODORI PARK!
HEY, GUY!
This is Minare Koda's *Wave*, Listen to…
Meeeheeee!
M'KAY.
IT'S CURRENTLY OCTOBER 4TH,
3:30 IN THE MORNING.

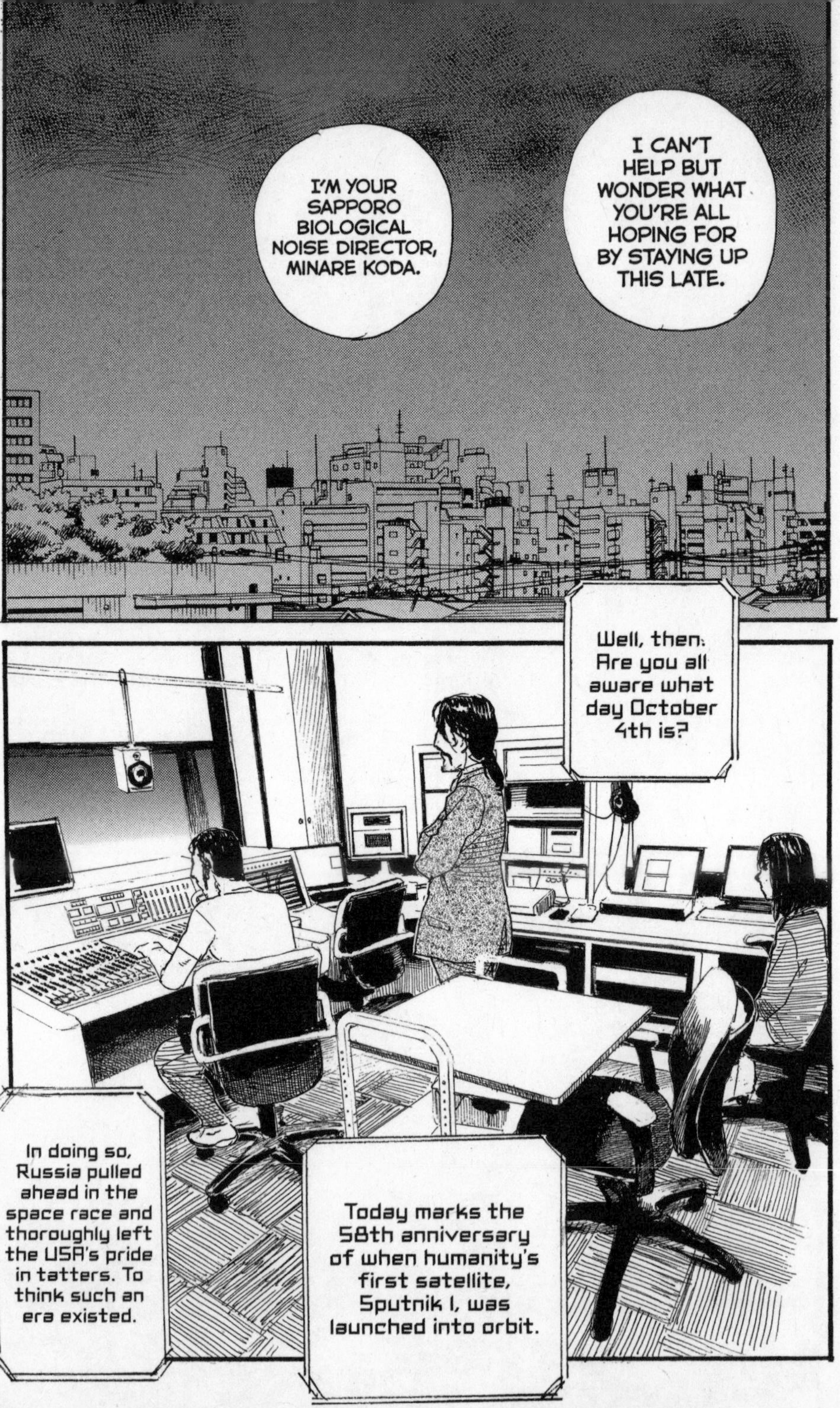

I CAN'T HELP BUT WONDER WHAT YOU'RE ALL HOPING FOR BY STAYING UP THIS LATE.
I'M YOUR SAPPORO BIOLOGICAL NOISE DIRECTOR, MINARE KODA.
Well, then: Are you all aware what day October 4th is?
Today marks the 58th anniversary of when humanity's first satellite, Sputnik I, was launched into orbit.
In doing so, Russia pulled ahead in the space race and thoroughly left the USA's pride in tatters. To think such an era existed.

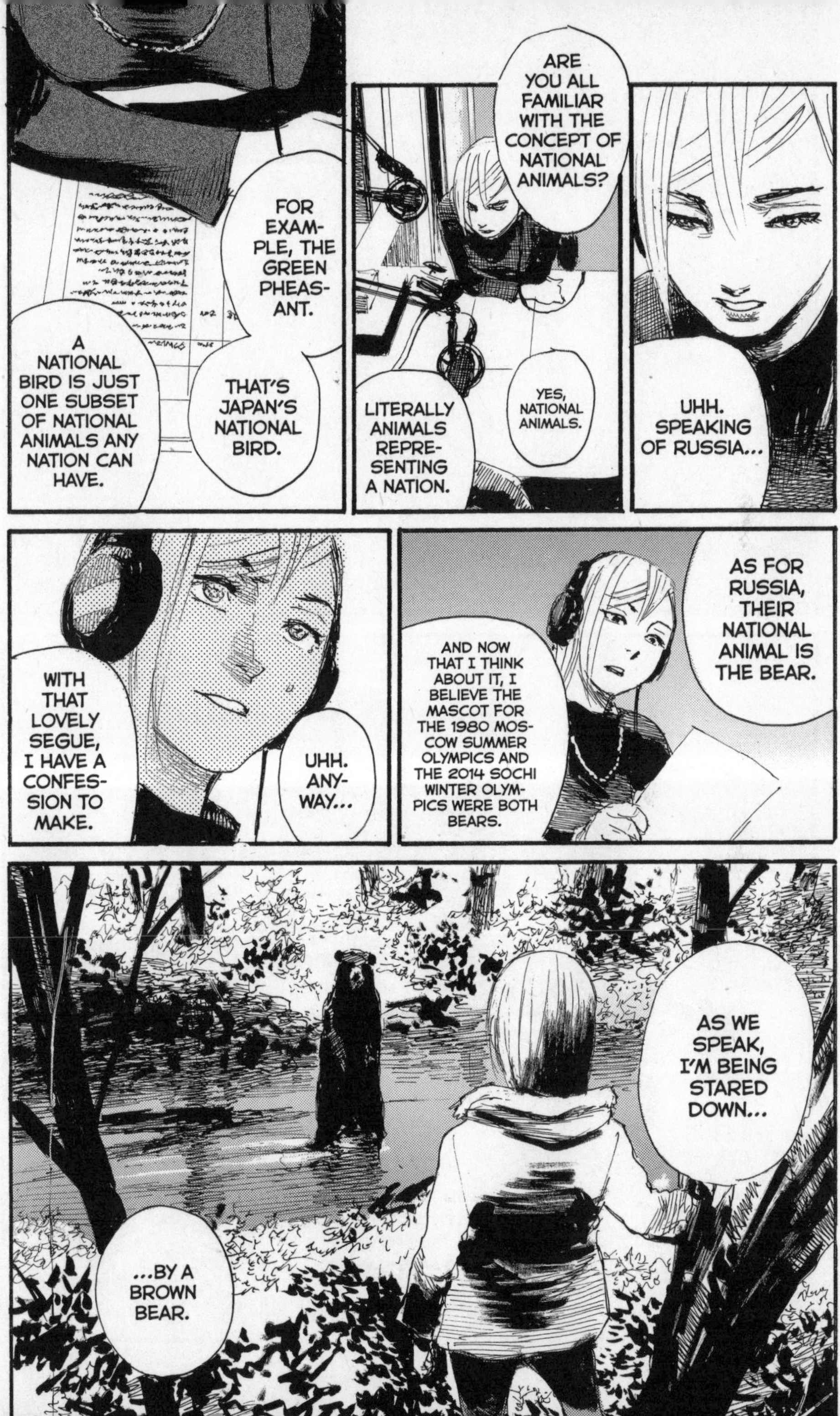
ARE YOU ALL FAMILIAR WITH THE CONCEPT OF NATIONAL ANIMALS?
UHH. SPEAKING OF RUSSIA...
YES, NATIONAL ANIMALS.
LITERALLY ANIMALS REPRE-SENTING A NATION.
FOR EXAM-PLE, THE GREEN PHEAS-ANT.
THAT'S JAPAN'S NATIONAL BIRD.
A NATIONAL BIRD IS JUST ONE SUBSET OF NATIONAL ANIMALS ANY NATION CAN HAVE.
AS FOR RUSSIA, THEIR NATIONAL ANIMAL IS THE BEAR.
AND NOW THAT I THINK ABOUT IT, I BELIEVE THE MASCOT FOR THE 1980 MOS-COW SUMMER OLYMPICS AND THE 2014 SOCHI WINTER OLYM-PICS WERE BOTH BEARS.
UHH. ANY-WAY...
WITH THAT LOVELY SEGUE, I HAVE A CONFES-SION TO MAKE.
AS WE SPEAK, I'M BEING STARED DOWN...
...BY A BROWN BEAR.

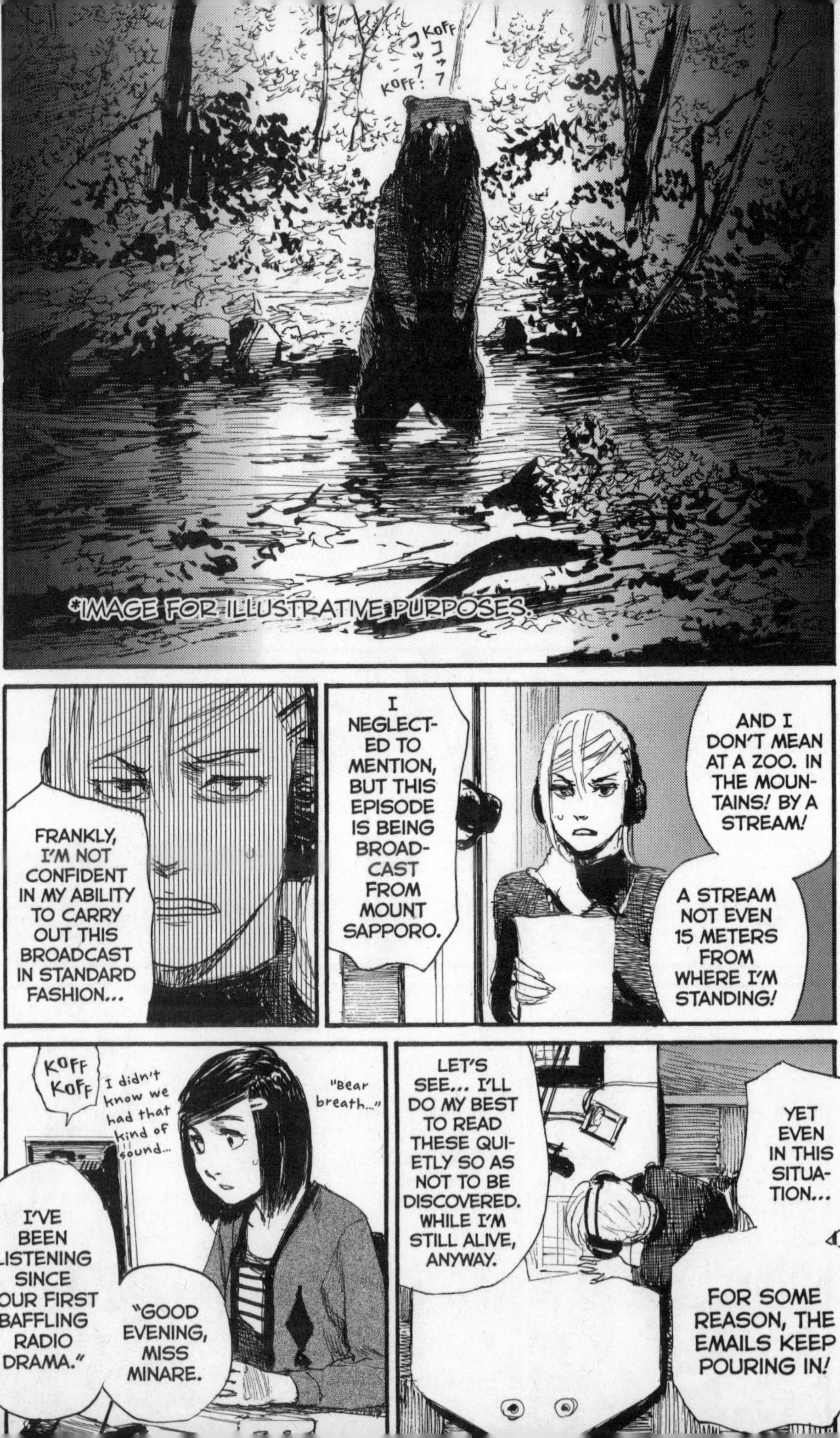
KOFF
KOFF:
*IMAGE FOR ILLUSTRATIVE PURPOSES.
AND I DON'T MEAN AT A ZOO. IN THE MOUNTAINS! BY A STREAM!
A STREAM NOT EVEN 15 METERS FROM WHERE I'M STANDING!
I NEGLECTED TO MENTION, BUT THIS EPISODE IS BEING BROADCAST FROM MOUNT SAPPORO.
FRANKLY, I'M NOT CONFIDENT IN MY ABILITY TO CARRY OUT THIS BROADCAST IN STANDARD FASHION...
YET EVEN IN THIS SITUATION...
FOR SOME REASON, THE EMAILS KEEP POURING IN!
LET'S SEE... I'LL DO MY BEST TO READ THESE QUIETLY SO AS NOT TO BE DISCOVERED. WHILE I'M STILL ALIVE, ANYWAY.
"Bear breath..."
I didn't know we had that kind of sound...
KOFF KOFF
"GOOD EVENING, MISS MINARE.
I'VE BEEN LISTENING SINCE YOUR FIRST BAFFLING RADIO DRAMA."

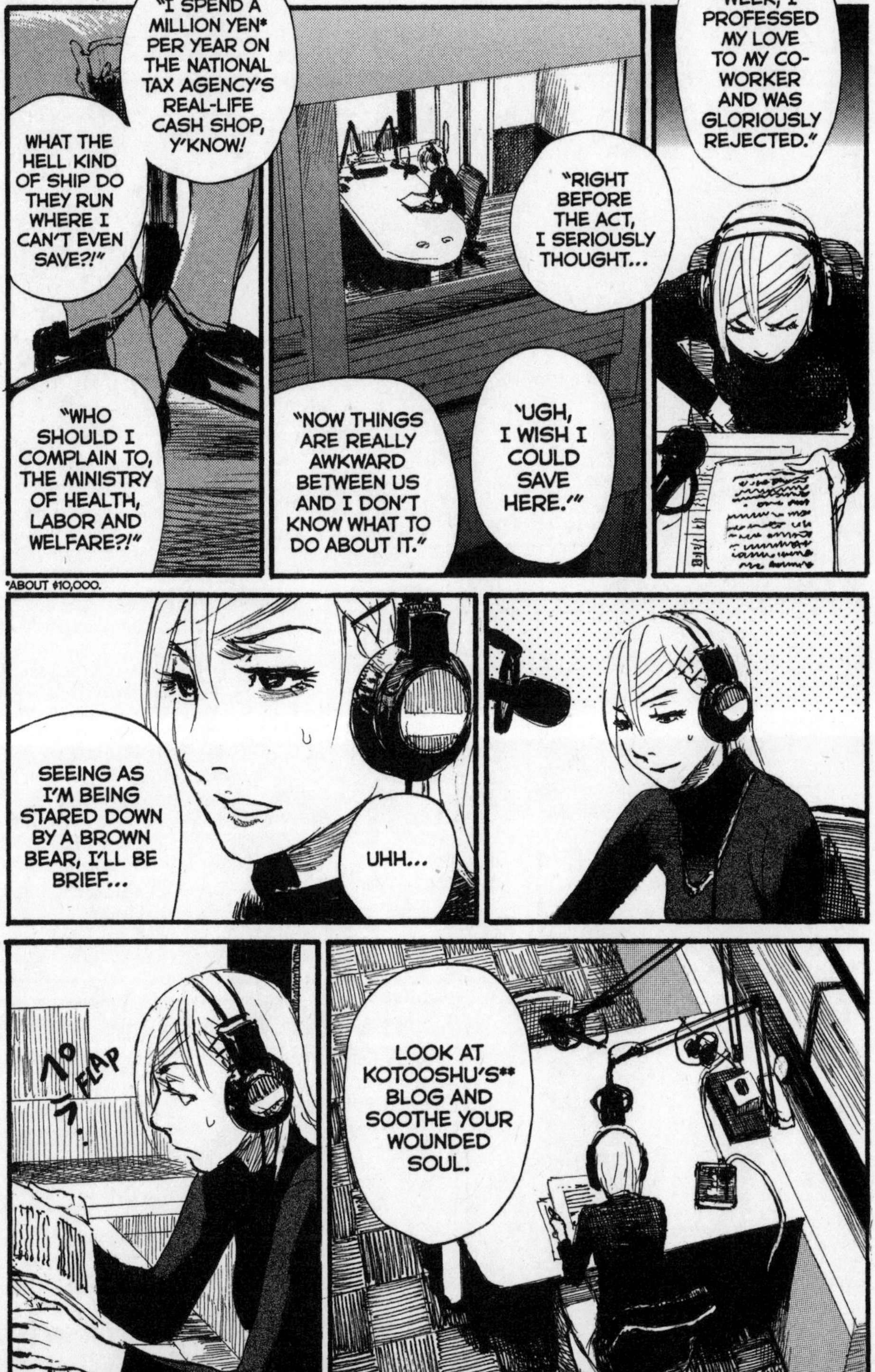
"LAST WEEK, I PROFESSED MY LOVE TO MY CO-WORKER AND WAS GLORIOUSLY REJECTED."
"RIGHT BEFORE THE ACT, I SERIOUSLY THOUGHT...
'UGH, I WISH I COULD SAVE HERE.'"
"NOW THINGS ARE REALLY AWKWARD BETWEEN US AND I DON'T KNOW WHAT TO DO ABOUT IT."
"I SPEND A MILLION YEN* PER YEAR ON THE NATIONAL TAX AGENCY'S REAL-LIFE CASH SHOP, Y'KNOW!
WHAT THE HELL KIND OF SHIP DO THEY RUN WHERE I CAN'T EVEN SAVE?!"
"WHO SHOULD I COMPLAIN TO, THE MINISTRY OF HEALTH, LABOR AND WELFARE?!"
UHH...
SEEING AS I'M BEING STARED DOWN BY A BROWN BEAR, I'LL BE BRIEF...
LOOK AT KOTOOSHU'S** BLOG AND SOOTHE YOUR WOUNDED SOUL.
FLAP

*ABOUT $10,000.

**KOTOOSHU KATSUNORI, A FORMER BULGARIA-BORN SUMO WRESTLER.

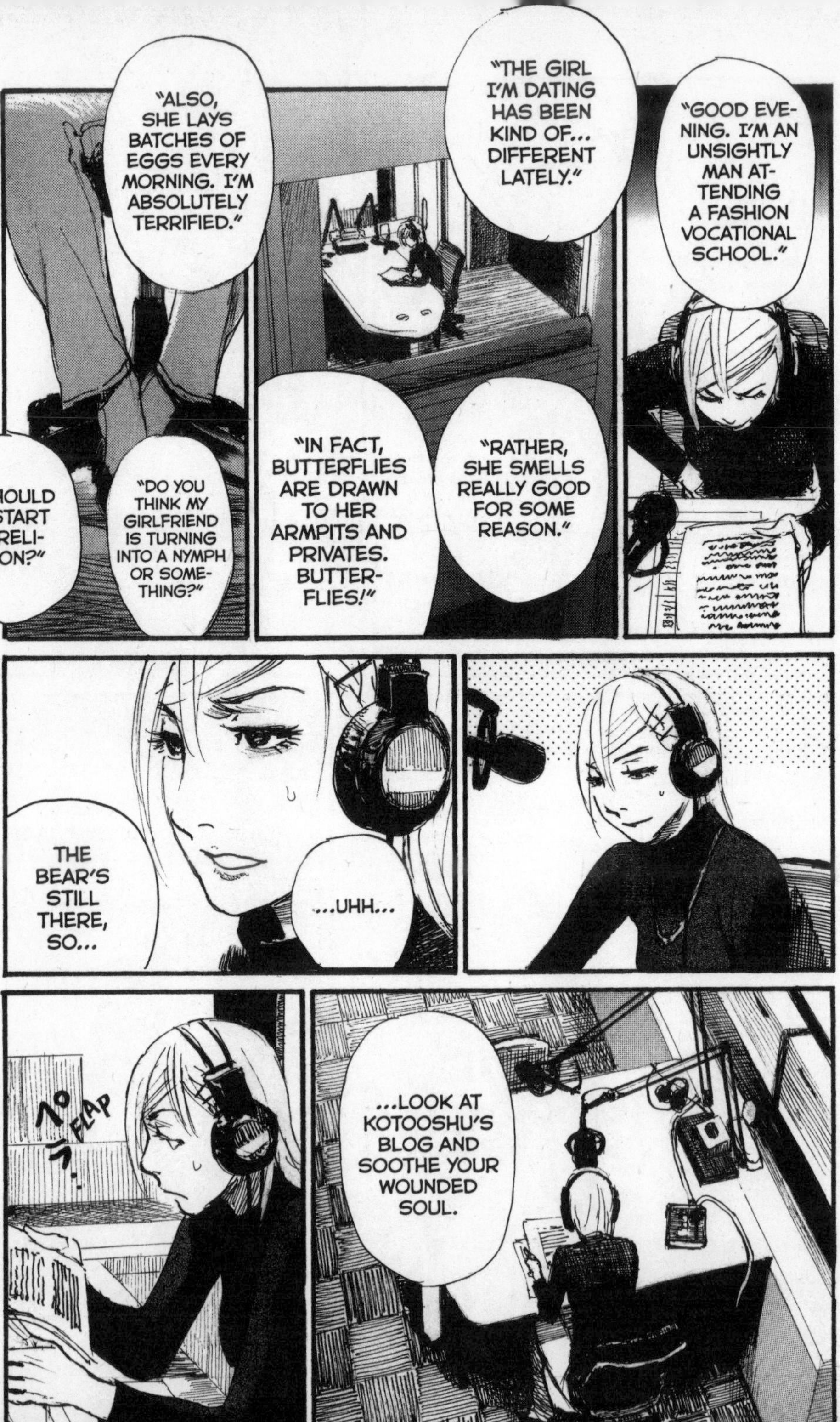
"GOOD EVE-NING. I'M AN UNSIGHTLY MAN AT-TENDING A FASHION VOCATIONAL SCHOOL."
"THE GIRL I'M DATING HAS BEEN KIND OF... DIFFERENT LATELY."
"RATHER, SHE SMELLS REALLY GOOD FOR SOME REASON."
"IN FACT, BUTTERFLIES ARE DRAWN TO HER ARMPITS AND PRIVATES. BUTTER-FLIES!"
"ALSO, SHE LAYS BATCHES OF EGGS EVERY MORNING. I'M ABSOLUTELY TERRIFIED."
"DO YOU THINK MY GIRLFRIEND IS TURNING INTO A NYMPH OR SOME-THING?"
"SHOULD I START A RELI-GION?"
...UHH...
THE BEAR'S STILL THERE, SO...
...LOOK AT KOTOOSHU'S BLOG AND SOOTHE YOUR WOUNDED SOUL.
FLAP

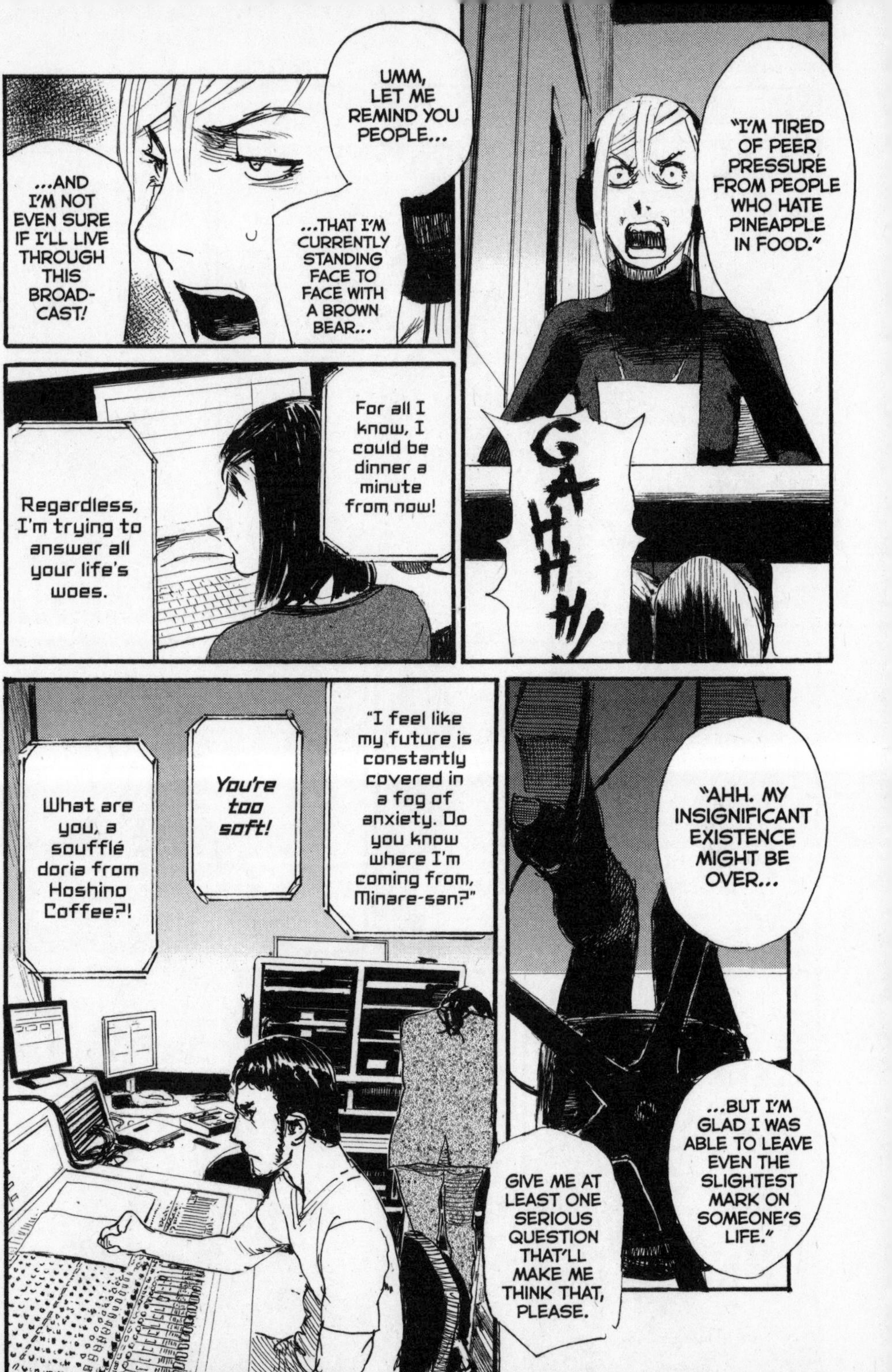
"I'M TIRED OF PEER PRESSURE FROM PEOPLE WHO HATE PINEAPPLE IN FOOD."
GAHHH!!
UMM, LET ME REMIND YOU PEOPLE...
...THAT I'M CURRENTLY STANDING FACE TO FACE WITH A BROWN BEAR...
...AND I'M NOT EVEN SURE IF I'LL LIVE THROUGH THIS BROAD-CAST!
For all I know, I could be dinner a minute from now!
Regardless, I'm trying to answer all your life's woes.
"AHH. MY INSIGNIFICANT EXISTENCE MIGHT BE OVER...
...BUT I'M GLAD I WAS ABLE TO LEAVE EVEN THE SLIGHTEST MARK ON SOMEONE'S LIFE."
"I feel like my future is constantly covered in a fog of anxiety. Do you know where I'm coming from, Minare-san?"
You're too soft!
What are you, a soufflé doria from Hoshino Coffee?!
GIVE ME AT LEAST ONE SERIOUS QUESTION THAT'LL MAKE ME THINK THAT, PLEASE.

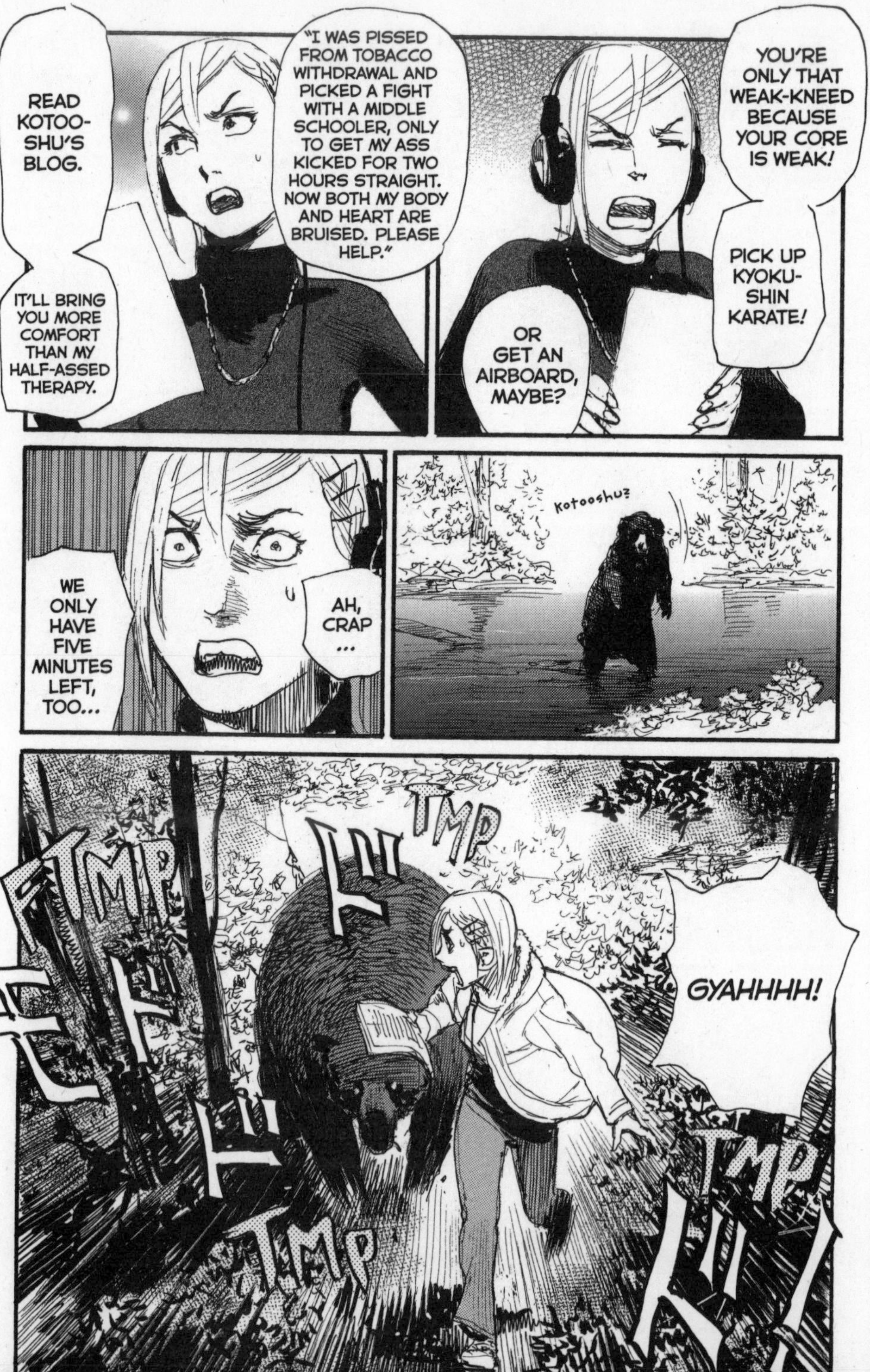
YOU'RE ONLY THAT WEAK-KNEED BECAUSE YOUR CORE IS WEAK!
PICK UP KYOKUSHIN KARATE!
OR GET AN AIRBOARD, MAYBE?
"I WAS PISSED FROM TOBACCO WITHDRAWAL AND PICKED A FIGHT WITH A MIDDLE SCHOOLER, ONLY TO GET MY ASS KICKED FOR TWO HOURS STRAIGHT. NOW BOTH MY BODY AND HEART ARE BRUISED. PLEASE HELP."
READ KOTOOSHU'S BLOG.
IT'LL BRING YOU MORE COMFORT THAN MY HALF-ASSED THERAPY.
Kotooshu?
AH, CRAP...
WE ONLY HAVE FIVE MINUTES LEFT, TOO...
GYAHHHH!
TMP
TMP
TMP
TMP

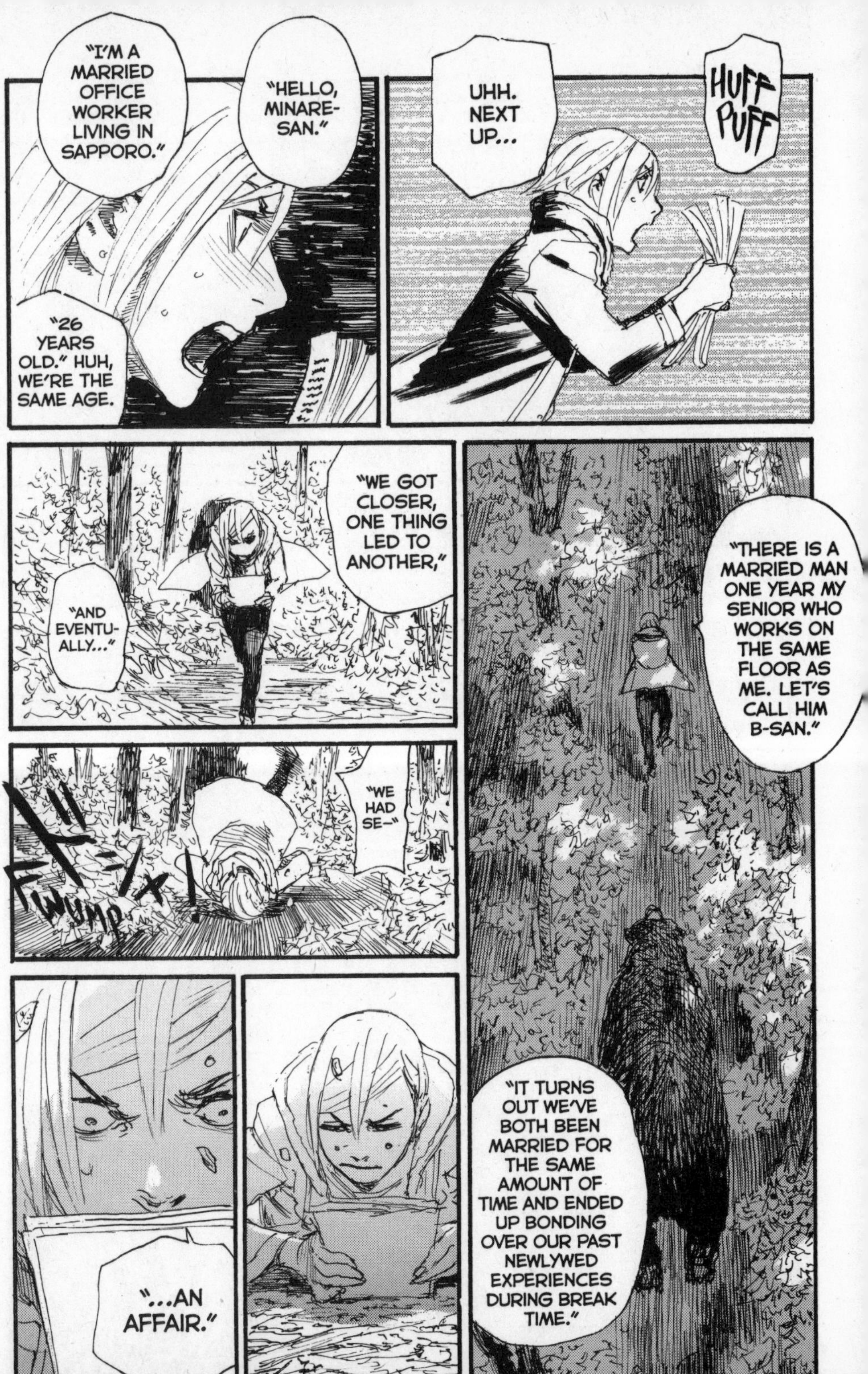
HUFF PUFF
UHH. NEXT UP...
"HELLO, MINARE-SAN."
"I'M A MARRIED OFFICE WORKER LIVING IN SAPPORO."
"26 YEARS OLD." HUH, WE'RE THE SAME AGE.
"THERE IS A MARRIED MAN ONE YEAR MY SENIOR WHO WORKS ON THE SAME FLOOR AS ME. LET'S CALL HIM B-SAN."
"IT TURNS OUT WE'VE BOTH BEEN MARRIED FOR THE SAME AMOUNT OF TIME AND ENDED UP BONDING OVER OUR PAST NEWLYWED EXPERIENCES DURING BREAK TIME."
"WE GOT CLOSER, ONE THING LED TO ANOTHER,"
"AND EVENTUALLY..."
"WE HAD SE—"
FWUMP
"...AN AFFAIR."

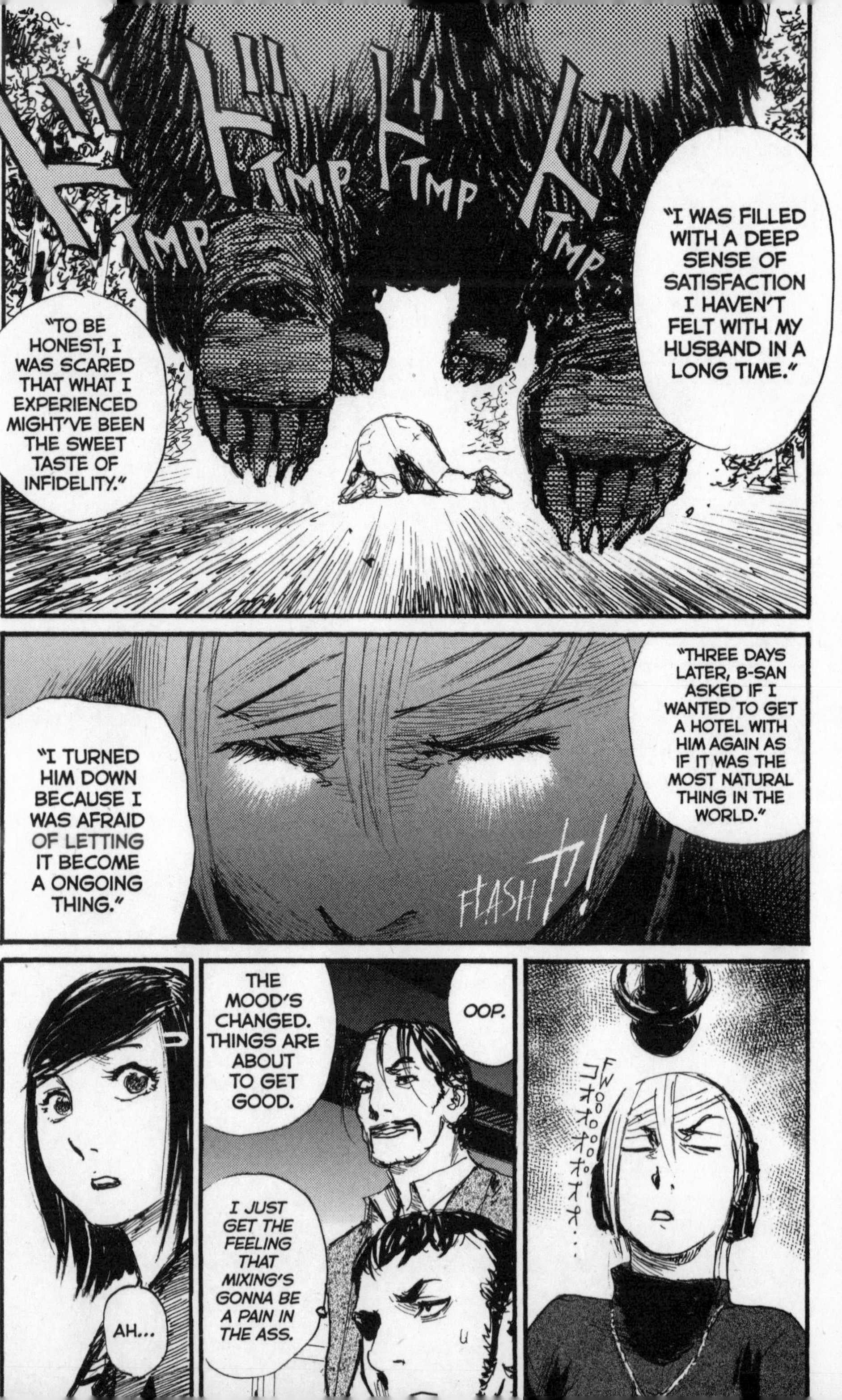
TMP TMP TMP TMP TMP
"I WAS FILLED WITH A DEEP SENSE OF SATISFACTION I HAVEN'T FELT WITH MY HUSBAND IN A LONG TIME."
"TO BE HONEST, I WAS SCARED THAT WHAT I EXPERIENCED MIGHT'VE BEEN THE SWEET TASTE OF INFIDELITY."
"THREE DAYS LATER, B-SAN ASKED IF I WANTED TO GET A HOTEL WITH HIM AGAIN AS IF IT WAS THE MOST NATURAL THING IN THE WORLD."
"I TURNED HIM DOWN BECAUSE I WAS AFRAID OF LETTING IT BECOME A ONGOING THING."
FLASH カッ!
FWOO コオオオオオオ…
OOP.
THE MOOD'S CHANGED. THINGS ARE ABOUT TO GET GOOD.
I JUST GET THE FEELING THAT MIXING'S GONNA BE A PAIN IN THE ASS.
AH...

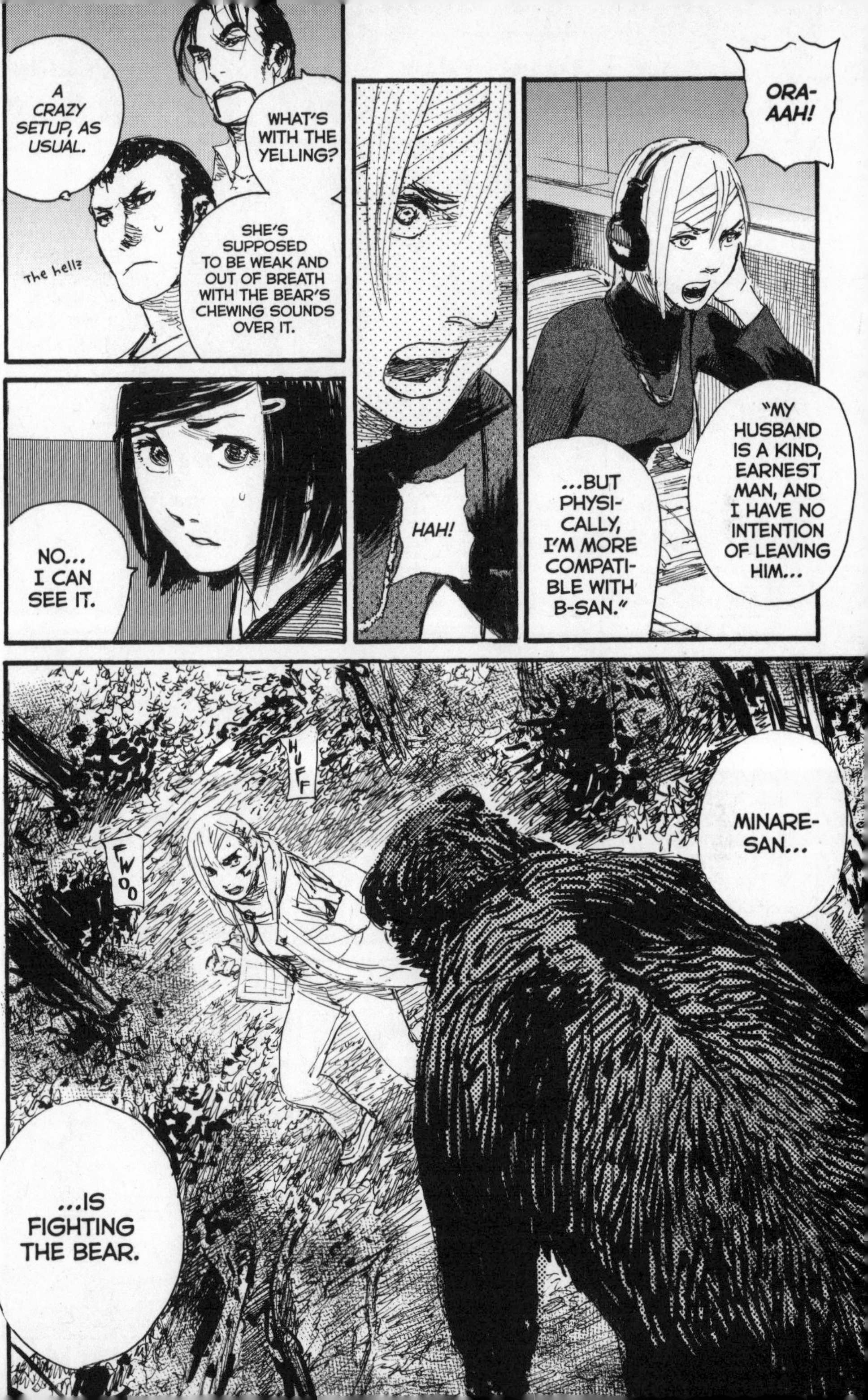
ORA-AAH!
"MY HUSBAND IS A KIND, EARNEST MAN, AND I HAVE NO INTENTION OF LEAVING HIM...
...BUT PHYSICALLY, I'M MORE COMPATIBLE WITH B-SAN."
HAH!
WHAT'S WITH THE YELLING?
A CRAZY SETUP, AS USUAL.
SHE'S SUPPOSED TO BE WEAK AND OUT OF BREATH WITH THE BEAR'S CHEWING SOUNDS OVER IT.
The hell?
NO... I CAN SEE IT.
MINARE-SAN...
HUFF
FWOO
...IS FIGHTING THE BEAR.

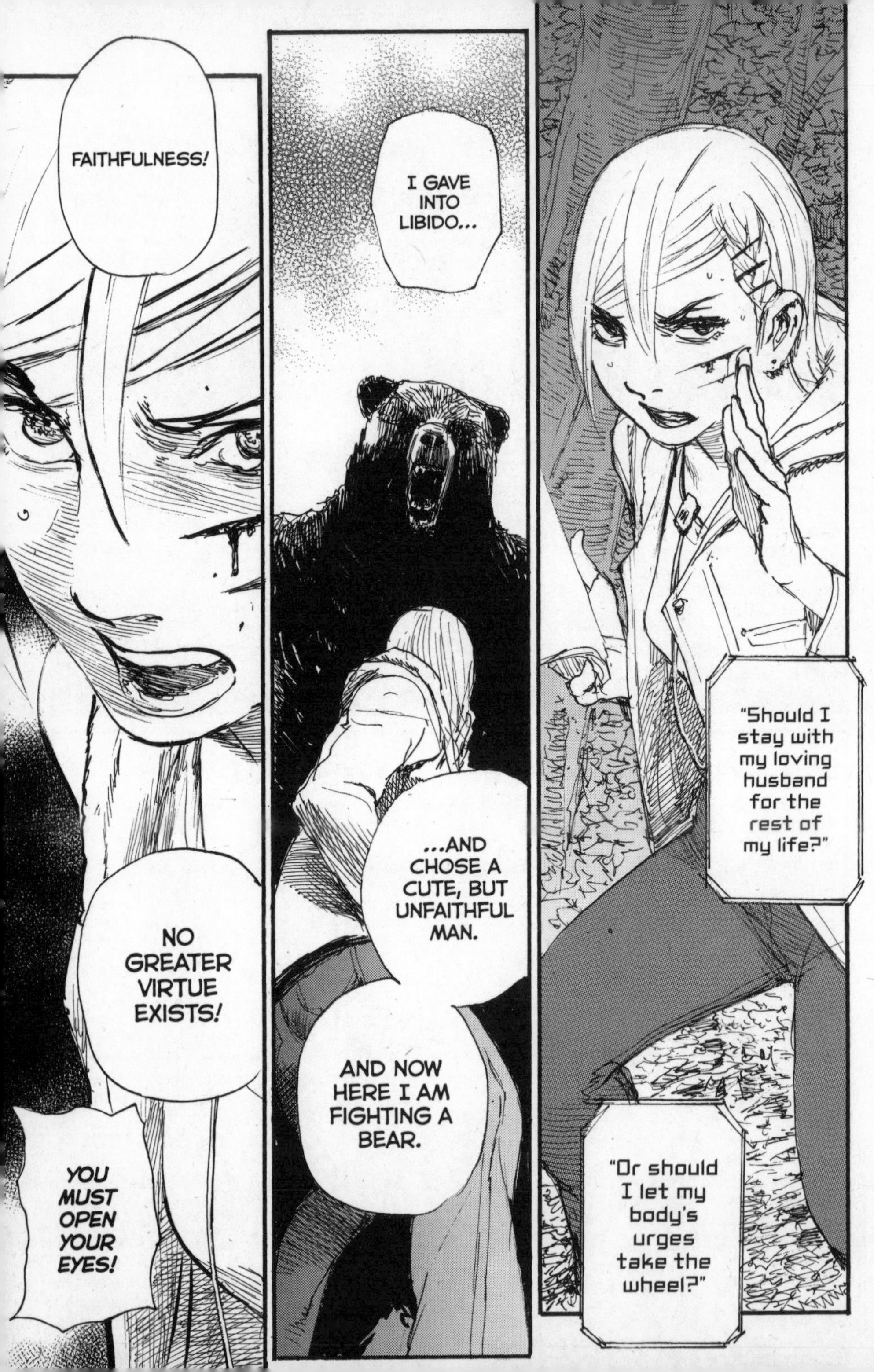
"Should I stay with my loving husband for the rest of my life?"
"Or should I let my body's urges take the wheel?"
I GAVE INTO LIBIDO...
...AND CHOSE A CUTE, BUT UNFAITHFUL MAN.
AND NOW HERE I AM FIGHTING A BEAR.
FAITHFULNESS!
NO GREATER VIRTUE EXISTS!
YOU MUST OPEN YOUR EYES!

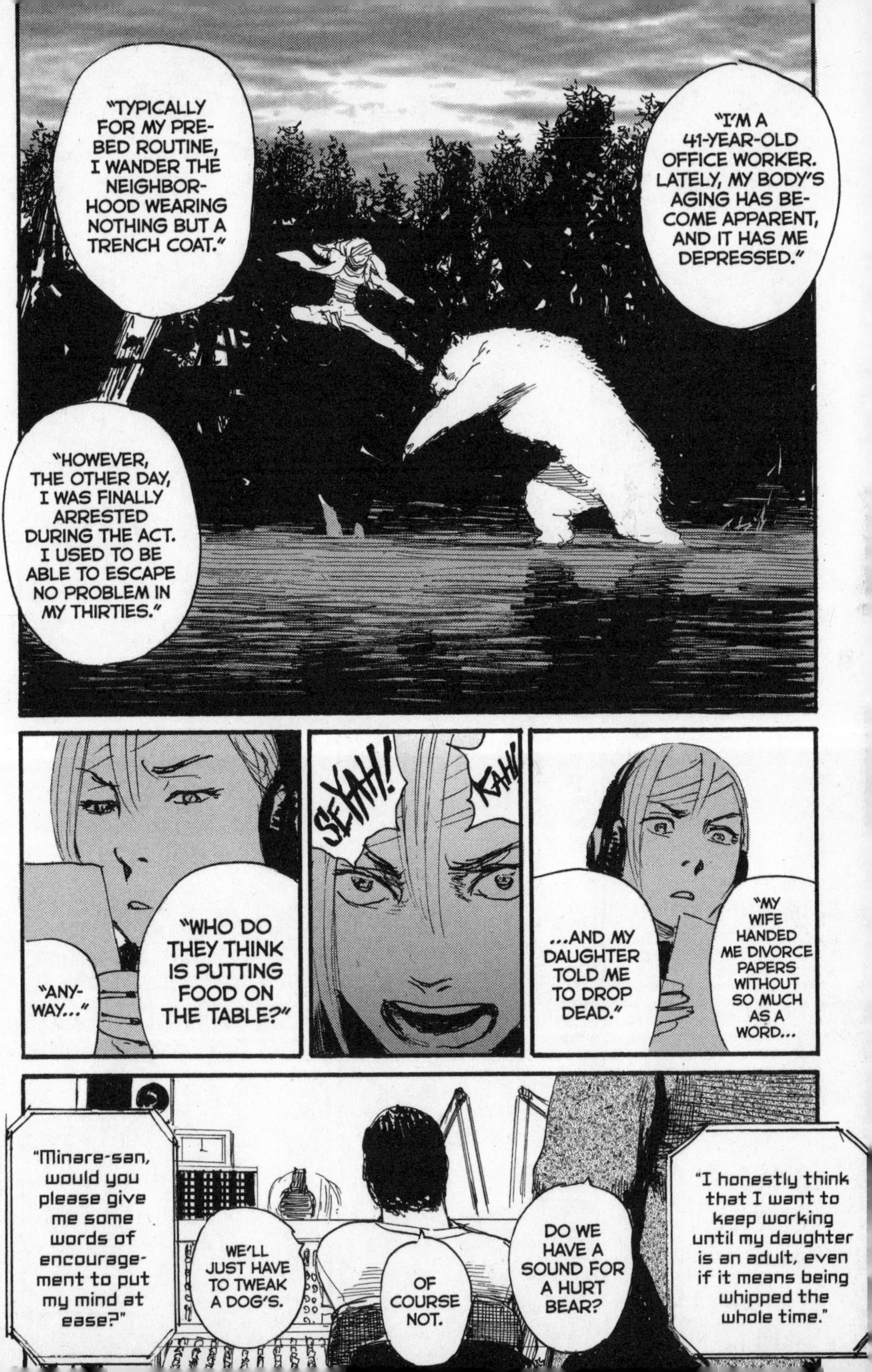
"I'M A 41-YEAR-OLD OFFICE WORKER. LATELY, MY BODY'S AGING HAS BECOME APPARENT, AND IT HAS ME DEPRESSED."
"TYPICALLY FOR MY PRE-BED ROUTINE, I WANDER THE NEIGHBORHOOD WEARING NOTHING BUT A TRENCH COAT."
"HOWEVER, THE OTHER DAY, I WAS FINALLY ARRESTED DURING THE ACT. I USED TO BE ABLE TO ESCAPE NO PROBLEM IN MY THIRTIES."
"MY WIFE HANDED ME DIVORCE PAPERS WITHOUT SO MUCH AS A WORD...
...AND MY DAUGHTER TOLD ME TO DROP DEAD."
KAH!
SEYAH!
"WHO DO THEY THINK IS PUTTING FOOD ON THE TABLE?"
"ANYWAY..."
"I honestly think that I want to keep working until my daughter is an adult, even if it means being whipped the whole time."
DO WE HAVE A SOUND FOR A HURT BEAR?
OF COURSE NOT.
WE'LL JUST HAVE TO TWEAK A DOG'S.
"Minare-san, would you please give me some words of encouragement to put my mind at ease?"

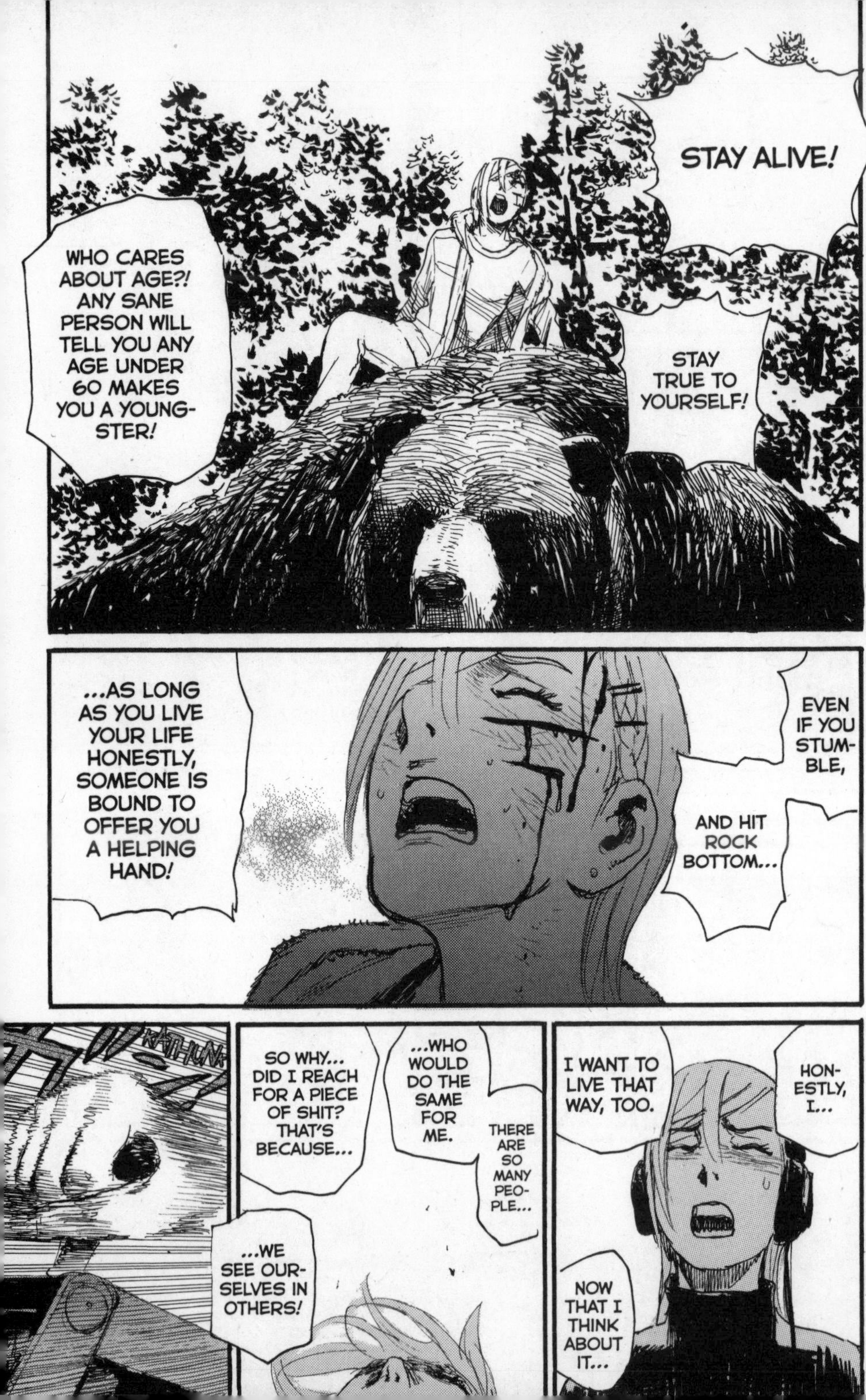
STAY ALIVE!
STAY TRUE TO YOURSELF!
WHO CARES ABOUT AGE?! ANY SANE PERSON WILL TELL YOU ANY AGE UNDER 60 MAKES YOU A YOUNG-STER!
EVEN IF YOU STUM-BLE,
AND HIT ROCK BOTTOM...
...AS LONG AS YOU LIVE YOUR LIFE HONESTLY, SOMEONE IS BOUND TO OFFER YOU A HELPING HAND!
HON-ESTLY, I...
I WANT TO LIVE THAT WAY, TOO.
NOW THAT I THINK ABOUT IT...
THERE ARE SO MANY PEO-PLE...
...WHO WOULD DO THE SAME FOR ME.
SO WHY... DID I REACH FOR A PIECE OF SHIT? THAT'S BECAUSE...
...WE SEE OUR-SELVES IN OTHERS!
KATHUNK

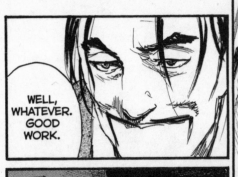

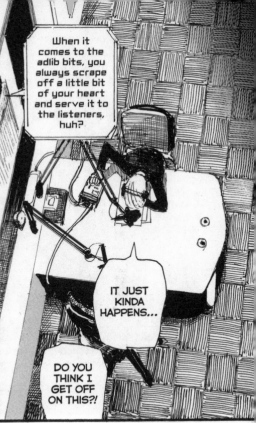

When it comes to the adlib bits, you always scrape off a little bit of your heart and serve it to the listeners, huh?
IT JUST KINDA HAPPENS...
DO YOU THINK I GET OFF ON THIS?!
WELL, WHATEVER. GOOD WORK.
TAK TAK TAK
COPYING DATA 72%
COPYING DATA 100%

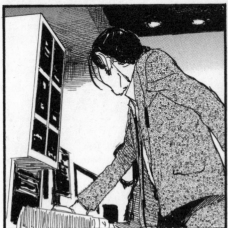

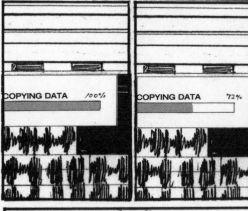

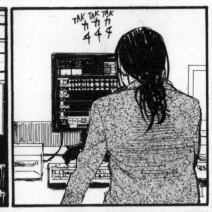

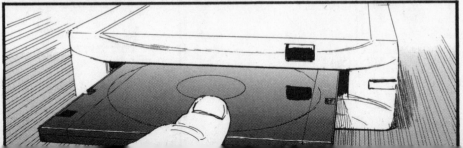

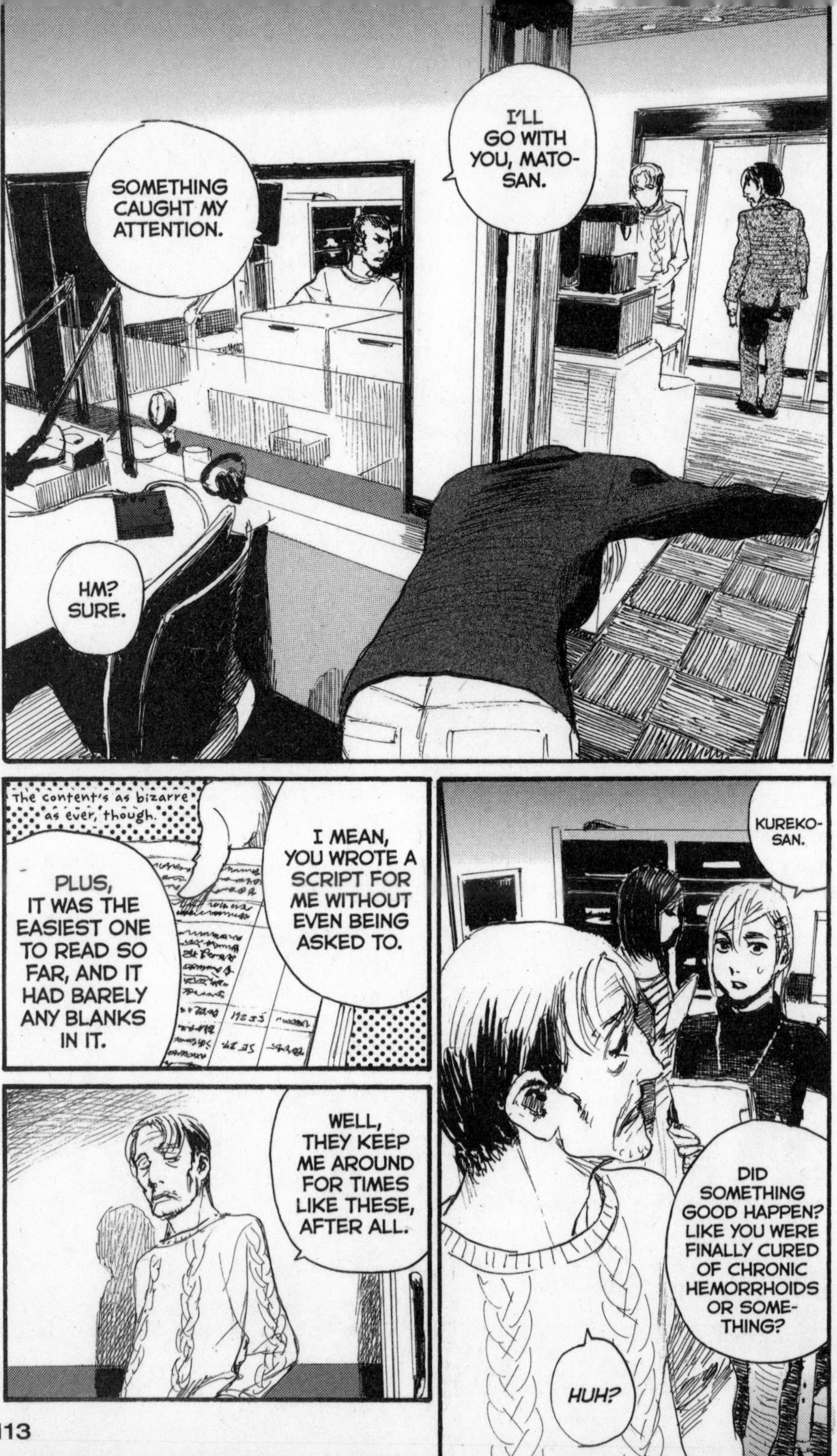
I'LL GO WITH YOU, MATO-SAN.
SOMETHING CAUGHT MY ATTENTION.
HM? SURE.
KUREKO-SAN.
DID SOMETHING GOOD HAPPEN? LIKE YOU WERE FINALLY CURED OF CHRONIC HEMORRHOIDS OR SOME-THING?
HUH?
I MEAN, YOU WROTE A SCRIPT FOR ME WITHOUT EVEN BEING ASKED TO.
PLUS, IT WAS THE EASIEST ONE TO READ SO FAR, AND IT HAD BARELY ANY BLANKS IN IT.
The content's as bizarre as ever, though.
WELL, THEY KEEP ME AROUND FOR TIMES LIKE THESE, AFTER ALL.

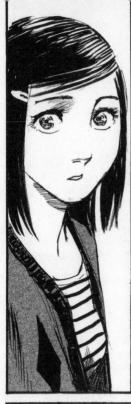

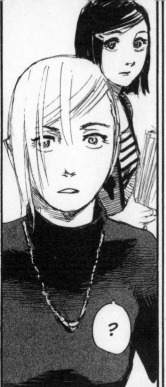

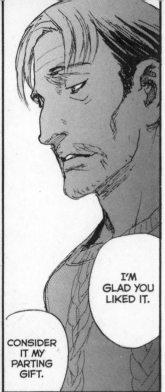

I'M GLAD YOU LIKED IT.

CONSIDER IT MY PARTING GIFT.

?

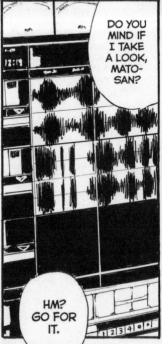

DO YOU MIND IF I TAKE A LOOK, MATO-SAN?

HM? GO FOR IT.

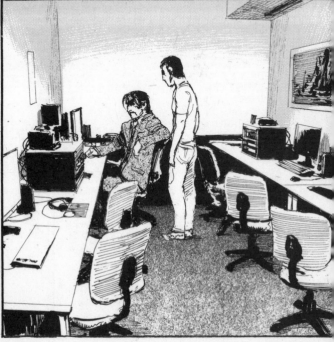

114

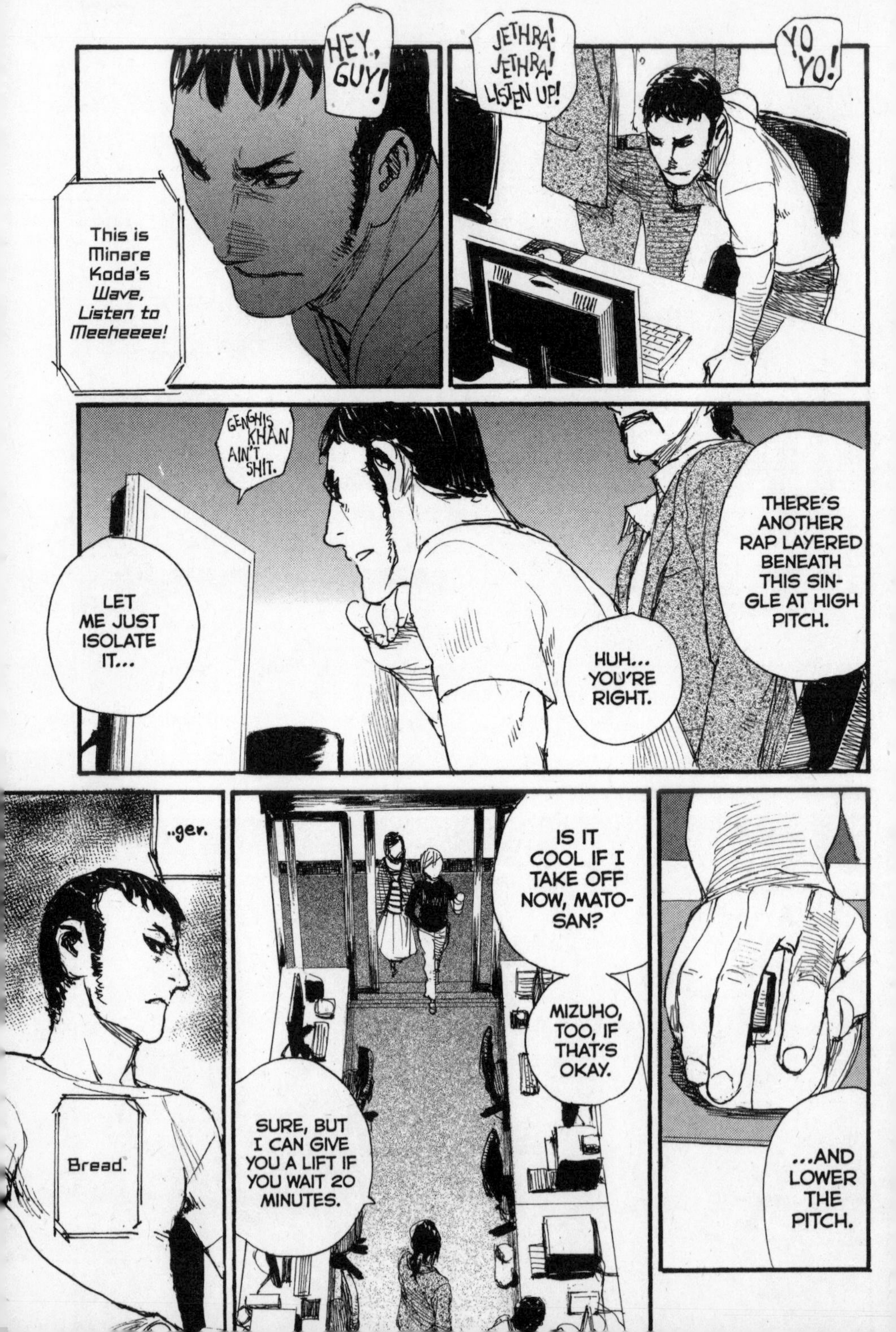

YO YO!
JETHRA! JETHRA! LISTEN UP!
HEY, GUY!
This is Minare Koda's *Wave, Listen to Meeheeee!*
THERE'S ANOTHER RAP LAYERED BENEATH THIS SINGLE AT HIGH PITCH.
GENGHIS KHAN AIN'T SHIT.
HUH... YOU'RE RIGHT.
LET ME JUST ISOLATE IT...
...AND LOWER THE PITCH.
IS IT COOL IF I TAKE OFF NOW, MATO-SAN?
MIZUHO, TOO, IF THAT'S OKAY.
SURE, BUT I CAN GIVE YOU A LIFT IF YOU WAIT 20 MINUTES.
..ger.
Bread.

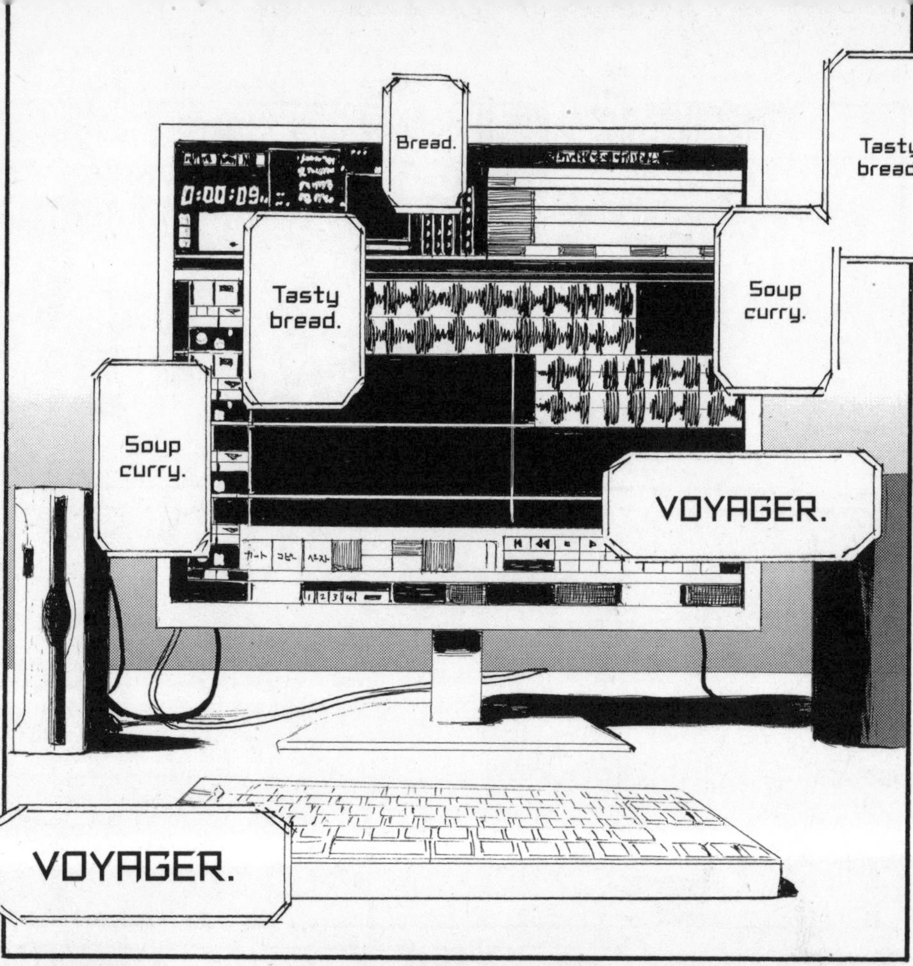
Tasty bread.
Bread.
Soup curry.
Tasty bread.
Soup curry.
VOYAGER.
VOYAGER.
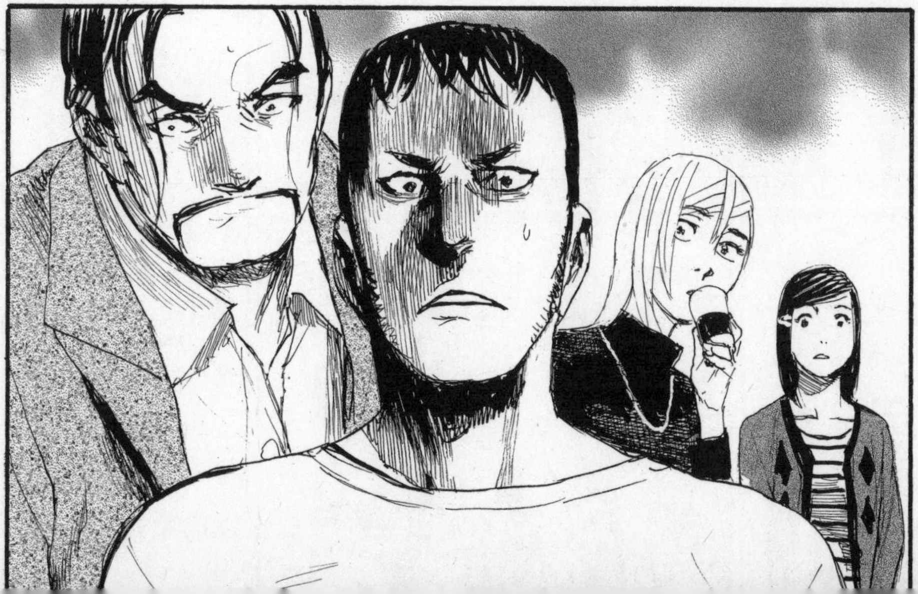

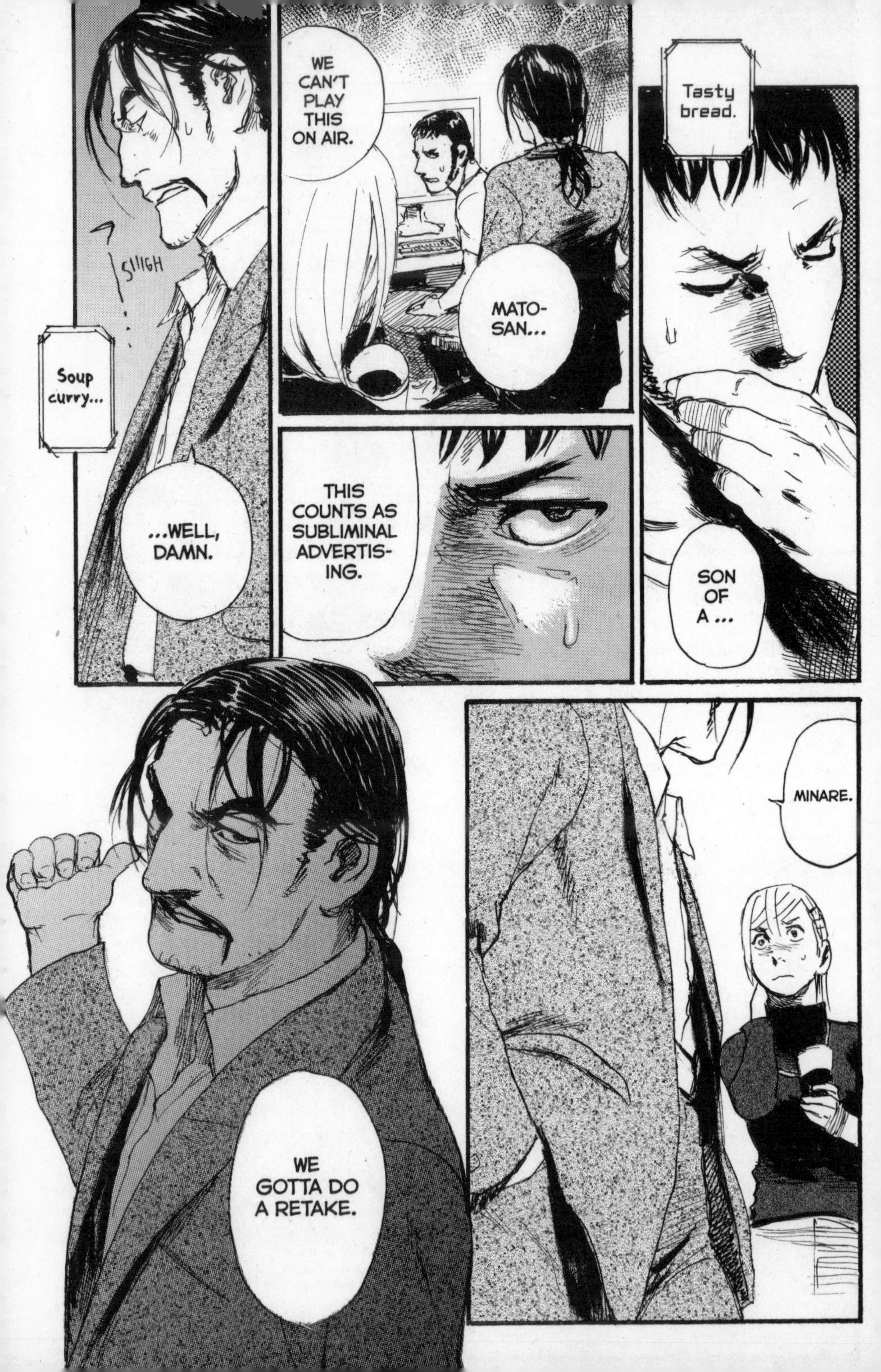
Tasty bread.
SON OF A ...
WE CAN'T PLAY THIS ON AIR.
MATO-SAN...
THIS COUNTS AS SUBLIMINAL ADVERTIS-ING.
SIIIGH
Soup curry...
...WELL, DAMN.
MINARE.
WE GOTTA DO A RETAKE.

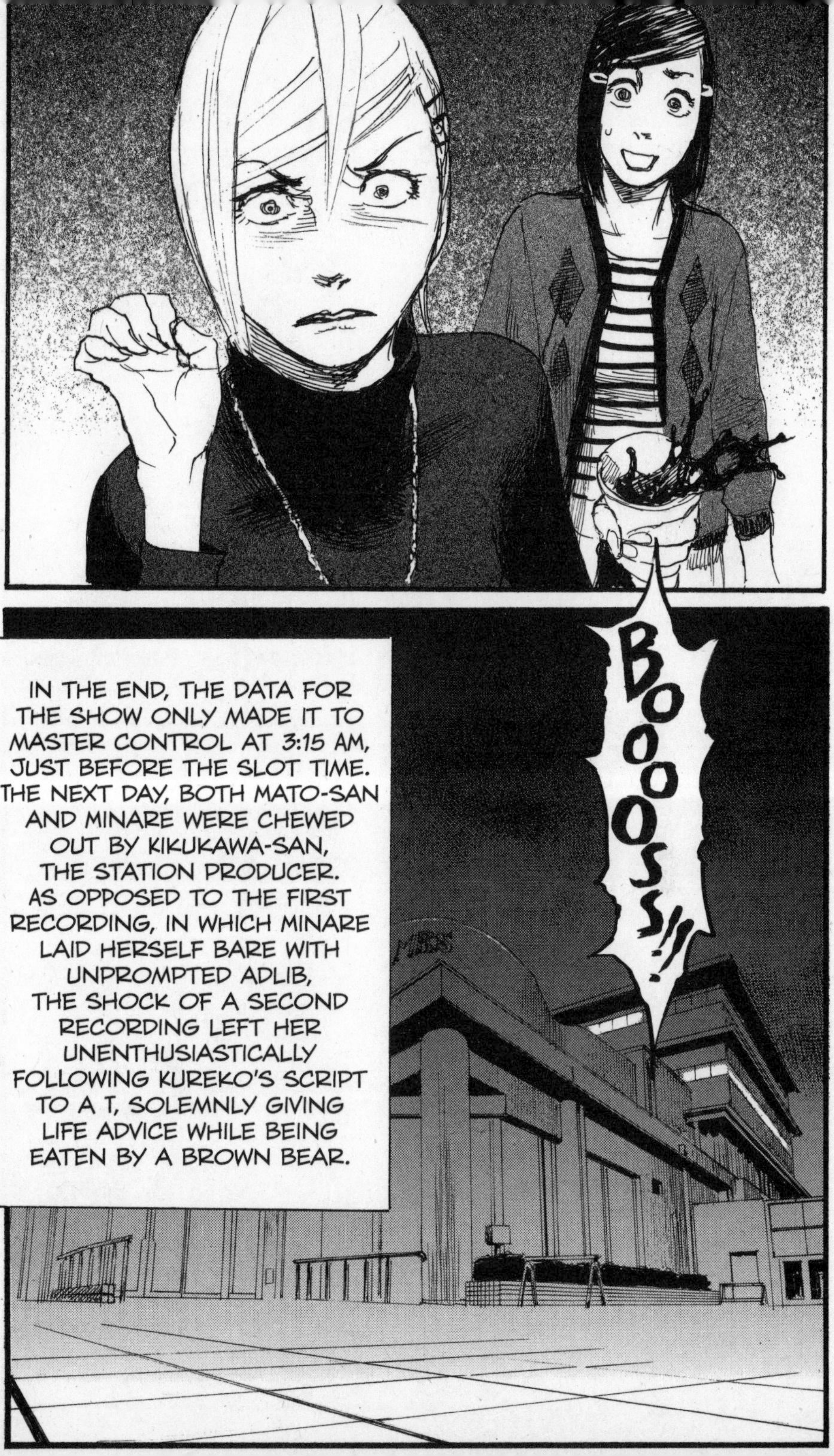
BOOOOSS!!
IN THE END, THE DATA FOR THE SHOW ONLY MADE IT TO MASTER CONTROL AT 3:15 AM, JUST BEFORE THE SLOT TIME. THE NEXT DAY, BOTH MATO-SAN AND MINARE WERE CHEWED OUT BY KIKUKAWA-SAN, THE STATION PRODUCER. AS OPPOSED TO THE FIRST RECORDING, IN WHICH MINARE LAID HERSELF BARE WITH UNPROMPTED ADLIB, THE SHOCK OF A SECOND RECORDING LEFT HER UNENTHUSIASTICALLY FOLLOWING KUREKO'S SCRIPT TO A T, SOLEMNLY GIVING LIFE ADVICE WHILE BEING EATEN BY A BROWN BEAR.

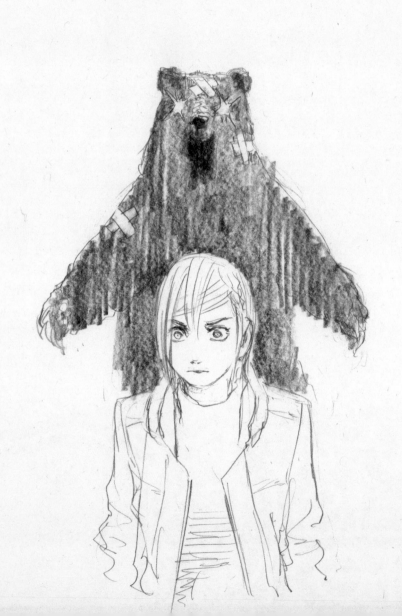

wave
LISTEN
TO ME!

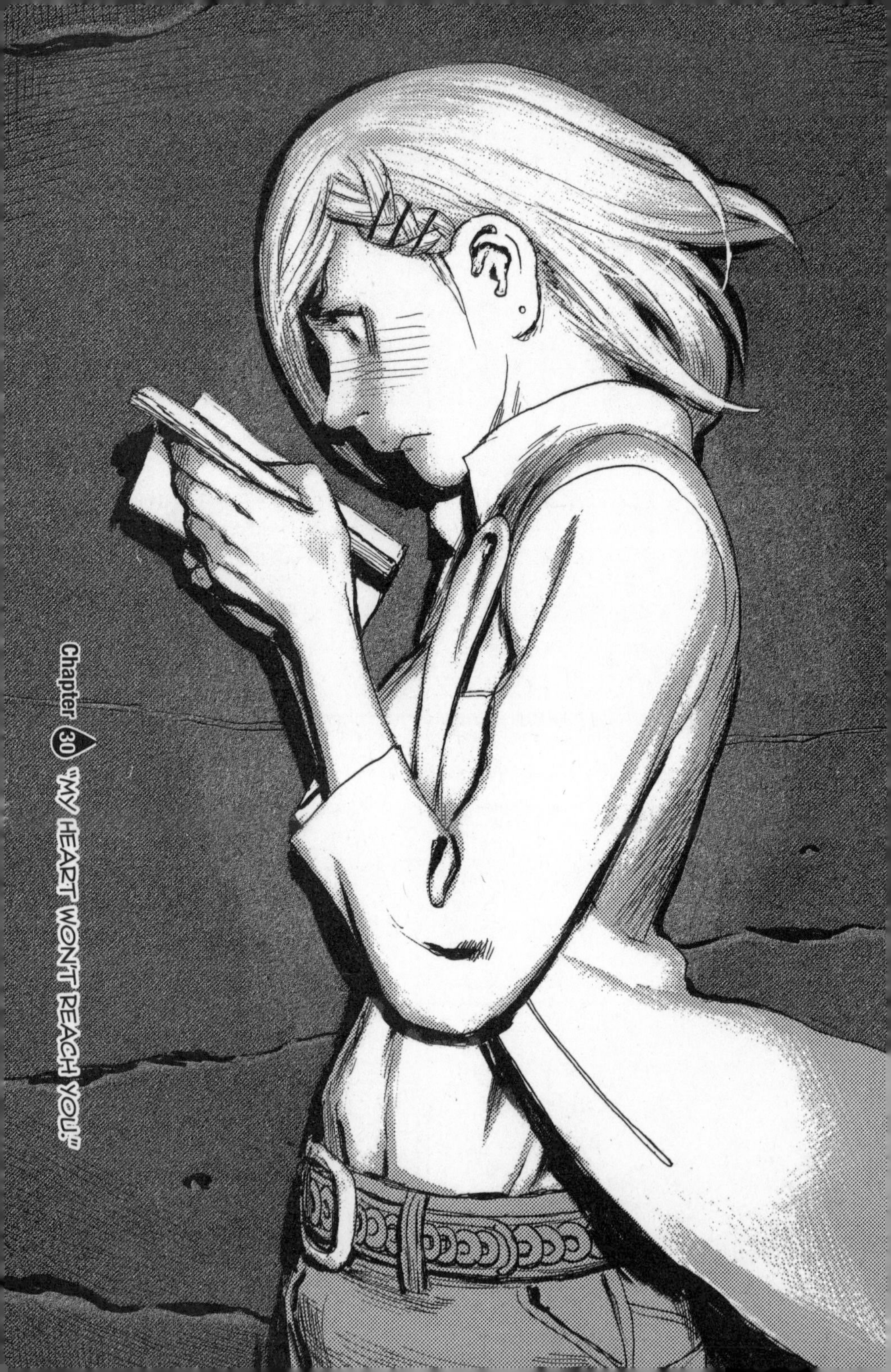
Chapter 30 "MY HEART WON'T REACH YOU."

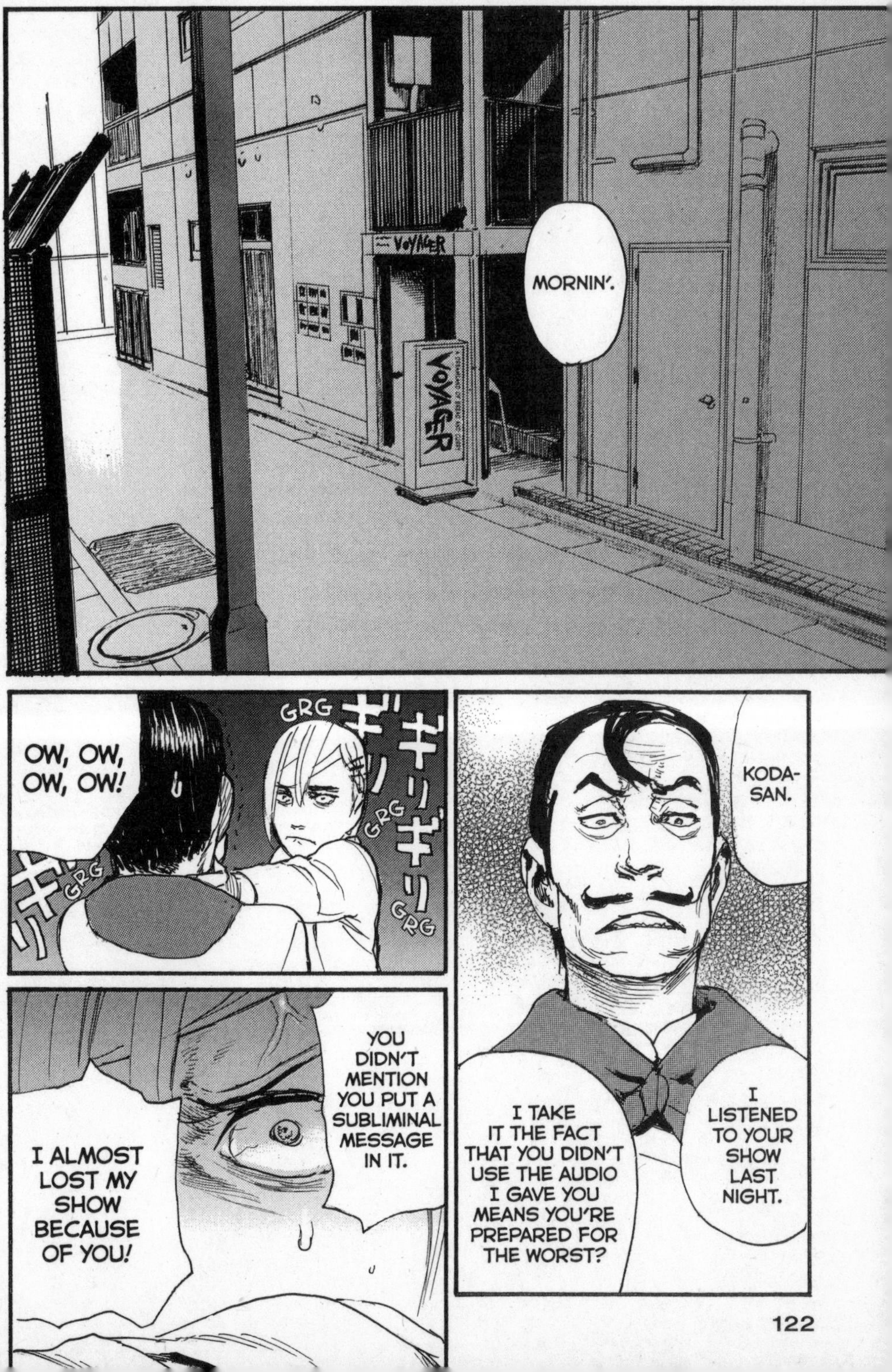
VOYAGER
VOYAGER
MORNIN'.
KODA-SAN.
I LISTENED TO YOUR SHOW LAST NIGHT.
I TAKE IT THE FACT THAT YOU DIDN'T USE THE AUDIO I GAVE YOU MEANS YOU'RE PREPARED FOR THE WORST?
GRG ギリ
ギリギリ
GRG
GRG
OW, OW, OW, OW!
ギリ GRG
YOU DIDN'T MENTION YOU PUT A SUBLIMINAL MESSAGE IN IT.
I ALMOST LOST MY SHOW BECAUSE OF YOU!

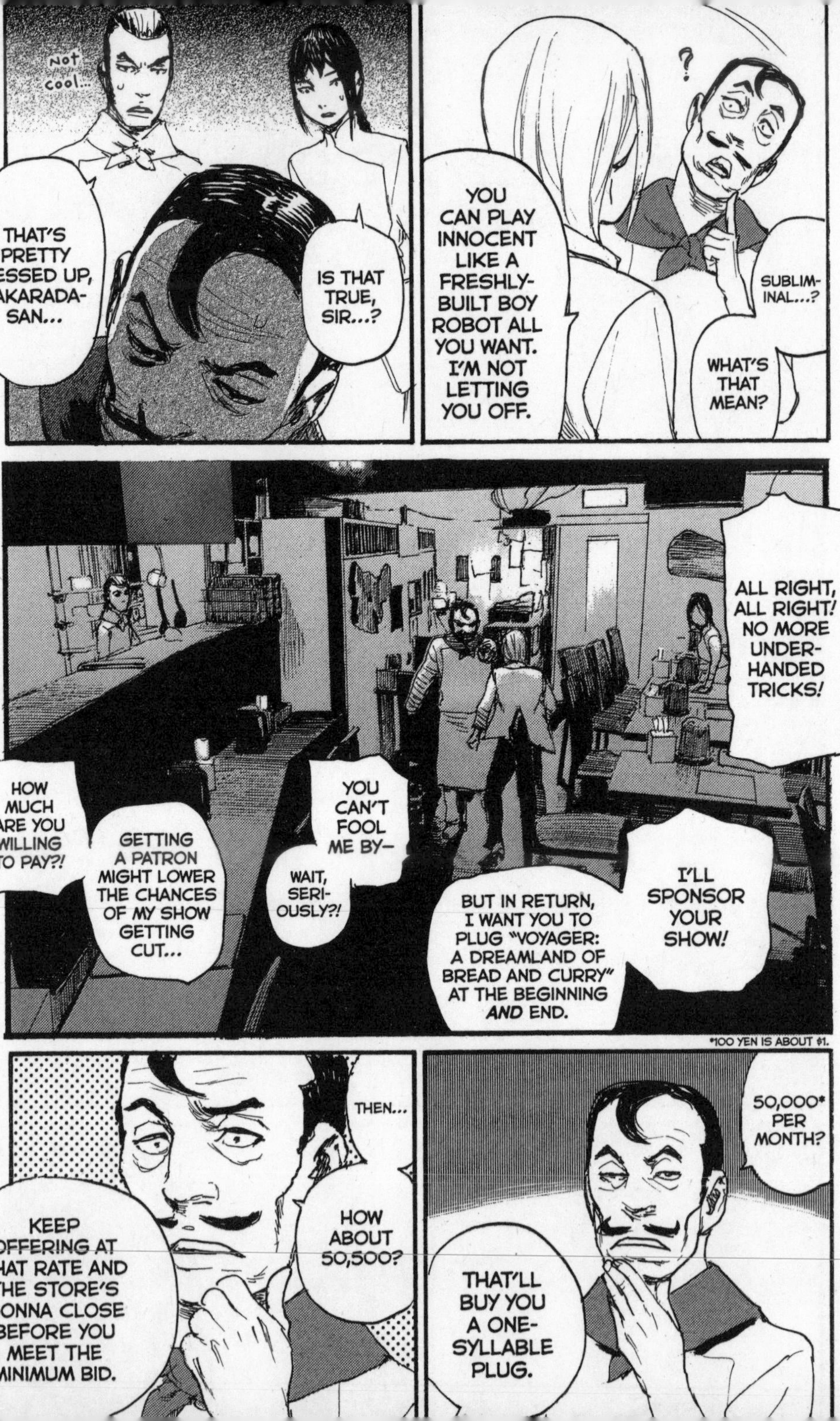
?
SUBLIMINAL...?
WHAT'S THAT MEAN?
YOU CAN PLAY INNOCENT LIKE A FRESHLY-BUILT BOY ROBOT ALL YOU WANT. I'M NOT LETTING YOU OFF.
Not cool...
IS THAT TRUE, SIR...?
THAT'S PRETTY MESSED UP, TAKARADA-SAN...
ALL RIGHT, ALL RIGHT! NO MORE UNDER-HANDED TRICKS!
I'LL SPONSOR YOUR SHOW!
BUT IN RETURN, I WANT YOU TO PLUG "VOYAGER: A DREAMLAND OF BREAD AND CURRY" AT THE BEGINNING *AND* END.
YOU CAN'T FOOL ME BY—
WAIT, SERIOUSLY?!
GETTING A PATRON MIGHT LOWER THE CHANCES OF MY SHOW GETTING CUT...
HOW MUCH ARE YOU WILLING TO PAY?!
50,000* PER MONTH?
THAT'LL BUY YOU A ONE-SYLLABLE PLUG.
THEN...
HOW ABOUT 50,500?
KEEP OFFERING AT THAT RATE AND THE STORE'S GONNA CLOSE BEFORE YOU MEET THE MINIMUM BID.

*100 YEN IS ABOUT $1.

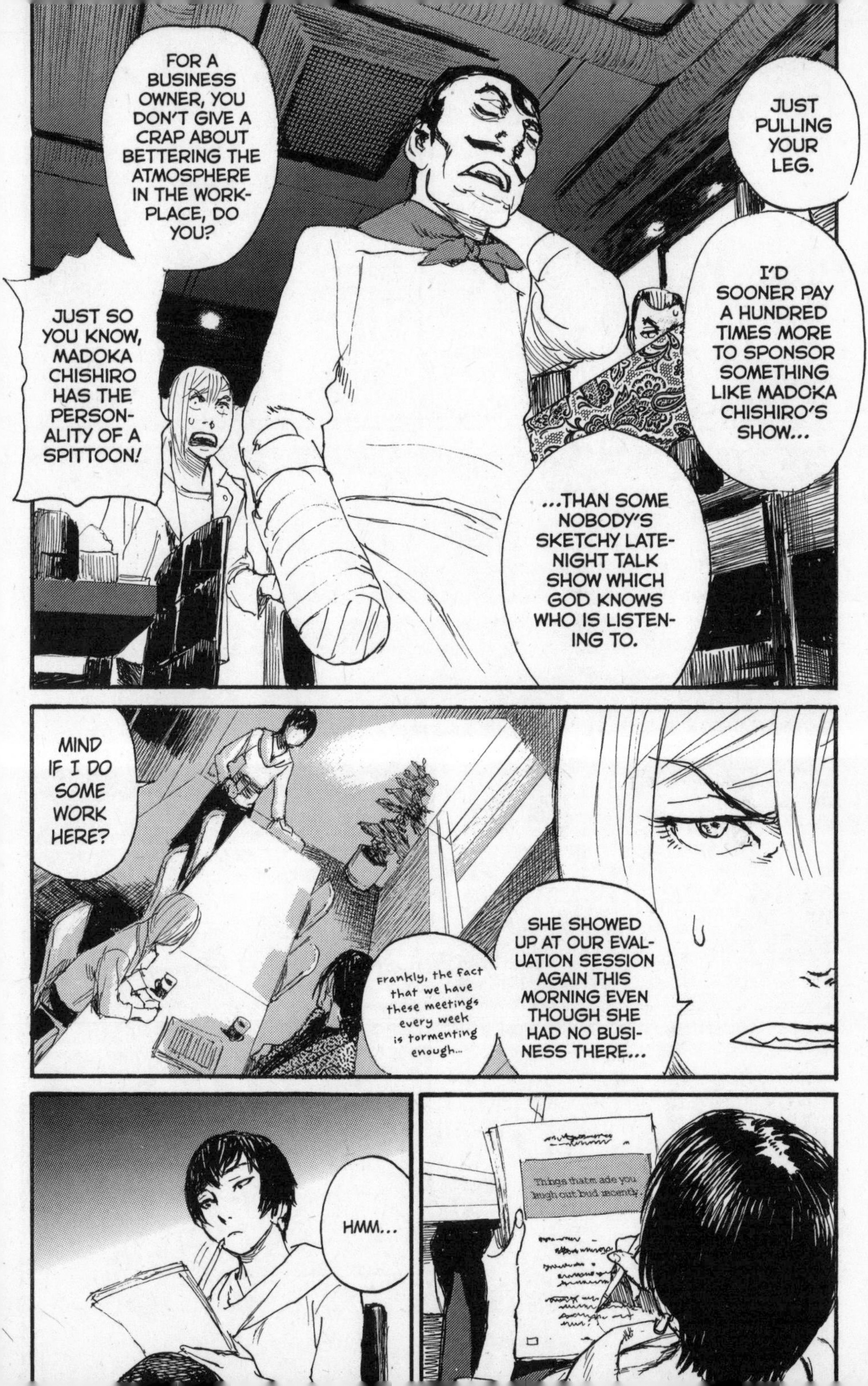
JUST PULLING YOUR LEG.
FOR A BUSINESS OWNER, YOU DON'T GIVE A CRAP ABOUT BETTERING THE ATMOSPHERE IN THE WORK-PLACE, DO YOU?
I'D SOONER PAY A HUNDRED TIMES MORE TO SPONSOR SOMETHING LIKE MADOKA CHISHIRO'S SHOW...
...THAN SOME NOBODY'S SKETCHY LATE-NIGHT TALK SHOW WHICH GOD KNOWS WHO IS LISTEN-ING TO.
JUST SO YOU KNOW, MADOKA CHISHIRO HAS THE PERSON-ALITY OF A SPITTOON!
SHE SHOWED UP AT OUR EVAL-UATION SESSION AGAIN THIS MORNING EVEN THOUGH SHE HAD NO BUSI-NESS THERE...
Frankly, the fact that we have these meetings every week is tormenting enough...
MIND IF I DO SOME WORK HERE?
Things that made you laugh out loud recently
HMM...

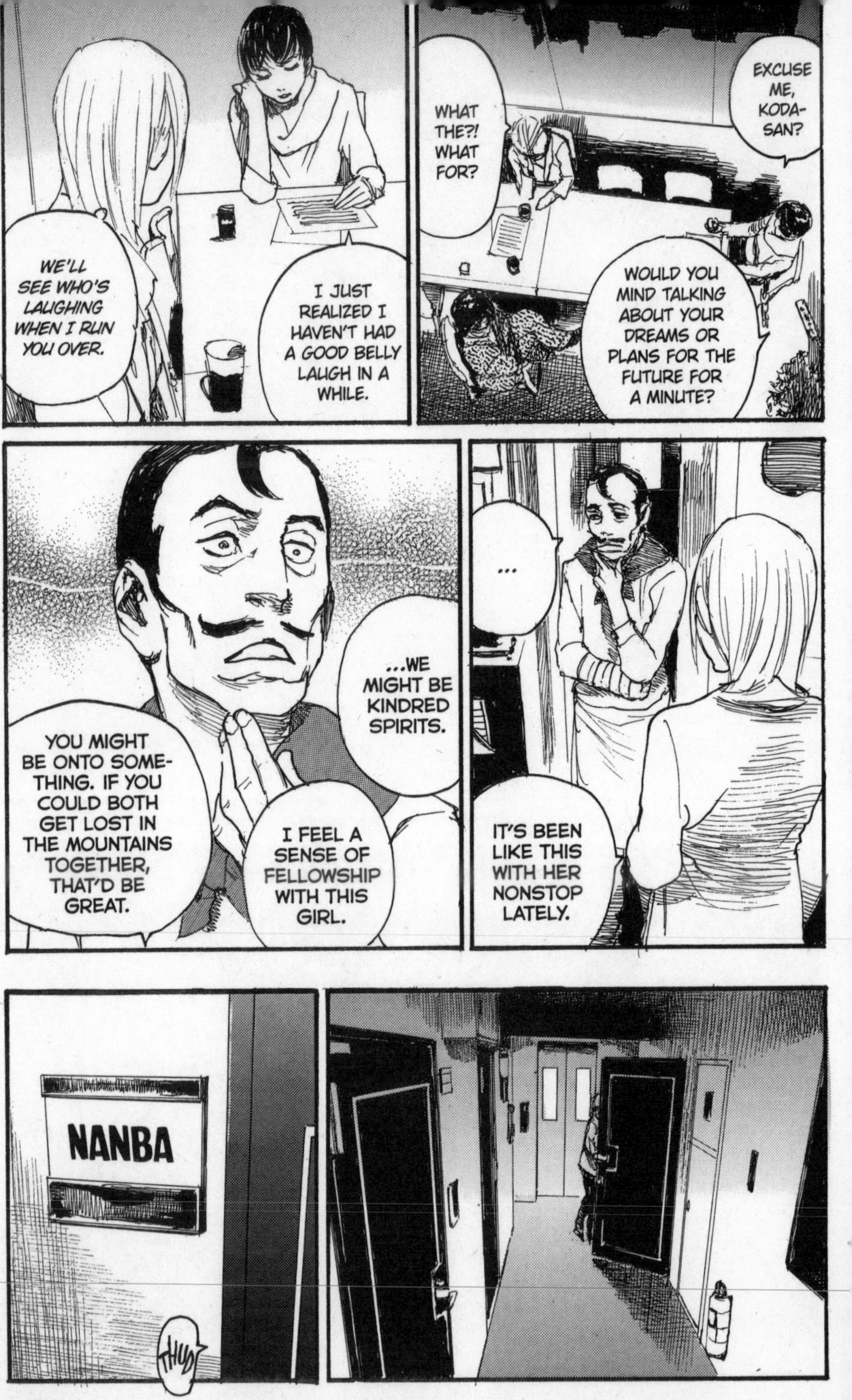

EXCUSE ME, KODA-SAN?
WHAT THE?! WHAT FOR?
WOULD YOU MIND TALKING ABOUT YOUR DREAMS OR PLANS FOR THE FUTURE FOR A MINUTE?
I JUST REALIZED I HAVEN'T HAD A GOOD BELLY LAUGH IN A WHILE.
WE'LL SEE WHO'S LAUGHING WHEN I RUN YOU OVER.
...
IT'S BEEN LIKE THIS WITH HER NONSTOP LATELY.
...WE MIGHT BE KINDRED SPIRITS.
I FEEL A SENSE OF FELLOWSHIP WITH THIS GIRL.
YOU MIGHT BE ONTO SOME-THING. IF YOU COULD BOTH GET LOST IN THE MOUNTAINS TOGETHER, THAT'D BE GREAT.
NANBA
THUD

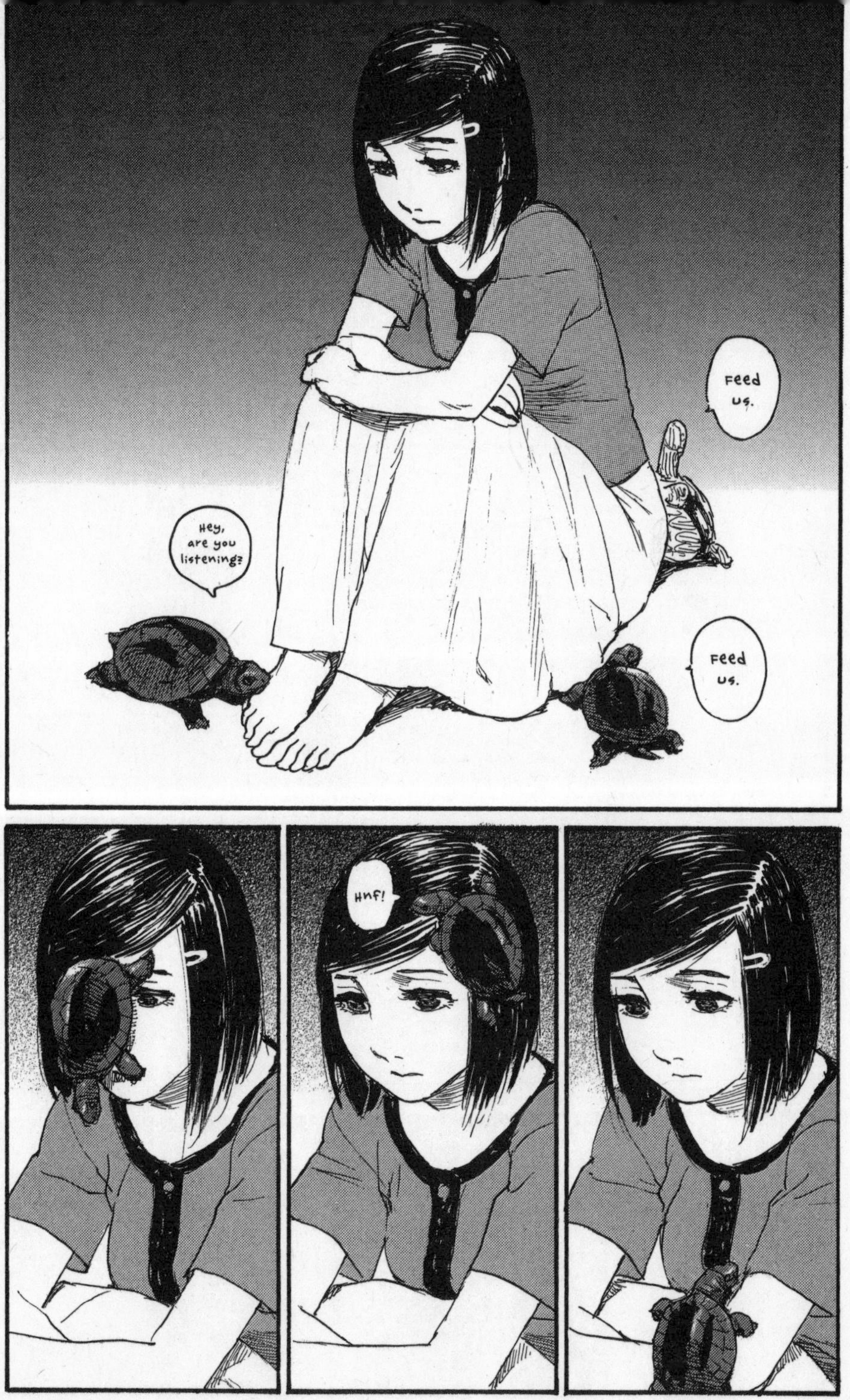

Feed us.
Hey, are you listening?
Feed us.
Hnf!

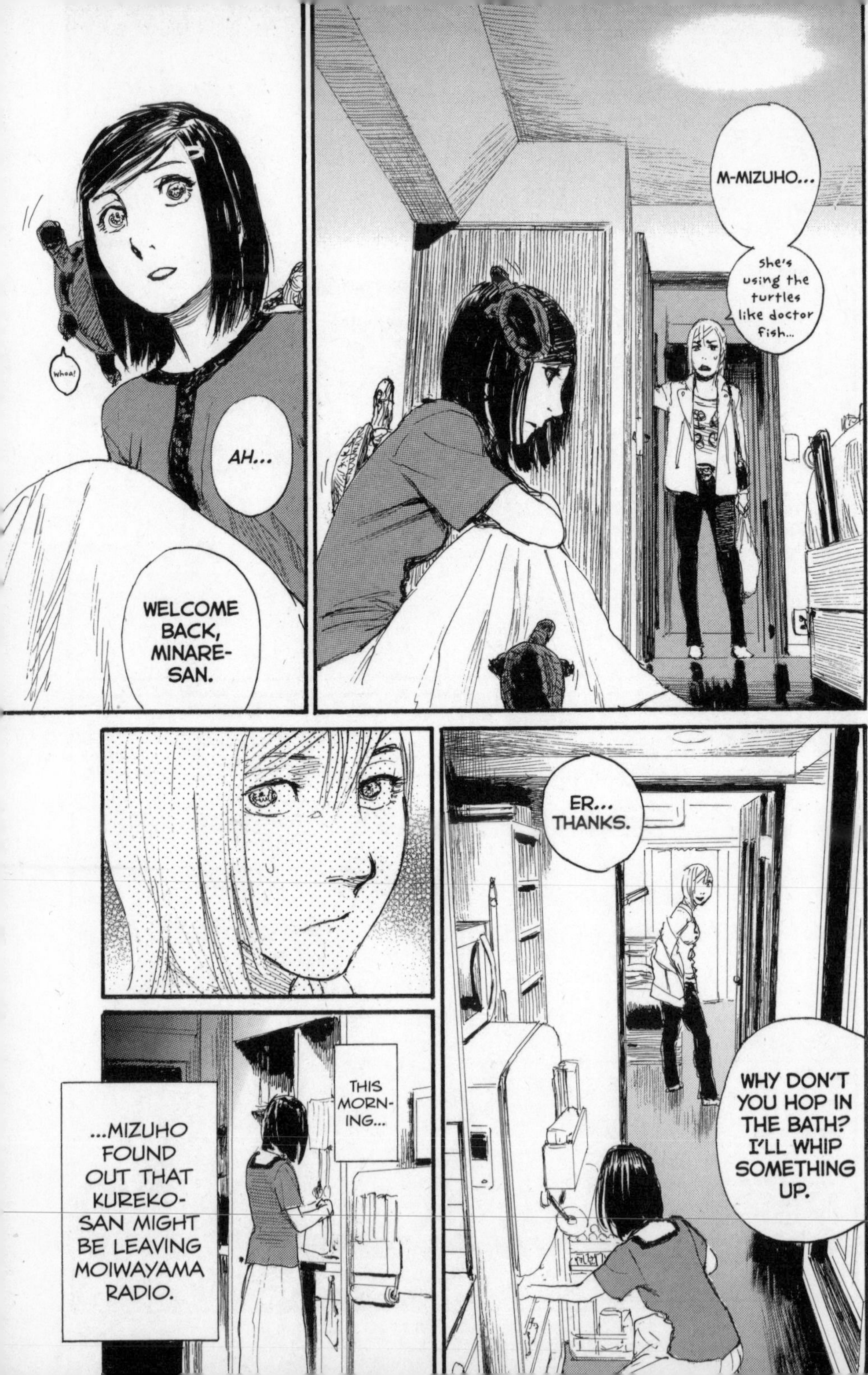
M-MIZUHO...
she's using the turtles like doctor fish...
Whoa!
AH...
WELCOME BACK, MINARE-SAN.
ER... THANKS.
WHY DON'T YOU HOP IN THE BATH? I'LL WHIP SOMETHING UP.
THIS MORNING...
...MIZUHO FOUND OUT THAT KUREKO-SAN MIGHT BE LEAVING MOIWAYAMA RADIO.

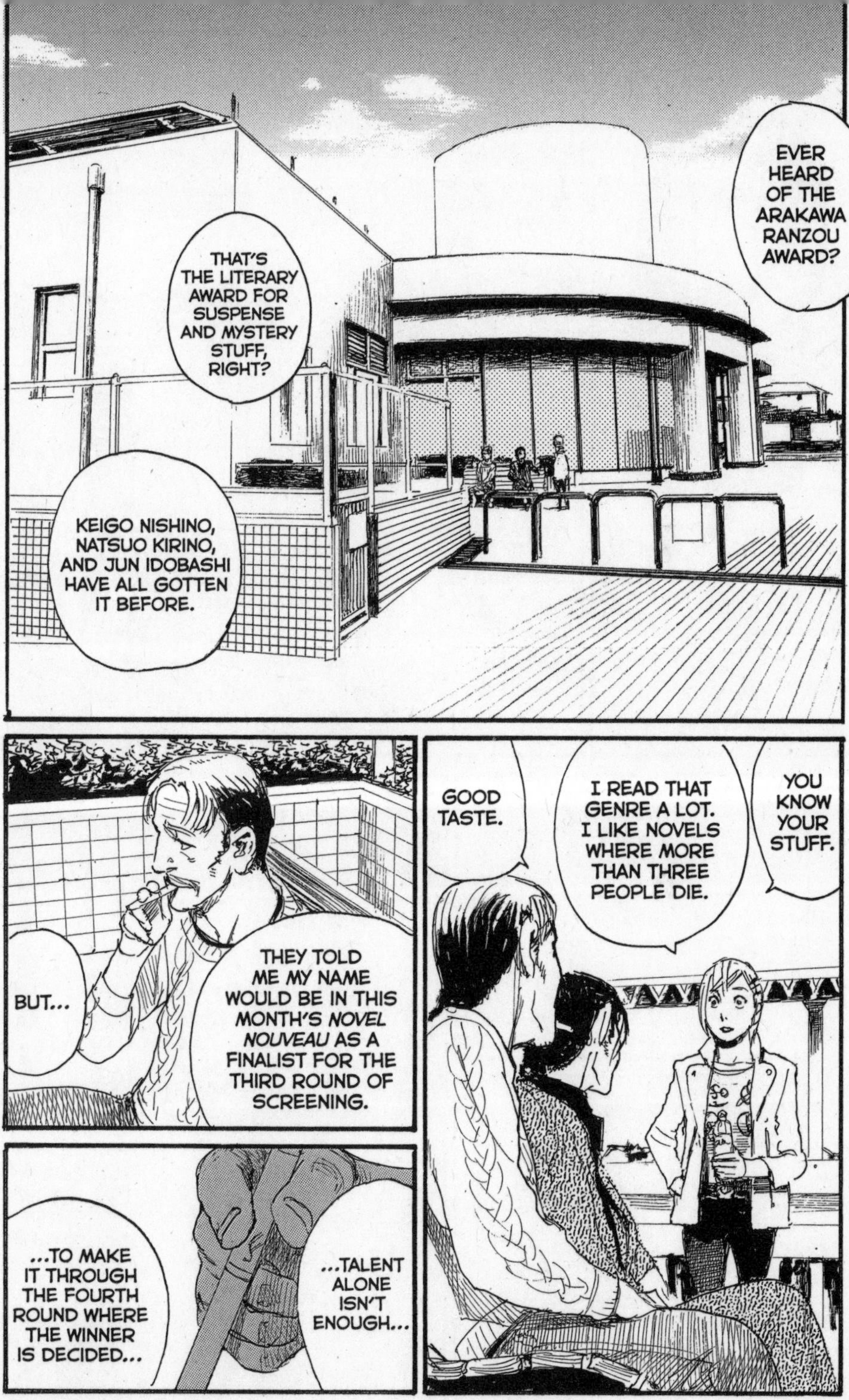
EVER HEARD OF THE ARAKAWA RANZOU AWARD?
THAT'S THE LITERARY AWARD FOR SUSPENSE AND MYSTERY STUFF, RIGHT?
KEIGO NISHINO, NATSUO KIRINO, AND JUN IDOBASHI HAVE ALL GOTTEN IT BEFORE.
YOU KNOW YOUR STUFF.
I READ THAT GENRE A LOT. I LIKE NOVELS WHERE MORE THAN THREE PEOPLE DIE.
GOOD TASTE.
THEY TOLD ME MY NAME WOULD BE IN THIS MONTH'S *NOVEL NOUVEAU* AS A FINALIST FOR THE THIRD ROUND OF SCREENING.
BUT...
...TALENT ALONE ISN'T ENOUGH...
...TO MAKE IT THROUGH THE FOURTH ROUND WHERE THE WINNER IS DECIDED...

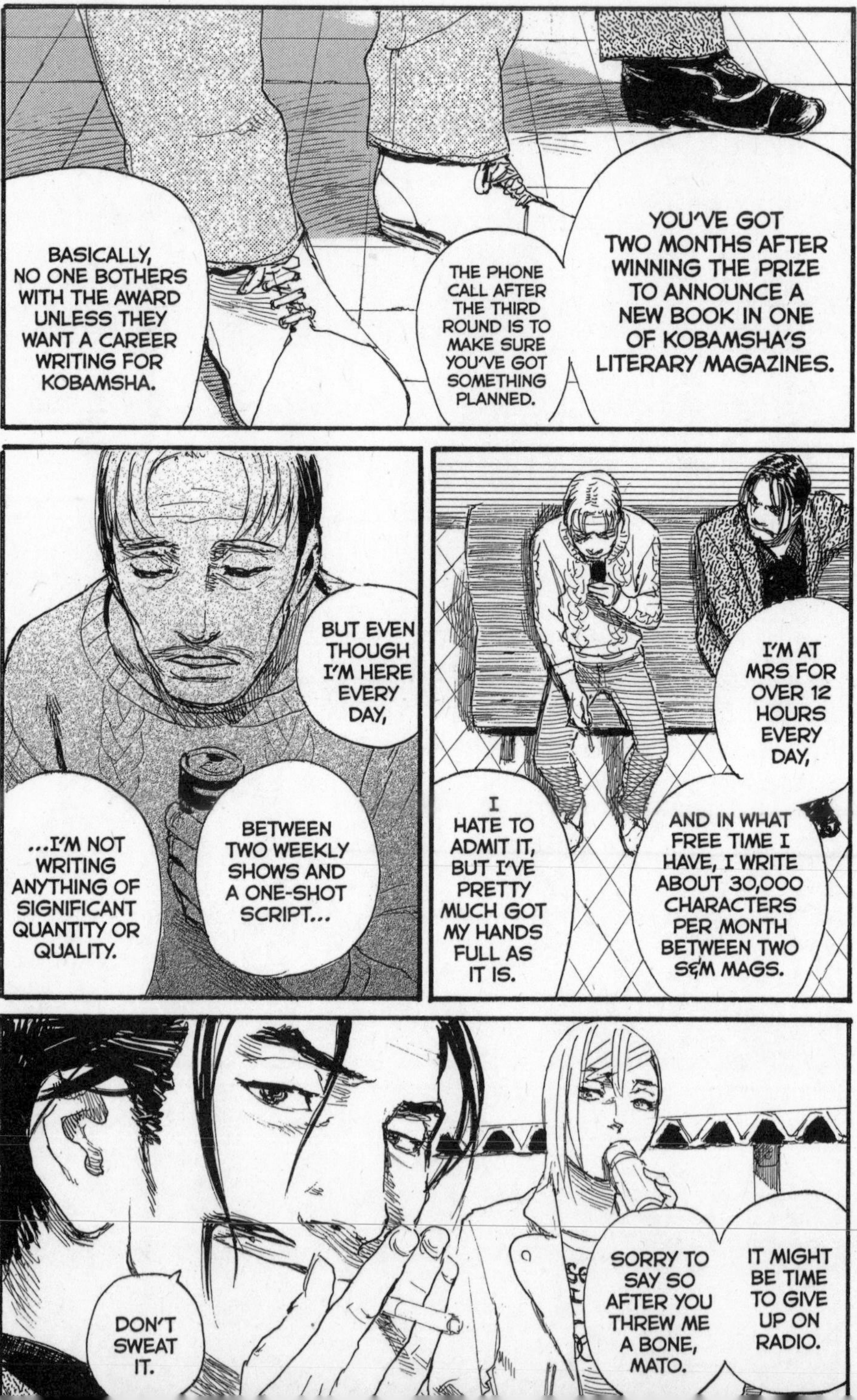
YOU'VE GOT TWO MONTHS AFTER WINNING THE PRIZE TO ANNOUNCE A NEW BOOK IN ONE OF KOBAMSHA'S LITERARY MAGAZINES.
THE PHONE CALL AFTER THE THIRD ROUND IS TO MAKE SURE YOU'VE GOT SOMETHING PLANNED.
BASICALLY, NO ONE BOTHERS WITH THE AWARD UNLESS THEY WANT A CAREER WRITING FOR KOBAMSHA.
I'M AT MRS FOR OVER 12 HOURS EVERY DAY,
AND IN WHAT FREE TIME I HAVE, I WRITE ABOUT 30,000 CHARACTERS PER MONTH BETWEEN TWO S&M MAGS.
I HATE TO ADMIT IT, BUT I'VE PRETTY MUCH GOT MY HANDS FULL AS IT IS.
BUT EVEN THOUGH I'M HERE EVERY DAY,
BETWEEN TWO WEEKLY SHOWS AND A ONE-SHOT SCRIPT...
...I'M NOT WRITING ANYTHING OF SIGNIFICANT QUANTITY OR QUALITY.
IT MIGHT BE TIME TO GIVE UP ON RADIO.
SORRY TO SAY SO AFTER YOU THREW ME A BONE, MATO.
DON'T SWEAT IT.

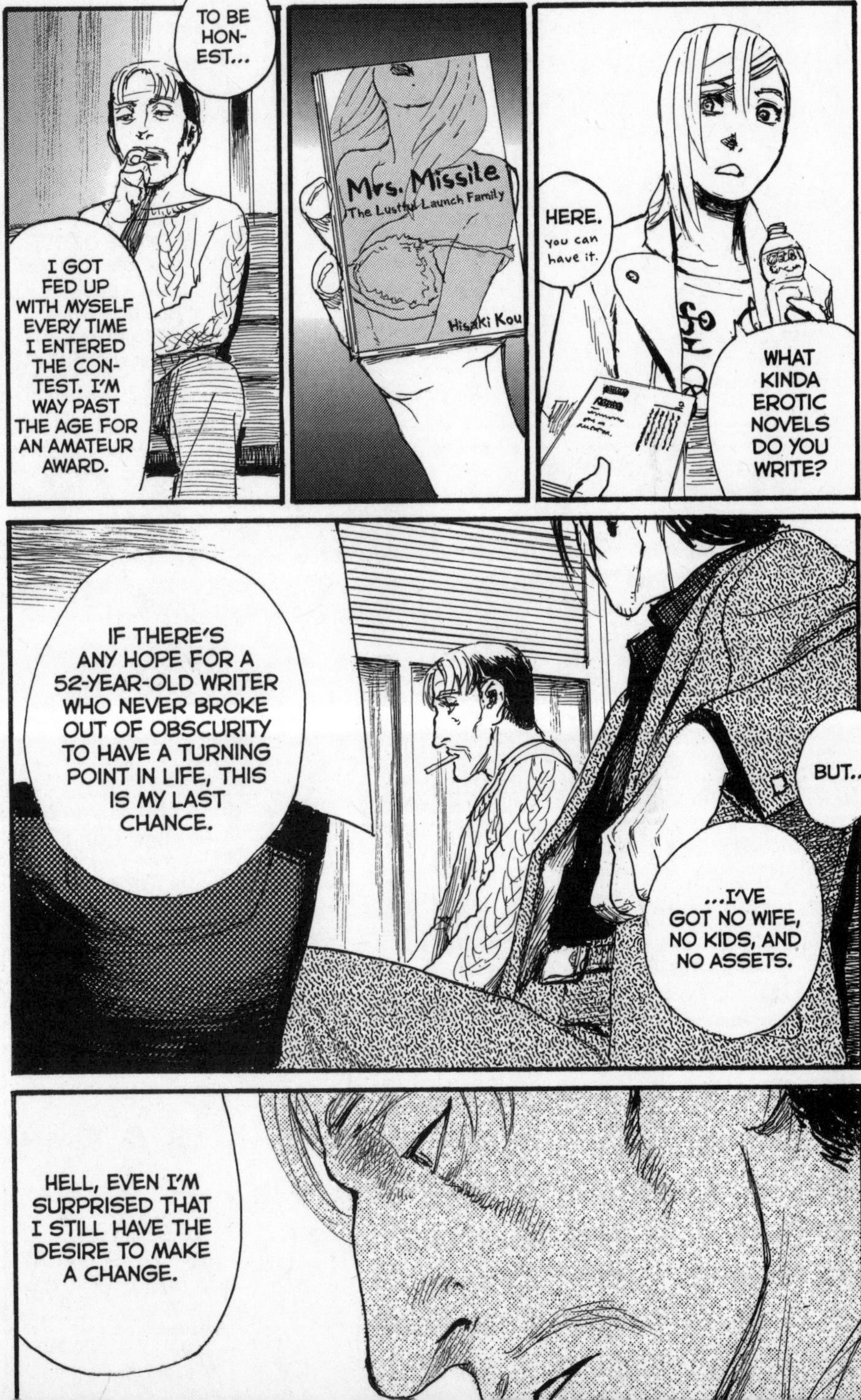
HERE.
you can have it.
WHAT KINDA EROTIC NOVELS DO YOU WRITE?
Mrs. Missile
The Lustful Launch Family
Hisaki Kou
TO BE HON-EST...
I GOT FED UP WITH MYSELF EVERY TIME I ENTERED THE CON-TEST. I'M WAY PAST THE AGE FOR AN AMATEUR AWARD.
BUT...
...I'VE GOT NO WIFE, NO KIDS, AND NO ASSETS.
IF THERE'S ANY HOPE FOR A 52-YEAR-OLD WRITER WHO NEVER BROKE OUT OF OBSCURITY TO HAVE A TURNING POINT IN LIFE, THIS IS MY LAST CHANCE.
HELL, EVEN I'M SURPRISED THAT I STILL HAVE THE DESIRE TO MAKE A CHANGE.

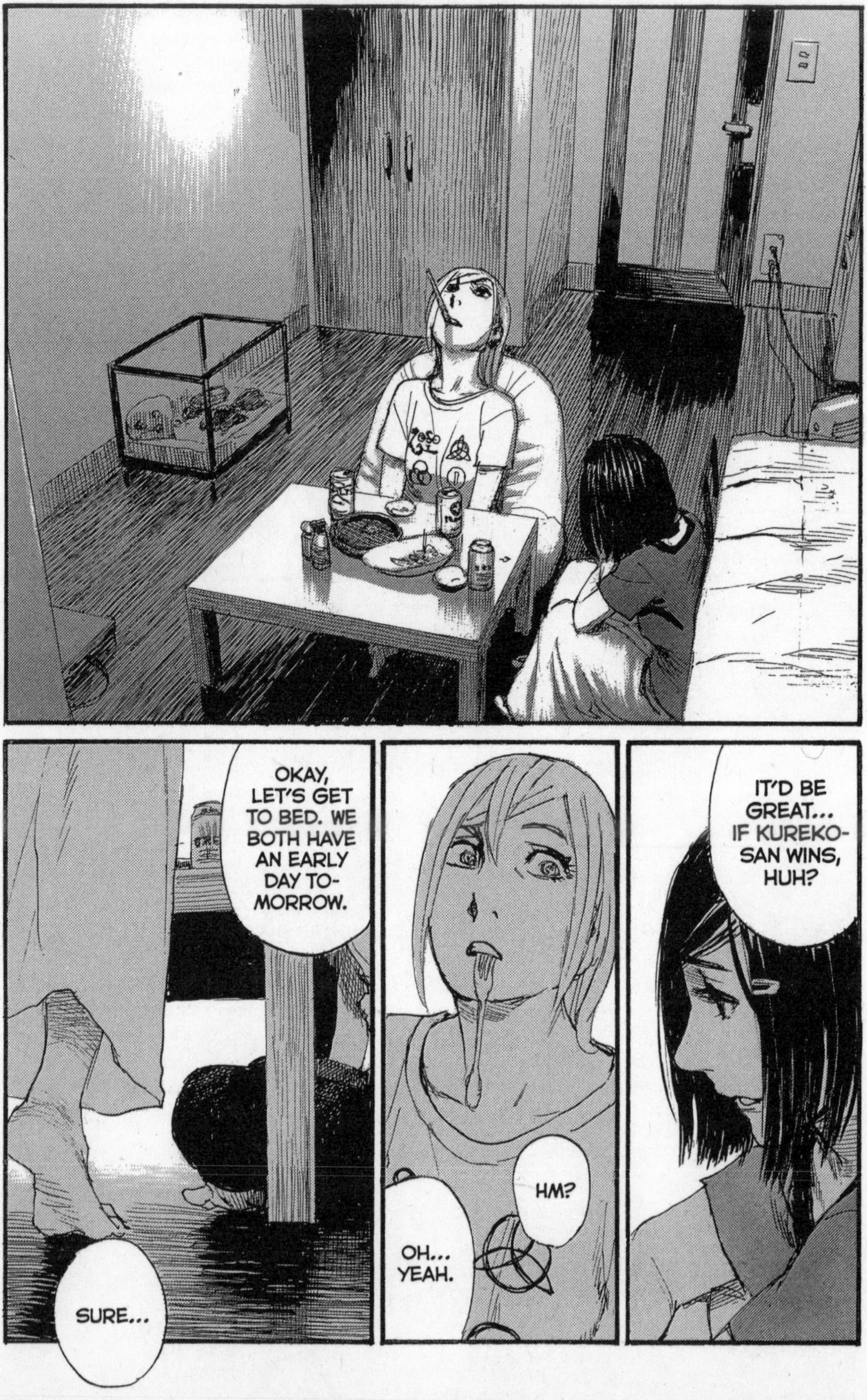
IT'D BE GREAT... IF KUREKO-SAN WINS, HUH?
HM?
OH... YEAH.
OKAY, LET'S GET TO BED. WE BOTH HAVE AN EARLY DAY TO-MORROW.
SURE...

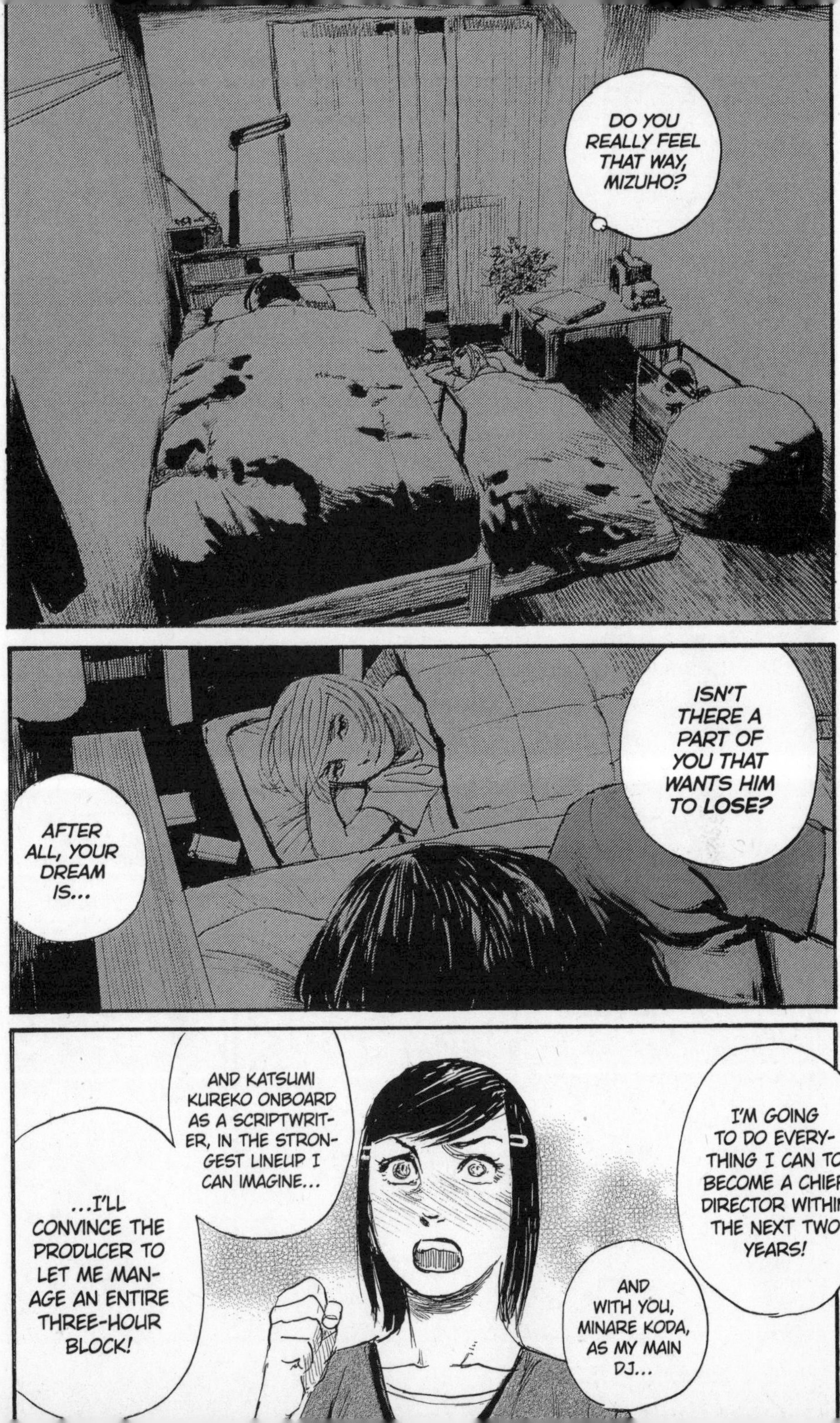
DO YOU REALLY FEEL THAT WAY, MIZUHO?
ISN'T THERE A PART OF YOU THAT WANTS HIM TO LOSE?
AFTER ALL, YOUR DREAM IS...
I'M GOING TO DO EVERYTHING I CAN TO BECOME A CHIEF DIRECTOR WITHIN THE NEXT TWO YEARS!
AND WITH YOU, MINARE KODA, AS MY MAIN DJ...
AND KATSUMI KUREKO ONBOARD AS A SCRIPTWRITER, IN THE STRONGEST LINEUP I CAN IMAGINE...
...I'LL CONVINCE THE PRODUCER TO LET ME MANAGE AN ENTIRE THREE-HOUR BLOCK!

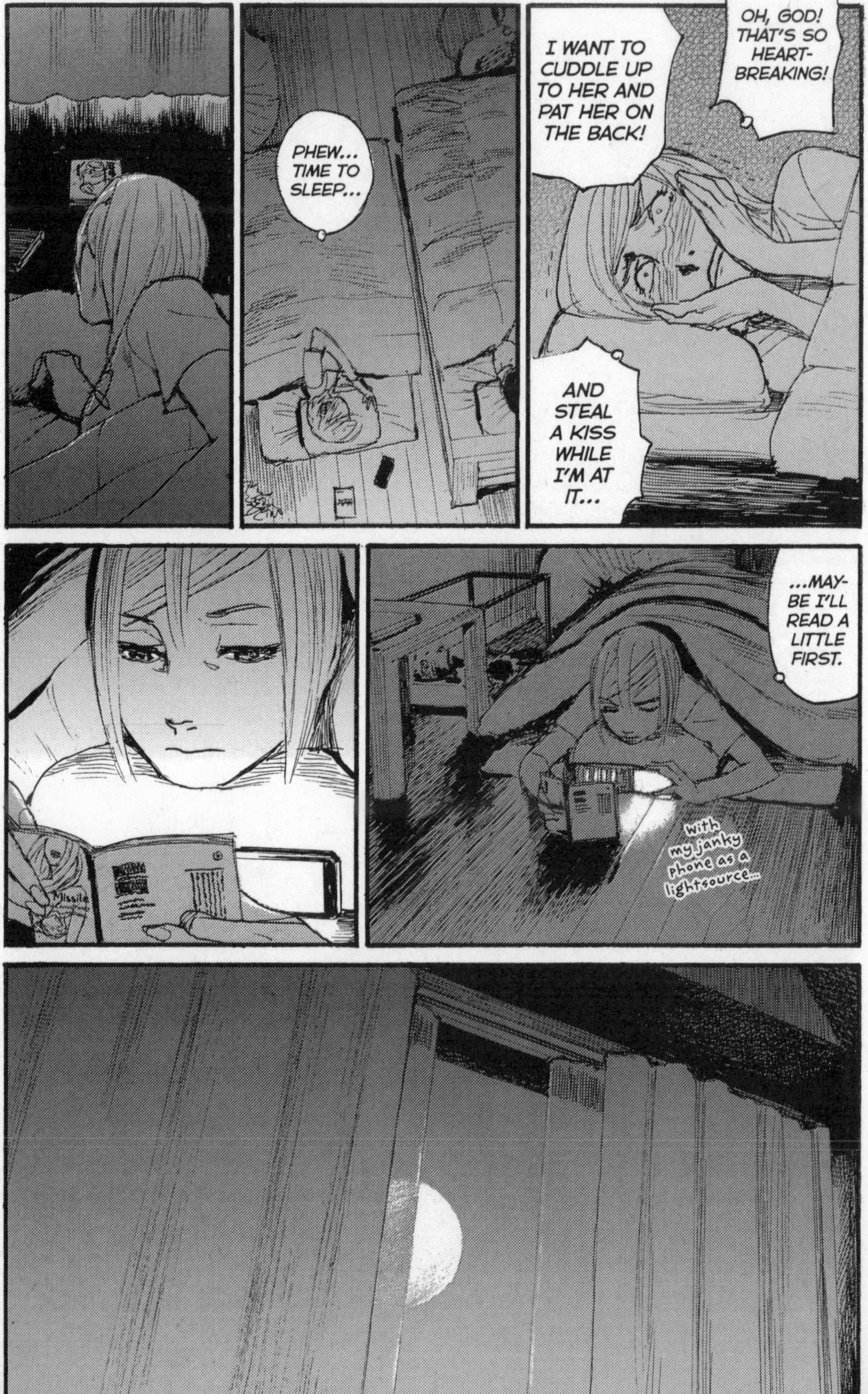
OH, GOD! THAT'S SO HEART-BREAKING!
I WANT TO CUDDLE UP TO HER AND PAT HER ON THE BACK!
AND STEAL A KISS WHILE I'M AT IT...
PHEW... TIME TO SLEEP...
...MAY-BE I'LL READ A LITTLE FIRST.
With my janky phone as a lightsource...
Missile

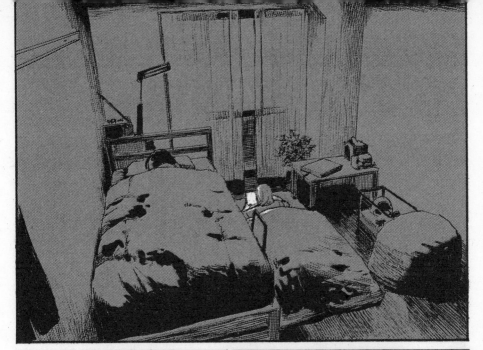

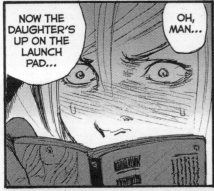

NOW THE DAUGHTER'S UP ON THE LAUNCH PAD...

OH, MAN...

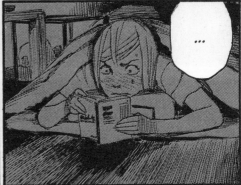

...

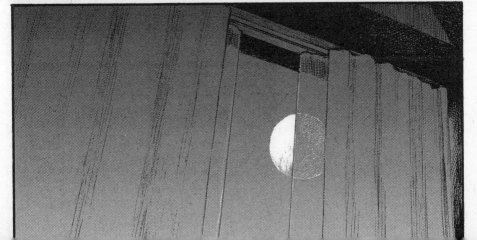

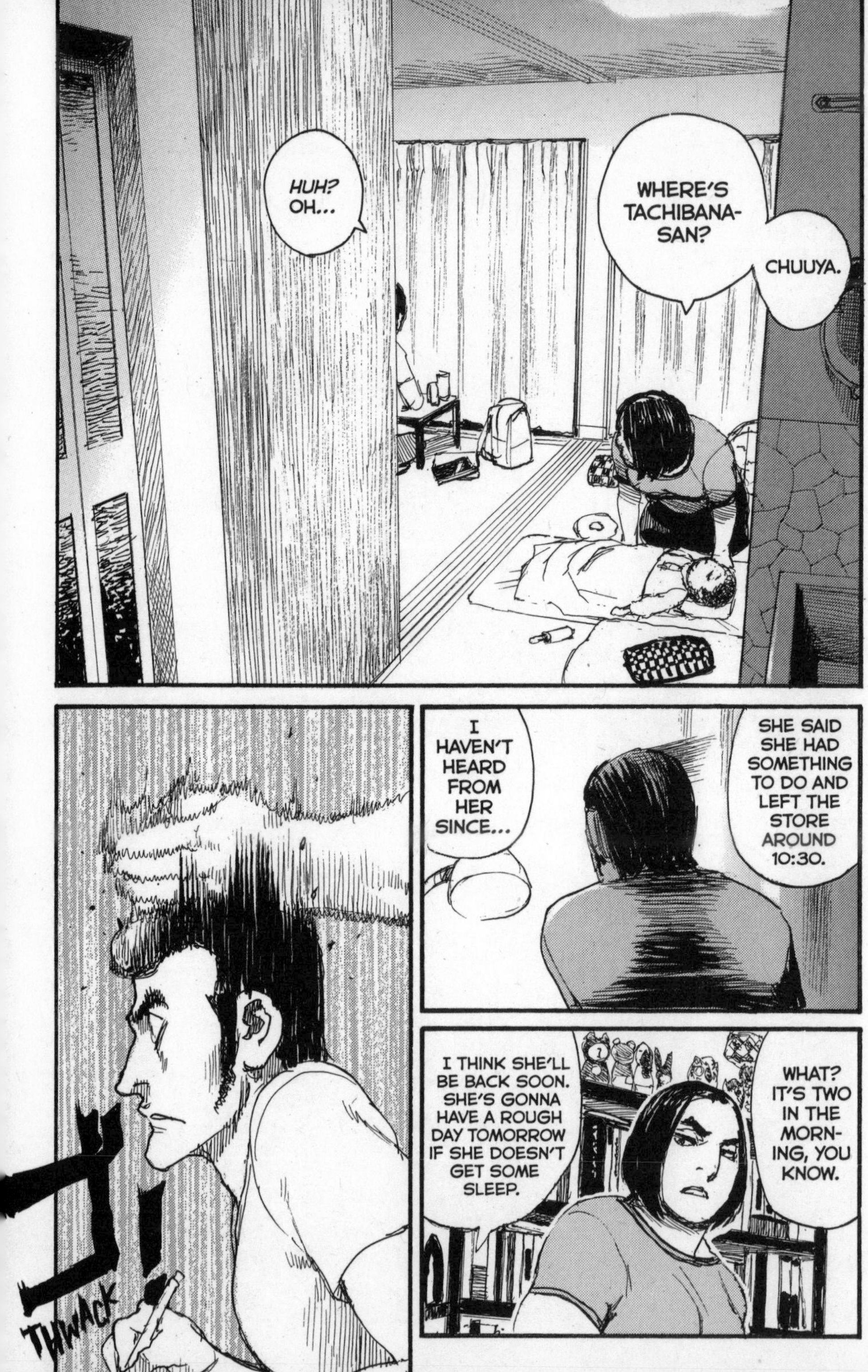
CHUUYA.
WHERE'S TACHIBANA-SAN?
HUH? OH...
SHE SAID SHE HAD SOMETHING TO DO AND LEFT THE STORE AROUND 10:30.
I HAVEN'T HEARD FROM HER SINCE...
WHAT? IT'S TWO IN THE MORNING, YOU KNOW.
I THINK SHE'LL BE BACK SOON. SHE'S GONNA HAVE A ROUGH DAY TOMORROW IF SHE DOESN'T GET SOME SLEEP.
THWACK

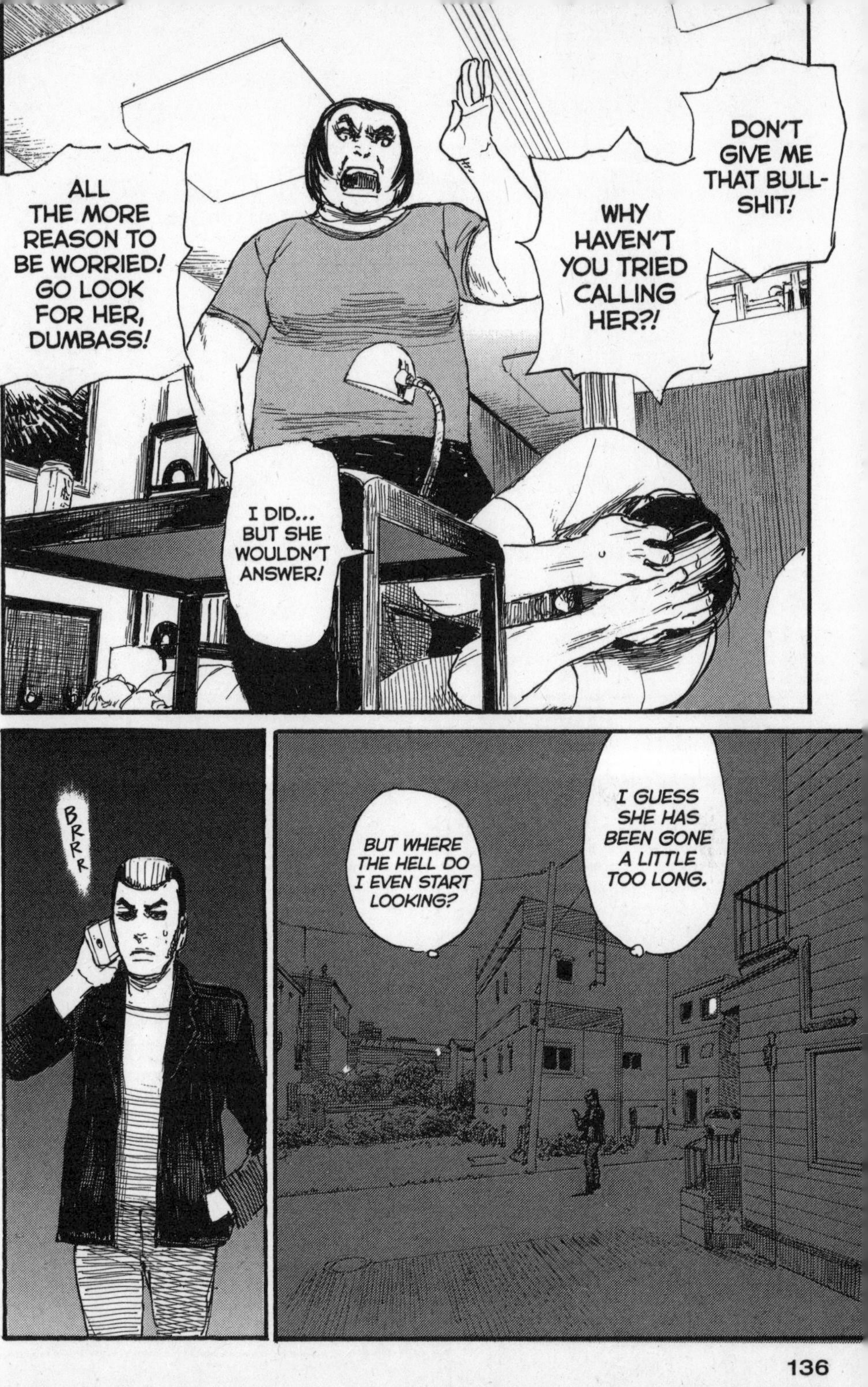
DON'T GIVE ME THAT BULL-SHIT!
WHY HAVEN'T YOU TRIED CALLING HER?!
ALL THE MORE REASON TO BE WORRIED! GO LOOK FOR HER, DUMBASS!
I DID... BUT SHE WOULDN'T ANSWER!
I GUESS SHE HAS BEEN GONE A LITTLE TOO LONG.
BUT WHERE THE HELL DO I EVEN START LOOKING?
BRRR

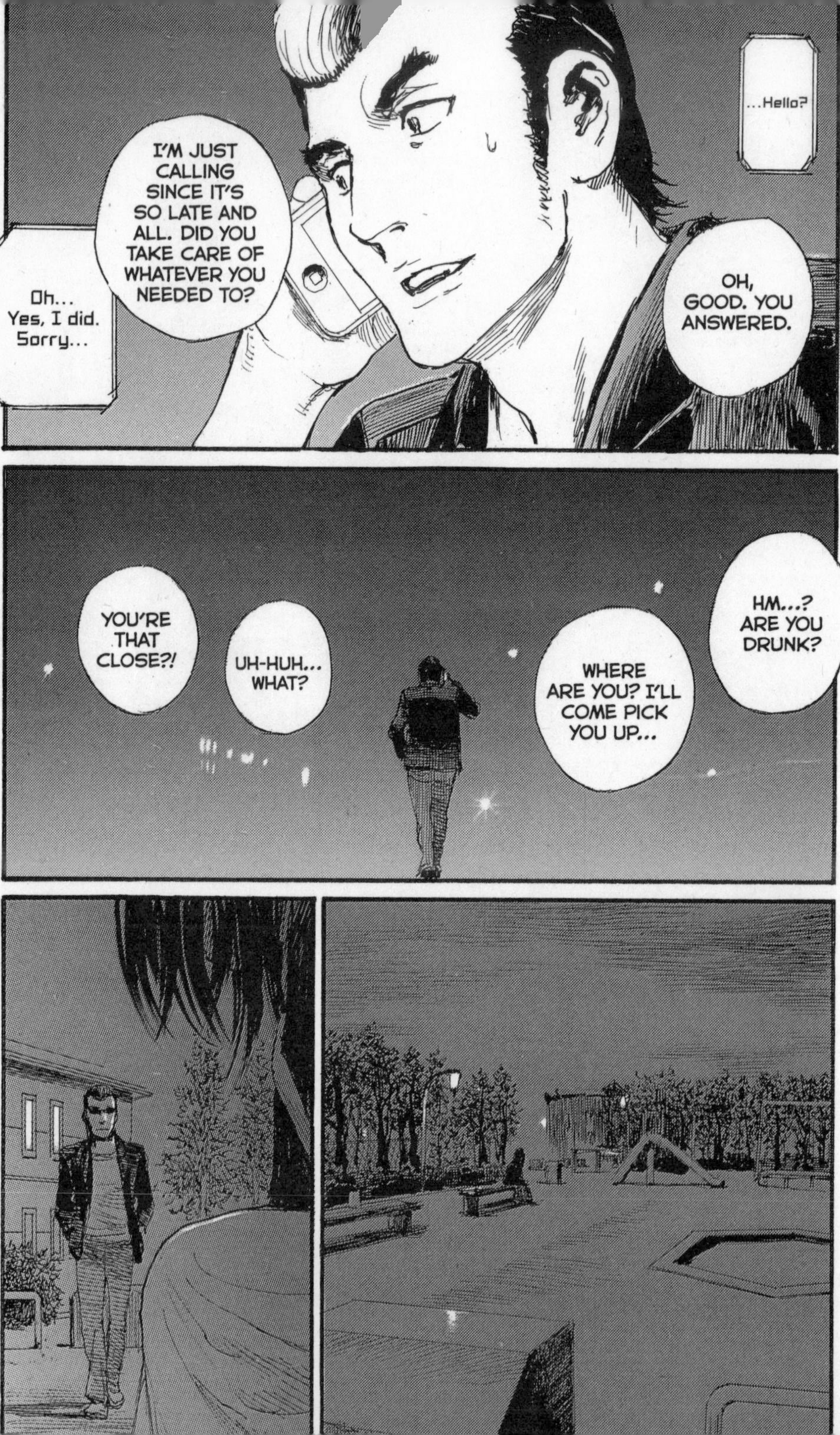
...Hello?
OH, GOOD. YOU ANSWERED.
I'M JUST CALLING SINCE IT'S SO LATE AND ALL. DID YOU TAKE CARE OF WHATEVER YOU NEEDED TO?
Oh... Yes, I did. Sorry...
HM...? ARE YOU DRUNK?
WHERE ARE YOU? I'LL COME PICK YOU UP...
UH-HUH... WHAT?
YOU'RE THAT CLOSE?!

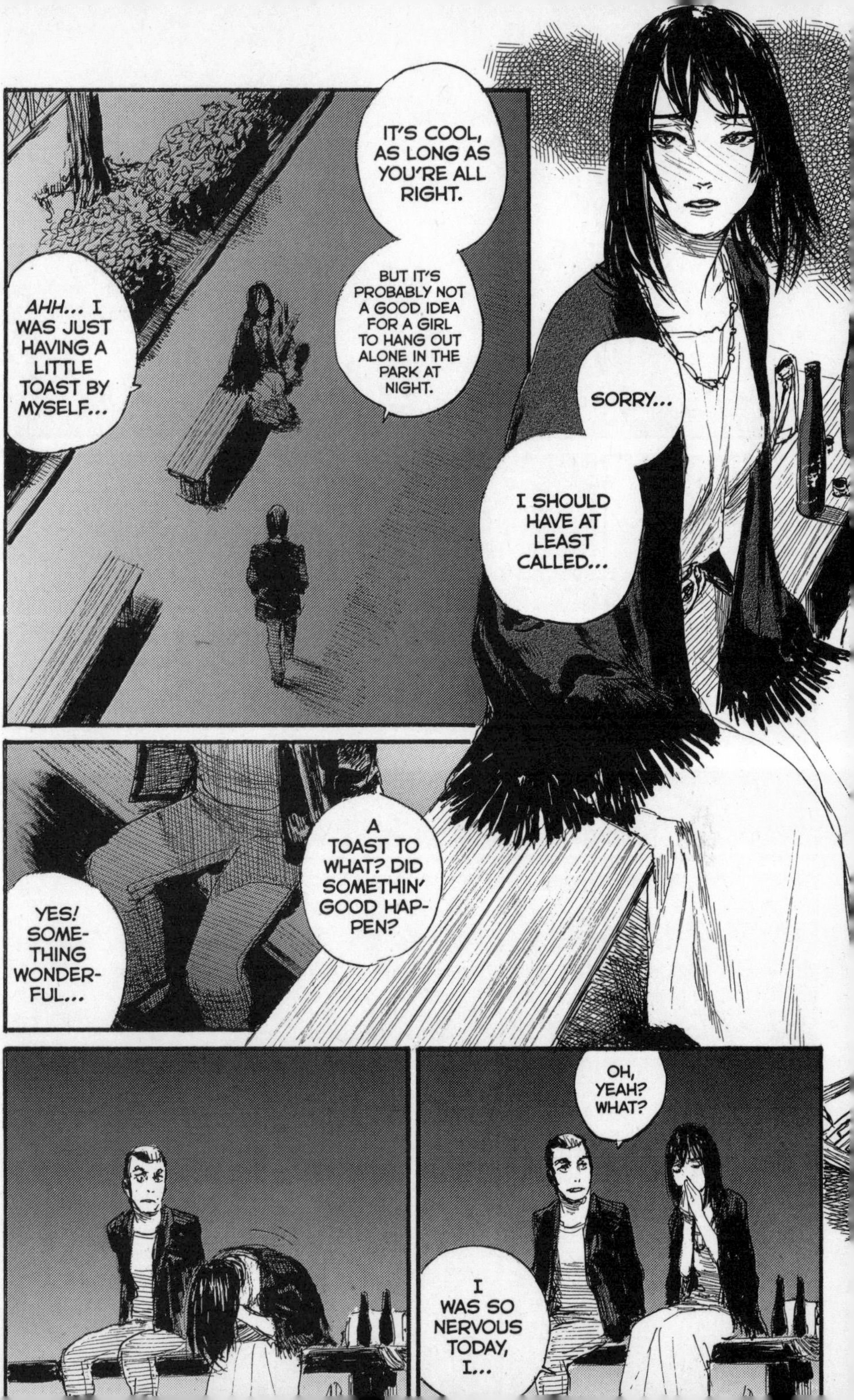
SORRY...
I SHOULD HAVE AT LEAST CALLED...
IT'S COOL, AS LONG AS YOU'RE ALL RIGHT.
BUT IT'S PROBABLY NOT A GOOD IDEA FOR A GIRL TO HANG OUT ALONE IN THE PARK AT NIGHT.
AHH... I WAS JUST HAVING A LITTLE TOAST BY MYSELF...
A TOAST TO WHAT? DID SOMETHIN' GOOD HAP-PEN?
YES! SOME-THING WONDER-FUL...
OH, YEAH? WHAT?
I WAS SO NERVOUS TODAY, I...

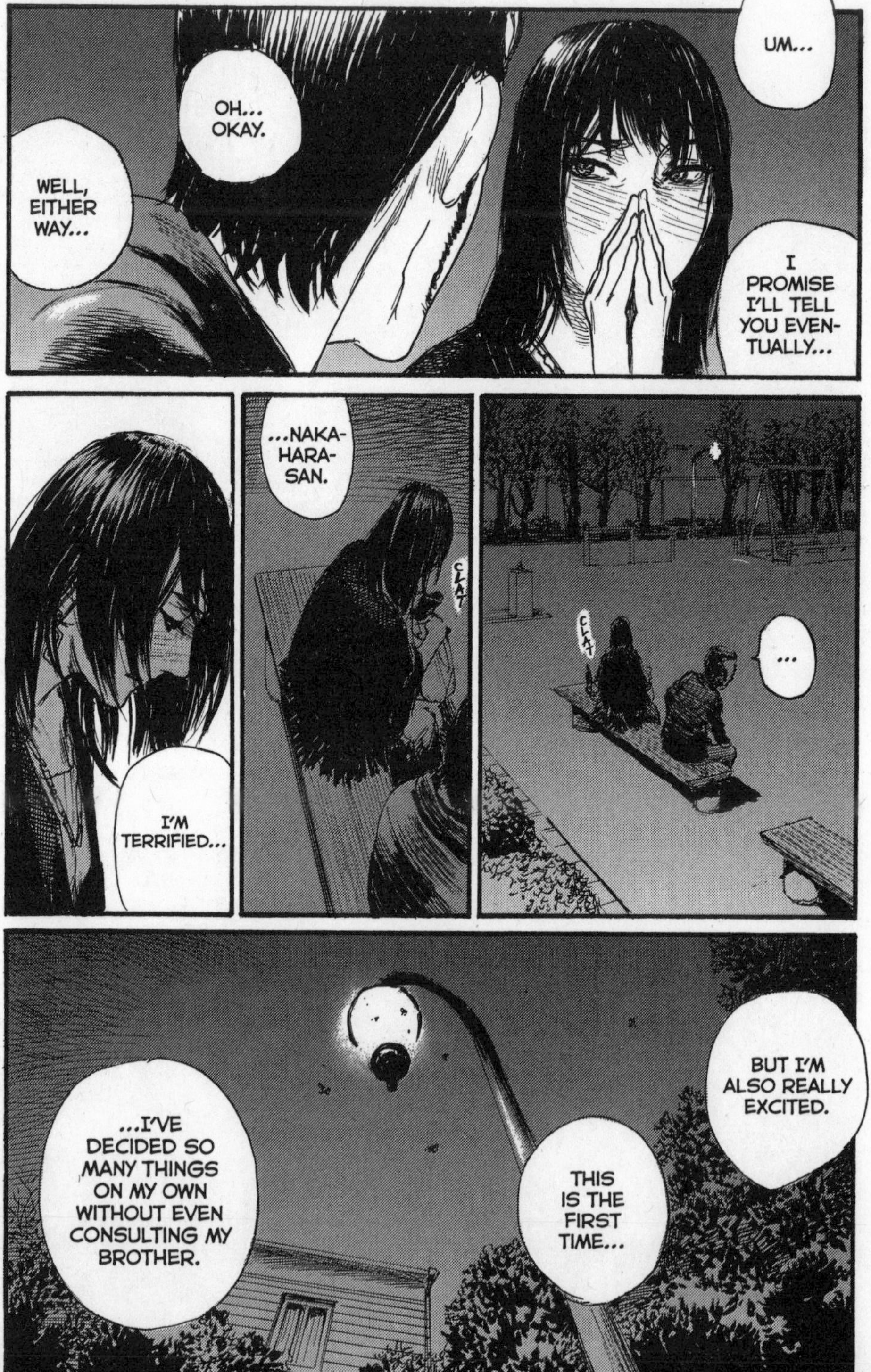
UM...
I PROMISE I'LL TELL YOU EVEN-TUALLY...
OH... OKAY.
WELL, EITHER WAY...
CLAT
...
...NAKA-HARA-SAN.
CLAT
I'M TERRIFIED...
BUT I'M ALSO REALLY EXCITED.
THIS IS THE FIRST TIME...
...I'VE DECIDED SO MANY THINGS ON MY OWN WITHOUT EVEN CONSULTING MY BROTHER.

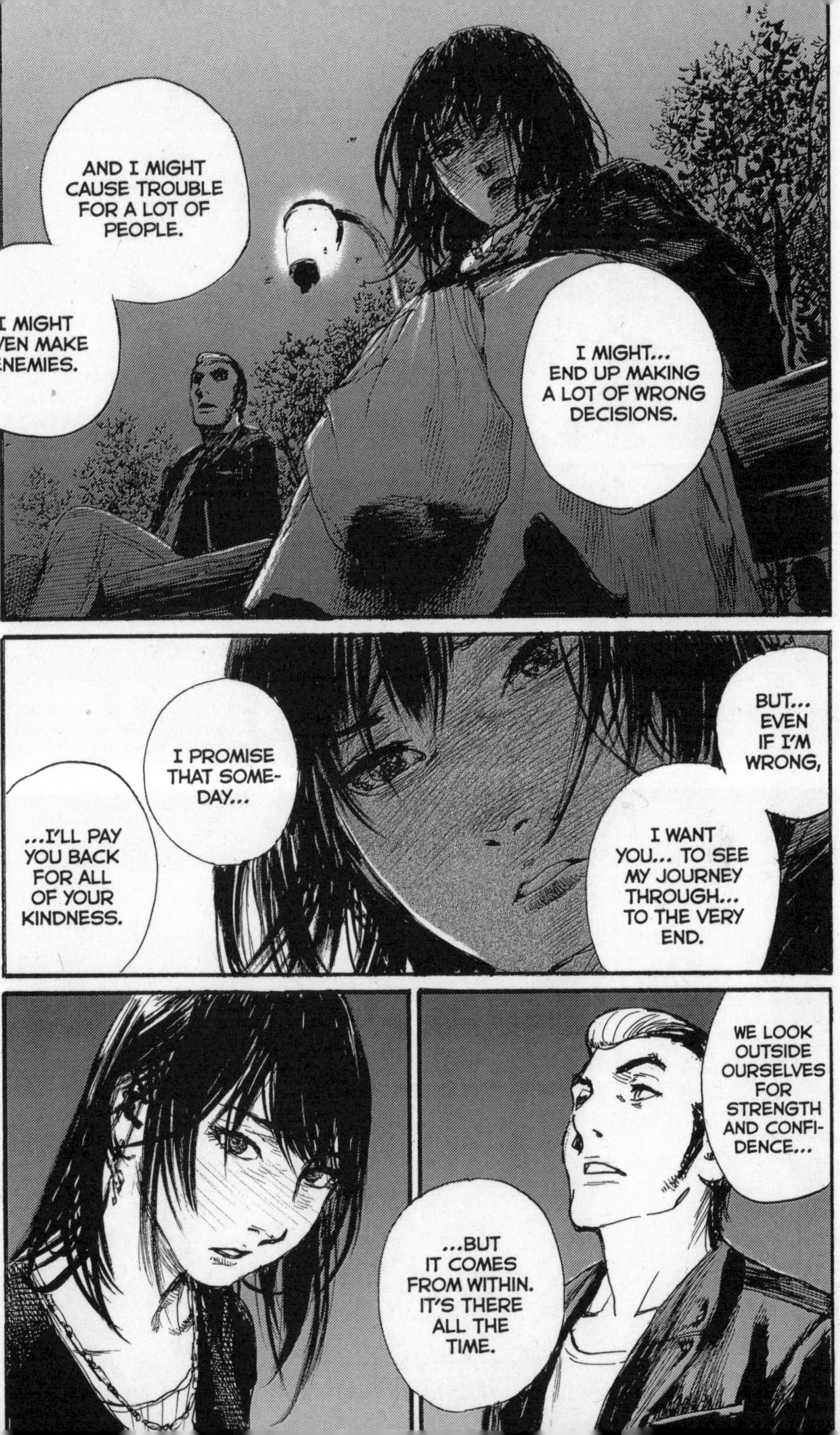
I MIGHT... END UP MAKING A LOT OF WRONG DECISIONS.
AND I MIGHT CAUSE TROUBLE FOR A LOT OF PEOPLE.
I MIGHT EVEN MAKE ENEMIES.
BUT... EVEN IF I'M WRONG,
I WANT YOU... TO SEE MY JOURNEY THROUGH... TO THE VERY END.
I PROMISE THAT SOME-DAY...
...I'LL PAY YOU BACK FOR ALL OF YOUR KINDNESS.
WE LOOK OUTSIDE OURSELVES FOR STRENGTH AND CONFI-DENCE...
...BUT IT COMES FROM WITHIN. IT'S THERE ALL THE TIME.

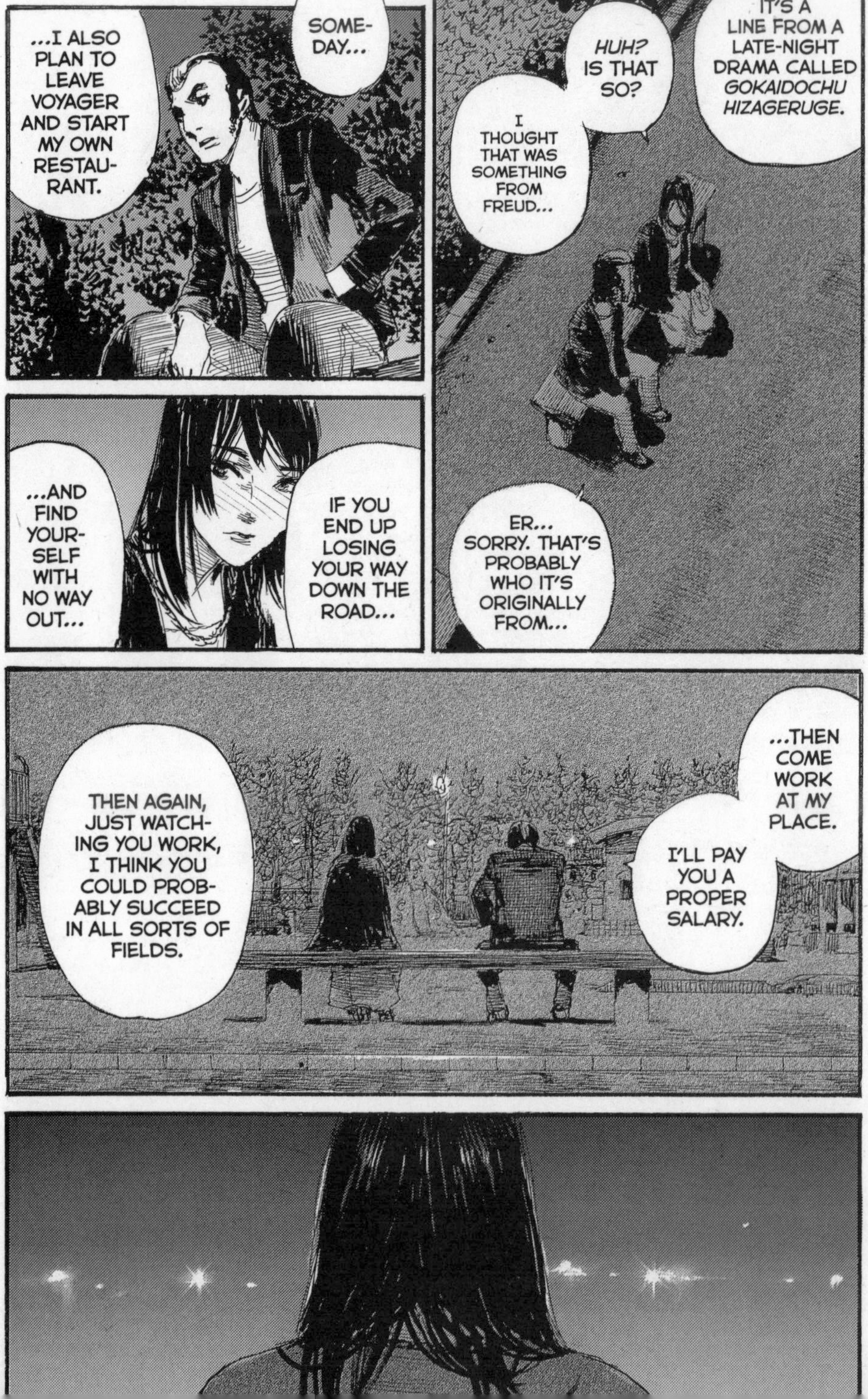
IT'S A LINE FROM A LATE-NIGHT DRAMA CALLED *GOKAIDOCHU HIZAGERUGE*.
HUH? IS THAT SO?
I THOUGHT THAT WAS SOMETHING FROM FREUD...
ER... SORRY. THAT'S PROBABLY WHO IT'S ORIGINALLY FROM...
SOME-DAY...
...I ALSO PLAN TO LEAVE VOYAGER AND START MY OWN RESTAU-RANT.
IF YOU END UP LOSING YOUR WAY DOWN THE ROAD...
...AND FIND YOUR-SELF WITH NO WAY OUT...
...THEN COME WORK AT MY PLACE.
I'LL PAY YOU A PROPER SALARY.
THEN AGAIN, JUST WATCH-ING YOU WORK, I THINK YOU COULD PROB-ABLY SUCCEED IN ALL SORTS OF FIELDS.

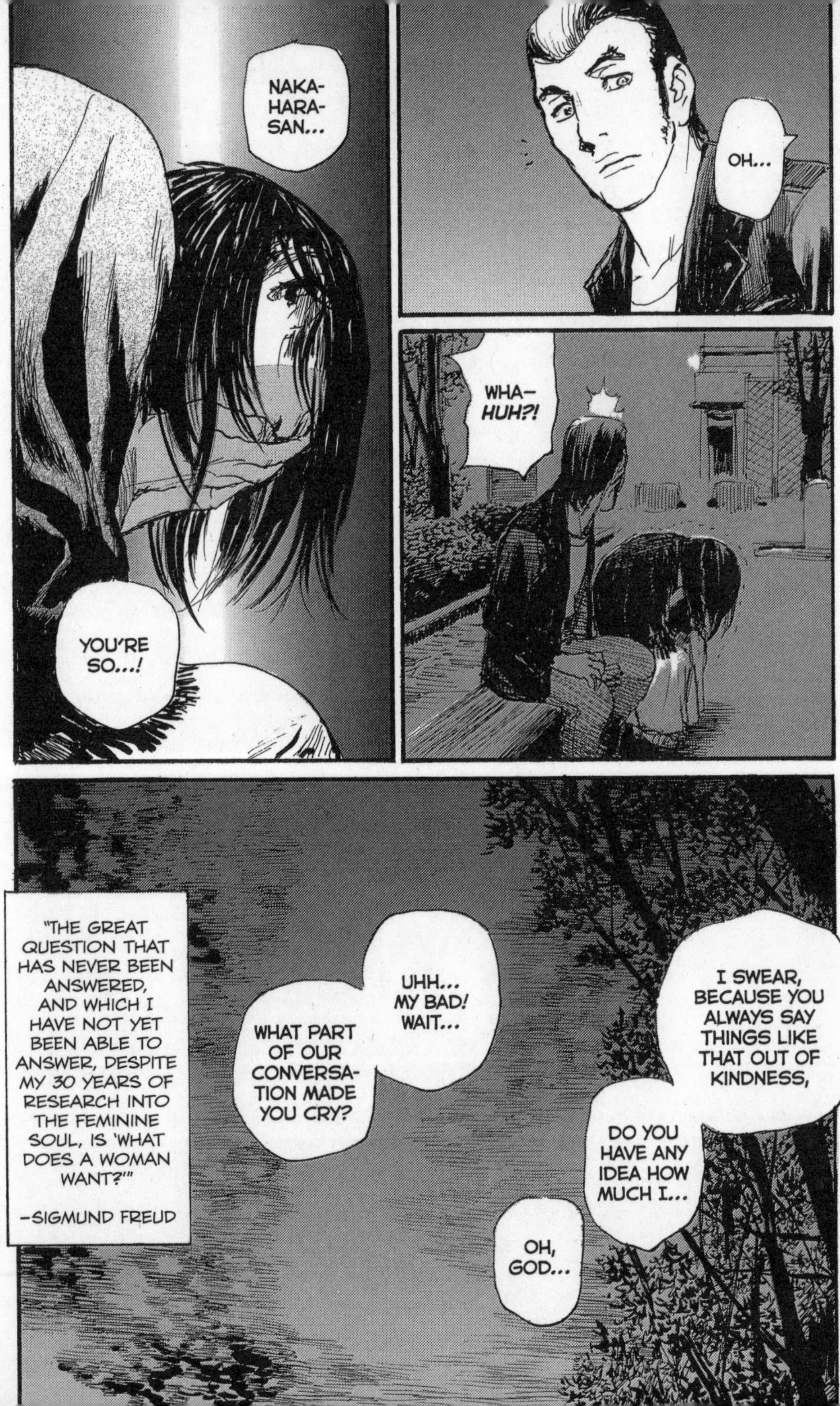
OH...
WHA-HUH?!
NAKA-HARA-SAN...
YOU'RE SO...!
I SWEAR, BECAUSE YOU ALWAYS SAY THINGS LIKE THAT OUT OF KINDNESS,
UHH... MY BAD! WAIT...
WHAT PART OF OUR CONVERSA-TION MADE YOU CRY?
DO YOU HAVE ANY IDEA HOW MUCH I...
OH, GOD...
"THE GREAT QUESTION THAT HAS NEVER BEEN ANSWERED, AND WHICH I HAVE NOT YET BEEN ABLE TO ANSWER, DESPITE MY 30 YEARS OF RESEARCH INTO THE FEMININE SOUL, IS 'WHAT DOES A WOMAN WANT?'"
–SIGMUND FREUD

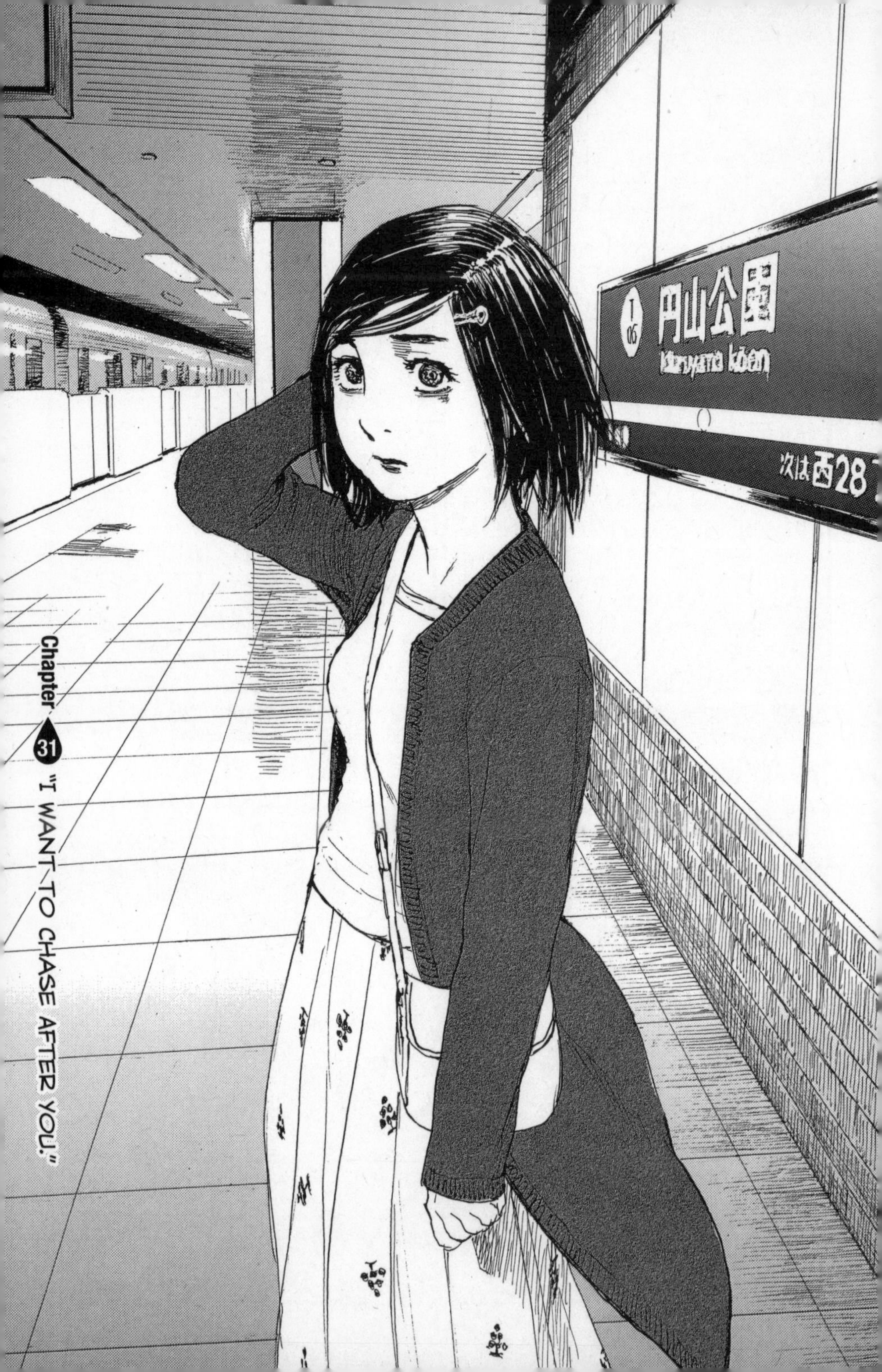
Chapter 31 "I WANT TO CHASE AFTER YOU."
円山公園
次は西28

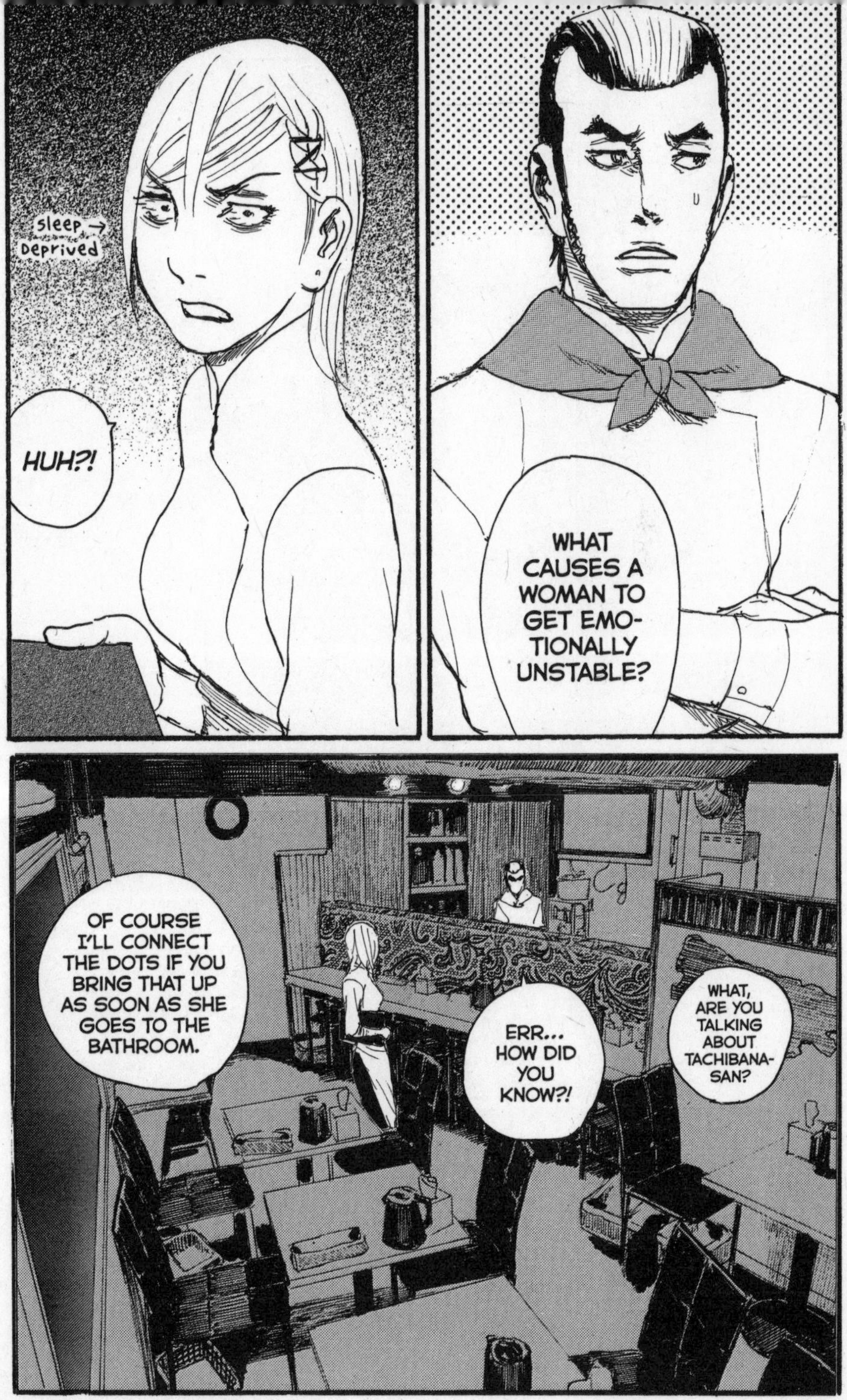
WHAT CAUSES A WOMAN TO GET EMO-TIONALLY UNSTABLE?
sleep → Deprived
HUH?!
WHAT, ARE YOU TALKING ABOUT TACHIBANA-SAN?
ERR... HOW DID YOU KNOW?!
OF COURSE I'LL CONNECT THE DOTS IF YOU BRING THAT UP AS SOON AS SHE GOES TO THE BATHROOM.

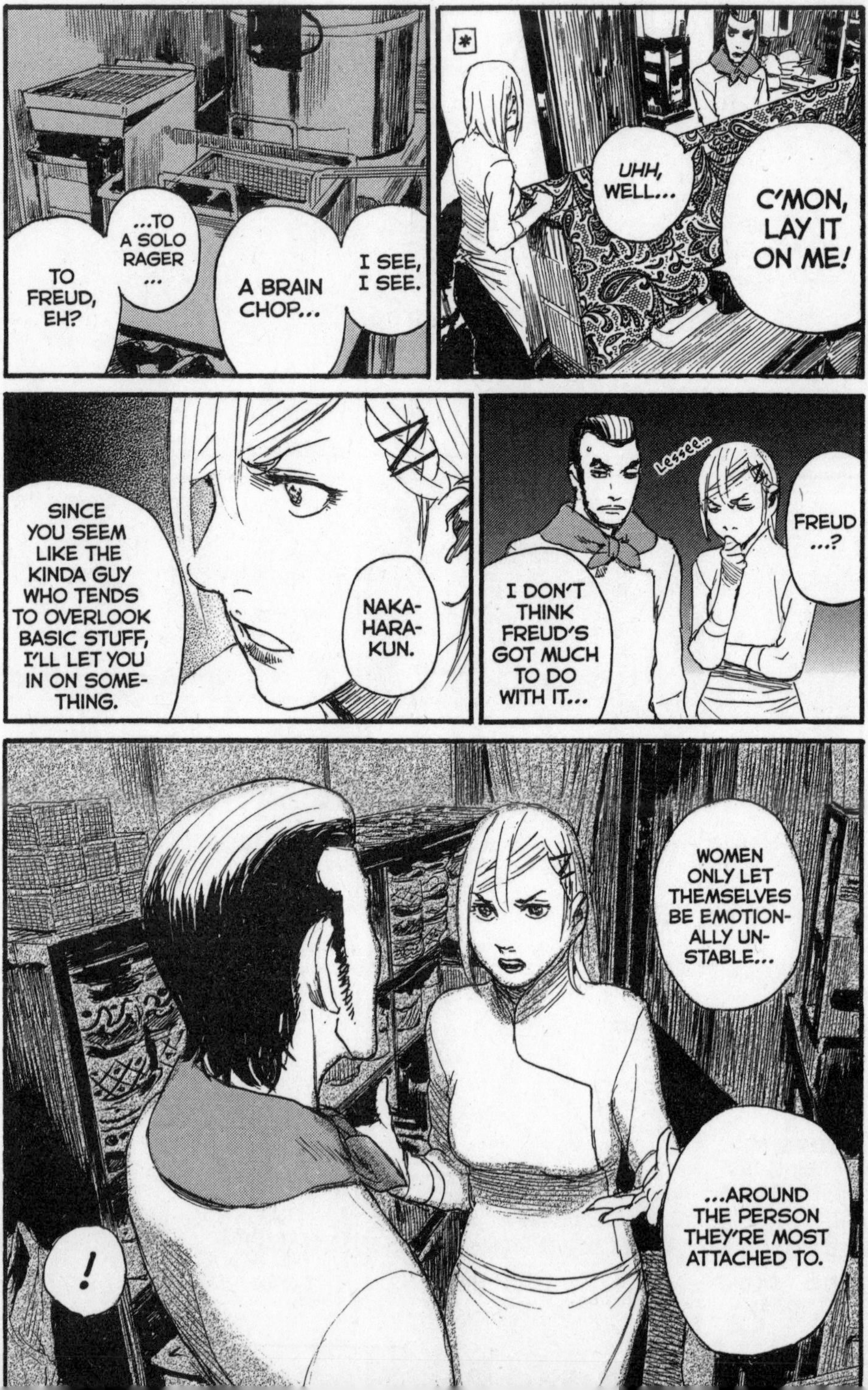

*
C'MON, LAY IT ON ME!
UHH, WELL...
I SEE, I SEE.
A BRAIN CHOP...
...TO A SOLO RAGER ...
TO FREUD, EH?
FREUD ...?
Lessee...
I DON'T THINK FREUD'S GOT MUCH TO DO WITH IT...
NAKA-HARA-KUN.
SINCE YOU SEEM LIKE THE KINDA GUY WHO TENDS TO OVERLOOK BASIC STUFF, I'LL LET YOU IN ON SOME-THING.
WOMEN ONLY LET THEMSELVES BE EMOTION-ALLY UN-STABLE...
...AROUND THE PERSON THEY'RE MOST ATTACHED TO.
!

*A WOMAN WHO COMES RUNNING AT THE SMELL OF GOSSIP

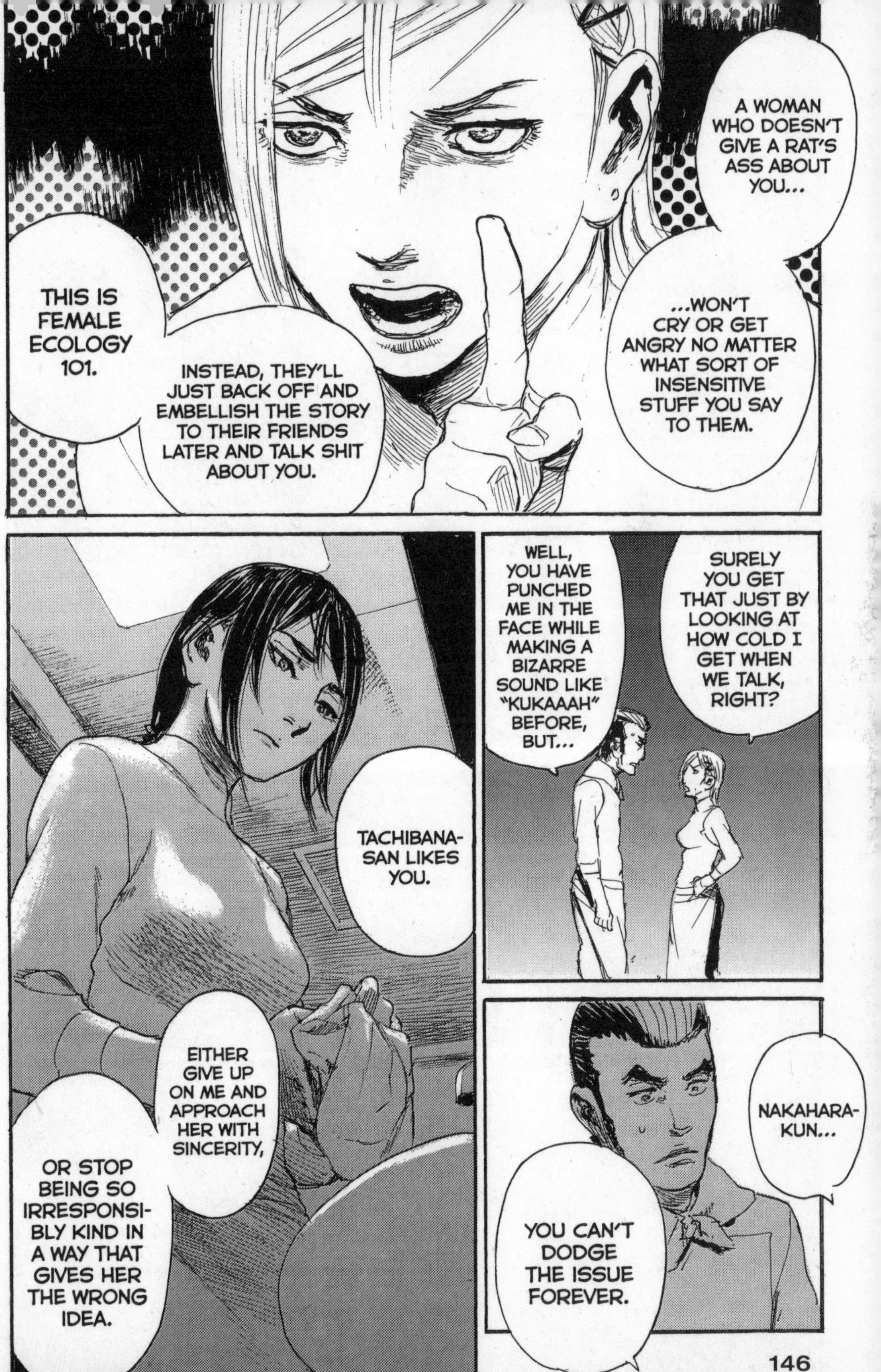
A WOMAN WHO DOESN'T GIVE A RAT'S ASS ABOUT YOU...
...WON'T CRY OR GET ANGRY NO MATTER WHAT SORT OF INSENSITIVE STUFF YOU SAY TO THEM.
INSTEAD, THEY'LL JUST BACK OFF AND EMBELLISH THE STORY TO THEIR FRIENDS LATER AND TALK SHIT ABOUT YOU.
THIS IS FEMALE ECOLOGY 101.
SURELY YOU GET THAT JUST BY LOOKING AT HOW COLD I GET WHEN WE TALK, RIGHT?
WELL, YOU HAVE PUNCHED ME IN THE FACE WHILE MAKING A BIZARRE SOUND LIKE "KUKAAAH" BEFORE, BUT...
NAKAHARA-KUN...
YOU CAN'T DODGE THE ISSUE FOREVER.
TACHIBANA-SAN LIKES YOU.
EITHER GIVE UP ON ME AND APPROACH HER WITH SINCERITY,
OR STOP BEING SO IRRESPONSIBLY KIND IN A WAY THAT GIVES HER THE WRONG IDEA.

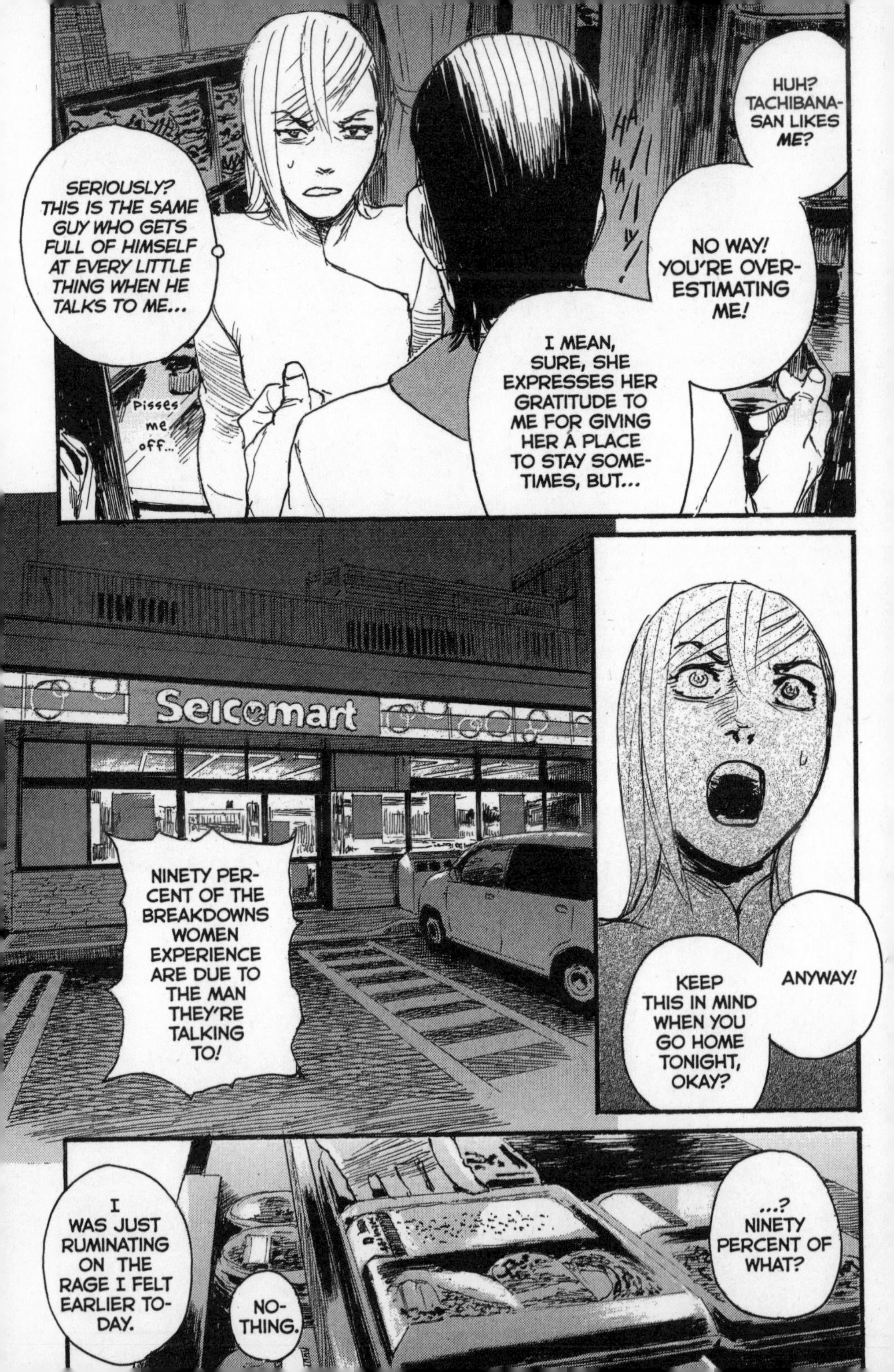

HUH? TACHIBANA-SAN LIKES ME?
NO WAY! YOU'RE OVER-ESTIMATING ME!
I MEAN, SURE, SHE EXPRESSES HER GRATITUDE TO ME FOR GIVING HER A PLACE TO STAY SOMETIMES, BUT...
SERIOUSLY? THIS IS THE SAME GUY WHO GETS FULL OF HIMSELF AT EVERY LITTLE THING WHEN HE TALKS TO ME...
Pisses me off...
ANYWAY!
KEEP THIS IN MIND WHEN YOU GO HOME TONIGHT, OKAY?
Seicomart
NINETY PERCENT OF THE BREAKDOWNS WOMEN EXPERIENCE ARE DUE TO THE MAN THEY'RE TALKING TO!
...? NINETY PERCENT OF WHAT?
NO-THING.
I WAS JUST RUMINATING ON THE RAGE I FELT EARLIER TODAY.

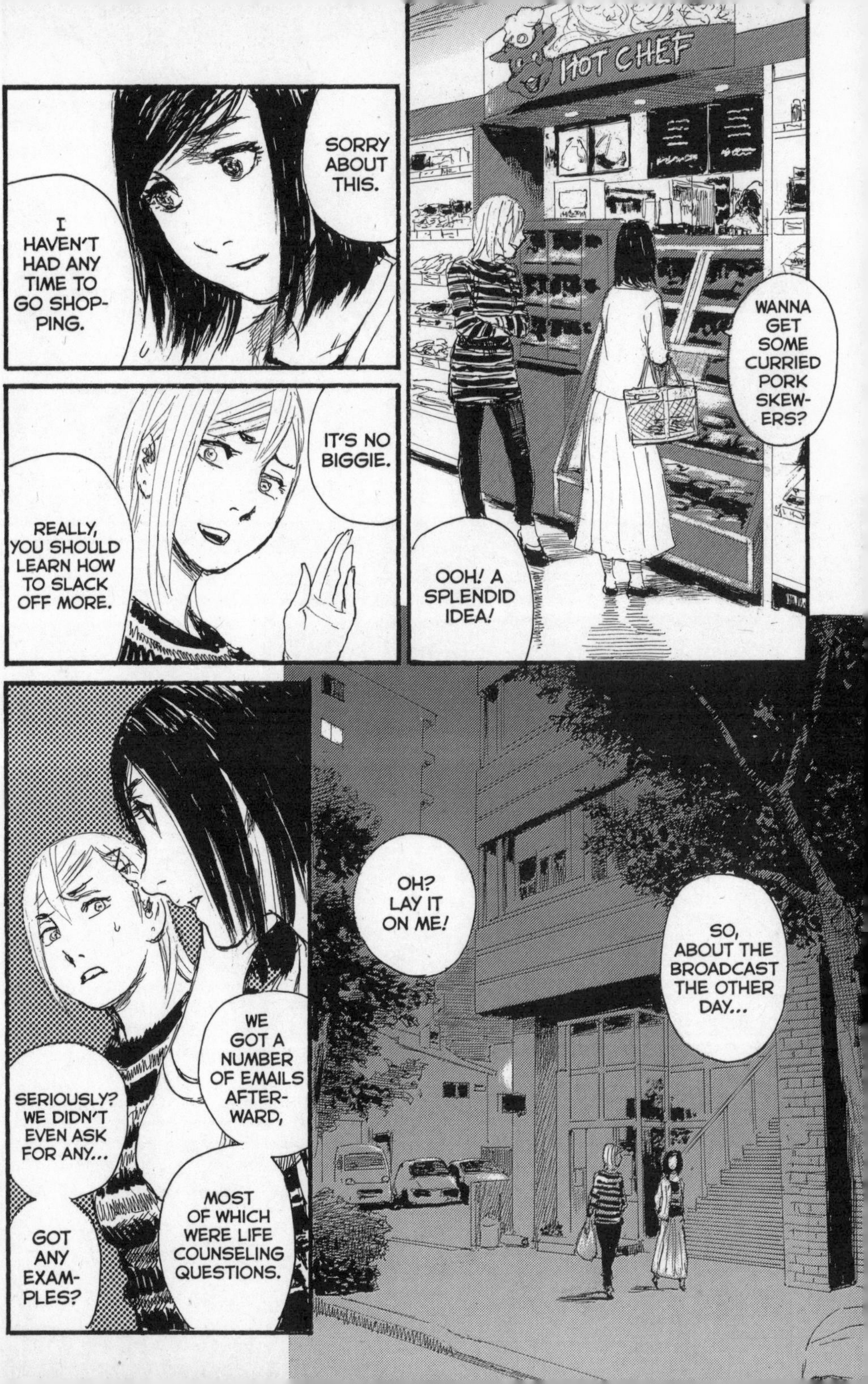
HOT CHEF
WANNA GET SOME CURRIED PORK SKEW-ERS?
OOH! A SPLENDID IDEA!
SORRY ABOUT THIS.
I HAVEN'T HAD ANY TIME TO GO SHOP-PING.
IT'S NO BIGGIE.
REALLY, YOU SHOULD LEARN HOW TO SLACK OFF MORE.
SO, ABOUT THE BROADCAST THE OTHER DAY...
OH? LAY IT ON ME!
WE GOT A NUMBER OF EMAILS AFTER-WARD,
SERIOUSLY? WE DIDN'T EVEN ASK FOR ANY...
MOST OF WHICH WERE LIFE COUNSELING QUESTIONS.
GOT ANY EXAM-PLES?

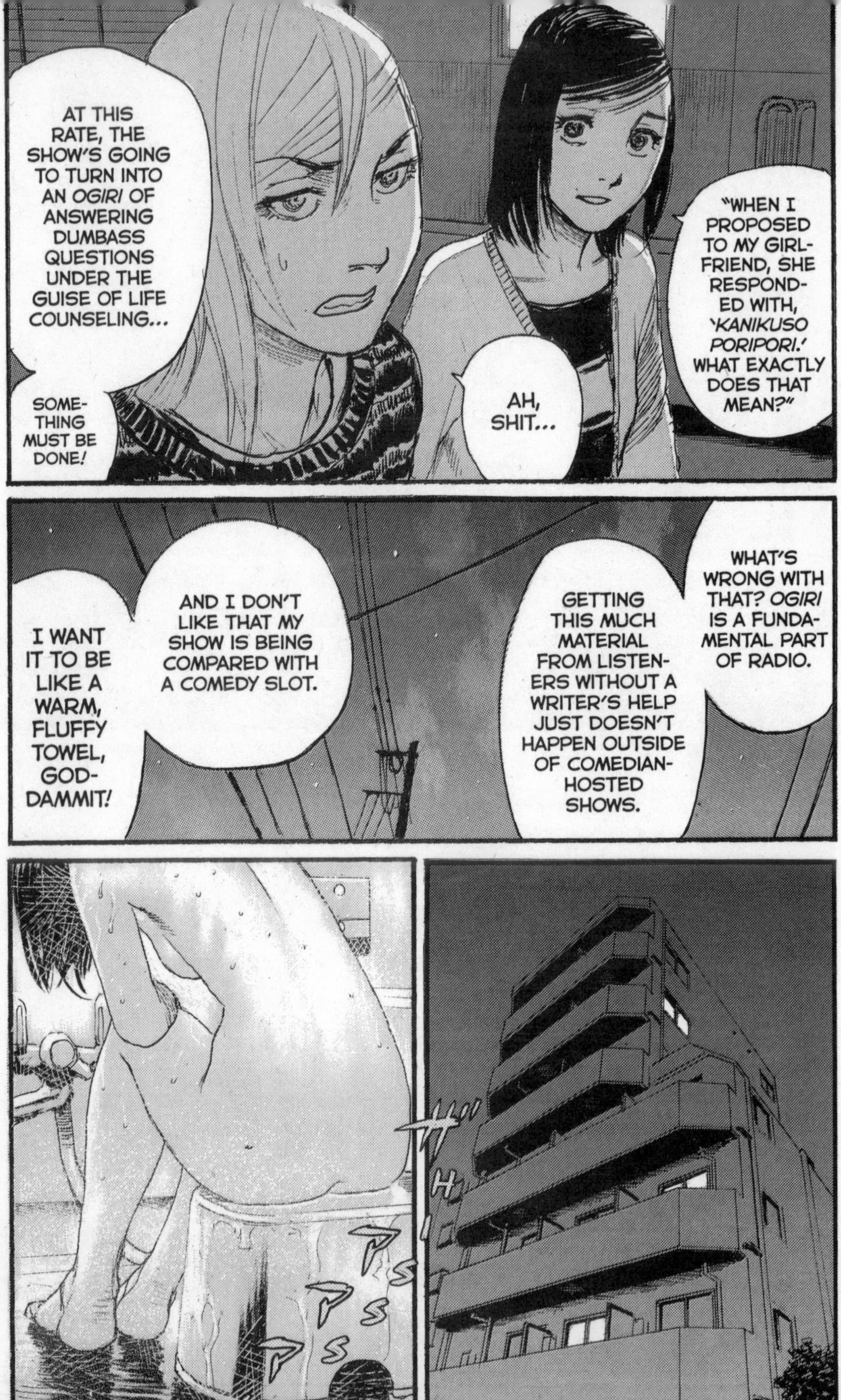
"WHEN I PROPOSED TO MY GIRLFRIEND, SHE RESPONDED WITH, '*KANIKUSO PORIPORI*.' WHAT EXACTLY DOES THAT MEAN?"
AH, SHIT...
AT THIS RATE, THE SHOW'S GOING TO TURN INTO AN *OGIRI* OF ANSWERING DUMBASS QUESTIONS UNDER THE GUISE OF LIFE COUNSELING...
SOMETHING MUST BE DONE!
WHAT'S WRONG WITH THAT? *OGIRI* IS A FUNDAMENTAL PART OF RADIO.
GETTING THIS MUCH MATERIAL FROM LISTENERS WITHOUT A WRITER'S HELP JUST DOESN'T HAPPEN OUTSIDE OF COMEDIAN-HOSTED SHOWS.
AND I DON'T LIKE THAT MY SHOW IS BEING COMPARED WITH A COMEDY SLOT.
I WANT IT TO BE LIKE A WARM, FLUFFY TOWEL, GODDAMMIT!

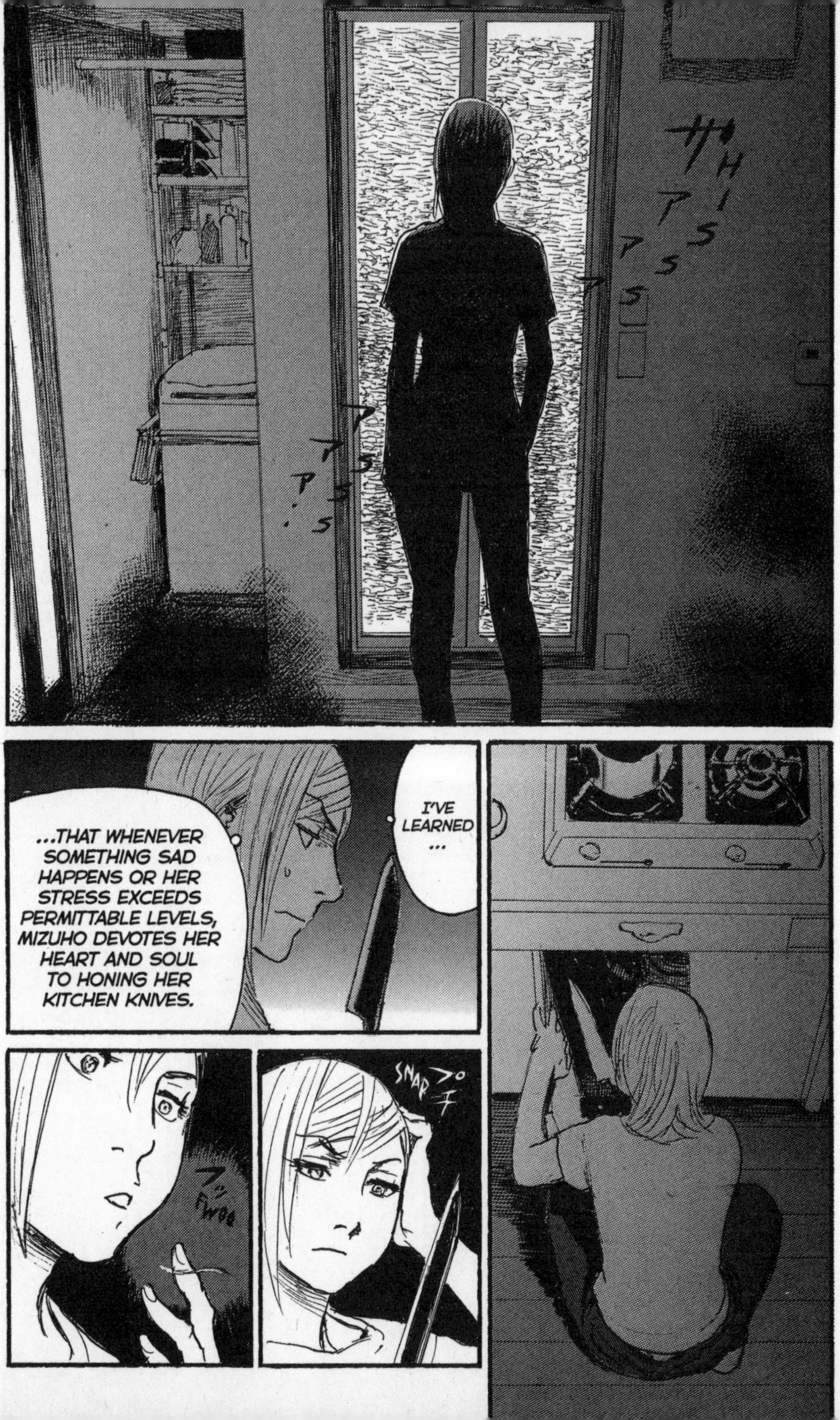
HISSSS
SSS..
I'VE LEARNED...
...THAT WHENEVER SOMETHING SAD HAPPENS OR HER STRESS EXCEEDS PERMITTABLE LEVELS, MIZUHO DEVOTES HER HEART AND SOUL TO HONING HER KITCHEN KNIVES.
SNAP
FWOO

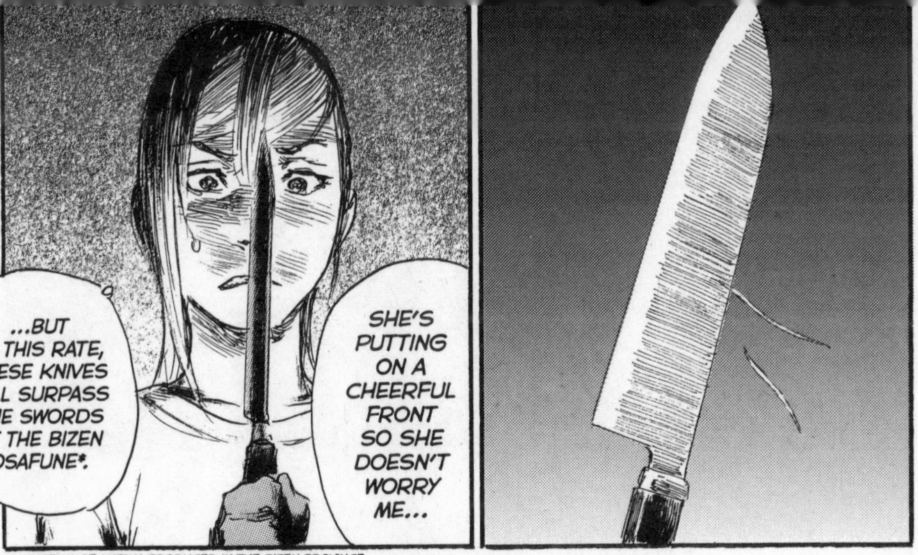
SHE'S PUTTING ON A CHEERFUL FRONT SO SHE DOESN'T WORRY ME...
...BUT AT THIS RATE, THESE KNIVES WILL SURPASS THE SWORDS AT THE BIZEN OSAFUNE*.

*A MUSEUM OF *KATANA* PRODUCED IN THE BIZEN PROVINCE.

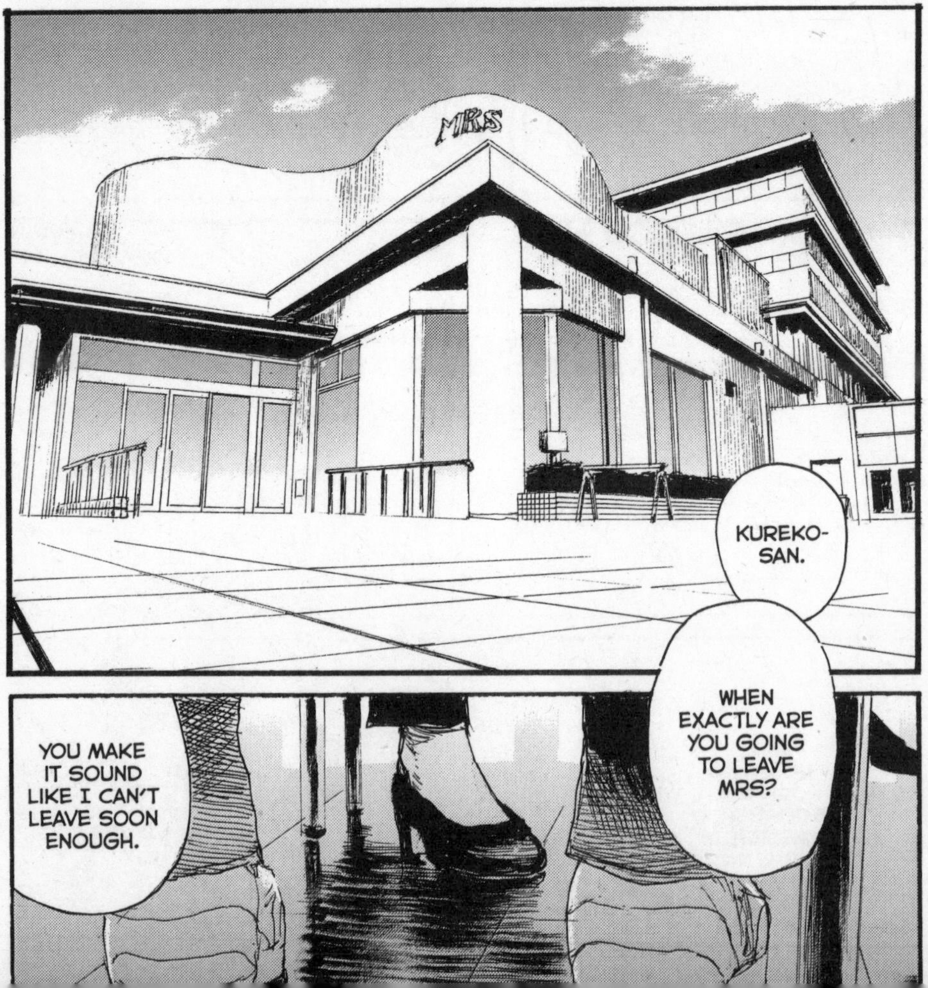
MRS
KUREKO-SAN.
WHEN EXACTLY ARE YOU GOING TO LEAVE MRS?
YOU MAKE IT SOUND LIKE I CAN'T LEAVE SOON ENOUGH.

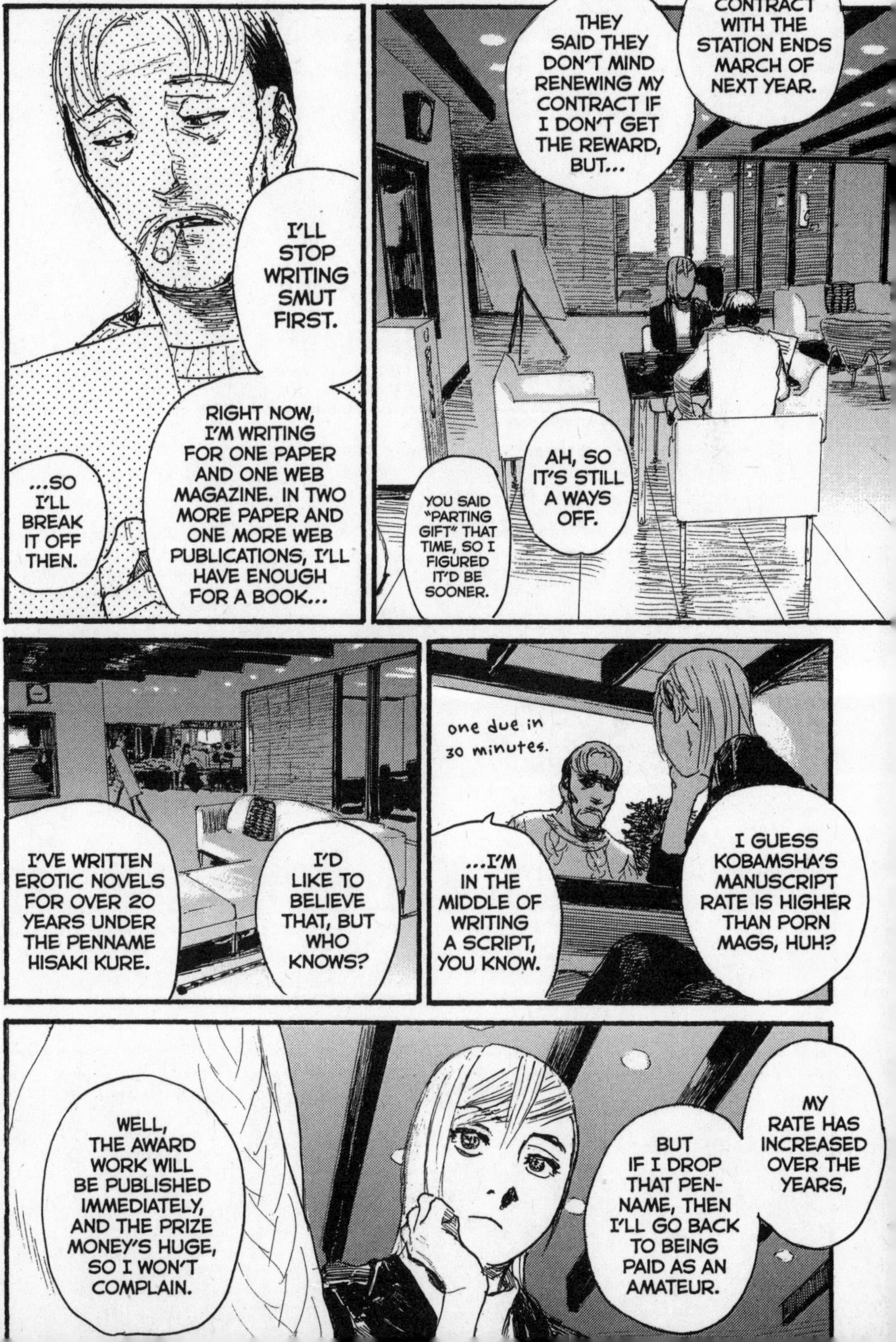
MY CONTRACT WITH THE STATION ENDS MARCH OF NEXT YEAR.
THEY SAID THEY DON'T MIND RENEWING MY CONTRACT IF I DON'T GET THE REWARD, BUT...
AH, SO IT'S STILL A WAYS OFF.
YOU SAID "PARTING GIFT" THAT TIME, SO I FIGURED IT'D BE SOONER.
I'LL STOP WRITING SMUT FIRST.
RIGHT NOW, I'M WRITING FOR ONE PAPER AND ONE WEB MAGAZINE. IN TWO MORE PAPER AND ONE MORE WEB PUBLICATIONS, I'LL HAVE ENOUGH FOR A BOOK...
...SO I'LL BREAK IT OFF THEN.
I GUESS KOBAMSHA'S MANUSCRIPT RATE IS HIGHER THAN PORN MAGS, HUH?
...I'M IN THE MIDDLE OF WRITING A SCRIPT, YOU KNOW.
one due in 30 minutes.
I'D LIKE TO BELIEVE THAT, BUT WHO KNOWS?
I'VE WRITTEN EROTIC NOVELS FOR OVER 20 YEARS UNDER THE PENNAME HISAKI KURE.
MY RATE HAS INCREASED OVER THE YEARS,
BUT IF I DROP THAT PEN-NAME, THEN I'LL GO BACK TO BEING PAID AS AN AMATEUR.
WELL, THE AWARD WORK WILL BE PUBLISHED IMMEDIATELY, AND THE PRIZE MONEY'S HUGE, SO I WON'T COMPLAIN.

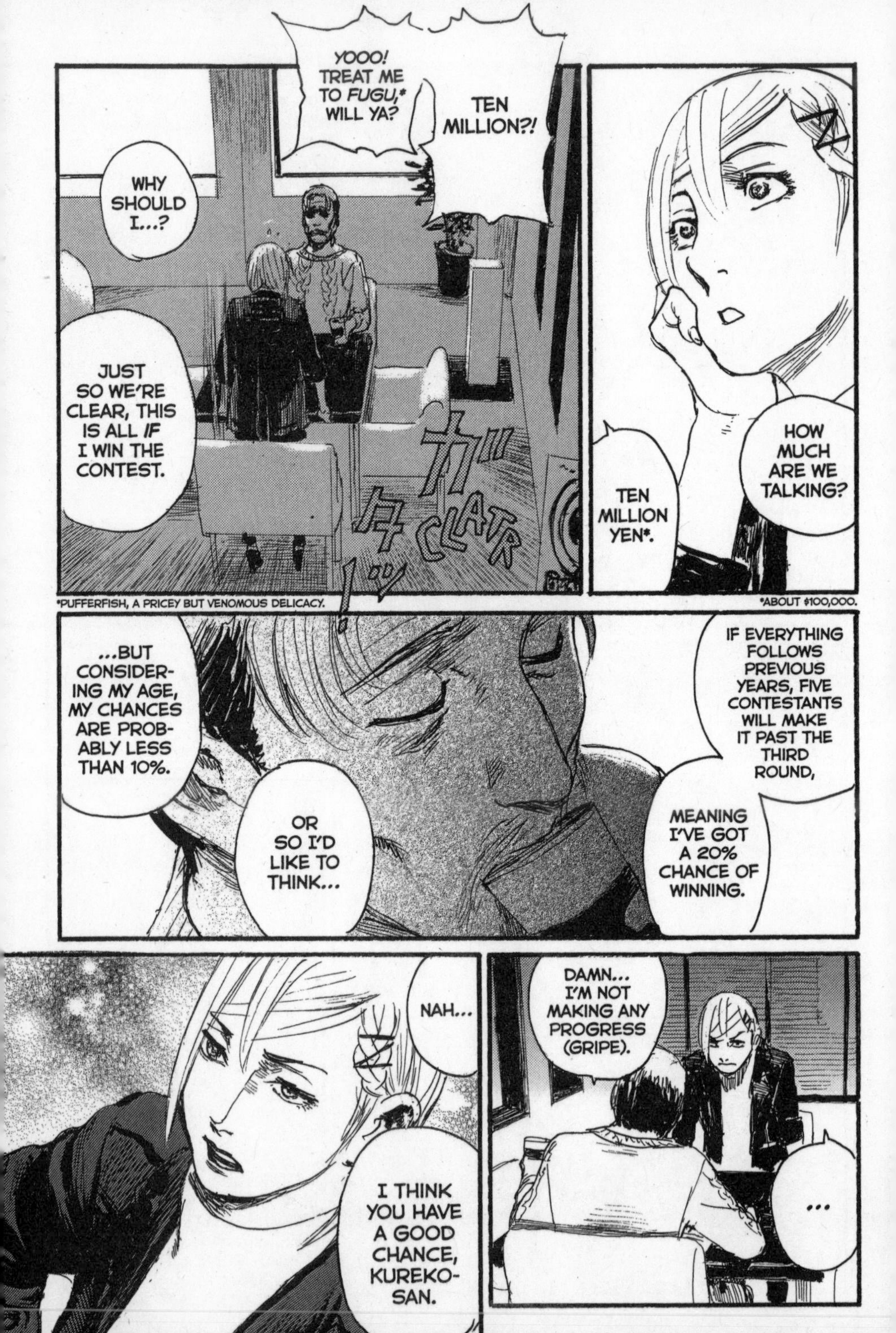
HOW MUCH ARE WE TALKING?
TEN MILLION YEN*.
TEN MILLION?!
YOOO! TREAT ME TO FUGU,* WILL YA?
WHY SHOULD I...?
JUST SO WE'RE CLEAR, THIS IS ALL IF I WIN THE CONTEST.
CLATR
IF EVERYTHING FOLLOWS PREVIOUS YEARS, FIVE CONTESTANTS WILL MAKE IT PAST THE THIRD ROUND,
MEANING I'VE GOT A 20% CHANCE OF WINNING.
...BUT CONSIDERING MY AGE, MY CHANCES ARE PROBABLY LESS THAN 10%.
OR SO I'D LIKE TO THINK...
DAMN... I'M NOT MAKING ANY PROGRESS (GRIPE).
...
NAH...
I THINK YOU HAVE A GOOD CHANCE, KUREKO-SAN.

*ABOUT $100,000.

*PUFFERFISH, A PRICEY BUT VENOMOUS DELICACY.

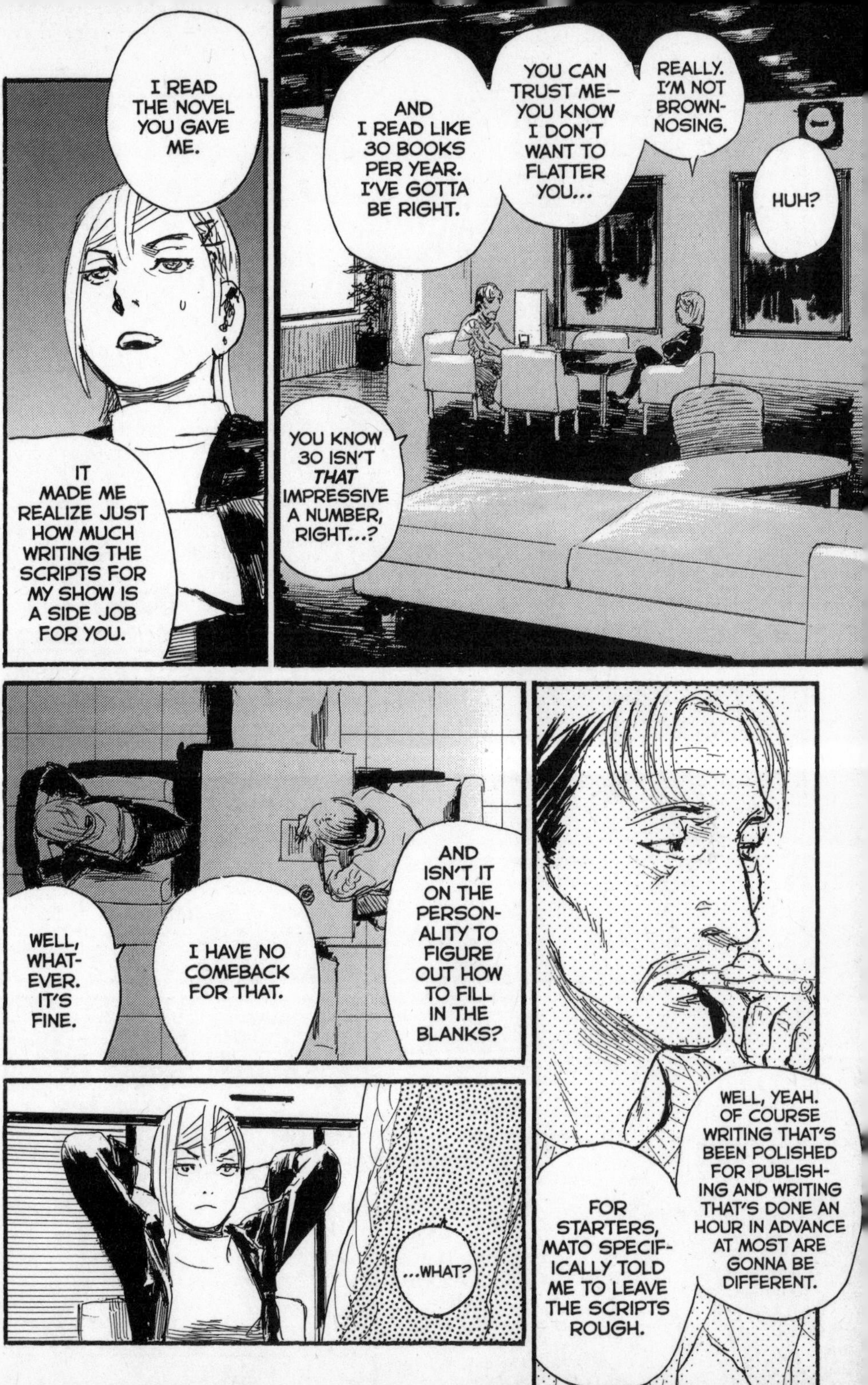
REALLY. I'M NOT BROWN-NOSING.
YOU CAN TRUST ME— YOU KNOW I DON'T WANT TO FLATTER YOU...
AND I READ LIKE 30 BOOKS PER YEAR. I'VE GOTTA BE RIGHT.
HUH?
YOU KNOW 30 ISN'T *THAT* IMPRESSIVE A NUMBER, RIGHT...?
I READ THE NOVEL YOU GAVE ME.
IT MADE ME REALIZE JUST HOW MUCH WRITING THE SCRIPTS FOR MY SHOW IS A SIDE JOB FOR YOU.
WELL, YEAH. OF COURSE WRITING THAT'S BEEN POLISHED FOR PUBLISHING AND WRITING THAT'S DONE AN HOUR IN ADVANCE AT MOST ARE GONNA BE DIFFERENT.
FOR STARTERS, MATO SPECIFICALLY TOLD ME TO LEAVE THE SCRIPTS ROUGH.
AND ISN'T IT ON THE PERSONALITY TO FIGURE OUT HOW TO FILL IN THE BLANKS?
I HAVE NO COMEBACK FOR THAT.
WELL, WHATEVER. IT'S FINE.
...WHAT?

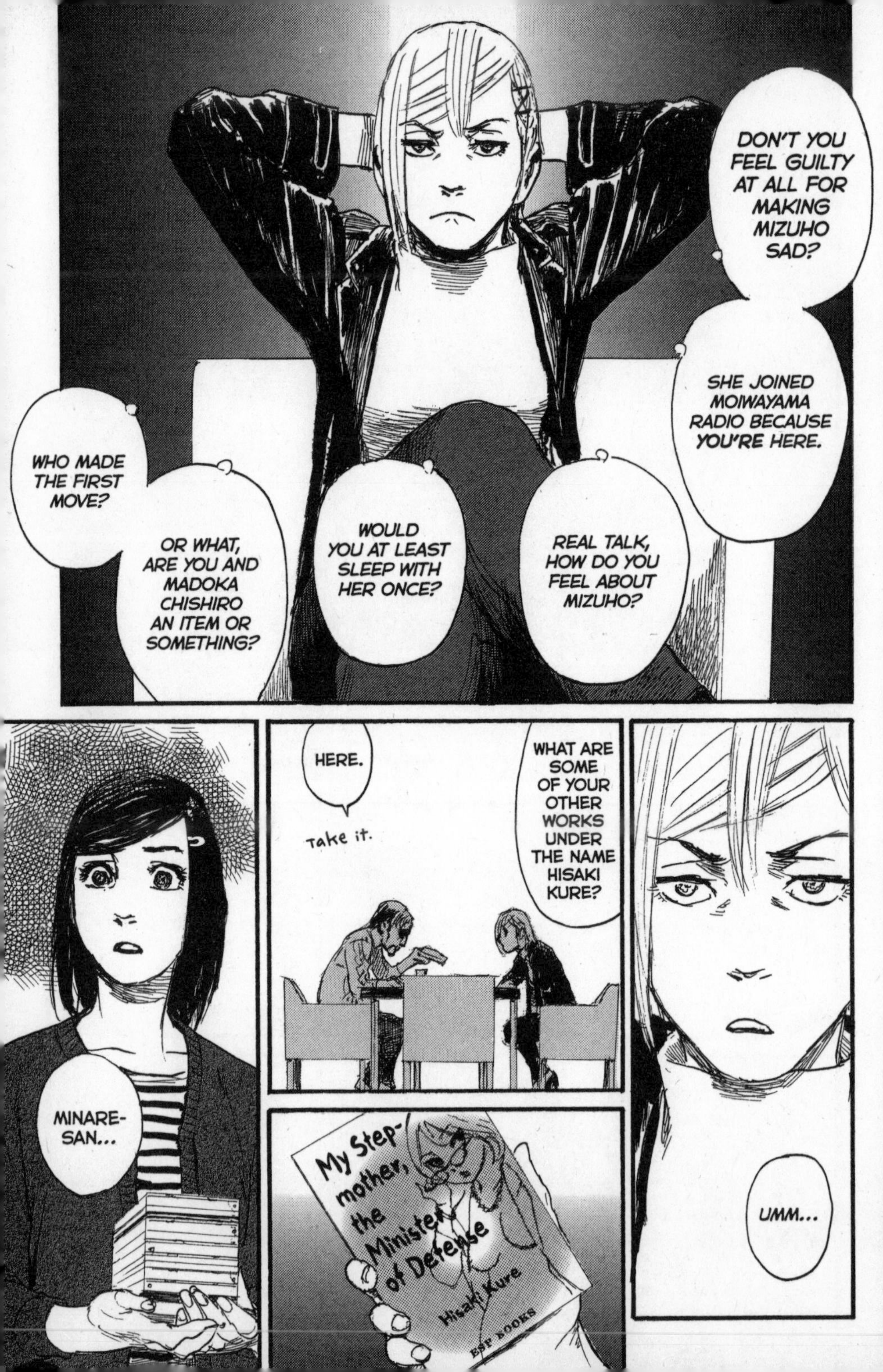
DON'T YOU FEEL GUILTY AT ALL FOR MAKING MIZUHO SAD?
SHE JOINED MOIWAYAMA RADIO BECAUSE YOU'RE HERE.
REAL TALK, HOW DO YOU FEEL ABOUT MIZUHO?
WOULD YOU AT LEAST SLEEP WITH HER ONCE?
OR WHAT, ARE YOU AND MADOKA CHISHIRO AN ITEM OR SOMETHING?
WHO MADE THE FIRST MOVE?
UMM...
WHAT ARE SOME OF YOUR OTHER WORKS UNDER THE NAME HISAKI KURE?
HERE.
Take it.
My Stepmother, the Minister of Defense
Hisaki Kure
ESP BOOKS
MINARE-SAN...

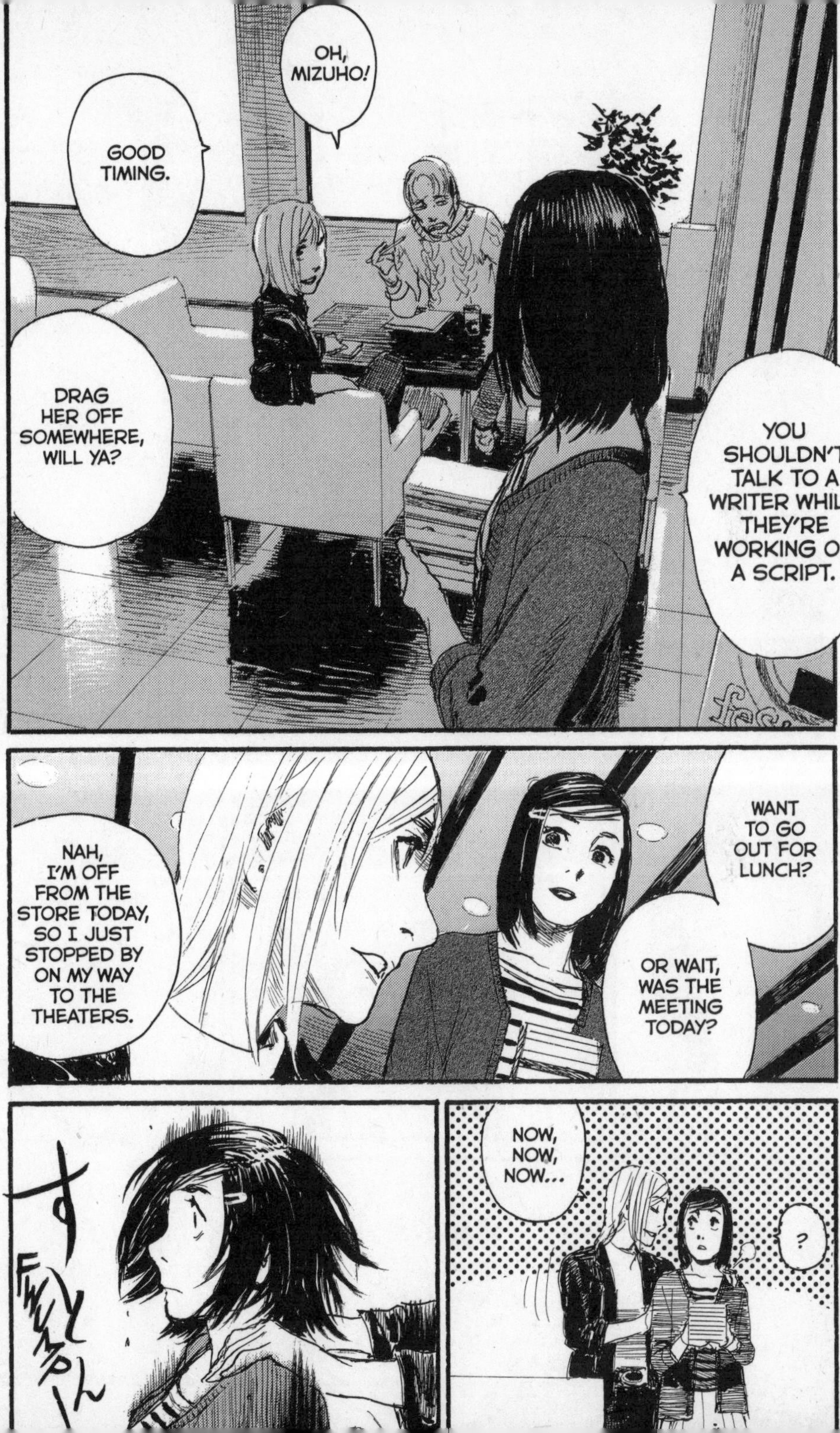
OH, MIZUHO!
GOOD TIMING.
DRAG HER OFF SOMEWHERE, WILL YA?
YOU SHOULDN'T TALK TO A WRITER WHILE THEY'RE WORKING ON A SCRIPT.
WANT TO GO OUT FOR LUNCH?
OR WAIT, WAS THE MEETING TODAY?
NAH, I'M OFF FROM THE STORE TODAY, SO I JUST STOPPED BY ON MY WAY TO THE THEATERS.
NOW, NOW, NOW...
?
FWUMP

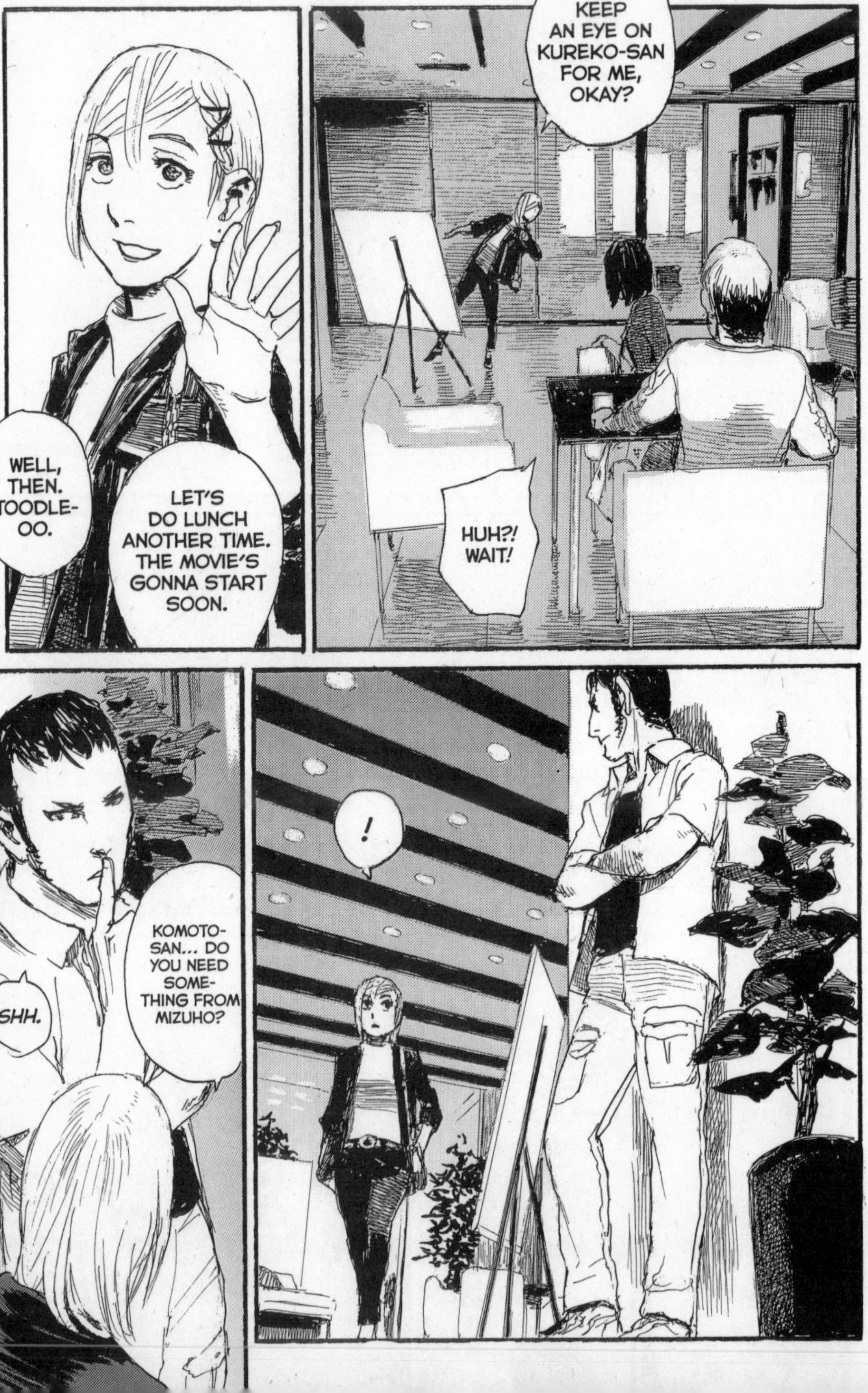
KEEP AN EYE ON KUREKO-SAN FOR ME, OKAY?
HUH?! WAIT!
LET'S DO LUNCH ANOTHER TIME. THE MOVIE'S GONNA START SOON.
WELL, THEN. TOODLE-OO.
!
KOMOTO-SAN... DO YOU NEED SOME-THING FROM MIZUHO?
SHH.

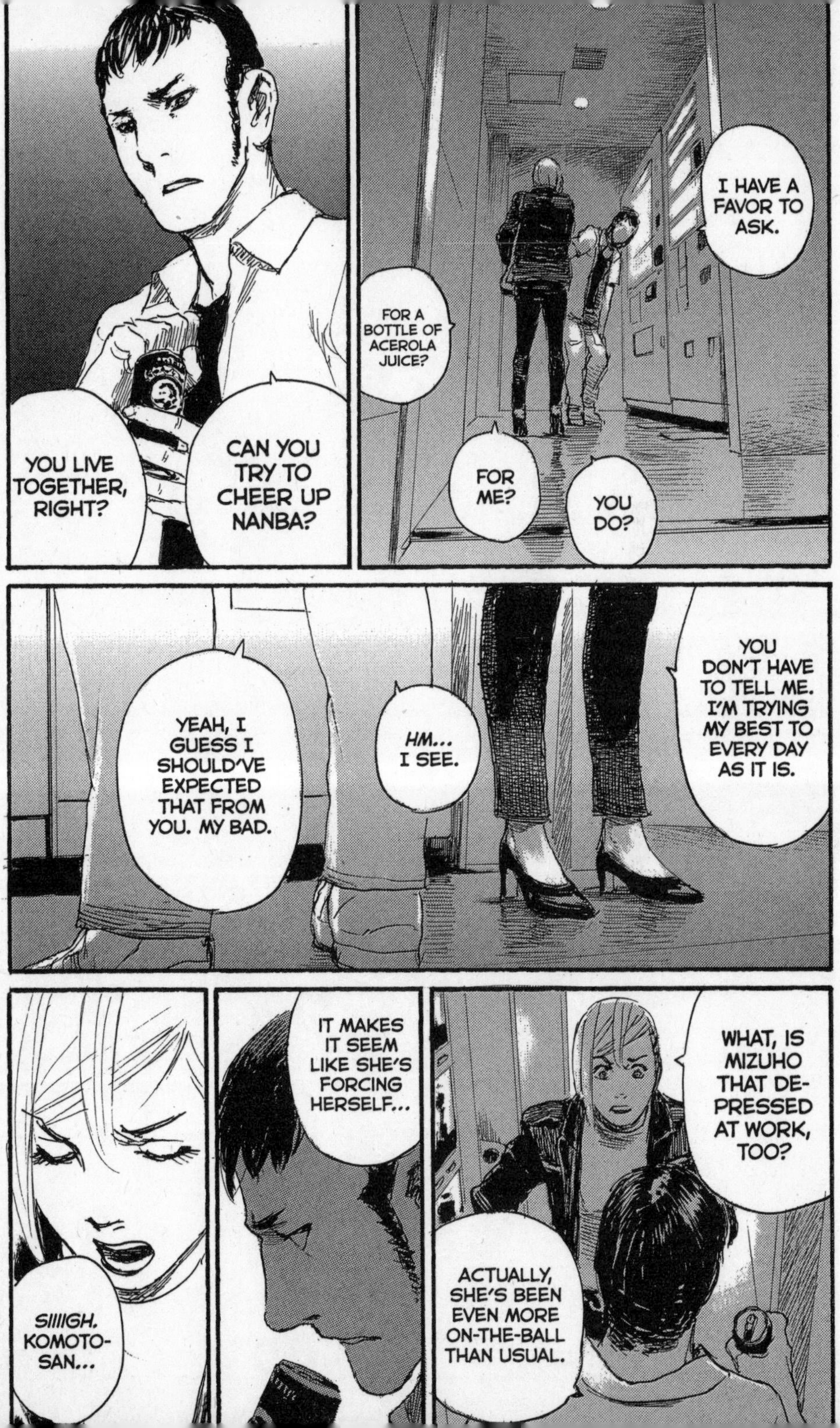
I HAVE A FAVOR TO ASK.
YOU DO?
FOR ME?
FOR A BOTTLE OF ACEROLA JUICE?
CAN YOU TRY TO CHEER UP NANBA?
YOU LIVE TOGETHER, RIGHT?
YOU DON'T HAVE TO TELL ME. I'M TRYING MY BEST TO EVERY DAY AS IT IS.
HM... I SEE.
YEAH, I GUESS I SHOULD'VE EXPECTED THAT FROM YOU. MY BAD.
WHAT, IS MIZUHO THAT DE-PRESSED AT WORK, TOO?
ACTUALLY, SHE'S BEEN EVEN MORE ON-THE-BALL THAN USUAL.
IT MAKES IT SEEM LIKE SHE'S FORCING HERSELF...
SIIIGH. KOMOTO-SAN...

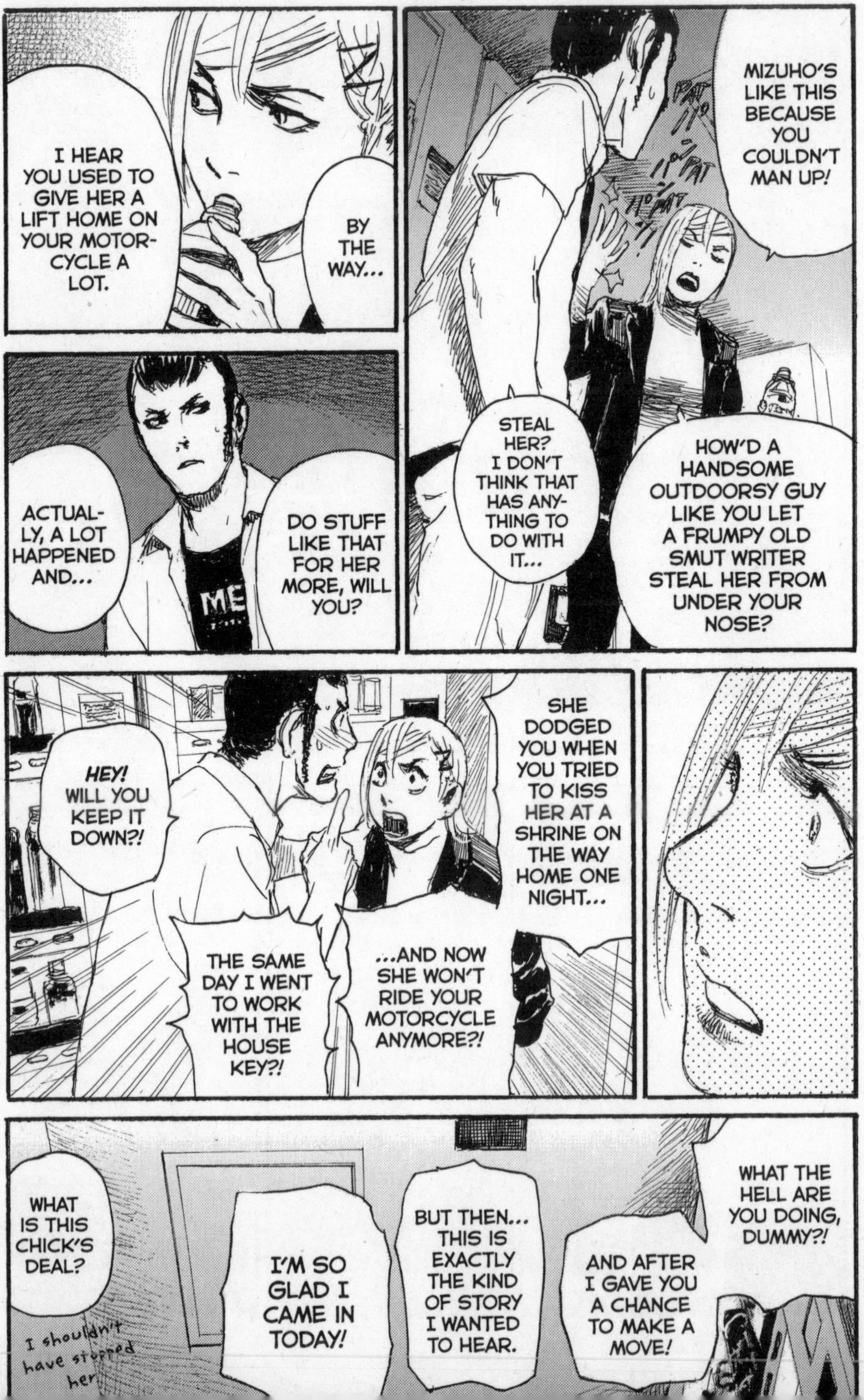

MIZUHO'S LIKE THIS BECAUSE YOU COULDN'T MAN UP!
PAT PAT PAT
HOW'D A HANDSOME OUTDOORSY GUY LIKE YOU LET A FRUMPY OLD SMUT WRITER STEAL HER FROM UNDER YOUR NOSE?
STEAL HER? I DON'T THINK THAT HAS ANY-THING TO DO WITH IT...
BY THE WAY...
I HEAR YOU USED TO GIVE HER A LIFT HOME ON YOUR MOTOR-CYCLE A LOT.
DO STUFF LIKE THAT FOR HER MORE, WILL YOU?
ACTUAL-LY, A LOT HAPPENED AND...
SHE DODGED YOU WHEN YOU TRIED TO KISS HER AT A SHRINE ON THE WAY HOME ONE NIGHT...
HEY! WILL YOU KEEP IT DOWN?!
...AND NOW SHE WON'T RIDE YOUR MOTORCYCLE ANYMORE?!
THE SAME DAY I WENT TO WORK WITH THE HOUSE KEY?!
WHAT THE HELL ARE YOU DOING, DUMMY?!
AND AFTER I GAVE YOU A CHANCE TO MAKE A MOVE!
BUT THEN... THIS IS EXACTLY THE KIND OF STORY I WANTED TO HEAR.
I'M SO GLAD I CAME IN TODAY!
WHAT IS THIS CHICK'S DEAL?
I shouldn't have stopped her

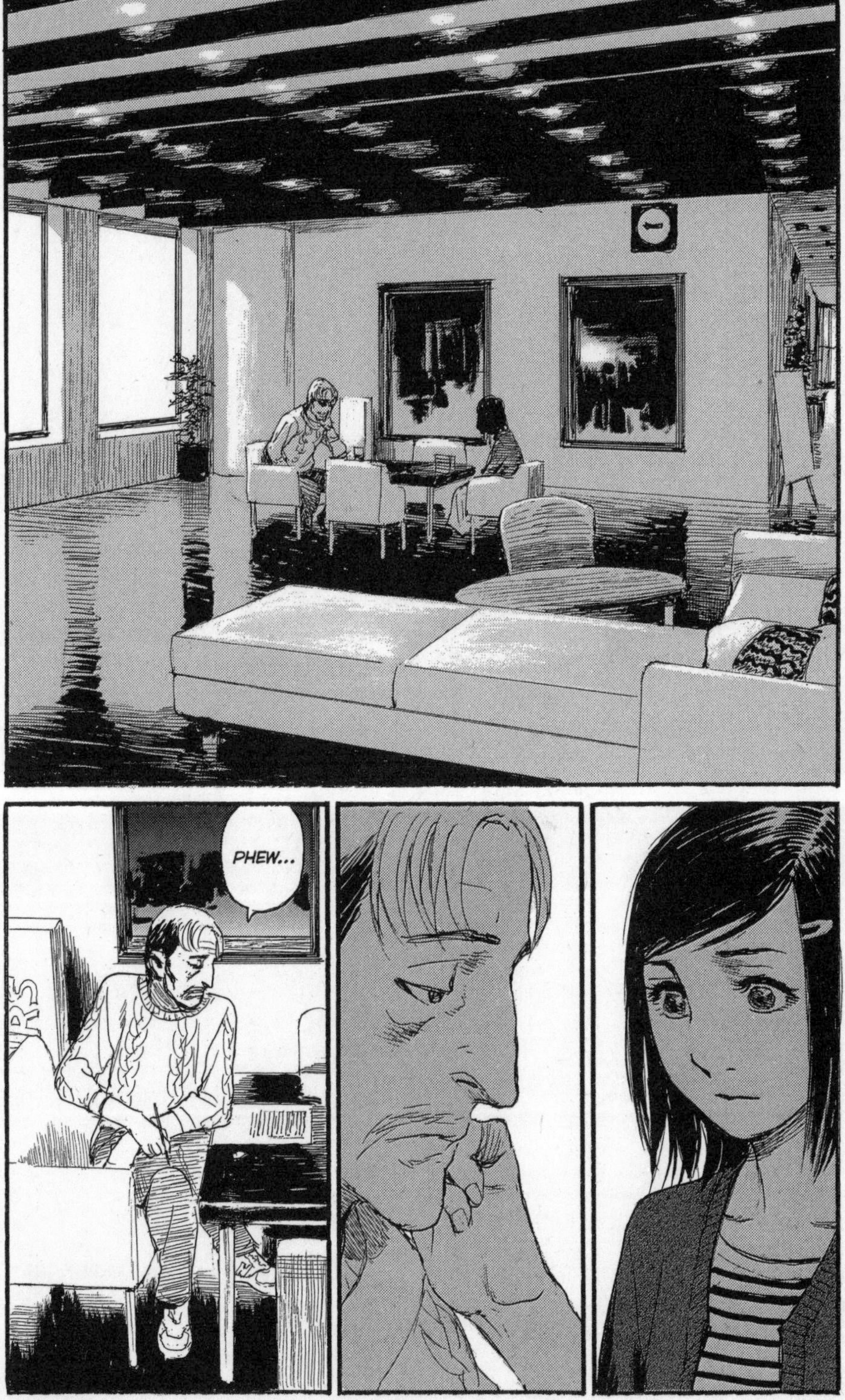
PHEW...

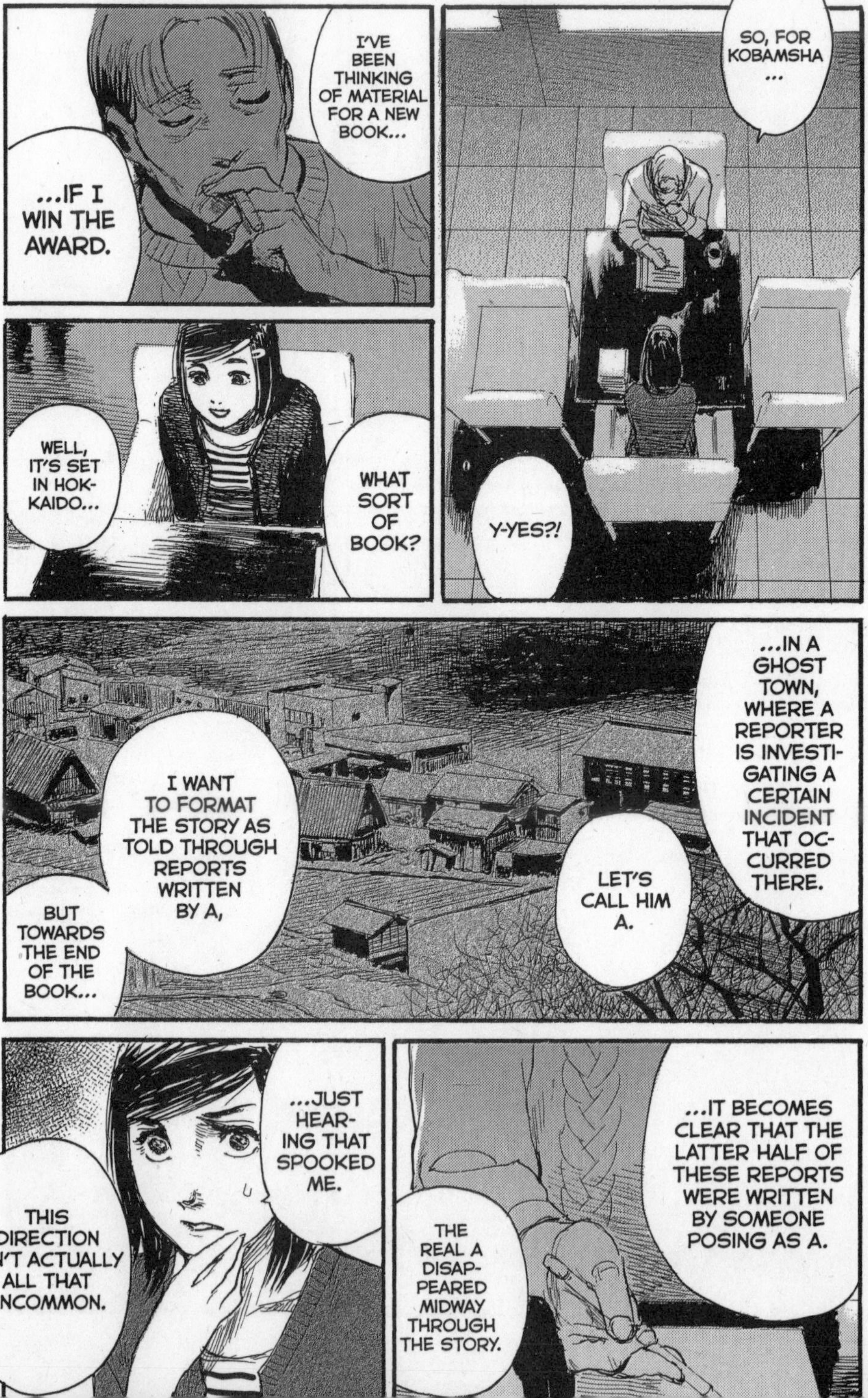
SO, FOR KOBAMSHA ...
Y-YES?!
I'VE BEEN THINKING OF MATERIAL FOR A NEW BOOK...
...IF I WIN THE AWARD.
WHAT SORT OF BOOK?
WELL, IT'S SET IN HOK-KAIDO...
...IN A GHOST TOWN, WHERE A REPORTER IS INVESTI-GATING A CERTAIN INCIDENT THAT OC-CURRED THERE.
LET'S CALL HIM A.
I WANT TO FORMAT THE STORY AS TOLD THROUGH REPORTS WRITTEN BY A,
BUT TOWARDS THE END OF THE BOOK...
...IT BECOMES CLEAR THAT THE LATTER HALF OF THESE REPORTS WERE WRITTEN BY SOMEONE POSING AS A.
THE REAL A DISAP-PEARED MIDWAY THROUGH THE STORY.
...JUST HEAR-ING THAT SPOOKED ME.
THIS DIRECTION ISN'T ACTUALLY ALL THAT UNCOMMON.

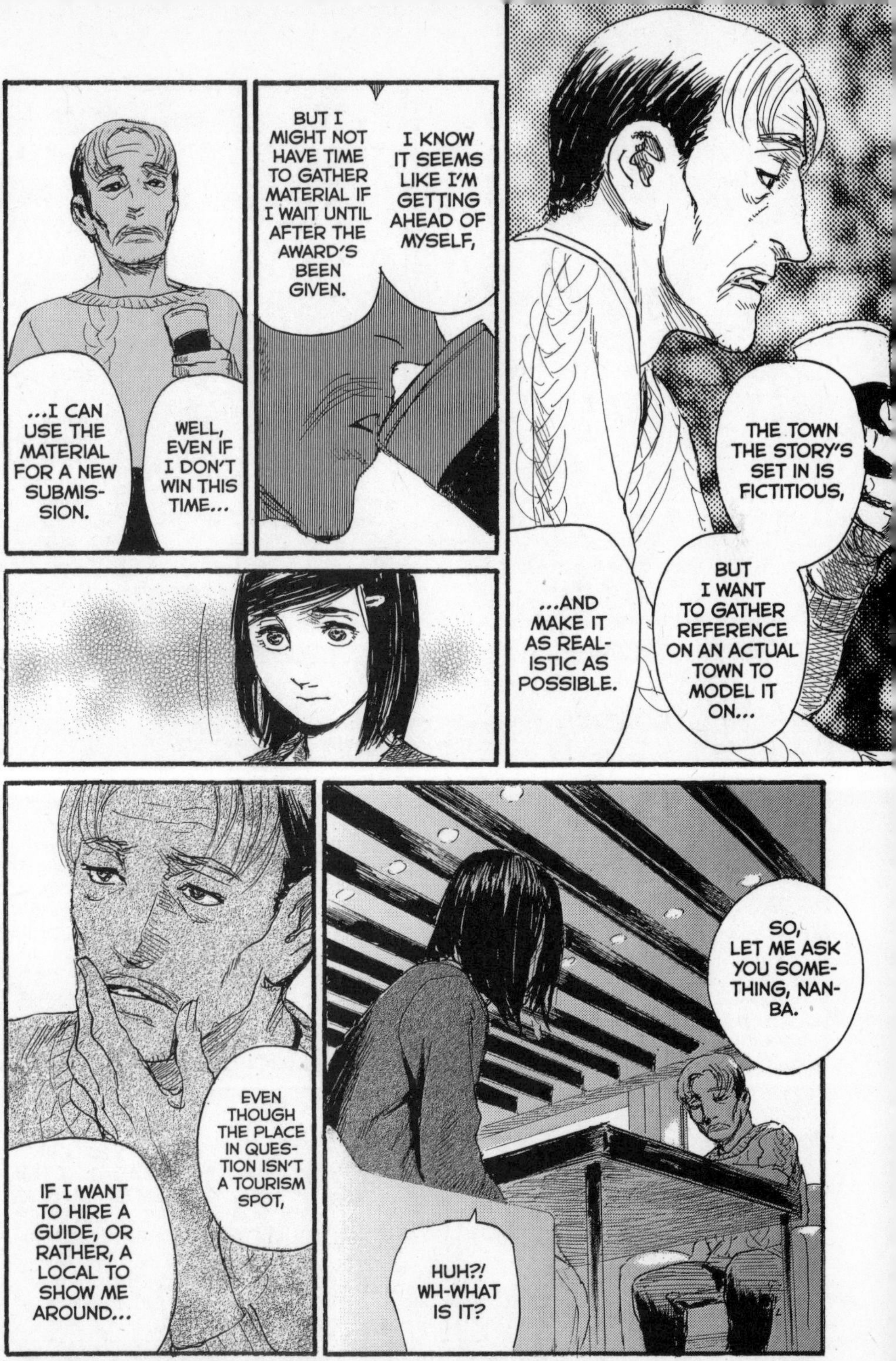
THE TOWN THE STORY'S SET IN IS FICTITIOUS,
BUT I WANT TO GATHER REFERENCE ON AN ACTUAL TOWN TO MODEL IT ON...
...AND MAKE IT AS REAL-ISTIC AS POSSIBLE.
I KNOW IT SEEMS LIKE I'M GETTING AHEAD OF MYSELF,
BUT I MIGHT NOT HAVE TIME TO GATHER MATERIAL IF I WAIT UNTIL AFTER THE AWARD'S BEEN GIVEN.
WELL, EVEN IF I DON'T WIN THIS TIME...
...I CAN USE THE MATERIAL FOR A NEW SUBMIS-SION.
SO, LET ME ASK YOU SOME-THING, NAN-BA.
HUH?! WH-WHAT IS IT?
EVEN THOUGH THE PLACE IN QUES-TION ISN'T A TOURISM SPOT,
IF I WANT TO HIRE A GUIDE, OR RATHER, A LOCAL TO SHOW ME AROUND...

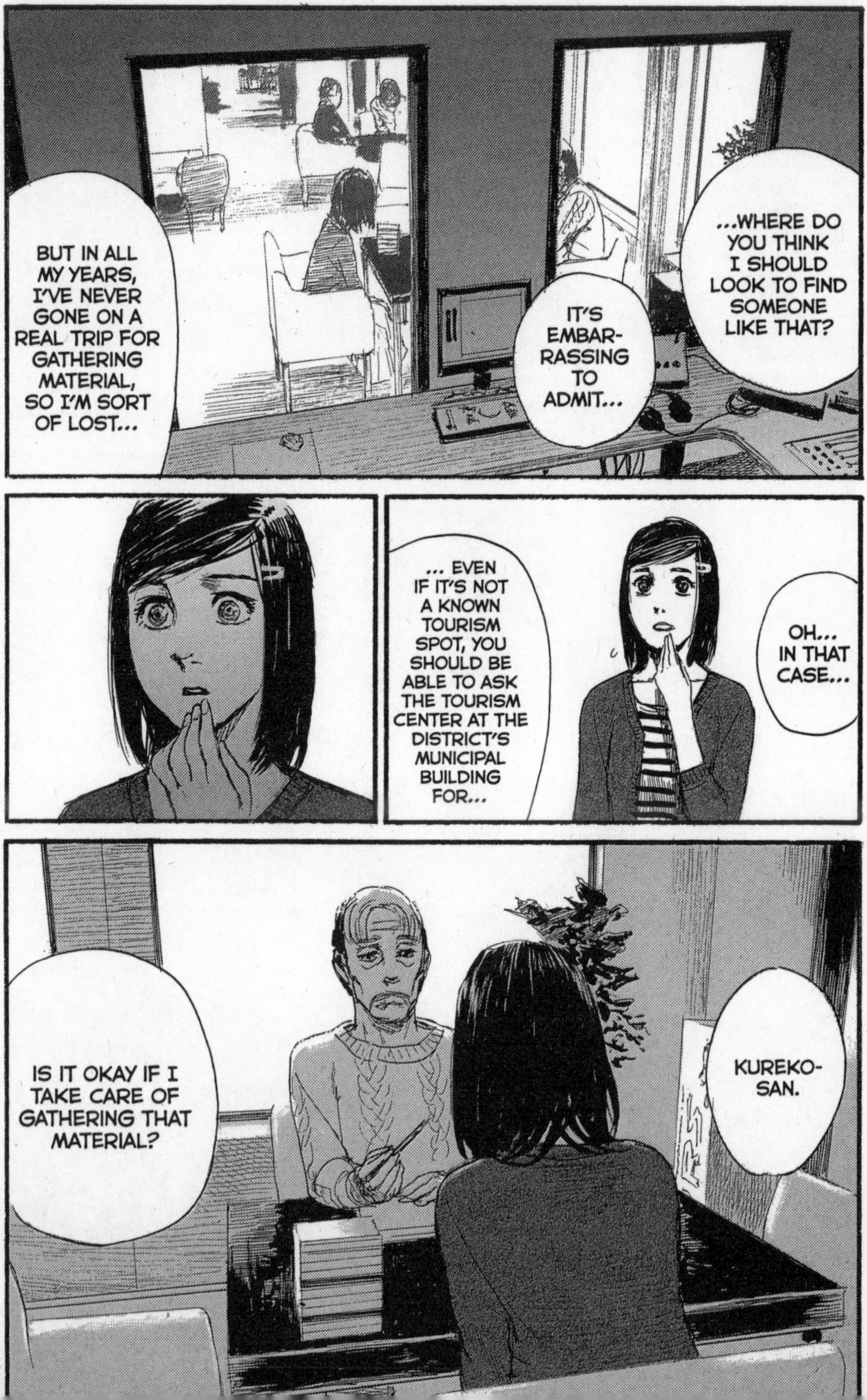
...WHERE DO YOU THINK I SHOULD LOOK TO FIND SOMEONE LIKE THAT?
IT'S EMBARRASSING TO ADMIT...
BUT IN ALL MY YEARS, I'VE NEVER GONE ON A REAL TRIP FOR GATHERING MATERIAL, SO I'M SORT OF LOST...
OH... IN THAT CASE...
... EVEN IF IT'S NOT A KNOWN TOURISM SPOT, YOU SHOULD BE ABLE TO ASK THE TOURISM CENTER AT THE DISTRICT'S MUNICIPAL BUILDING FOR...
KUREKO-SAN.
IS IT OKAY IF I TAKE CARE OF GATHERING THAT MATERIAL?

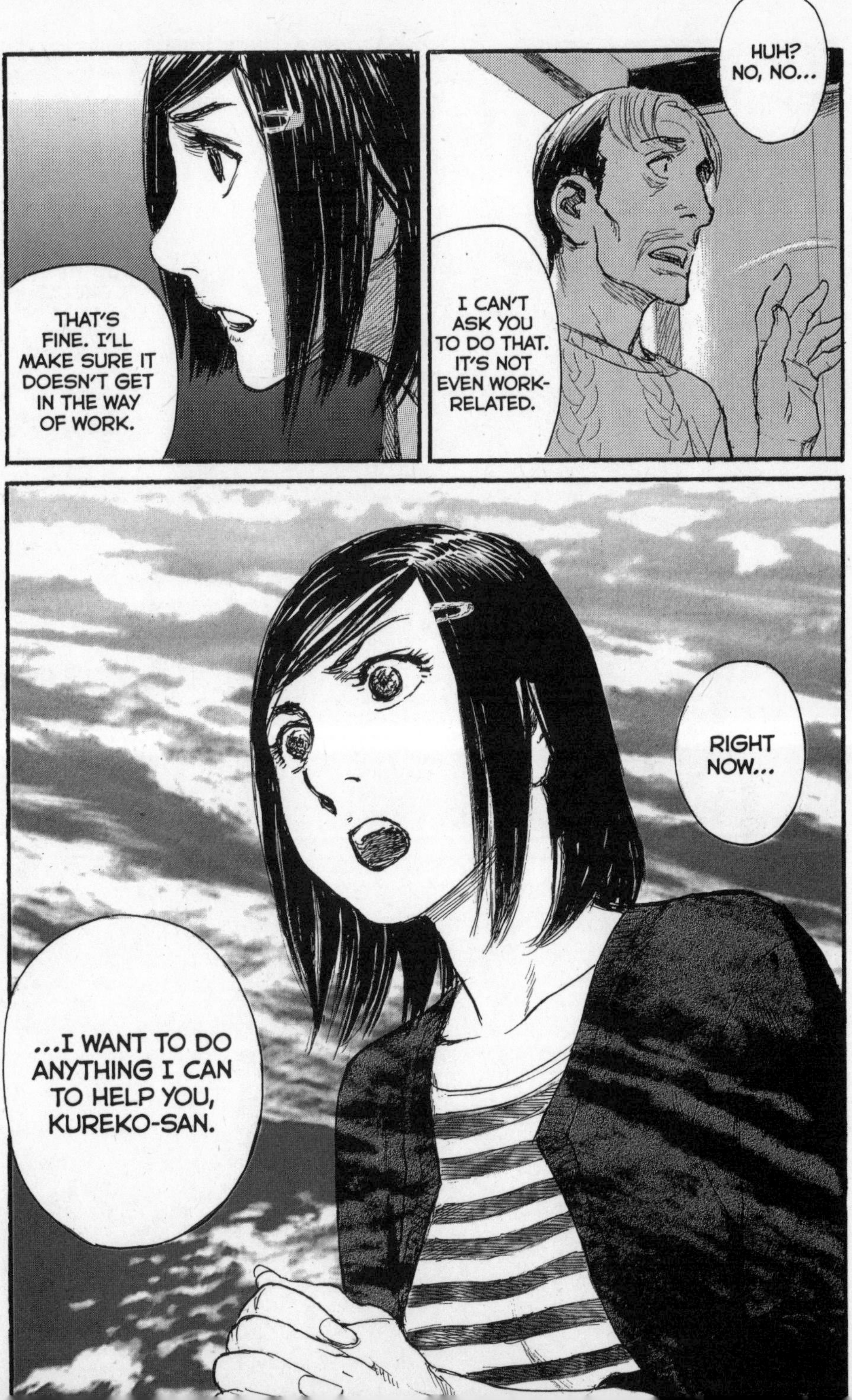
HUH? NO, NO...
I CAN'T ASK YOU TO DO THAT. IT'S NOT EVEN WORK-RELATED.
THAT'S FINE. I'LL MAKE SURE IT DOESN'T GET IN THE WAY OF WORK.
RIGHT NOW...
...I WANT TO DO ANYTHING I CAN TO HELP YOU, KUREKO-SAN.

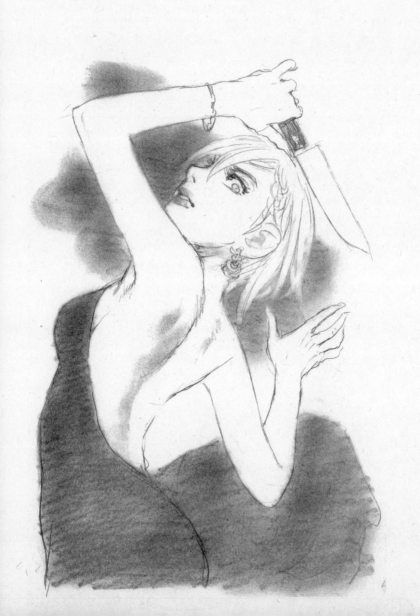

wave
LISTEN
TO ME!

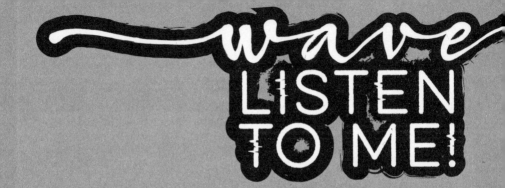

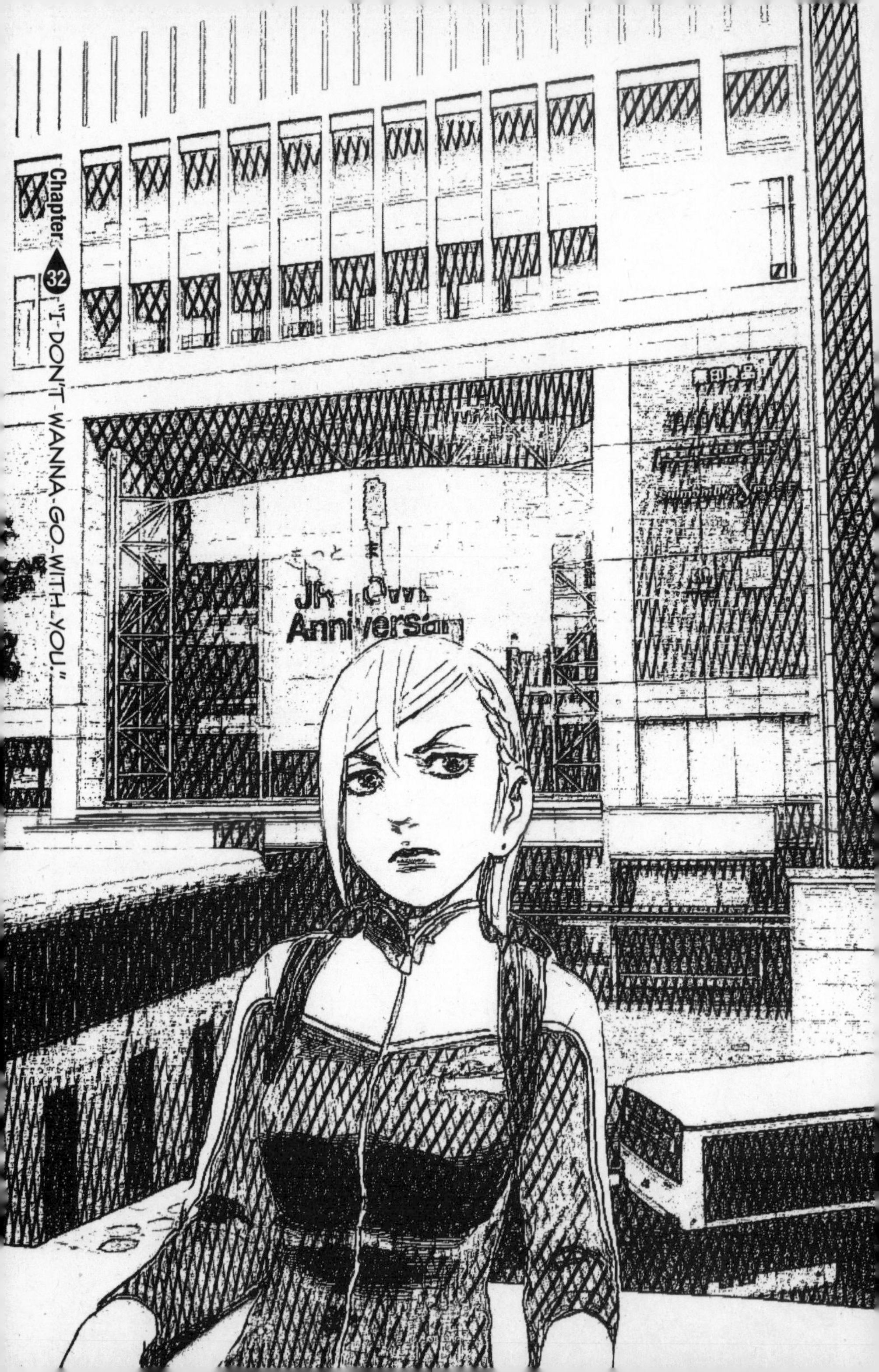
Chapter 32
"I-DON'T-WANNA-GO-WITH-YOU."

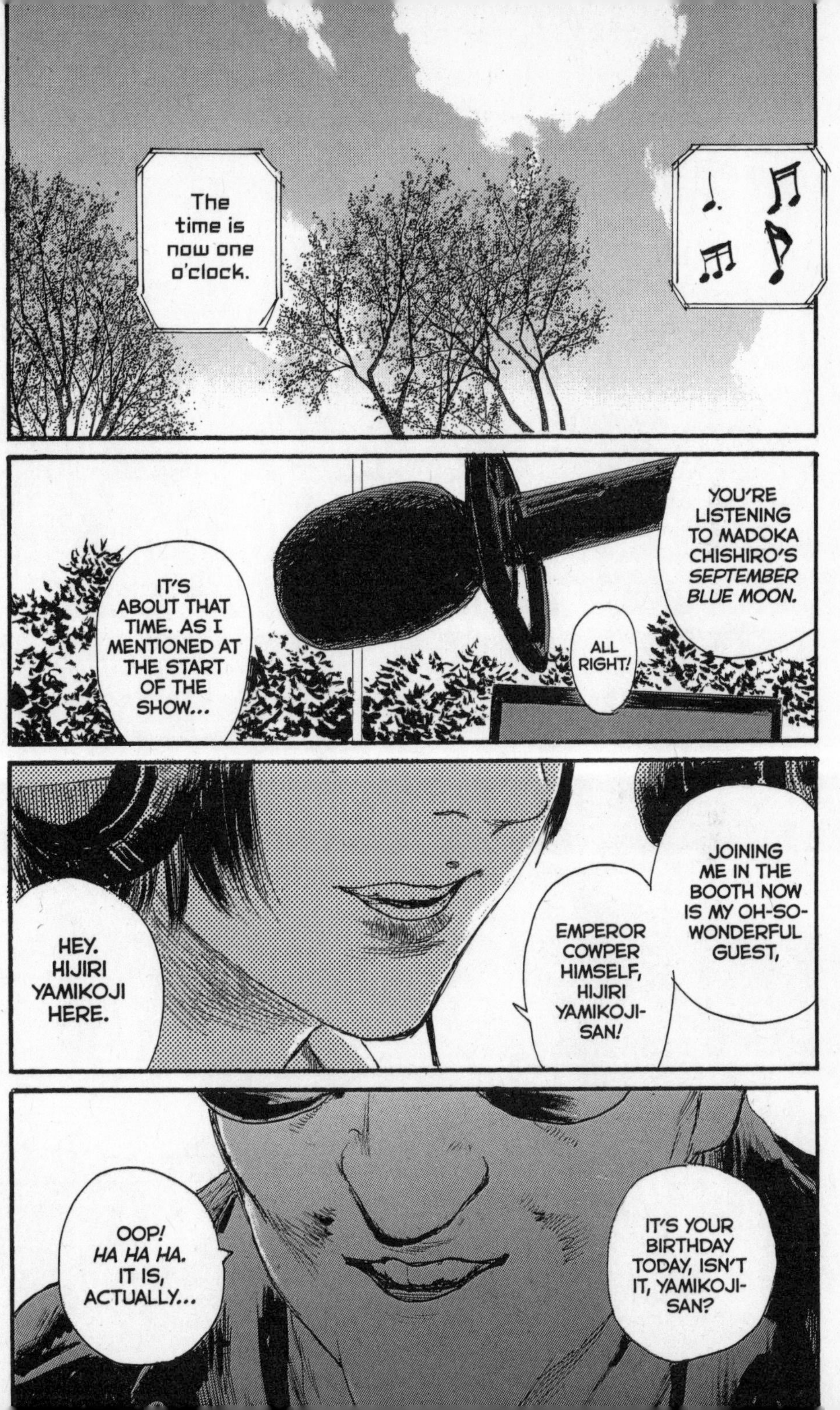
The time is now one o'clock.
YOU'RE LISTENING TO MADOKA CHISHIRO'S *SEPTEMBER BLUE MOON.*
ALL RIGHT!
IT'S ABOUT THAT TIME. AS I MENTIONED AT THE START OF THE SHOW...
JOINING ME IN THE BOOTH NOW IS MY OH-SO-WONDERFUL GUEST,
EMPEROR COWPER HIMSELF, HIJIRI YAMIKOJI-SAN!
HEY. HIJIRI YAMIKOJI HERE.
IT'S YOUR BIRTHDAY TODAY, ISN'T IT, YAMIKOJI-SAN?
OOP! *HA HA HA.* IT IS, ACTUALLY...

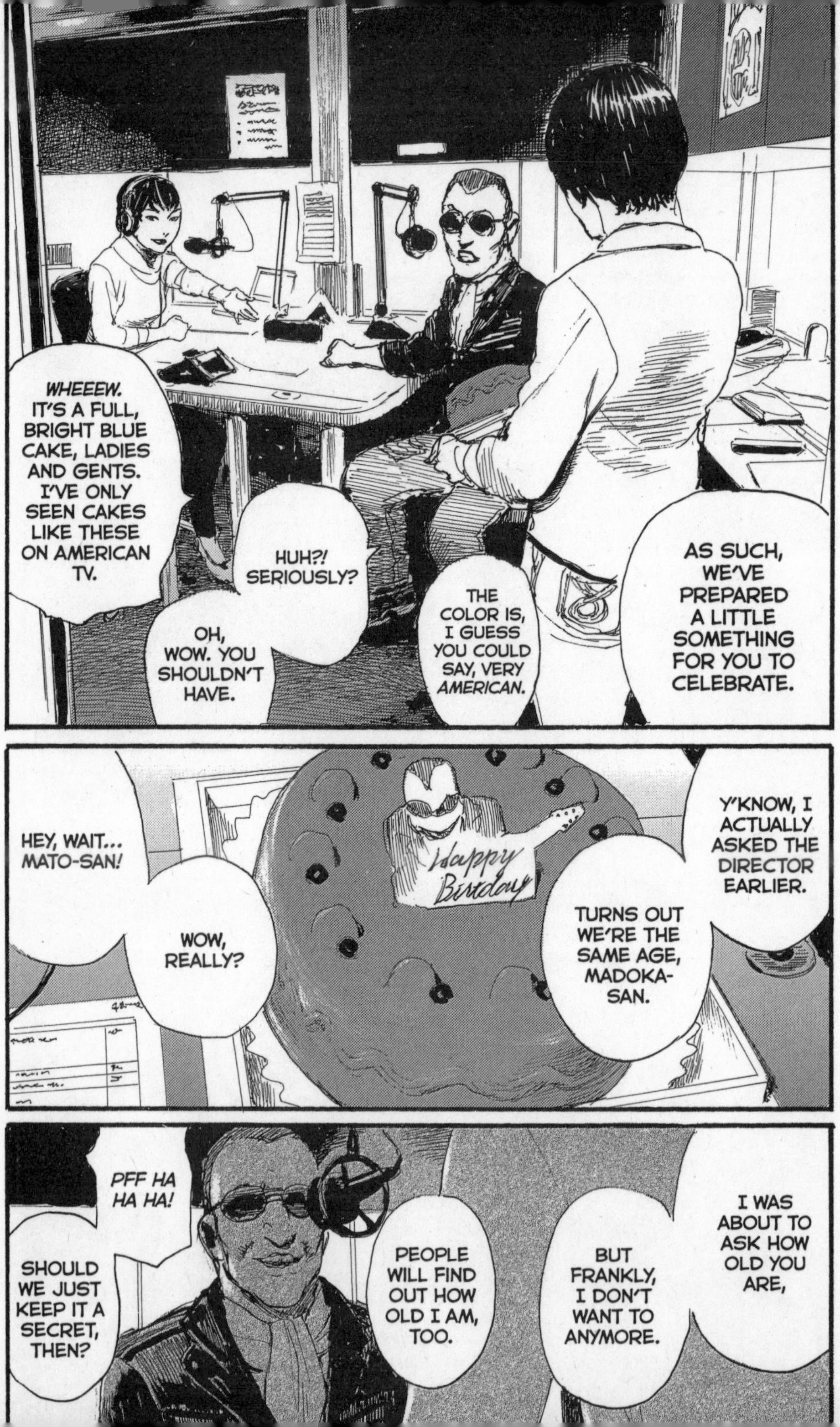
AS SUCH, WE'VE PREPARED A LITTLE SOMETHING FOR YOU TO CELEBRATE.
OH, WOW. YOU SHOULDN'T HAVE.
THE COLOR IS, I GUESS YOU COULD SAY, VERY *AMERICAN.*
HUH?! SERIOUSLY?
WHEEEW. IT'S A FULL, BRIGHT BLUE CAKE, LADIES AND GENTS. I'VE ONLY SEEN CAKES LIKE THESE ON AMERICAN TV.
Y'KNOW, I ACTUALLY ASKED THE DIRECTOR EARLIER.
TURNS OUT WE'RE THE SAME AGE, MADOKA-SAN.
HEY, WAIT... MATO-SAN!
WOW, REALLY?
Happy Birthday
I WAS ABOUT TO ASK HOW OLD YOU ARE,
BUT FRANKLY, I DON'T WANT TO ANYMORE.
PEOPLE WILL FIND OUT HOW OLD I AM, TOO.
PFF HA HA HA!
SHOULD WE JUST KEEP IT A SECRET, THEN?

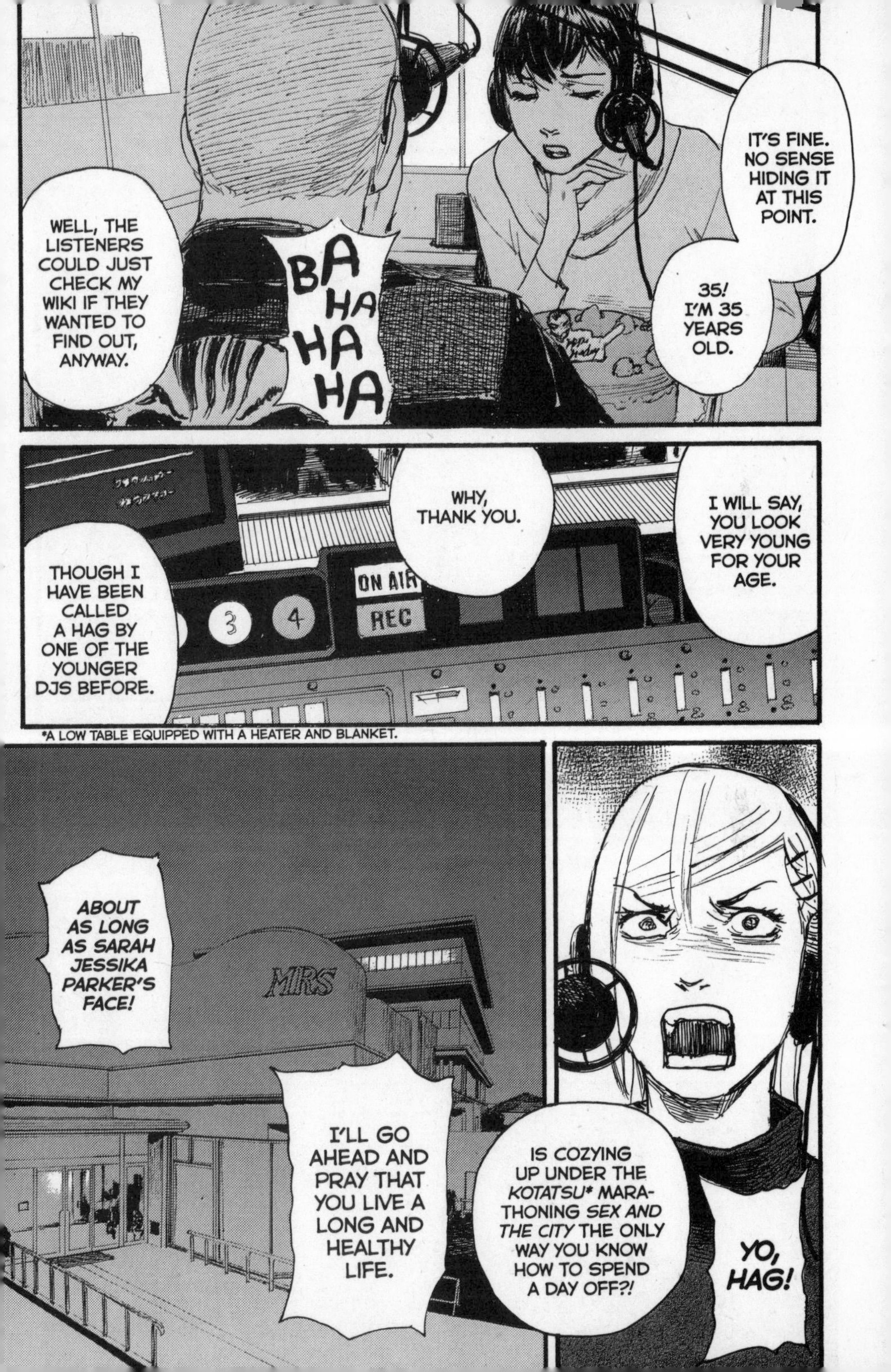
IT'S FINE. NO SENSE HIDING IT AT THIS POINT.
35! I'M 35 YEARS OLD.
WELL, THE LISTENERS COULD JUST CHECK MY WIKI IF THEY WANTED TO FIND OUT, ANYWAY.
BA HA HA HA
I WILL SAY, YOU LOOK VERY YOUNG FOR YOUR AGE.
WHY, THANK YOU.
THOUGH I HAVE BEEN CALLED A HAG BY ONE OF THE YOUNGER DJS BEFORE.
ON AIR
REC
YO, HAG!
IS COZYING UP UNDER THE *KOTATSU** MARA-THONING *SEX AND THE CITY* THE ONLY WAY YOU KNOW HOW TO SPEND A DAY OFF?!
I'LL GO AHEAD AND PRAY THAT YOU LIVE A LONG AND HEALTHY LIFE.
ABOUT AS LONG AS SARAH JESSIKA PARKER'S FACE!
MRS

*A LOW TABLE EQUIPPED WITH A HEATER AND BLANKET.

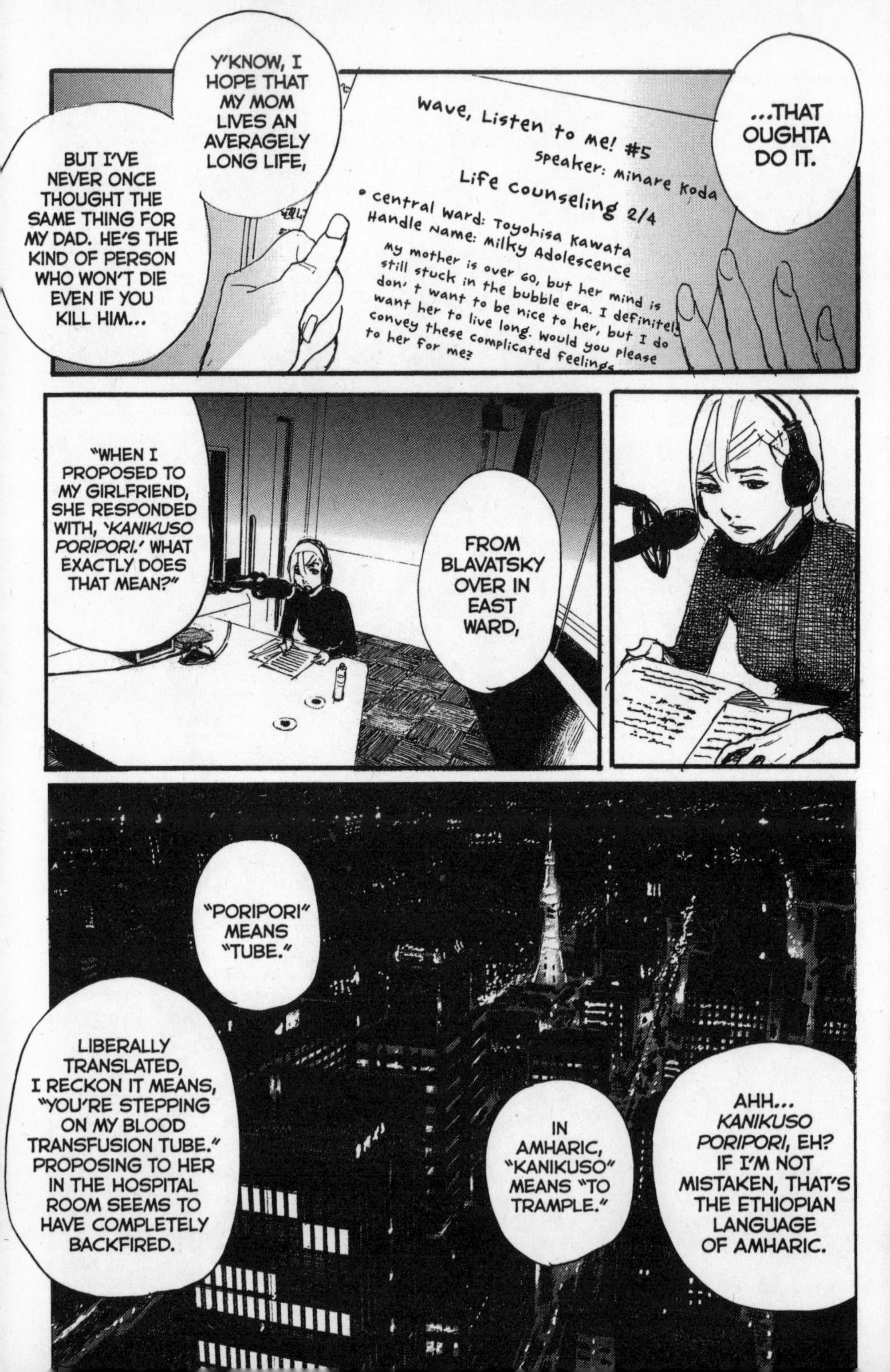
...THAT OUGHTA DO IT.
Wave, Listen to me! #5
Speaker: Minare Koda
Life counseling 2/4
• Central Ward: Toyohisa Kawata
Handle Name: Milky Adolescence
My mother is over 60, but her mind is still stuck in the bubble era. I definitel don't want to be nice to her, but I do want her to live long. Would you please convey these complicated feelings to her for me?
Y'KNOW, I HOPE THAT MY MOM LIVES AN AVERAGELY LONG LIFE,
BUT I'VE NEVER ONCE THOUGHT THE SAME THING FOR MY DAD. HE'S THE KIND OF PERSON WHO WON'T DIE EVEN IF YOU KILL HIM...
FROM BLAVATSKY OVER IN EAST WARD,
"WHEN I PROPOSED TO MY GIRLFRIEND, SHE RESPONDED WITH, '*KANIKUSO PORIPORI.*' WHAT EXACTLY DOES THAT MEAN?"
AHH... *KANIKUSO PORIPORI*, EH? IF I'M NOT MISTAKEN, THAT'S THE ETHIOPIAN LANGUAGE OF AMHARIC.
IN AMHARIC, "KANIKUSO" MEANS "TO TRAMPLE."
"PORIPORI" MEANS "TUBE."
LIBERALLY TRANSLATED, I RECKON IT MEANS, "YOU'RE STEPPING ON MY BLOOD TRANSFUSION TUBE." PROPOSING TO HER IN THE HOSPITAL ROOM SEEMS TO HAVE COMPLETELY BACKFIRED.

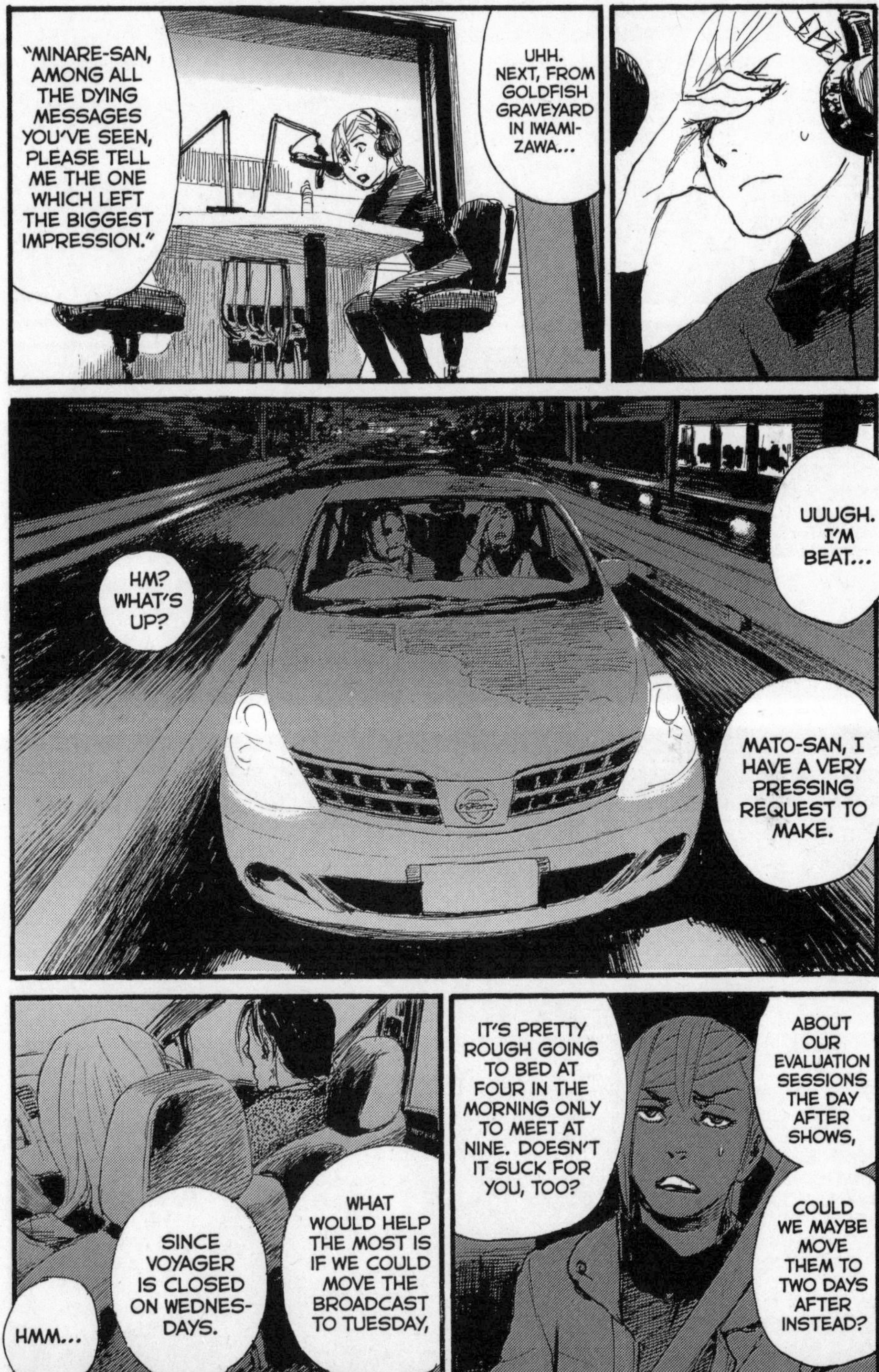
UHH. NEXT, FROM GOLDFISH GRAVEYARD IN IWAMI-ZAWA...
"MINARE-SAN, AMONG ALL THE DYING MESSAGES YOU'VE SEEN, PLEASE TELL ME THE ONE WHICH LEFT THE BIGGEST IMPRESSION."
UUUGH. I'M BEAT...
HM? WHAT'S UP?
MATO-SAN, I HAVE A VERY PRESSING REQUEST TO MAKE.
ABOUT OUR EVALUATION SESSIONS THE DAY AFTER SHOWS,
COULD WE MAYBE MOVE THEM TO TWO DAYS AFTER INSTEAD?
IT'S PRETTY ROUGH GOING TO BED AT FOUR IN THE MORNING ONLY TO MEET AT NINE. DOESN'T IT SUCK FOR YOU, TOO?
WHAT WOULD HELP THE MOST IS IF WE COULD MOVE THE BROADCAST TO TUESDAY,
SINCE VOYAGER IS CLOSED ON WEDNES-DAYS.
HMM...

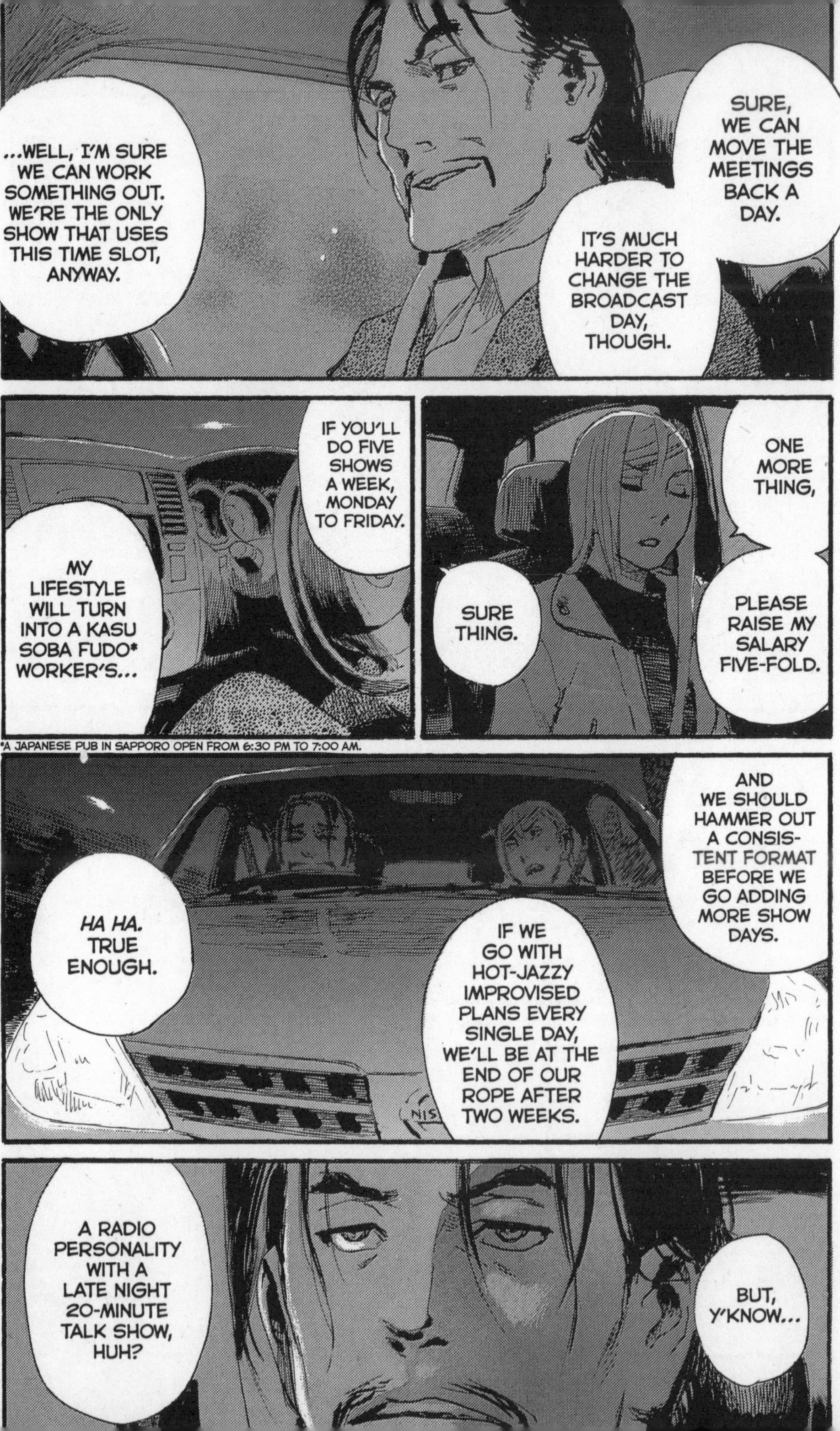
SURE, WE CAN MOVE THE MEETINGS BACK A DAY.
IT'S MUCH HARDER TO CHANGE THE BROADCAST DAY, THOUGH.
...WELL, I'M SURE WE CAN WORK SOMETHING OUT. WE'RE THE ONLY SHOW THAT USES THIS TIME SLOT, ANYWAY.
ONE MORE THING,
PLEASE RAISE MY SALARY FIVE-FOLD.
SURE THING.
IF YOU'LL DO FIVE SHOWS A WEEK, MONDAY TO FRIDAY.
MY LIFESTYLE WILL TURN INTO A KASU SOBA FUDO* WORKER'S...
AND WE SHOULD HAMMER OUT A CONSIS-TENT FORMAT BEFORE WE GO ADDING MORE SHOW DAYS.
IF WE GO WITH HOT-JAZZY IMPROVISED PLANS EVERY SINGLE DAY, WE'LL BE AT THE END OF OUR ROPE AFTER TWO WEEKS.
HA HA. TRUE ENOUGH.
BUT, Y'KNOW...
A RADIO PERSONALITY WITH A LATE NIGHT 20-MINUTE TALK SHOW, HUH?

*A JAPANESE PUB IN SAPPORO OPEN FROM 6:30 PM TO 7:00 AM.

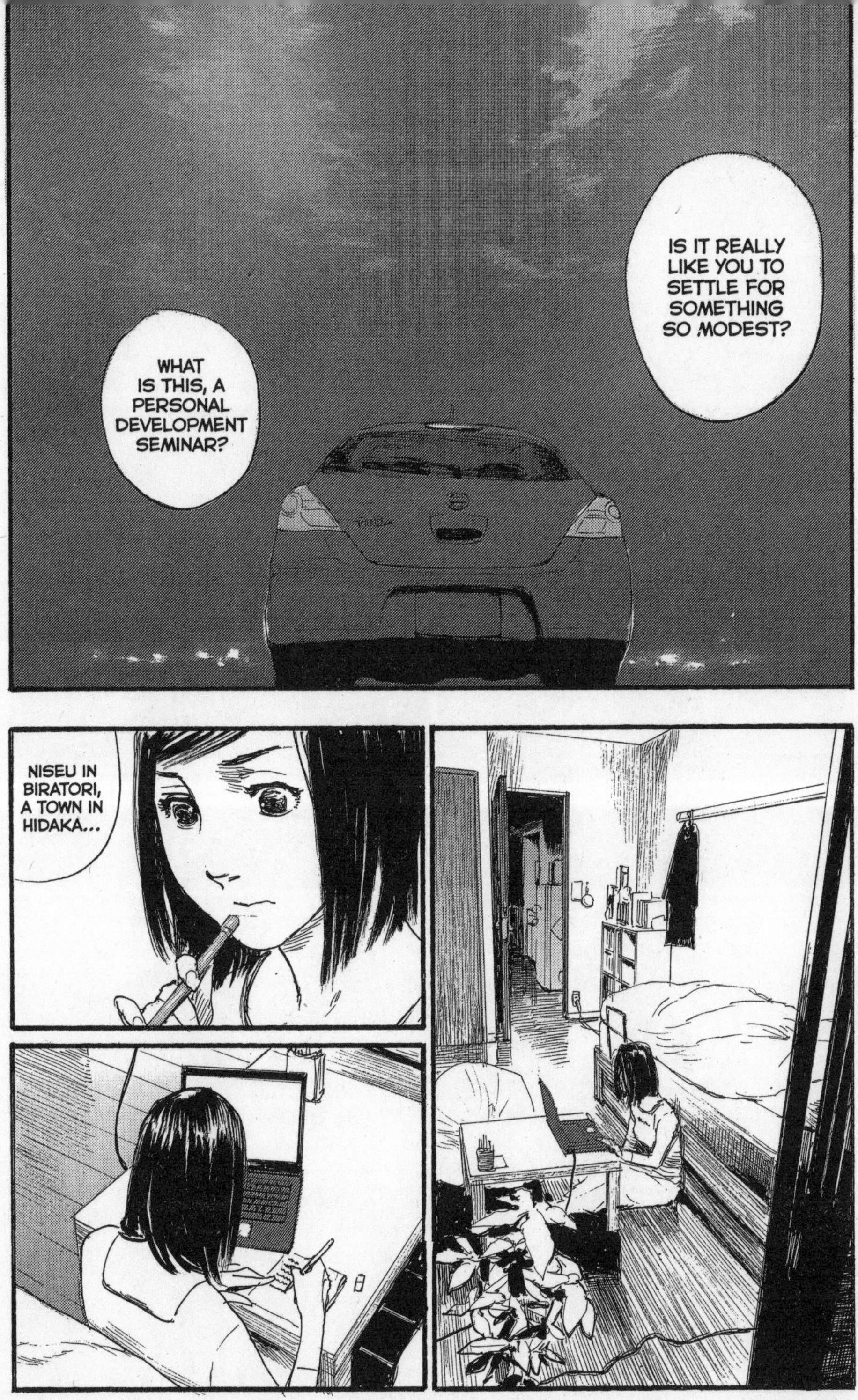
IS IT REALLY LIKE YOU TO SETTLE FOR SOMETHING SO MODEST?
WHAT IS THIS, A PERSONAL DEVELOPMENT SEMINAR?
NISEU IN BIRATORI, A TOWN IN HIDAKA...

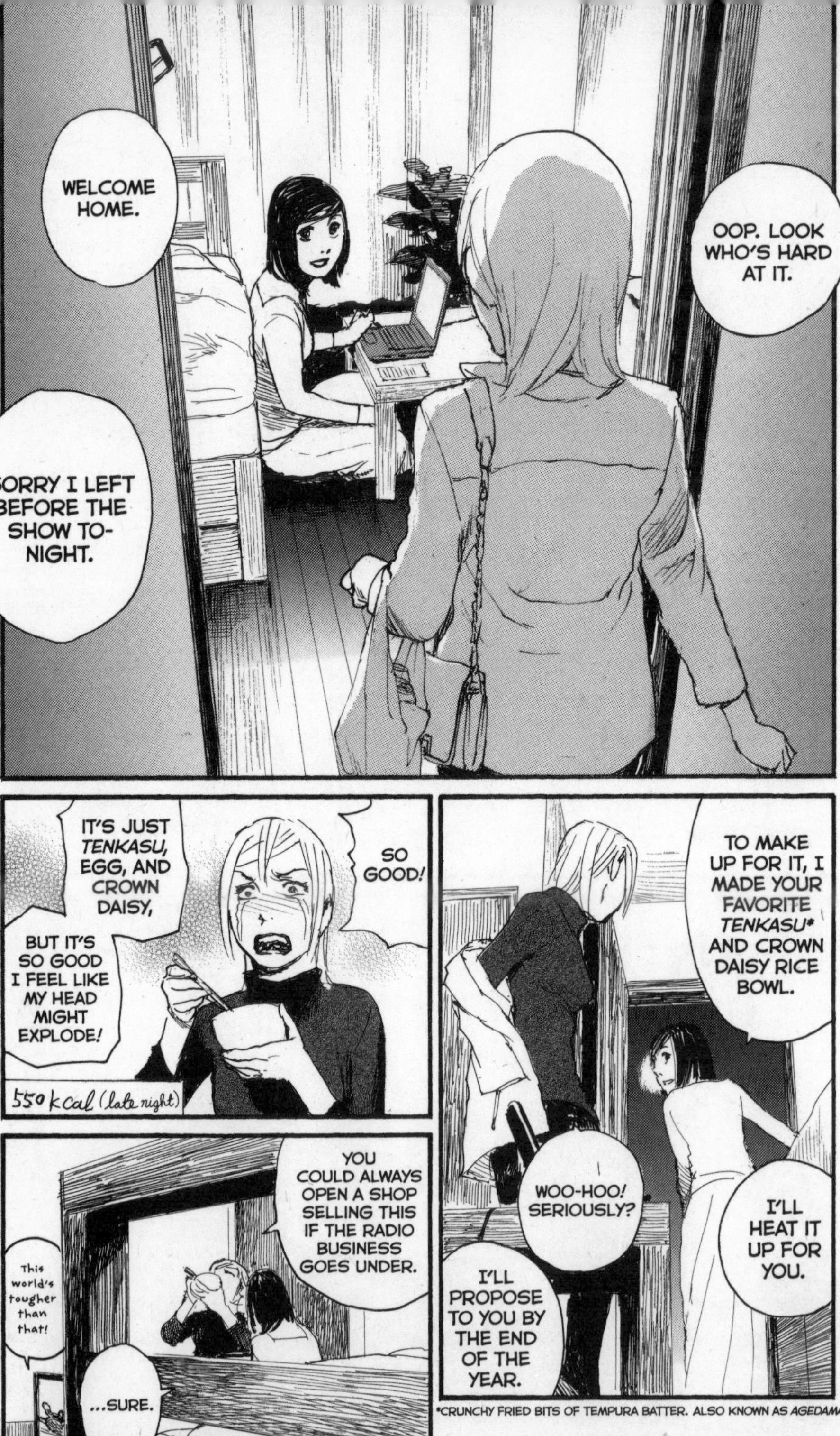
OOP. LOOK WHO'S HARD AT IT.
WELCOME HOME.
SORRY I LEFT BEFORE THE SHOW TO-NIGHT.
TO MAKE UP FOR IT, I MADE YOUR FAVORITE *TENKASU** AND CROWN DAISY RICE BOWL.
I'LL HEAT IT UP FOR YOU.
WOO-HOO! SERIOUSLY?
I'LL PROPOSE TO YOU BY THE END OF THE YEAR.
SO GOOD!
IT'S JUST *TENKASU*, EGG, AND CROWN DAISY,
BUT IT'S SO GOOD I FEEL LIKE MY HEAD MIGHT EXPLODE!
550 kcal (late night)
YOU COULD ALWAYS OPEN A SHOP SELLING THIS IF THE RADIO BUSINESS GOES UNDER.
This world's tougher than that!
...SURE.

*CRUNCHY FRIED BITS OF TEMPURA BATTER. ALSO KNOWN AS *AGEDAMA*.

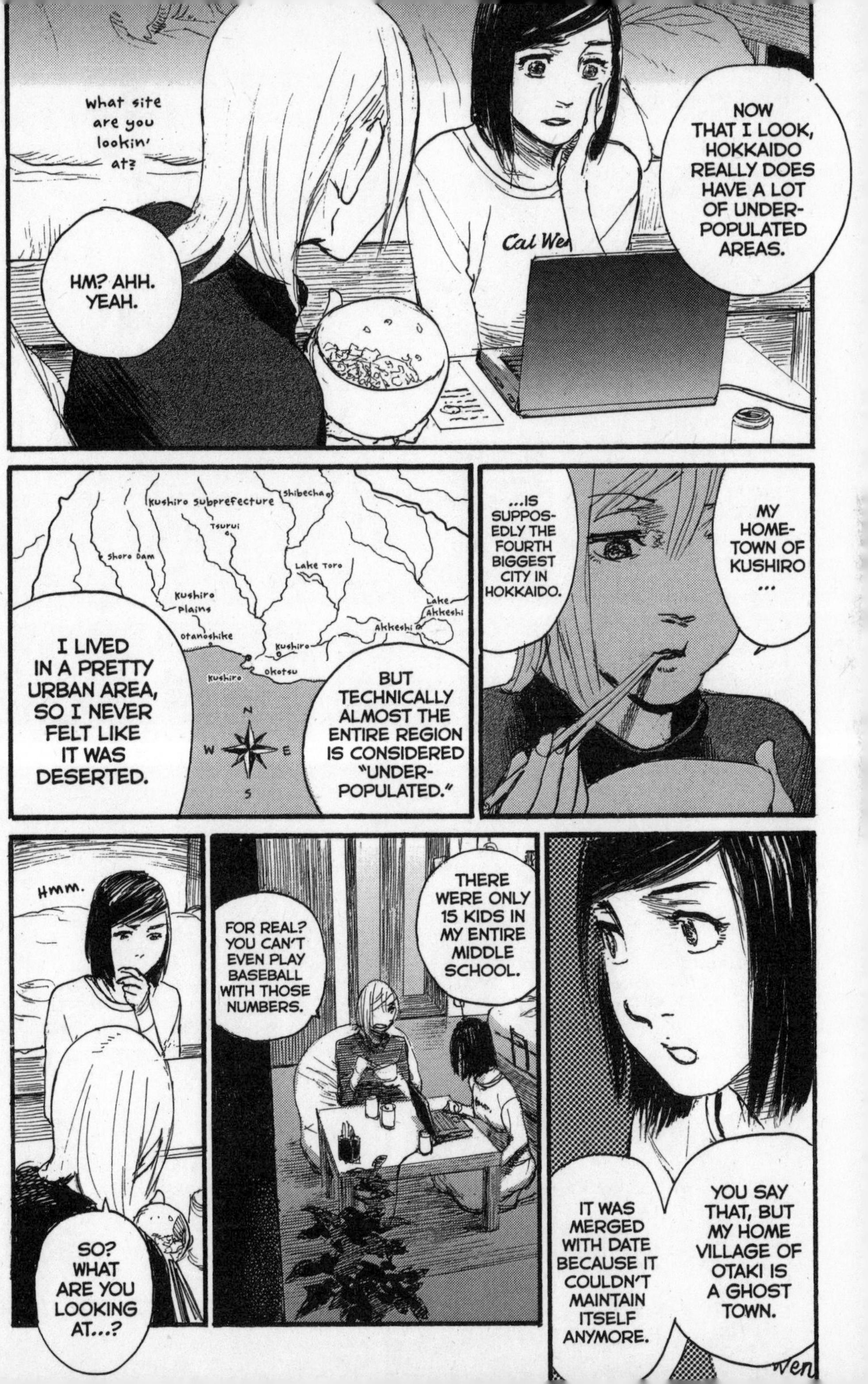
NOW THAT I LOOK, HOKKAIDO REALLY DOES HAVE A LOT OF UNDER-POPULATED AREAS.
Cal We
what site are you lookin' at?
HM? AHH. YEAH.
MY HOME-TOWN OF KUSHIRO ...
...IS SUPPOS-EDLY THE FOURTH BIGGEST CITY IN HOKKAIDO.
Kushiro subprefecture
Shibecha
Tsurui
Shoro Dam
Lake Toro
Kushiro plains
Lake Akkeshi
Akkeshi
Otanoshike
Kushiro
Kushiro
Okotsu
N
W
E
S
BUT TECHNICALLY ALMOST THE ENTIRE REGION IS CONSIDERED "UNDER-POPULATED."
I LIVED IN A PRETTY URBAN AREA, SO I NEVER FELT LIKE IT WAS DESERTED.
YOU SAY THAT, BUT MY HOME VILLAGE OF OTAKI IS A GHOST TOWN.
IT WAS MERGED WITH DATE BECAUSE IT COULDN'T MAINTAIN ITSELF ANYMORE.
THERE WERE ONLY 15 KIDS IN MY ENTIRE MIDDLE SCHOOL.
FOR REAL? YOU CAN'T EVEN PLAY BASEBALL WITH THOSE NUMBERS.
Hmm.
SO? WHAT ARE YOU LOOKING AT...?

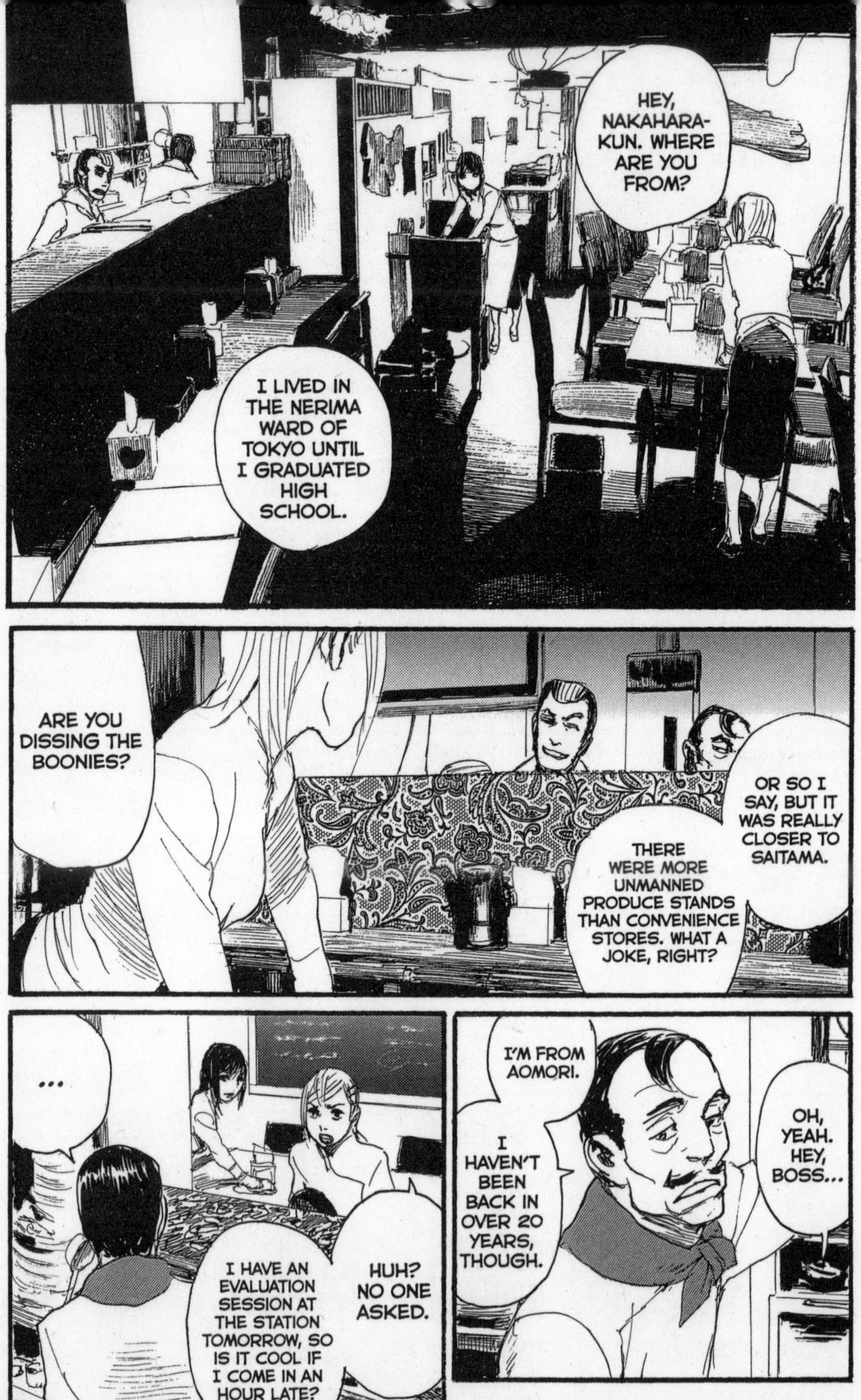
HEY, NAKAHARA-KUN. WHERE ARE YOU FROM?
I LIVED IN THE NERIMA WARD OF TOKYO UNTIL I GRADUATED HIGH SCHOOL.
OR SO I SAY, BUT IT WAS REALLY CLOSER TO SAITAMA.
THERE WERE MORE UNMANNED PRODUCE STANDS THAN CONVENIENCE STORES. WHAT A JOKE, RIGHT?
ARE YOU DISSING THE BOONIES?
I'M FROM AOMORI.
I HAVEN'T BEEN BACK IN OVER 20 YEARS, THOUGH.
OH, YEAH. HEY, BOSS...
HUH? NO ONE ASKED.
...
I HAVE AN EVALUATION SESSION AT THE STATION TOMORROW, SO IS IT COOL IF I COME IN AN HOUR LATE?

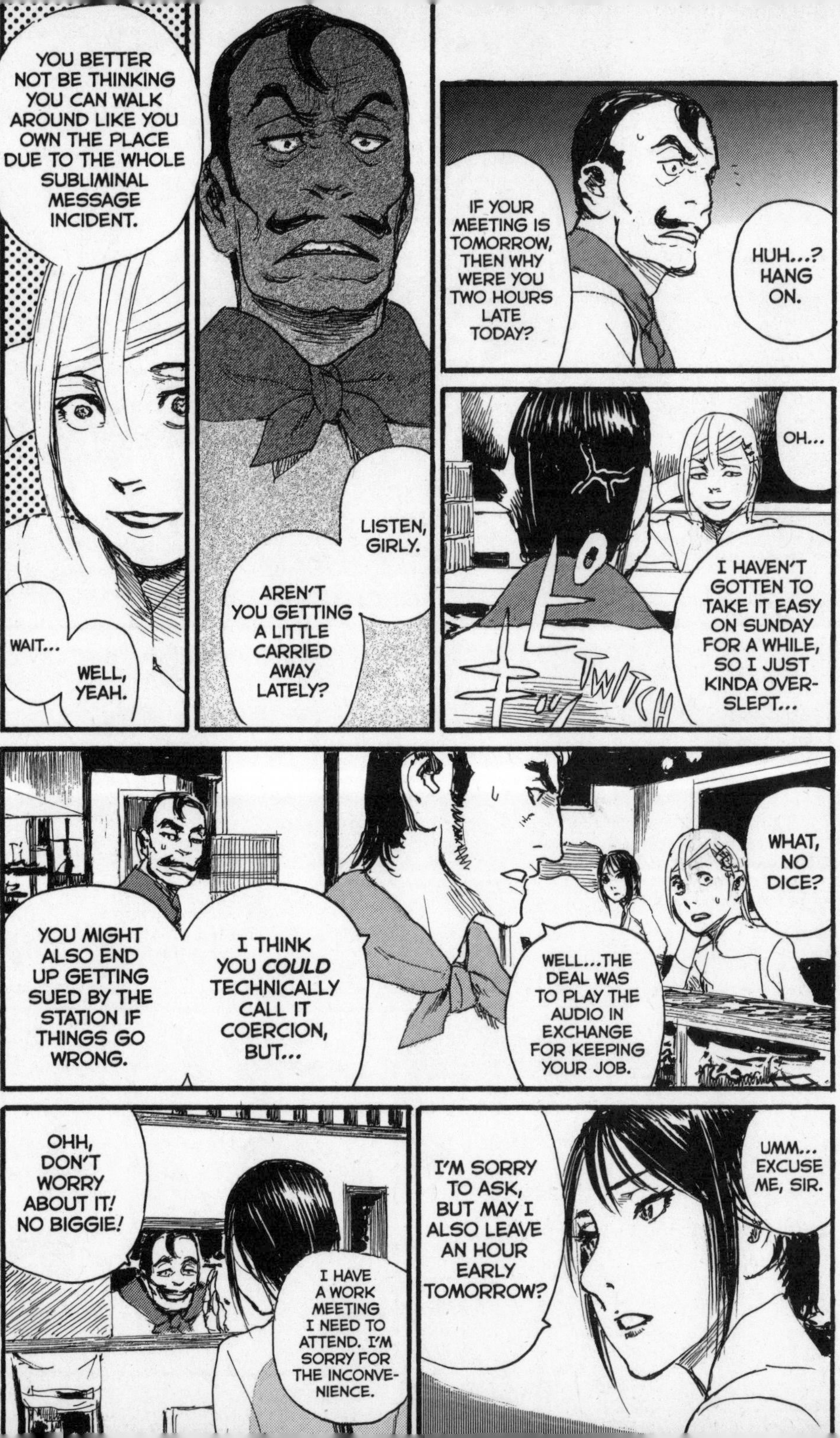
HUH...? HANG ON.
IF YOUR MEETING IS TOMORROW, THEN WHY WERE YOU TWO HOURS LATE TODAY?
OH...
I HAVEN'T GOTTEN TO TAKE IT EASY ON SUNDAY FOR A WHILE, SO I JUST KINDA OVER-SLEPT...
TWITCH
LISTEN, GIRLY.
AREN'T YOU GETTING A LITTLE CARRIED AWAY LATELY?
YOU BETTER NOT BE THINKING YOU CAN WALK AROUND LIKE YOU OWN THE PLACE DUE TO THE WHOLE SUBLIMINAL MESSAGE INCIDENT.
WAIT...
WELL, YEAH.
WHAT, NO DICE?
WELL...THE DEAL WAS TO PLAY THE AUDIO IN EXCHANGE FOR KEEPING YOUR JOB.
I THINK YOU *COULD* TECHNICALLY CALL IT COERCION, BUT...
YOU MIGHT ALSO END UP GETTING SUED BY THE STATION IF THINGS GO WRONG.
UMM... EXCUSE ME, SIR.
I'M SORRY TO ASK, BUT MAY I ALSO LEAVE AN HOUR EARLY TOMORROW?
I HAVE A WORK MEETING I NEED TO ATTEND. I'M SORRY FOR THE INCONVE-NIENCE.
OHH, DON'T WORRY ABOUT IT! NO BIGGIE!

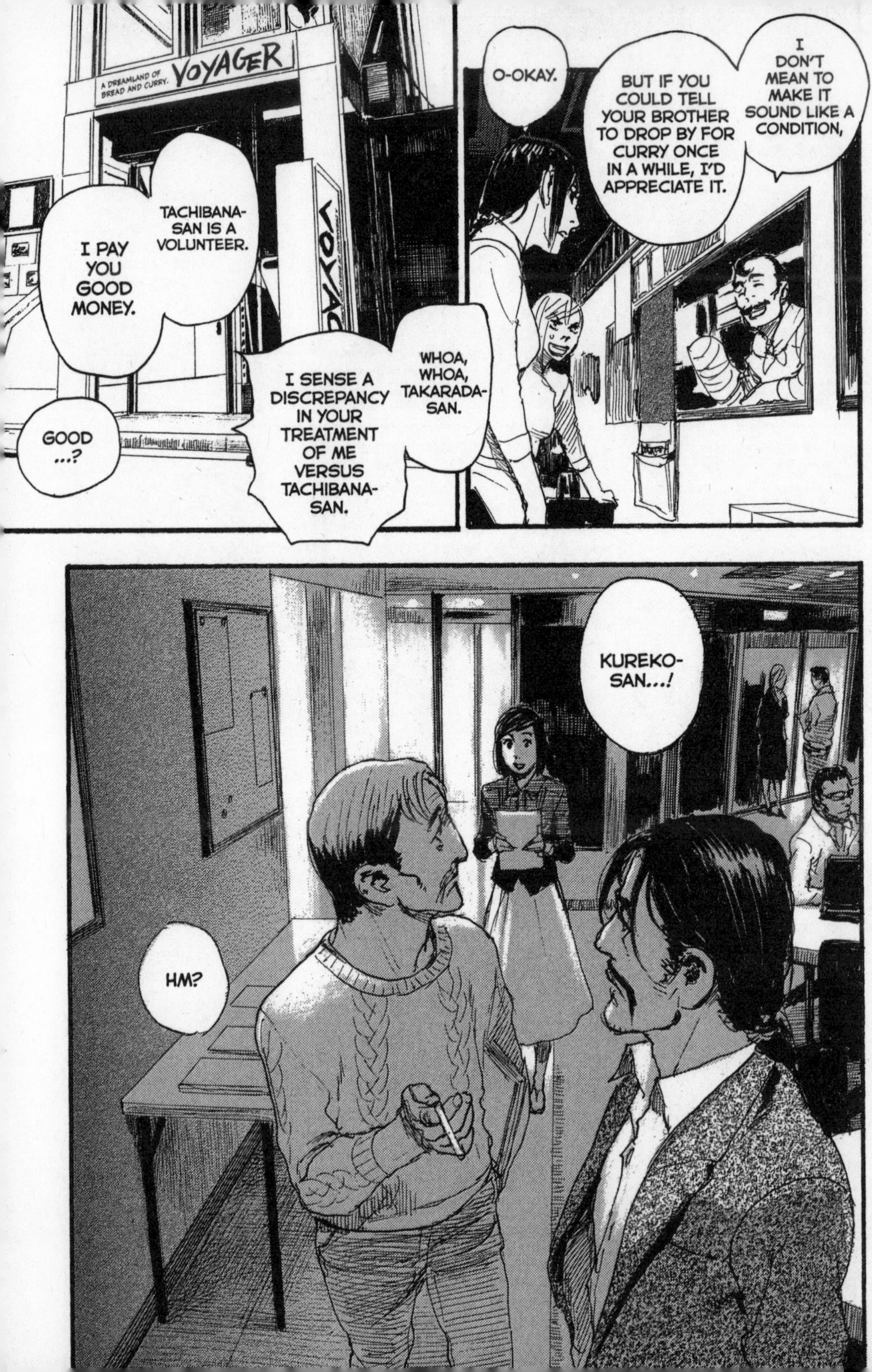
I DON'T MEAN TO MAKE IT SOUND LIKE A CONDITION,
BUT IF YOU COULD TELL YOUR BROTHER TO DROP BY FOR CURRY ONCE IN A WHILE, I'D APPRECIATE IT.
O-OKAY.
A DREAMLAND OF BREAD AND CURRY. VOYAGER
TACHIBANA-SAN IS A VOLUNTEER.
I PAY YOU GOOD MONEY.
WHOA, WHOA, TAKARADA-SAN.
I SENSE A DISCREPANCY IN YOUR TREATMENT OF ME VERSUS TACHIBANA-SAN.
GOOD ...?
KUREKO-SAN...!
HM?

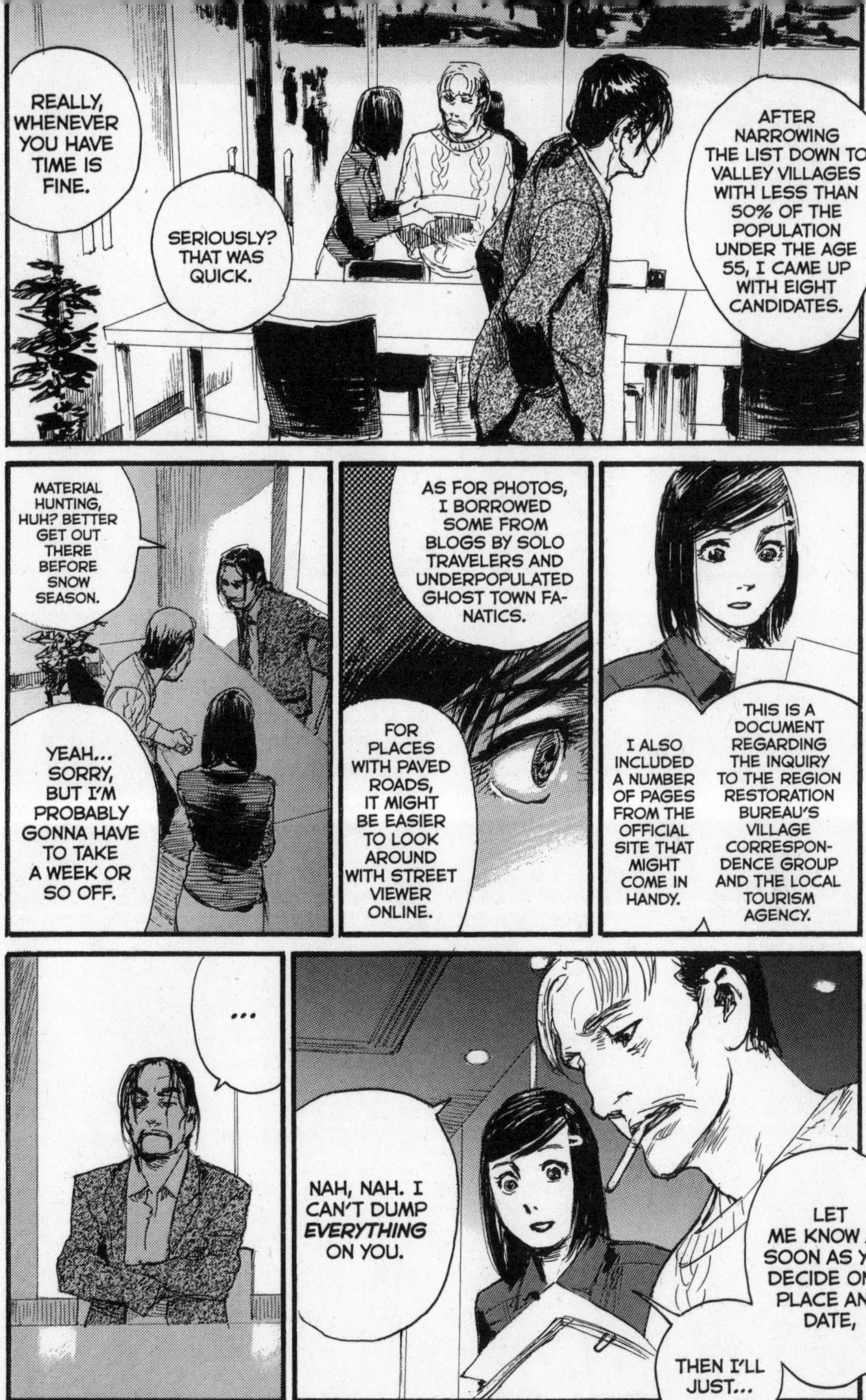
AFTER NARROWING THE LIST DOWN TO VALLEY VILLAGES WITH LESS THAN 50% OF THE POPULATION UNDER THE AGE 55, I CAME UP WITH EIGHT CANDIDATES.
REALLY, WHENEVER YOU HAVE TIME IS FINE.
SERIOUSLY? THAT WAS QUICK.
THIS IS A DOCUMENT REGARDING THE INQUIRY TO THE REGION RESTORATION BUREAU'S VILLAGE CORRESPONDENCE GROUP AND THE LOCAL TOURISM AGENCY.
I ALSO INCLUDED A NUMBER OF PAGES FROM THE OFFICIAL SITE THAT MIGHT COME IN HANDY.
AS FOR PHOTOS, I BORROWED SOME FROM BLOGS BY SOLO TRAVELERS AND UNDERPOPULATED GHOST TOWN FANATICS.
FOR PLACES WITH PAVED ROADS, IT MIGHT BE EASIER TO LOOK AROUND WITH STREET VIEWER ONLINE.
MATERIAL HUNTING, HUH? BETTER GET OUT THERE BEFORE SNOW SEASON.
YEAH... SORRY, BUT I'M PROBABLY GONNA HAVE TO TAKE A WEEK OR SO OFF.
LET ME KNOW AS SOON AS YOU DECIDE ON A PLACE AND DATE,
THEN I'LL JUST...
NAH, NAH. I CAN'T DUMP *EVERYTHING* ON YOU.
...

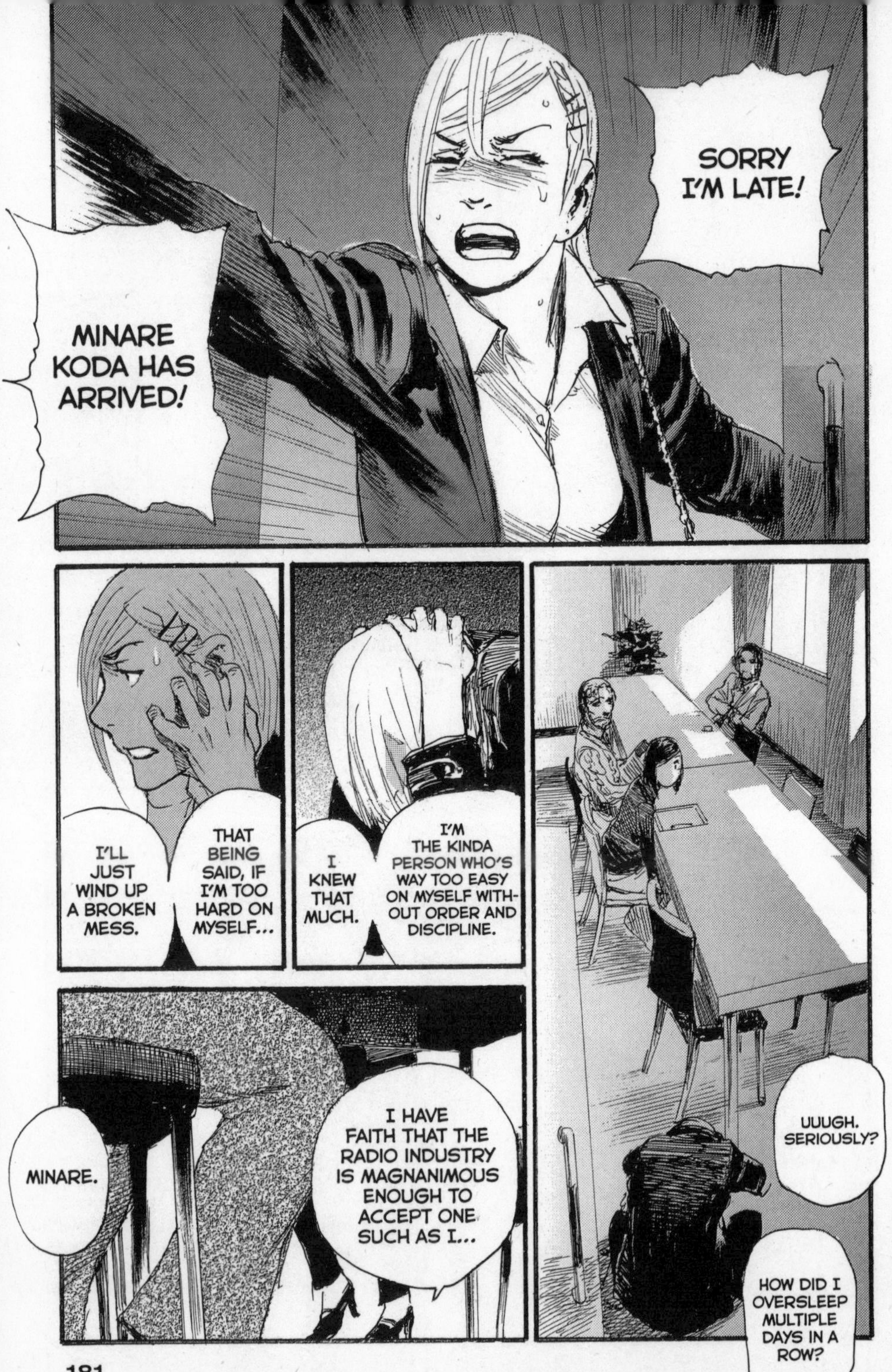
SORRY I'M LATE!
MINARE KODA HAS ARRIVED!
UUUGH. SERIOUSLY?
HOW DID I OVERSLEEP MULTIPLE DAYS IN A ROW?
I'M THE KINDA PERSON WHO'S WAY TOO EASY ON MYSELF WITH-OUT ORDER AND DISCIPLINE.
I KNEW THAT MUCH.
THAT BEING SAID, IF I'M TOO HARD ON MYSELF...
I'LL JUST WIND UP A BROKEN MESS.
I HAVE FAITH THAT THE RADIO INDUSTRY IS MAGNANIMOUS ENOUGH TO ACCEPT ONE SUCH AS I...
MINARE.

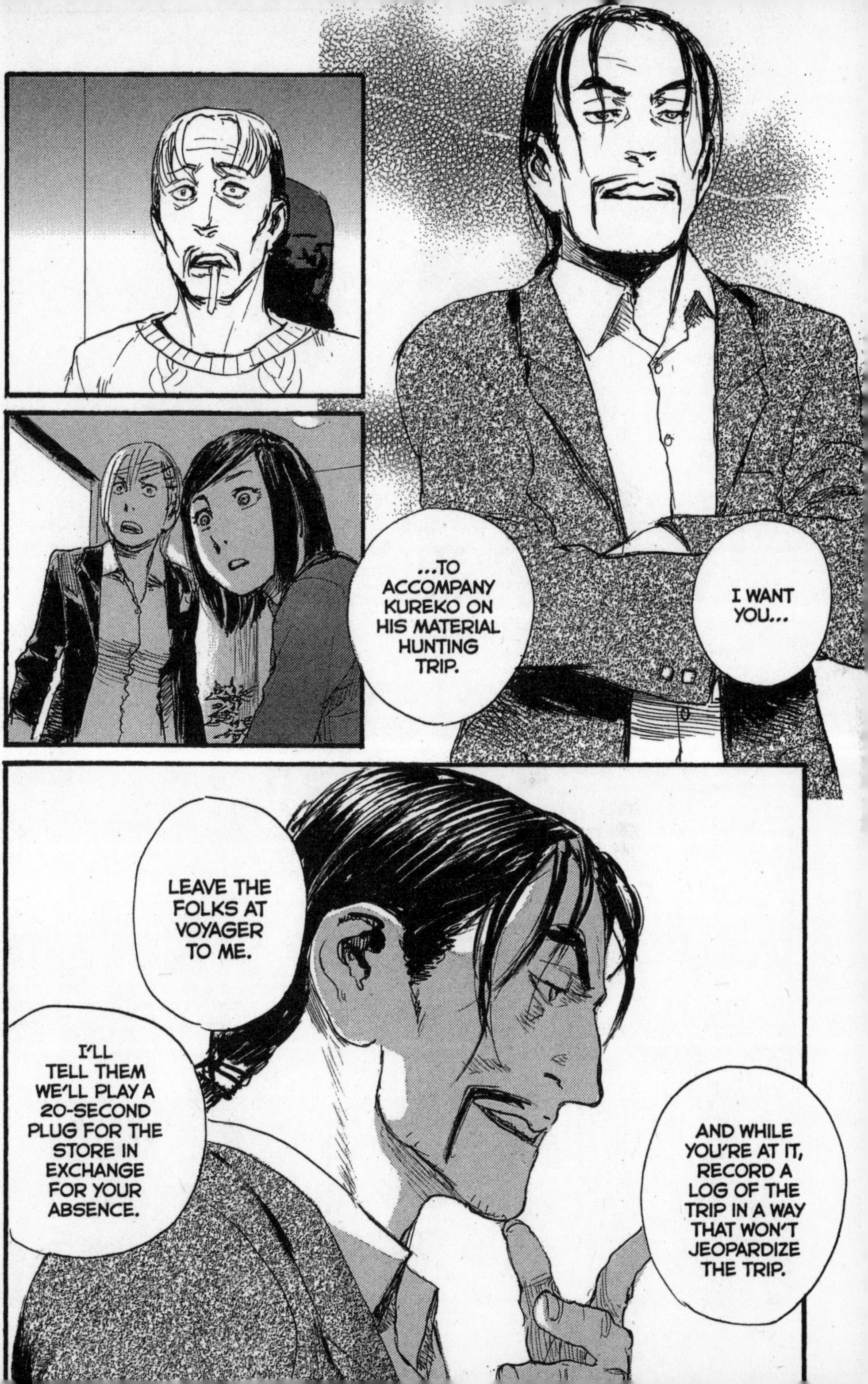
I WANT YOU...
...TO ACCOMPANY KUREKO ON HIS MATERIAL HUNTING TRIP.
LEAVE THE FOLKS AT VOYAGER TO ME.
I'LL TELL THEM WE'LL PLAY A 20-SECOND PLUG FOR THE STORE IN EXCHANGE FOR YOUR ABSENCE.
AND WHILE YOU'RE AT IT, RECORD A LOG OF THE TRIP IN A WAY THAT WON'T JEOPARDIZE THE TRIP.

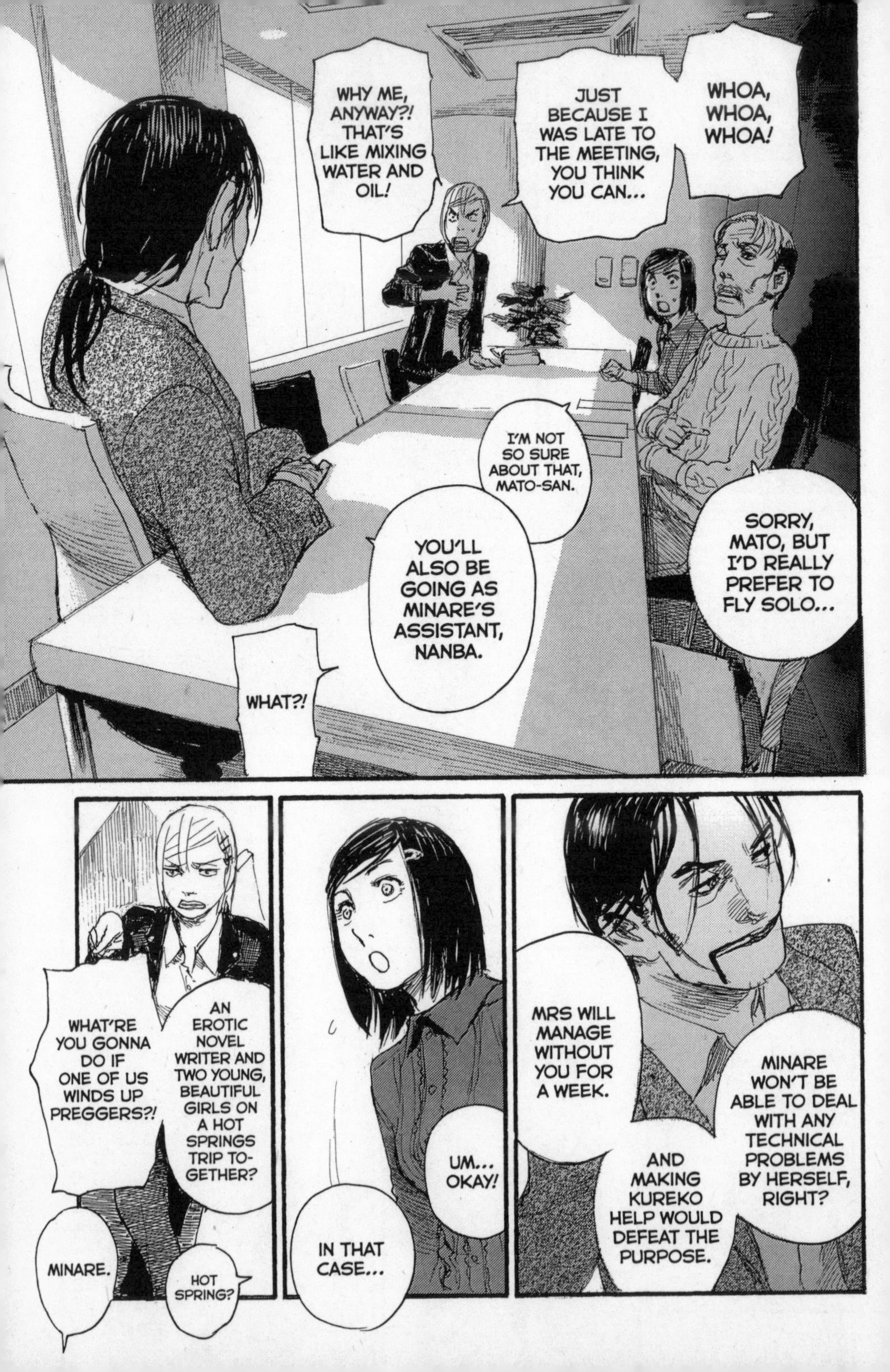
WHOA, WHOA, WHOA!
JUST BECAUSE I WAS LATE TO THE MEETING, YOU THINK YOU CAN...
WHY ME, ANYWAY?! THAT'S LIKE MIXING WATER AND OIL!
SORRY, MATO, BUT I'D REALLY PREFER TO FLY SOLO...
I'M NOT SO SURE ABOUT THAT, MATO-SAN.
YOU'LL ALSO BE GOING AS MINARE'S ASSISTANT, NANBA.
WHAT?!
MINARE WON'T BE ABLE TO DEAL WITH ANY TECHNICAL PROBLEMS BY HERSELF, RIGHT?
MRS WILL MANAGE WITHOUT YOU FOR A WEEK.
AND MAKING KUREKO HELP WOULD DEFEAT THE PURPOSE.
UM... OKAY!
IN THAT CASE...
AN EROTIC NOVEL WRITER AND TWO YOUNG, BEAUTIFUL GIRLS ON A HOT SPRINGS TRIP TO-GETHER?
WHAT'RE YOU GONNA DO IF ONE OF US WINDS UP PREGGERS?!
HOT SPRING?
MINARE.

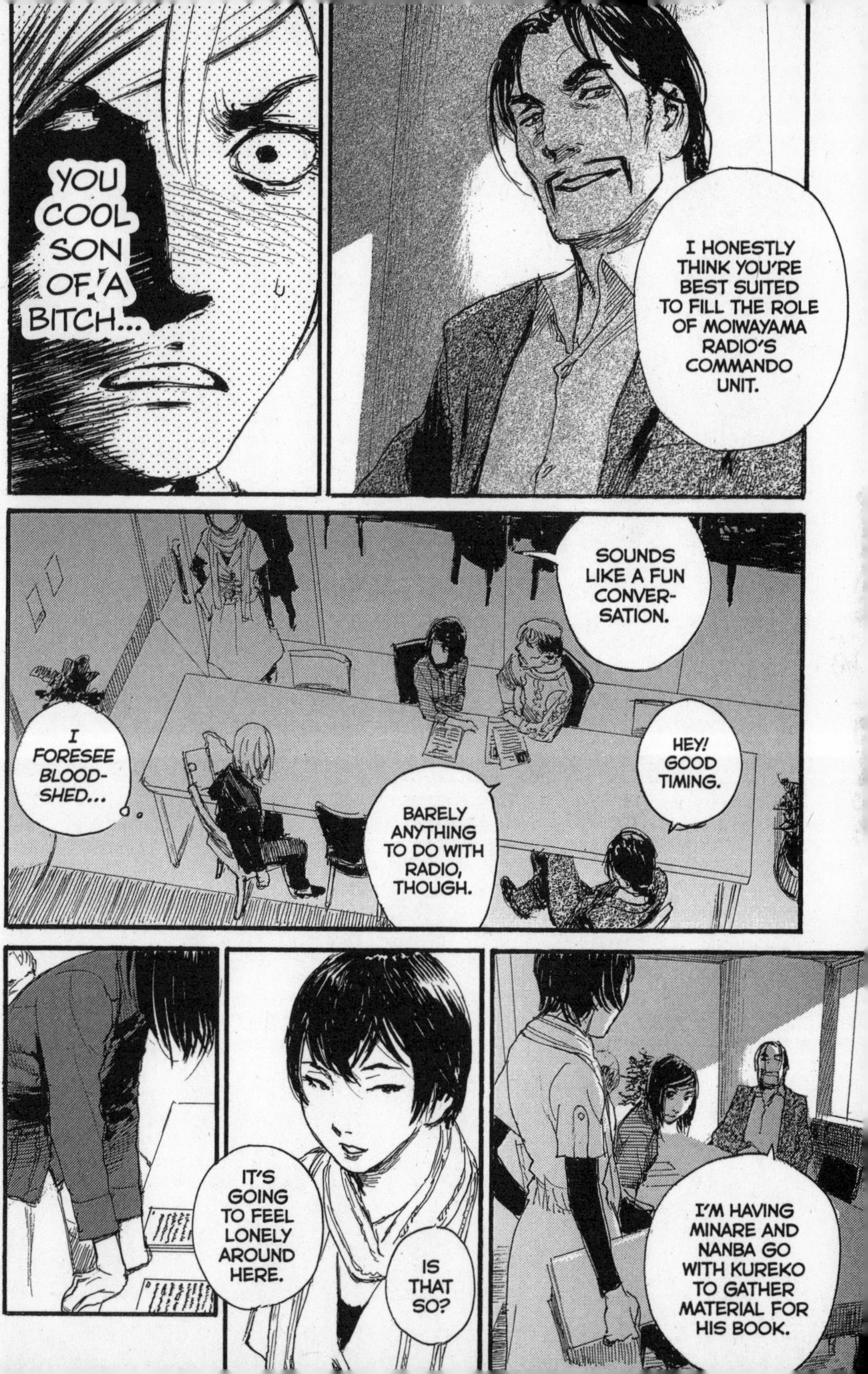
I HONESTLY THINK YOU'RE BEST SUITED TO FILL THE ROLE OF MOIWAYAMA RADIO'S COMMANDO UNIT.
YOU COOL SON OF A BITCH...
SOUNDS LIKE A FUN CONVERSATION.
HEY! GOOD TIMING.
BARELY ANYTHING TO DO WITH RADIO, THOUGH.
I FORESEE BLOODSHED...
I'M HAVING MINARE AND NANBA GO WITH KUREKO TO GATHER MATERIAL FOR HIS BOOK.
IS THAT SO?
IT'S GOING TO FEEL LONELY AROUND HERE.

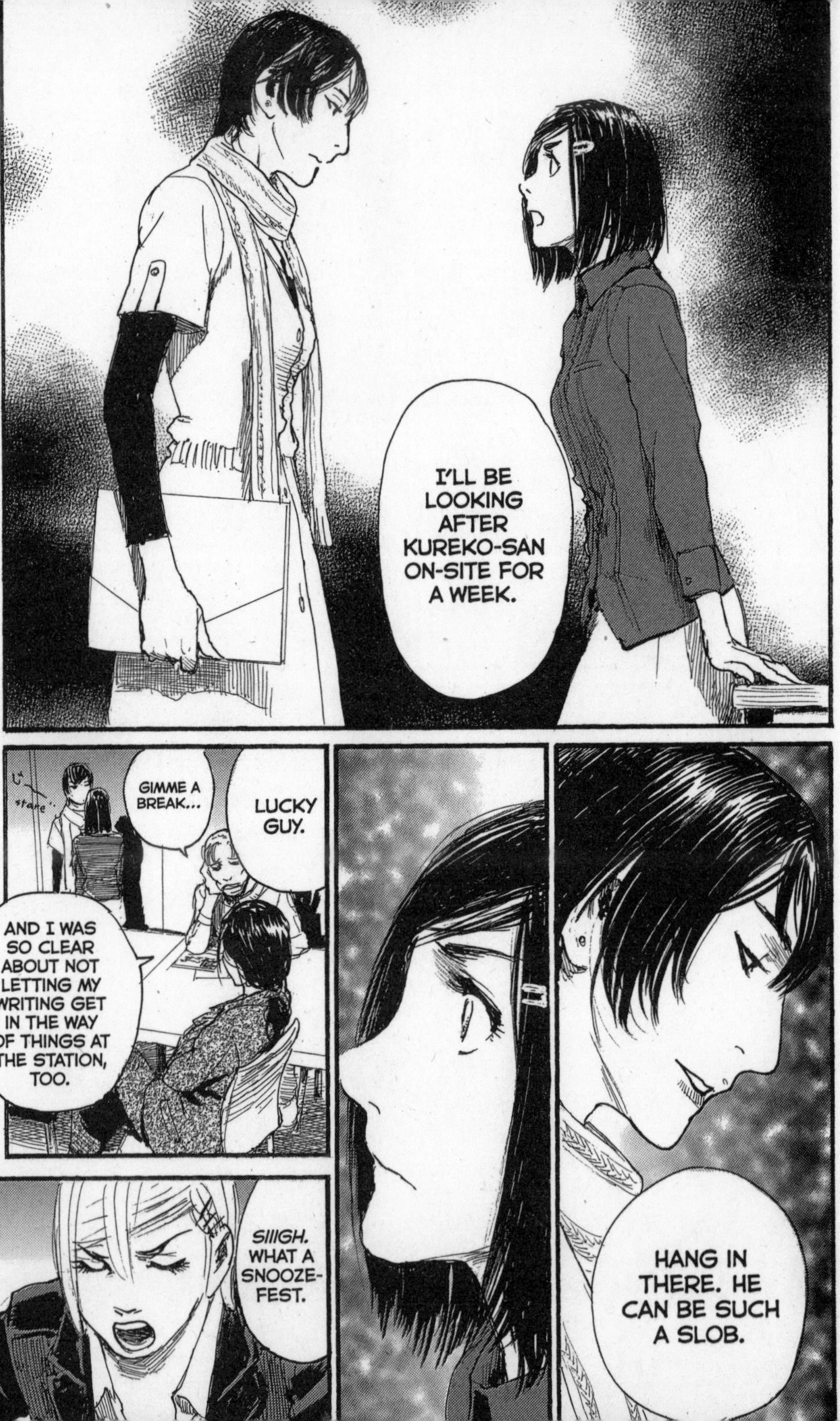

I'LL BE LOOKING AFTER KUREKO-SAN ON-SITE FOR A WEEK.
HANG IN THERE. HE CAN BE SUCH A SLOB.
LUCKY GUY.
GIMME A BREAK...
stare
AND I WAS SO CLEAR ABOUT NOT LETTING MY WRITING GET IN THE WAY OF THINGS AT THE STATION, TOO.
SIIIGH. WHAT A SNOOZE-FEST.

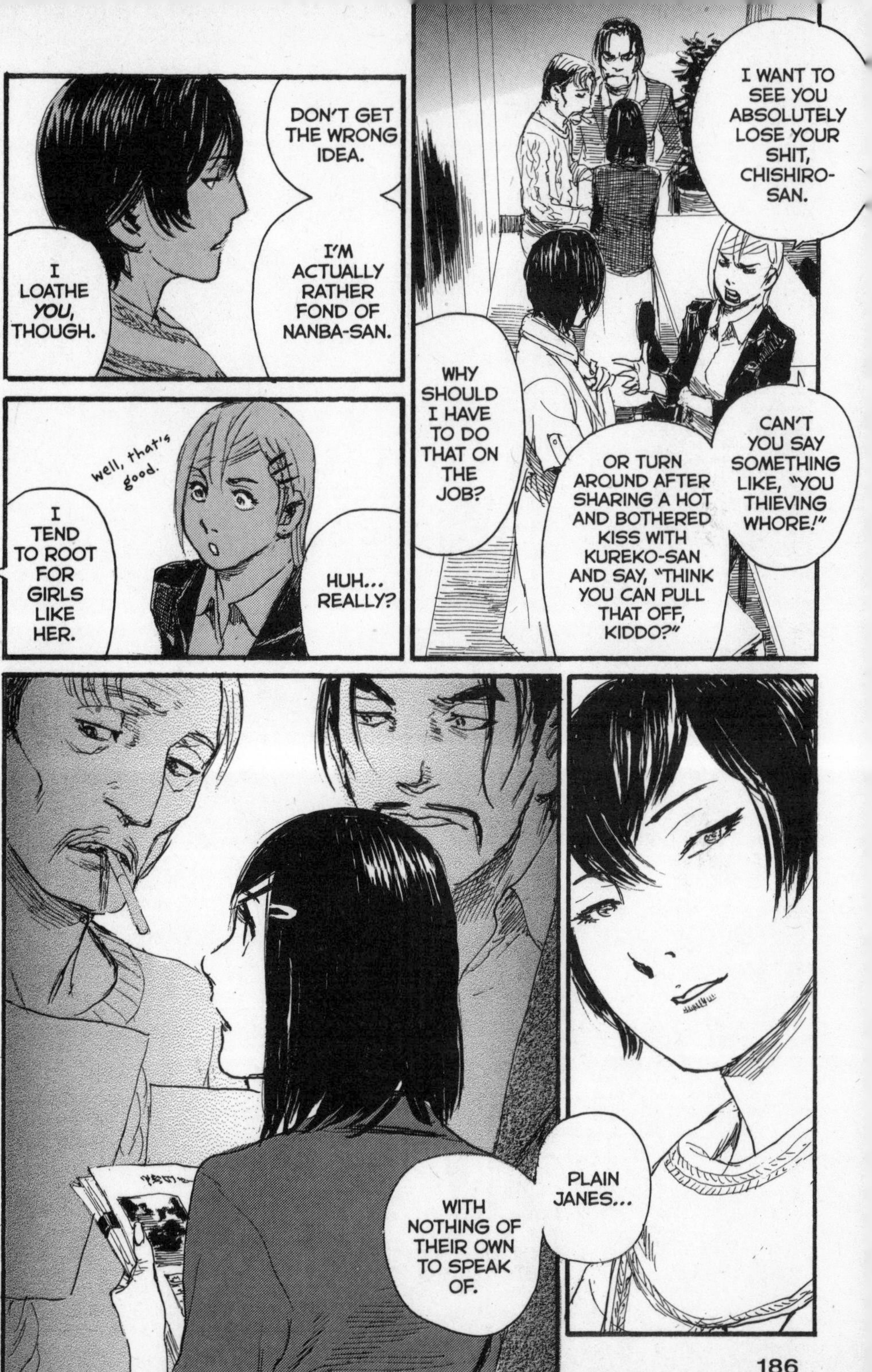
I WANT TO SEE YOU ABSOLUTELY LOSE YOUR SHIT, CHISHIRO-SAN.
CAN'T YOU SAY SOMETHING LIKE, "YOU THIEVING WHORE!"
OR TURN AROUND AFTER SHARING A HOT AND BOTHERED KISS WITH KUREKO-SAN AND SAY, "THINK YOU CAN PULL THAT OFF, KIDDO?"
WHY SHOULD I HAVE TO DO THAT ON THE JOB?
DON'T GET THE WRONG IDEA.
I'M ACTUALLY RATHER FOND OF NANBA-SAN.
I LOATHE *YOU*, THOUGH.
HUH... REALLY?
well, that's good.
I TEND TO ROOT FOR GIRLS LIKE HER.
PLAIN JANES...
WITH NOTHING OF THEIR OWN TO SPEAK OF.

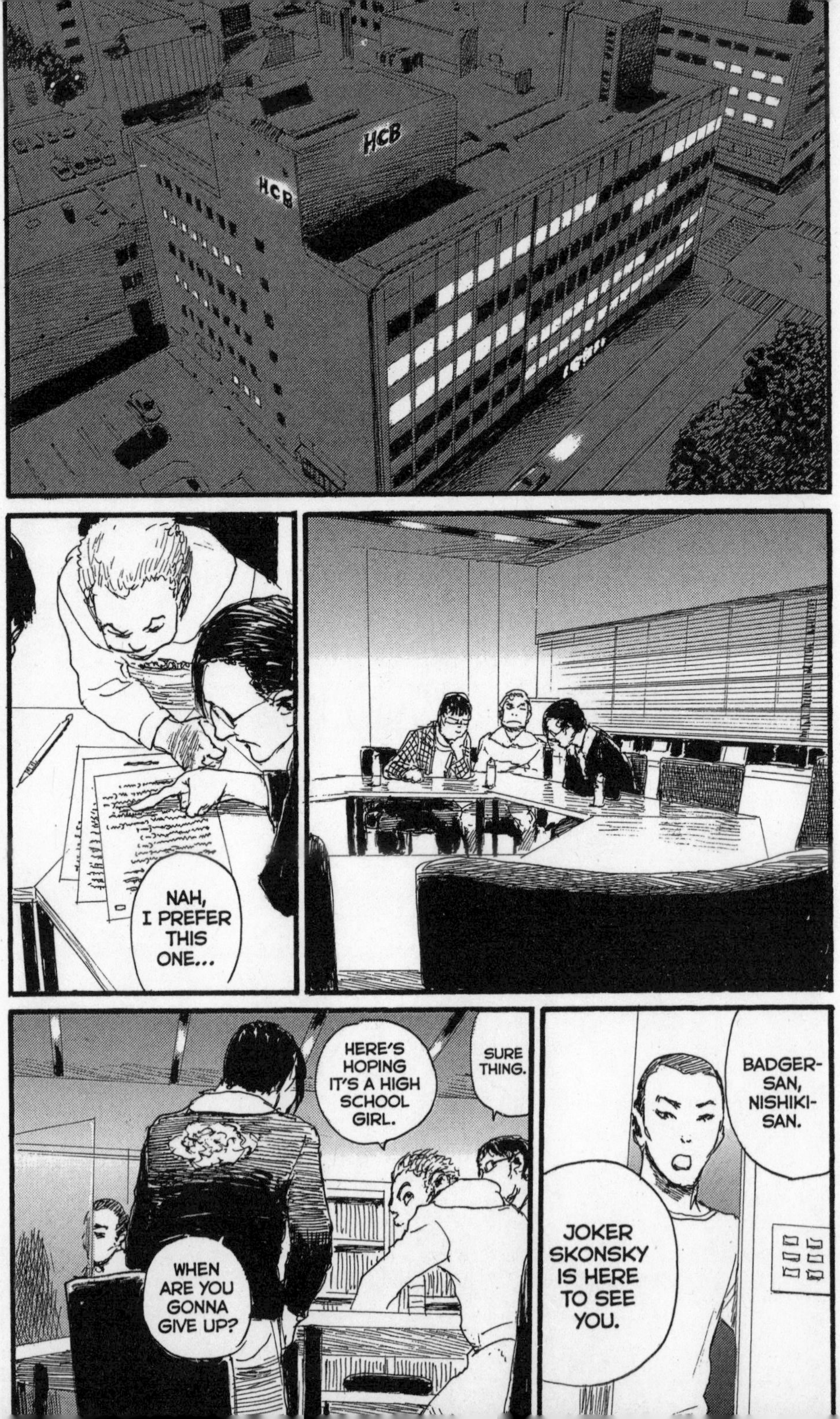
HCB
HCB
NAH, I PREFER THIS ONE...
BADGER-SAN, NISHIKI-SAN.
JOKER SKONSKY IS HERE TO SEE YOU.
SURE THING.
HERE'S HOPING IT'S A HIGH SCHOOL GIRL.
WHEN ARE YOU GONNA GIVE UP?

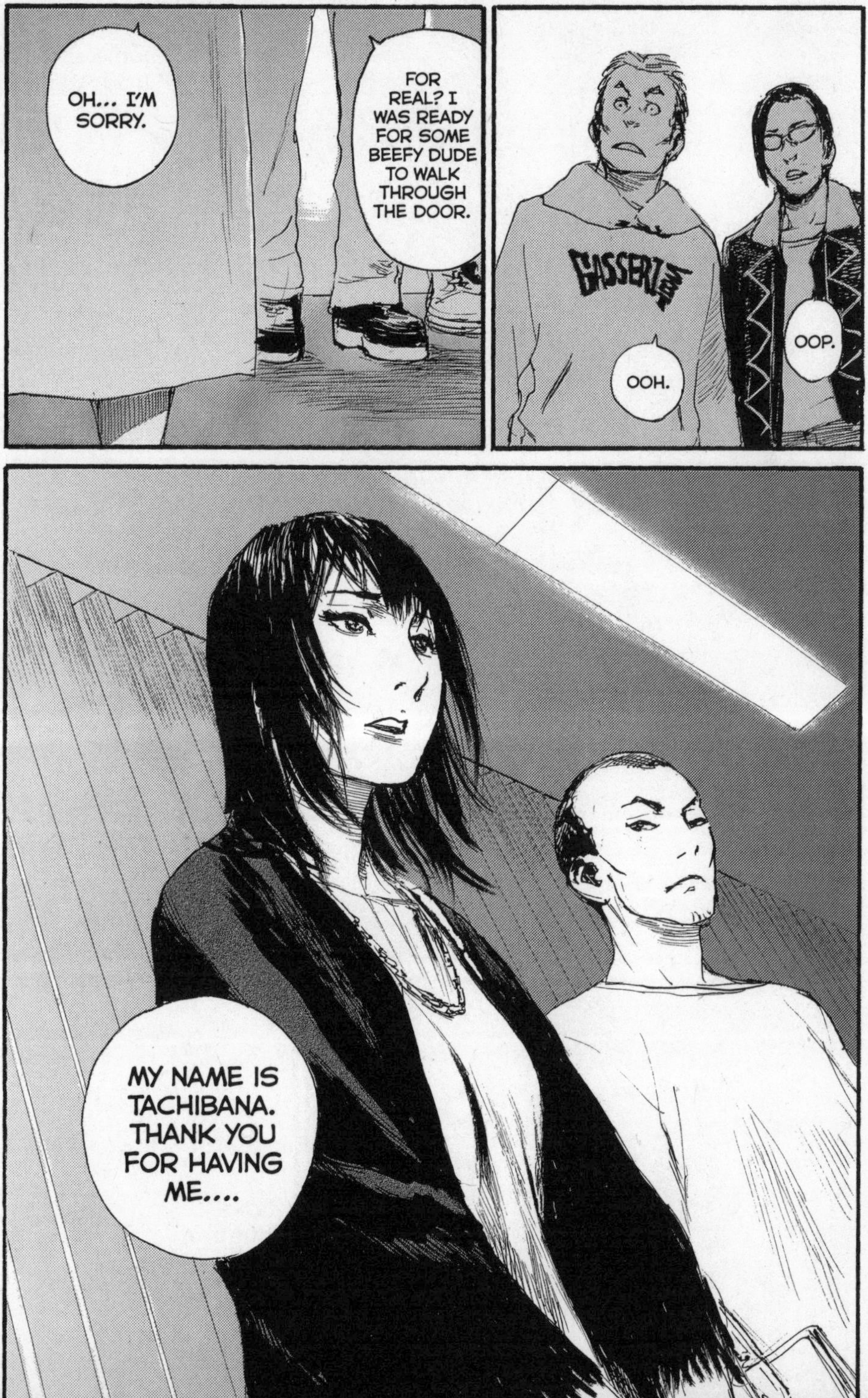
OOP.
OOH.
FOR REAL? I WAS READY FOR SOME BEEFY DUDE TO WALK THROUGH THE DOOR.
OH... I'M SORRY.
MY NAME IS TACHIBANA. THANK YOU FOR HAVING ME....

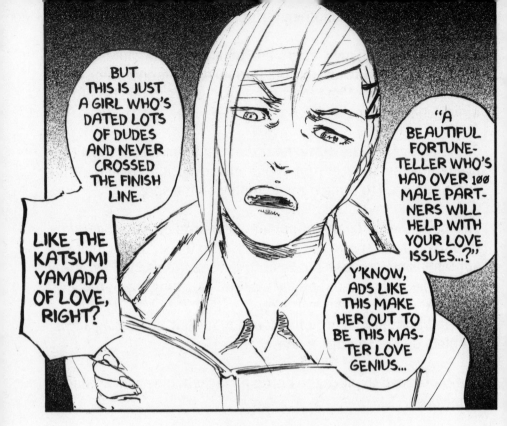

"A BEAUTIFUL FORTUNE-TELLER WHO'S HAD OVER 100 MALE PARTNERS WILL HELP WITH YOUR LOVE ISSUES...?"

Y'KNOW, ADS LIKE THIS MAKE HER OUT TO BE THIS MASTER LOVE GENIUS...

BUT THIS IS JUST A GIRL WHO'S DATED LOTS OF DUDES AND NEVER CROSSED THE FINISH LINE.

LIKE THE KATSUMI YAMADA OF LOVE, RIGHT?

AFTERWORD

Hello, everyone. What did you think of volume 4 of *Wave, Listen to Me!*—a dreamland of curry and radio, featuring a drunk woman whining about her life as the sun sets? This is, as you know, a manga whose author has been eternally drooling, mouth half-agape, over the prospect of making this into a romantic story, but now that we're at volume 4, I think we're starting to kind of see an atmosphere like that, finally—more or less. Not the protagonist, but still. The town of Kushiro gets namechecked a lot in this volume, but there's actually a lot of people in my life who were born there. Y-da-san, my first editor when I made my manga debut, and Yukari Takinami-san, an artist whom I may as well call the official supervisor of *Wave, Listen to Me!*, are two of them. That's why I wanted to give Kushiro a ton of good press when it came time to cover it in the story...but plans tend to go awry in many ways. Also, if you look at online reviews of Seicomart, the conventional wisdom for their food seems to be "the Hot Chef brand is awesome, everything else is sh*t," but to tell the truth, I've only gotten to shop there one time. Research trips for my work are generally two-night journeys, and for some reason, neither me nor my editor tend to suggest we have one of our meals at a convenience store when we go. Well, the reason's pretty obvious, I guess—but still, I wish I had a chance to just go up to Hokkaido and chill out for like half a month or so. Anyway, see you later. **—Hiroaki Samura**

"Have a seat," said my stepmother, pointing to the white loveseat she'd allegedly purchased off of Karimoku the month prior, before removing her jacket and tossing it vaguely threateningly onto the dining chair to her side.

She then opened the refrigerator door and retrieved a two-liter bottle of mineral water from the drink rack inside, twisted off the cap, and began to drink from it audibly on the spot.

Staring at the silhouette of her ample breasts displayed daringly through her violet sweater, I sat back onto the sofa with mild apprehension, grabbed the Eastern-Europe themed pillow sitting beside me and placed it on my lap. Still clutching the bottle, my stepmother walked across the room with a sliding stride and free-fell bottom-first onto the couch to my left, spattering a few droplets on her smooth, nylon-wrapped knee.

She proceeded to place the bottle on my left knee as if urging me to partake.

"So... about the letter you mentioned," I said, broaching the subject of our taxi-ride discussion once more and took the water bottle in hand—oddly cold to the touch, considering how short the AC had been running.

"From the Chief Cabinet Secretary? You're actually curious about that?" she replied quizzically.

"Well, certain—Sure, why wouldn't I be?" I said, catching myself mid-sentence.

My stepmother turned to face me, her cheeks flushed from an evening's worth of cocktails, and stared at me in silent admonishment for having slipped into my old habit of speaking as a proper congressional secretary in her presence.

Though perhaps due to the alcohol coursing through her veins, her eyes lacked their usual luster, replaced instead with a fervor unlike anything I'd seen from her before. She slowly allowed her body to lean against mine, removing her glasses and folding them with one hand, and tilted her head to rest a cheek on my shoulder.

"...I mean, it was from when I was first elected, and that was over a decade ago. I don't really see the point of only explaining that part of it, but if you really want to know, I'll tell you."

Feeling the full weight and warmth of my stepmother's body through my left arm, paired with the realization that they belonged to a woman only four years my senior, immediately turned my throat as dry as the Sahara Dessert. I drew the lipstick-smeared mouth of the bottle to my lips and threw back a third of the remaining water in a single gulp.

Then followed an awkward silence that spanned an eternity, or so it seemed anyway. In truth, it couldn't have lasted for even two minutes. Checking to see if she'd dozed off, I placed my hand on her thigh and lightly squeezed the supple flesh...an act I'd never done once since we began living together, let alone the time I spent working under her.

While I predicted that she would slap my hand away should she be awake, such a sensation never came. Rather, she lazily placed her hand on mine and, much to my surprise, slowly guided it into the slight crevice formed by her legs. Sitting there frozen with my hand clasped between her thighs, yet another three minutes passed in silence. Despite the still-chilly atmosphere of the room, I felt my left fingertips begin to sweat and tingle from the warmth, unsure if it was hers or my own.

Just then, I heard my stepmother part her lips and say, "He blackmailed me. Suga-san, that is. Back when he was still the Prime Minister."

Translation Notes

Yumi Matsutoya lyrics, page 22

Takarada appears to be such a big fan of music artist Yumi Matsutoya that his dialogue in this panel is paraphrasing the lyrics from her song *LATE SUMMER LAKE.* Similarly, as Nakahara suggests, the restaurant name VOYAGER could be a homage to Matsutoya's album and/or single of the same name.

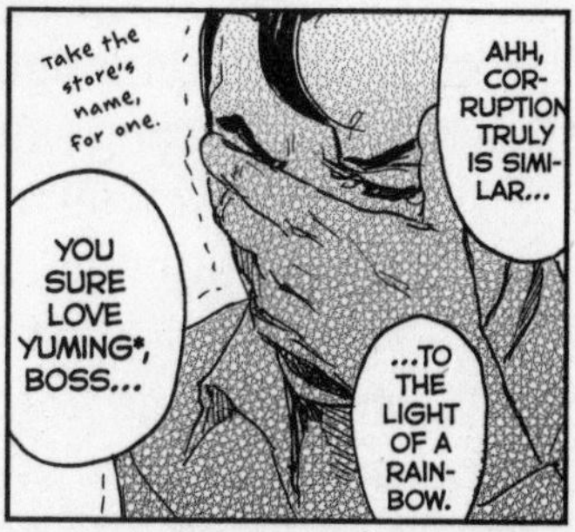

AHH, CORRUPTION TRULY IS SIMILAR...
...TO THE LIGHT OF A RAINBOW.
Take the store's name, for one.
YOU SURE LOVE YUMING*, BOSS...

Nusamai Bridge, page 30

A European-style bridge that spans across the Kushiro River to connect the northern and southern sections of the city. There are four (naked) bronze statues along the path, meant to represent each of the four seasons. It is one of the three most famous bridges in Hokkaido, along with Sapporo's Toyohira Bridge and Asahikawa's Asahi Bridge.

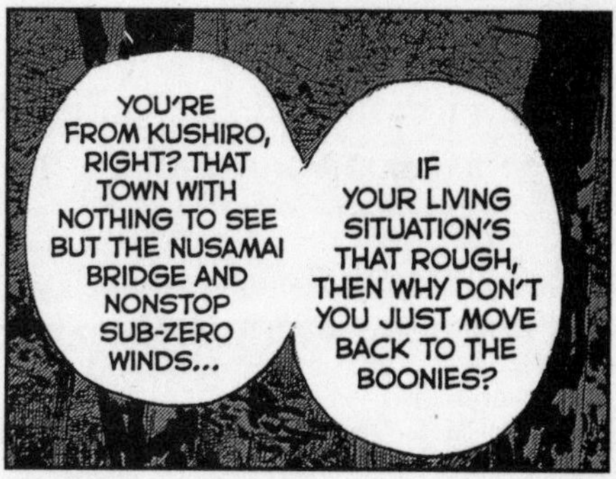

IF YOUR LIVING SITUATION'S THAT ROUGH, THEN WHY DON'T YOU JUST MOVE BACK TO THE BOONIES?
YOU'RE FROM KUSHIRO, RIGHT? THAT TOWN WITH NOTHING TO SEE BUT THE NUSAMAI BRIDGE AND NONSTOP SUB-ZERO WINDS...

Miyoshi Combo, page 33

A set meal from the curry restaurant chain Miyoshi, popular in Sapporo. Minare walks by one in volume 1.

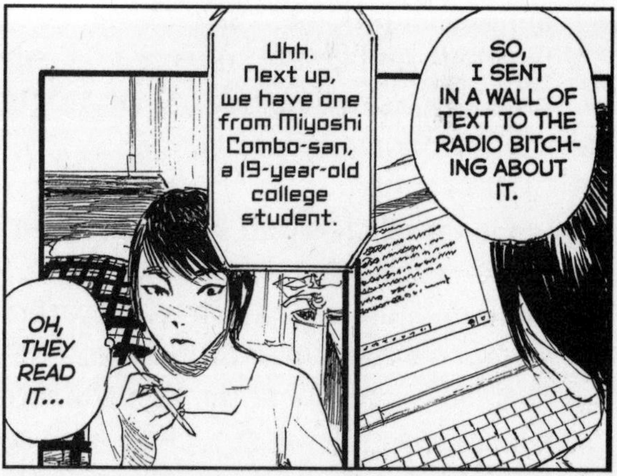

SO, I SENT IN A WALL OF TEXT TO THE RADIO BITCHING ABOUT IT.
Uhh. Next up, we have one from Miyoshi Combo-san, a 19-year-old college student.
OH, THEY READ IT...

Mount Ichankoppe, page 41

This ridge bears an Ainu name meaning "salmon spawning ground river," and sports one of the best views of Lake Shikotsu. As the reader may recall from volume 3, Lake Shikotsu is a popular ghost spot.

Marriage hunting parties, page 47

Marriage hunting, or *konkatsu,* refers to one's active pursuit of a spouse much in the same way "job hunting" refers to seeking employment. In Japan, traditional matchmaking, or *omiai,* usually brings the families of potential spouses together because the parents figure largely into the overall process. In the case of modern marriage hunting, which often involves parties at upscale venues with marriageable singles, there's more freedom among participants to pursue or give up on prospects, but the main idea is still that if you're attending, you're in it to get hitched.

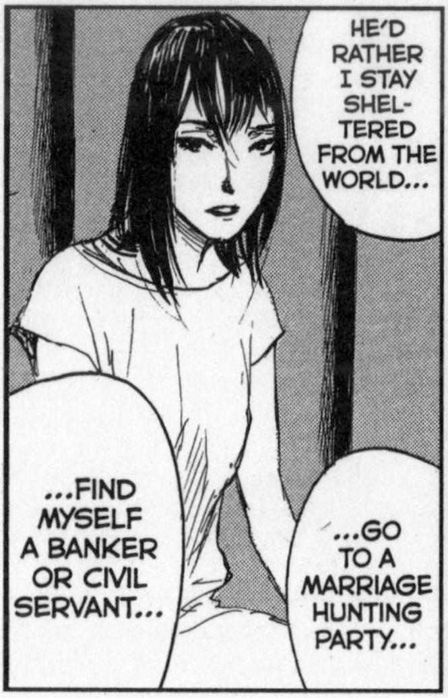
HE'D RATHER I STAY SHEL-TERED FROM THE WORLD...
...GO TO A MARRIAGE HUNTING PARTY...
...FIND MYSELF A BANKER OR CIVIL SERVANT...

Badger Taiji and *The No Badger-Hunting Hour*, page 41

This comedy duo name and radio show title appear to be a contradicting play on words. The "Taiji" in the duo's name "Badger Taiji" is the combination of their individual stage names, borrowing the "Tai" in "Taizo" and the "Ji" in "Jiro." This *taiji* is homophonous with the Japanese word meaning "extermination," so it's as if their radio show title is ironically meant to exclude them for an hour.

Kureko's books, page 77

The rightmost book lists Sadaji Yamato as the author, a sound effects veteran with decades of experience in both television and radio. His biography published in 2001 details his life experiences, including as chief sound effects director at NHK, Japan's national broadcasting organization. Additionally, the obscured book to the left of Kureko's hand looks to be a work from Tadao Chigusa, an older smut author who passed away in 1995.

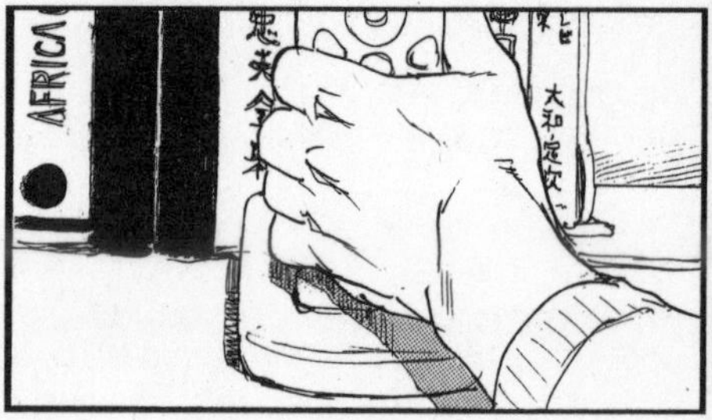
AFRICA

General-interest magazines, page 81

The rack in this panel features various magazines that borrow the aesthetic of real-life publications, but of course with slightly altered names. Of note, the magazine that catches Minare's father's eye, "Neoteric Weekly" (*Shuukan kindai*) is based on the magazine "Modern Weekly" (*Shuukan gendai*), which, like many publications in this genre, runs the gamut of celebrity news to politics when it comes to content.

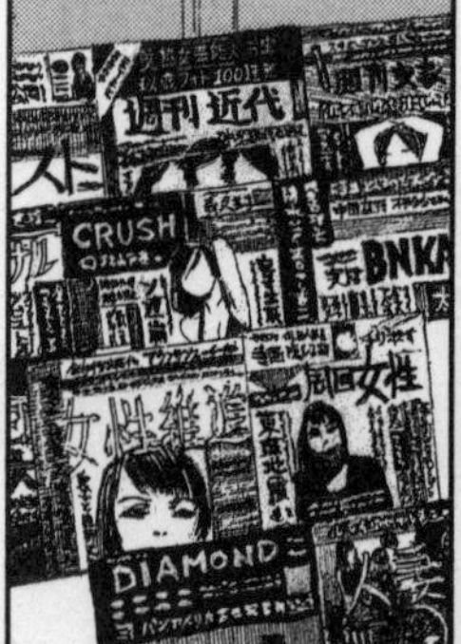
週刊近代
CRUSH
DIAMOND

Arakawa Ranzou Award, page 93

A fictionalized name of the *Edogawa Rampo Prize* given every year by the Mystery Writers of Japan. The real prize is named for a novelist instrumental in the development of Japanese mystery fiction writing, who lived during the mid-to late-1900s. Much like with the Arakawa award in this series, the winner of the Edogawa prize has their mystery novel published and receives 10,000,000 yen (about $100,000) in prize money.

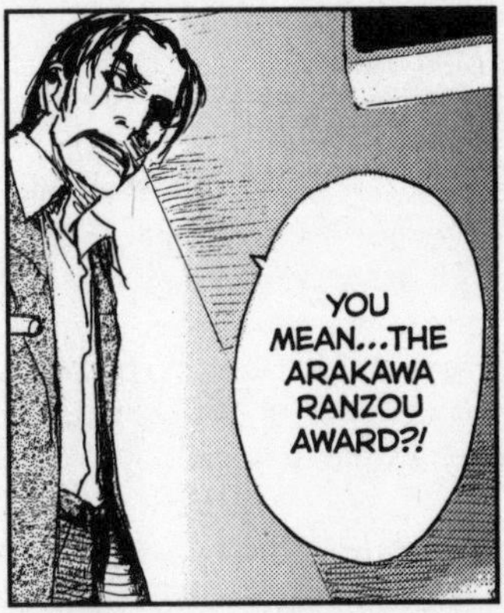
YOU MEAN...THE ARAKAWA RANZOU AWARD?!

Kotooshu's blog, page 103

Katsunori Kotooshu was the professional name of Kaloyan Stefanov Mahlyanov, a former professional sumo wrestler of Bulgarian descent. He rose to *ozeki,* the second-highest rank in sumo, in the early 2000s, but retired without achieving the top designation of *yokozuna,* and now trains up-and-coming sumo wrestlers. His blog mainly consists of photos of food, daily life, and his students, all with minimal captions.

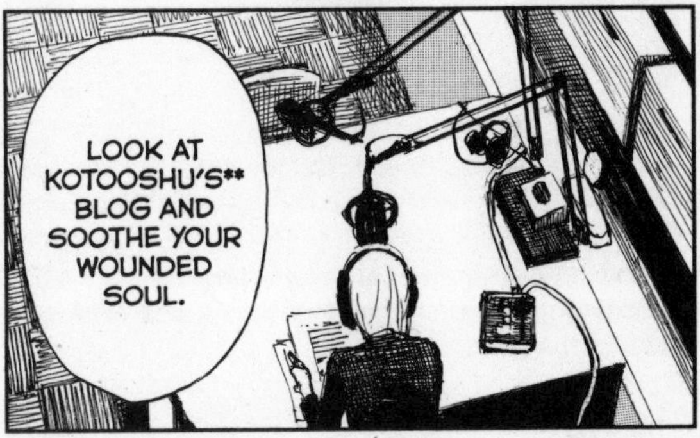
LOOK AT KOTOOSHU'S** BLOG AND SOOTHE YOUR WOUNDED SOUL.

Soufflé doria, page 104

Hoshino Coffee is a hand-drip coffee chain with locations throughout Japan and in select Asian countries. Doria is a common Western-style dish in Japan best equated to rice gratin, and the soufflé twist Hoshino adds to it is a whipped egg on top that's so fluffy, it's practically overflowing from the bowl the doria is served in.

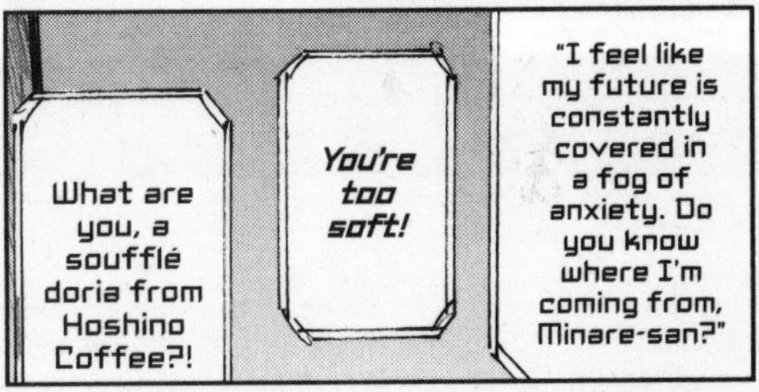
"I feel like my future is constantly covered in a fog of anxiety. Do you know where I'm coming from, Minare-san?"
You're too soft!
What are you, a soufflé doria from Hoshino Coffee?!

Kyokushin karate, page 105

One of the 8 main styles of karate, Kyokushin features more full-contact, knockdown sparring as compared with other styles.

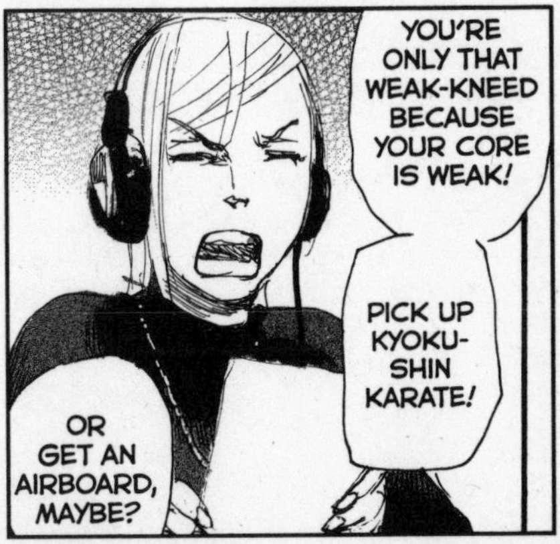
YOU'RE ONLY THAT WEAK-KNEED BECAUSE YOUR CORE IS WEAK!
PICK UP KYOKU-SHIN KARATE!
OR GET AN AIRBOARD, MAYBE?

Boy robot, page 123
A reference to the titular character in Osamu Tezuka's classic manga series *Astro Boy* (*Tetsuwan Atomu*), in which a scientist creates an android boy to replace his late son. When Astro Boy first awakens, he needs to be taught language and manners, much like any human child.

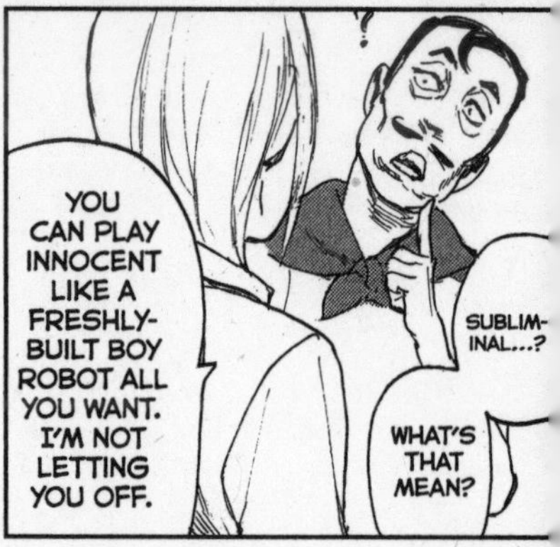
SUBLIM-INAL...?
WHAT'S THAT MEAN?
YOU CAN PLAY INNOCENT LIKE A FRESHLY-BUILT BOY ROBOT ALL YOU WANT. I'M NOT LETTING YOU OFF.

Keigo Nishino, Natsuo Kirino, and Jun Idobashi, page 128
These are all fictionalized names of real mystery authors who also won the *Edogawa Rampo Prize.* The actual author names are Keigo Higashino, Natsuo Kirino (takes a different spelling in Japanese), and Jun Ikeido respectively.

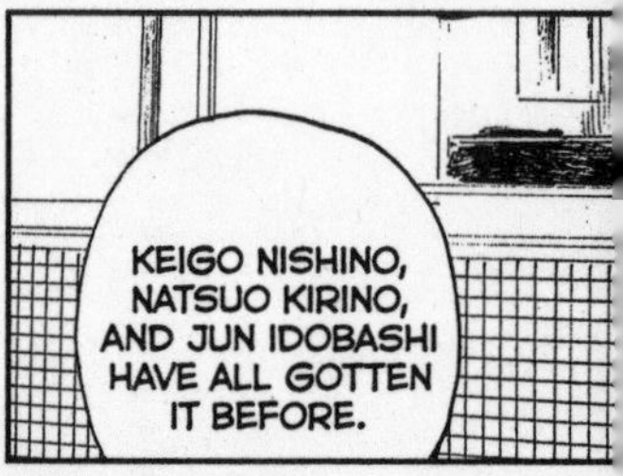
KEIGO NISHINO, NATSUO KIRINO, AND JUN IDOBASHI HAVE ALL GOTTEN IT BEFORE.

***Gokaidochu Hizakeruge*, page 181**
A parody of the comic novel *Tokaidochu Hizakurige*, known in translation as *Shank's Mare.* The original novel was published in the Edo period (1603-1868) and documented the misadventures of two travelers on the road from Edo (now Tokyo) to Kyoto. The story is told in the fashion of a travel guide written through the lens of supposedly "cultured" Edo men who often found themselves in hilarious situations whilst traveling among country bumpkins.

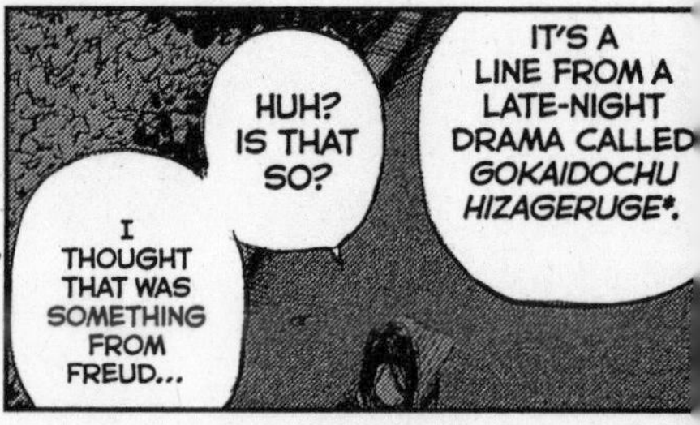
IT'S A LINE FROM A LATE-NIGHT DRAMA CALLED *GOKAIDOCHU HIZAGERUGE**.
HUH? IS THAT SO?
I THOUGHT THAT WAS SOMETHING FROM FREUD...

Katsumi Yamada, page 189
An athlete and veteran competitor on the TV show SASUKE (also known as *American Ninja Warrior*).

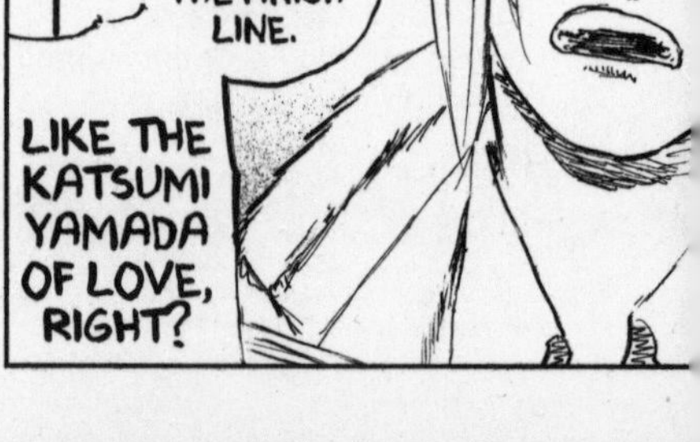
BUT THIS IS JUST A GIRL WHO'S DATED LOTS OF DUDES AND NEVER CROSSED THE FINISH LINE.
LIKE THE KATSUMI YAMADA OF LOVE, RIGHT?

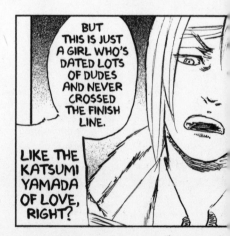

PERFECT WORLD

Rie Aruga

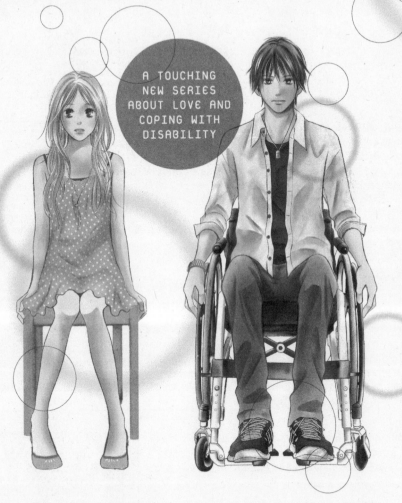

A TOUCHING NEW SERIES ABOUT LOVE AND COPING WITH DISABILITY

An office party reunites Tsugumi with her high school crush Itsuki. He's realized his dream of becoming an architect, but along the way, he experienced a spinal injury that put him in a wheelchair. Now Tsugumi's rekindled feelings will butt up against prejudices she never considered — and Itsuki will have to decide if he's ready to let someone into his heart...

"Depicts with great delicacy and courage the difficulties some with disabilities experience getting involved in romantic relationships... Rie Aruga refuses to romanticize, pushing her heroine to face the reality of disability. She invites her readers to the same tasks of empathy, knowledge and recognition."
—Slate.fr

"An important entry [in manga romance]... The emotional core of both plot and characters indicates thoughtfulness... [Aruga's] research is readily apparent in the text and artwork, making this feel like a real story."
—Anime News Network

KC KODANSHA COMICS

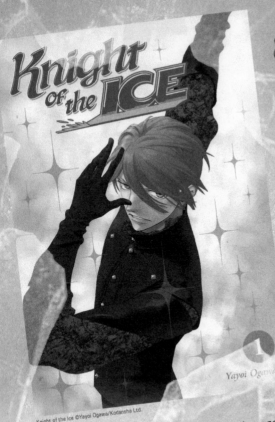

Knight of the Ice ©Yayoi Ogawa/Kodansha Ltd.

SKATING THRILLS AND ICY CHILLS WITH THIS NEW TINGLY ROMANCE SERIES!

A rom-com on ice, perfect for fans of *Princess Jellyfish* and *Wotakoi*. Kokoro is the talk of the figure-skating world, winning trophies and hearts. But little do they know... he's actually a huge nerd! From the beloved creator of *You're My Pet* (*Tramps Like Us*).

Chitose is a serious young woman, working for the health magazine *SASSO*. Or at least, she would be, if she wasn't constantly getting distracted by her childhood friend, international figure skating star Kokoro Kijinami! In the public eye and on the ice, Kokoro is a gallant, flawless knight, but behind his glittery costumes and breathtaking spins lies a secret: He's actually a hopelessly romantic otaku, who can only land his quad jumps when Chitose is on hand to recite a spell from his favorite magical girl anime!

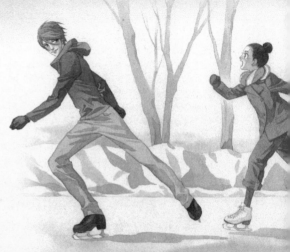

KC
KODANSHA
COMICS

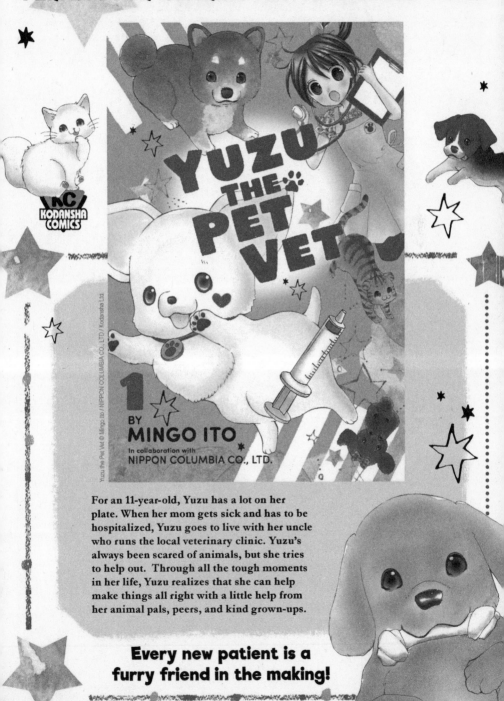

The adorable new odd-couple cat comedy manga from the creator of the beloved *Chi's Sweet Home*, in full color!

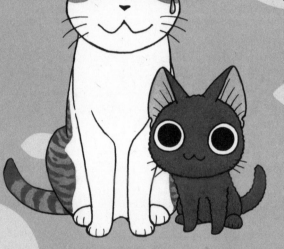

Sue & Tai-chan

Konami Kanata

Sue is an aging housecat who's looking forward to living out her life in peace... but her plans change when the mischievous black tomcat Tai-chan enters the picture! Hey! Sue never signed up to be a catsitter! *Sue & Tai-chan* is the latest from the reigning meow-narch of cute kitty comics, Konami Kanata.

KC KODANSHA COMICS

A SMART, NEW ROMANTIC COMEDY FOR FANS OF *SHORTCAKE CAKE* AND *TERRACE HOUSE!*

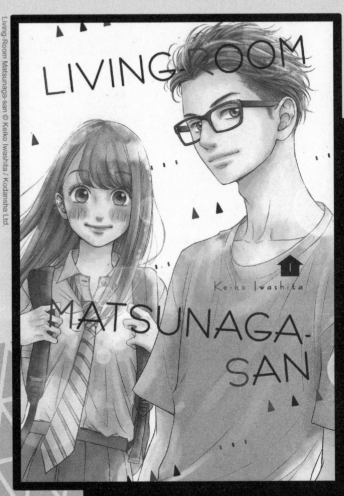

KC KODANSHA COMICS

A romance manga starring high school girl Meeko, who learns to live on her own in a boarding house whose living room is home to the odd (but handsome) Matsunaga-san. She begins to adjust to her new life away from her parents, but Meeko soon learns that no matter how far away from home she is, she's still a young girl at heart — especially when she finds herself falling for Matsunaga-san.

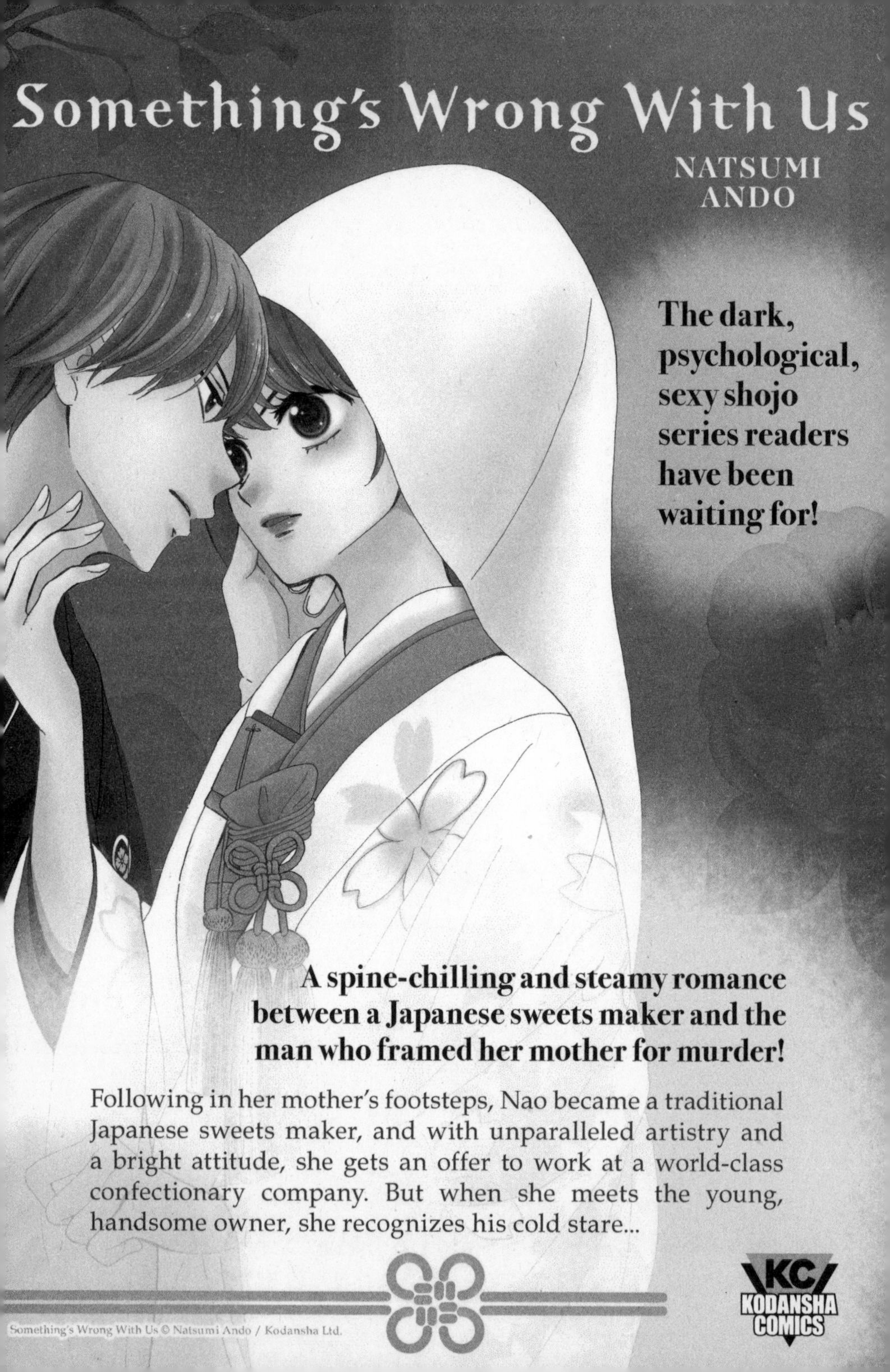
Something's Wrong With Us
NATSUMI ANDO
The dark, psychological, sexy shojo series readers have been waiting for!
A spine-chilling and steamy romance between a Japanese sweets maker and the man who framed her mother for murder!
Following in her mother's footsteps, Nao became a traditional Japanese sweets maker, and with unparalleled artistry and a bright attitude, she gets an offer to work at a world-class confectionary company. But when she meets the young, handsome owner, she recognizes his cold stare...
Something's Wrong With Us © Natsumi Ando / Kodansha Ltd.

The boys are back, in 400-page hardcovers that are as pretty and badass as they are!

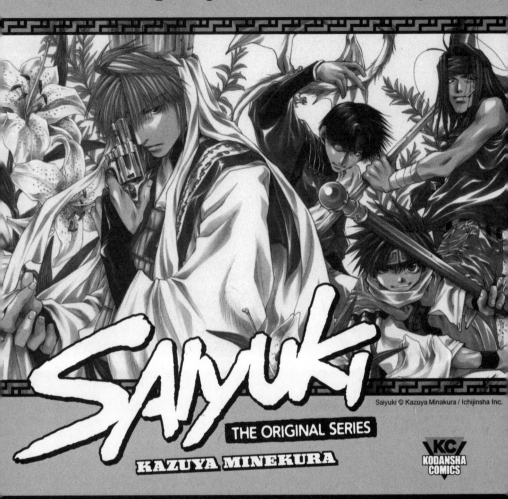

Saiyuki © Kazuya Minekura / Ichijinsha Inc.

Saiyuki
THE ORIGINAL SERIES
KAZUYA MINEKURA

KC / KODANSHA COMICS

"AN EDGY COMIC LOOK AT AN ANCIENT CHINESE TALE." —YALSA

Genjo Sanzo is a Buddhist priest in the city of Togenkyo, which is being ravaged by yokai spirits that have fallen out of balance with the natural order. His superiors send him on a journey far to the west to discover why this is happening and how to stop it. His companions are three yokai with human souls. But this is no day trip — the four will encounter many discoveries and horrors on the way.

FEATURES NEW TRANSLATION, COLOR PAGES, AND BEAUTIFUL WRAPAROUND COVER ART!

THE SWEET SCENT OF LOVE IS IN THE AIR! FOR FANS OF OFFBEAT ROMANCES LIKE *WOTAKOI*

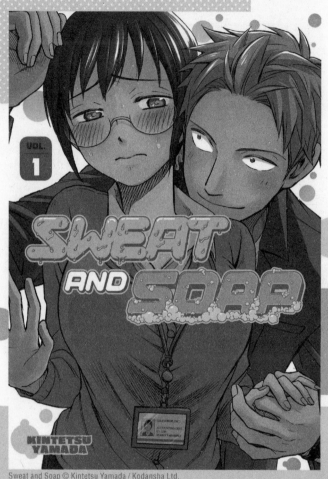

Sweat and Soap © Kintetsu Yamada / Kodansha Ltd.

In an office romance, there's a fine line between sexy and awkward... and that line is where Asako — a woman who sweats copiously — meets Koutarou — a perfume developer who can't get enough of Asako's, er, scent. Don't miss a romcom manga like no other!

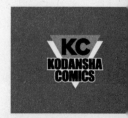

KC
KODANSHA COMICS

Young characters and steampunk setting, like *Howl's Moving Castle* and *Battle Angel Alita*

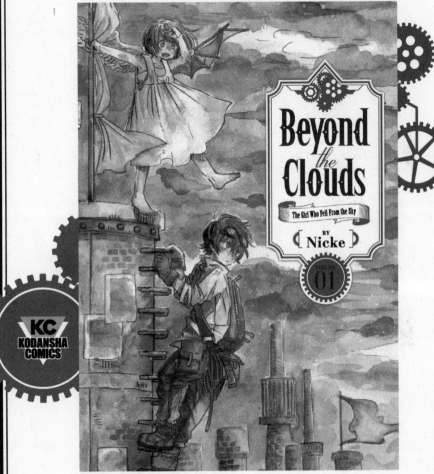

Beyond the Clouds © 2018 Nicke / Ki-oon

A boy with a talent for machines and a mysterious girl whose wings he's fixed will take you beyond the clouds! In the tradition of the high-flying, resonant adventure stories of Studio Ghibli comes a gorgeous tale about the longing of young hearts for adventure and friendship!

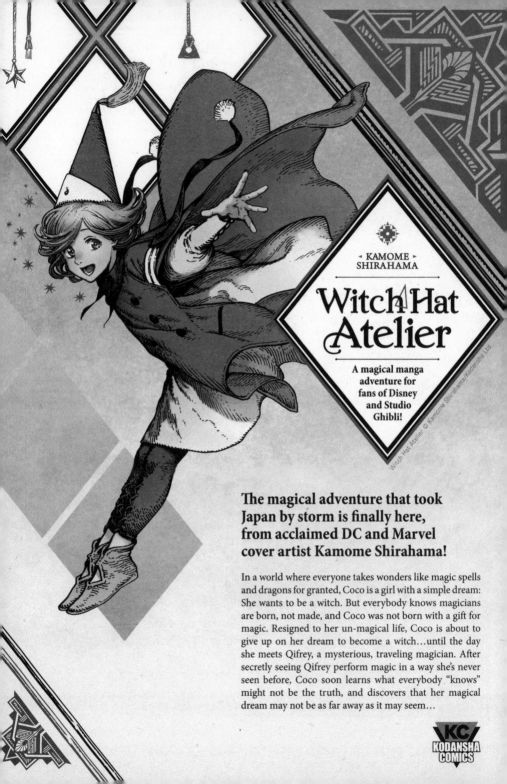

◂ KAMOME ▸
SHIRAHAMA

Witch Hat Atelier

A magical manga
adventure for
fans of Disney
and Studio
Ghibli!

Witch Hat Atelier © Kamome Shirahama/Kodansha Ltd.

The magical adventure that took Japan by storm is finally here, from acclaimed DC and Marvel cover artist Kamome Shirahama!

In a world where everyone takes wonders like magic spells and dragons for granted, Coco is a girl with a simple dream: She wants to be a witch. But everybody knows magicians are born, not made, and Coco was not born with a gift for magic. Resigned to her un-magical life, Coco is about to give up on her dream to become a witch...until the day she meets Qifrey, a mysterious, traveling magician. After secretly seeing Qifrey perform magic in a way she's never seen before, Coco soon learns what everybody "knows" might not be the truth, and discovers that her magical dream may not be as far away as it may seem...

KC
KODANSHA
COMICS

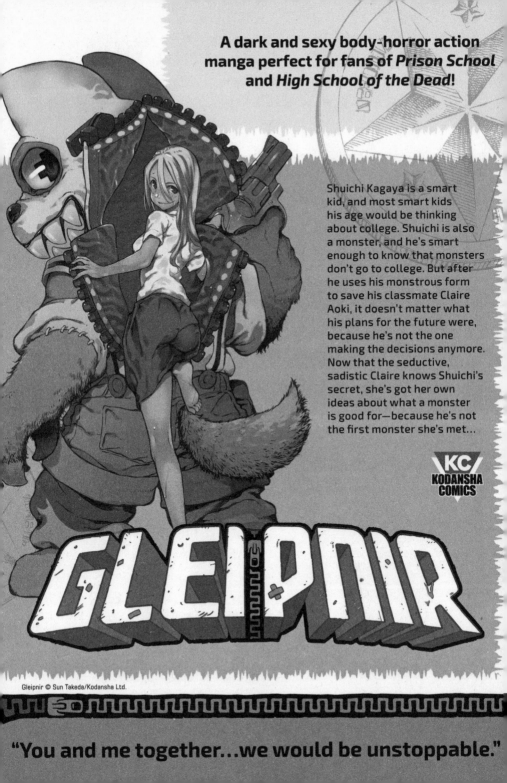

A dark and sexy body-horror action manga perfect for fans of *Prison School* and *High School of the Dead*!

Shuichi Kagaya is a smart kid, and most smart kids his age would be thinking about college. Shuichi is also a monster, and he's smart enough to know that monsters don't go to college. But after he uses his monstrous form to save his classmate Claire Aoki, it doesn't matter what his plans for the future were, because he's not the one making the decisions anymore. Now that the seductive, sadistic Claire knows Shuichi's secret, she's got her own ideas about what a monster is good for—because he's not the first monster she's met...

KC / KODANSHA COMICS

GLEIPNIR

"You and me together...we would be unstoppable."

SAINT ☆ YOUNG MEN

A LONG AWAITED ARRIVAL IN PREMIUM 2-IN-1 HARDCOVER

After centuries of hard work, Jesus and Buddha take a break from their heavenly duties to relax among the people of Japan, and their adventures in this lighthearted buddy comedy are sure to bring mirth and merriment to all!

"Brilliant...the physical comedy and facial expressions will make you literally LOL."
—Sam Humphries
(host of *DC Daily*; writer, *Green Lanterns*, *Legendary Star-Lord*)

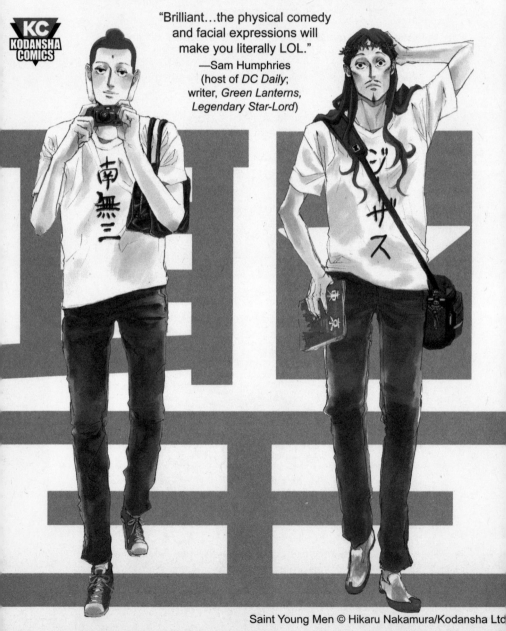

Kingston Frontenac PL/ARPs

Dec 2020

39011015010160

A Kodansha Comics Trade Paperback Original
Wave, Listen to Me! 4 copyright © 2017 Hiroaki Samura
English translation copyright © 2020 Hiroaki Samura

Published in the United States by Kodansha Comics, an imprint of
Kodansha USA Publishing, LLC, New York.

Publication rights for this English edition arranged through
Kodansha Ltd., Tokyo.

First published in Japan in 2017 by Kodansha Ltd., Tokyo
as Nami yo kiitekure, volume 4.

ISBN 978-1-63236-870-6

Original cover design by Tadashi Hisamochi (hive&co.,ltd.)

Printed in the United States of America.

www.kodanshacomics.com

9 8 7 6 5 4 3 2 1
Translation: Adam Hirsch
Additional Translation: Kevin Gifford
Lettering: Darren Smith
Additional lettering and layout: Michael Martin
Editing: Alexandra Swanson, Vanessa Tenazas
YKS Services LLC/SKY Japan, INC.
Kodansha Comics edition cover design by Adam D[...]

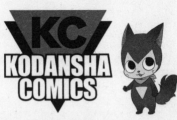

Publisher: Kiichiro Sugawara

Director of publishing services: Ben Applegate
Associate director of operations: Stephen Pakula
Publishing services managing editor: Noelle Webster
Assistant production manager: Emi Lotto, Angela Zurlo
Logo and character art ©Kodansha USA Publishing, LLC